TEACHING ALL NATIONS

# TEACHING ALL NATIONS

*A Symposium on Modern Catechetics*

*Edited by*
JOHANNES HOFINGER, S.J.
*English Version*
*Revised and partly translated*
*by*
CLIFFORD HOWELL, S.J.



HERDER
FREIBURG

BURNS AND OATES, LTD.
LONDON

Original edition "Katechetik heute", Herder, Freiburg



Nihil Obstat: Daniel Duivestijn, S.T.D.
Censor deputatus.

Imprimatur: E. Morrogh Bernard
Vic. Gen.
Westmonasterii, die 4a Aprilis, 1961

The Nihil Obstat and Imprimatur are a declaration that a book or pamphlet is considered to be free from doctrinal or moral error.
It is not implied that those who have granted the Nihil Obstat and Imprimatur agree with the contents, opinions or statements expressed.

Library of Congress Catalog Card Number: 61-9371

Made and printed in West Germany by Herder

## CONTENTS

*The Role of the Catechumenate in Christian Training*



*Training and Helping Catechists*



*Appendices*

Notes: –

(1) Papers marked with an asterisk (*) were not read at the Congress, but were circulated in typescript form to all participants.

(2) Unless the immediate context implies otherwise, the words "catechesis" and "catechist" as used in this book should be understood in their broadest sense; that is, they do not refer to the training of children only, but to any activity designed to impart knowledge of and love for the faith to any persons of any age, by all who teach religion in any capacity – whether as priests, brothers, nuns, school teachers or catechists.

(3) Only some of the papers in this English edition were translated by Fr. Clifford Howell, S.J. from the French or German originals. Those which do not have his initials in brackets at the end were translated by others and merely edited by him.

(4) The Index was compiled by Miss Martha Newman.

# FOREWORD

LISTENING to these lectures was a revelation; working on them to prepare the English version for the press has but confirmed the impression of their excellence and tremendous importance for the cause of catechesis throughout the world. Though a missionary meeting was the occasion for their delivery, no one should think that they are of interest and use only to missionaries. On the contrary; the series taken as a whole is a magnificent exposition of the principles and practice of catechesis – probably the most authoritative exposition ever yet given in one book.

There have been other catechetical congresses, and some have not been confined to a national basis. But no congress so far has been so truly and representatively *international* as this one. Almost every acknowledged leader of catechetical science throughout the world was present, and many of the lectures were given by them. It is a book for the world, and not just for the missions. That is why it is being published in four editions – German, French, English and Spanish – so that it may reach everybody. It is a book for bishops, priests, brothers, nuns and any of the laity concerned with catechetics in any capacity. All will find it interesting and useful, for it makes it quite clear what the greatest experts of the whole Catholic world are thinking *now*.

If anybody wants to disagree with them he is, no doubt, at liberty to do so. But if anybody claims to be really up to date in modern catechetical knowledge and yet says that he has not read this book, his claim – and the views he expresses – would deserve to be treated with scepticism.

It is a wonderful book; it has been a privilege to prepare its English version for the press, and thus to be associated with the work of spreading to the whole human race the Good Tidings of the salvation brought to men by Christ our Lord.

CLIFFORD HOWELL, S.J.

# LETTER FROM CARDINAL AGAGIANIAN TO THE EDITOR

Reverend Father,

I am grateful and pleased to have the two volumes with the papers in English and French which were delivered at the Congress for Mission Catechetics at Eichstätt on July 21–28, 1960.

Great praise is due to all those who prepared the Congress so industriously and carefully, to the knowledge and experience of the speakers and to the lively participation of those who came merely to listen. They strengthen the hope that the studies which have been undertaken mainly in Europe by several eminent scholars will bear rich fruit also in the missions.

Conferences of this kind as well as the publications of specialists will be of the greatest value above all for the ordinaries in the missions who, while respecting the wishes and suggestions of the experts, will have to use their own judgment in which way religious instructions in their missions are best to be carried out.

May God grant that this Congress will be an encouragement for the wider and deeper study of problems which confront the teaching of the faith in the missions.

Assuring you of my sincere appreciation,

I am

Yours sincerely in Christ,

G. P. CARDINAL AGAGIANIAN, Prefect.

† P. SIGISMONDI, Secretary.

Sacred Congregation for the Propagation
of the Faith, Rome.

This letter was written in Latin to Rev. J. Hofinger, S.J., Manila

# INTRODUCTION

AS we finished the International Study Week on Missionary Catechetics with a solemn Service of Thanksgiving in the Cathedral at Eichstätt on July 28th, 1960, we all felt that our meeting would have a decisive and permanent influence on the renewal of catechetics in the missions. We had two good reasons for this, apart from the manifest blessing of God which favoured the undertaking from its very beginning.

The first reason, beyond doubt, is the general situation regarding catechetics in the missions today. The Eichstätt Congress, to an extent unparalleled almost by any other congress, was both evoked and fostered by the circumstances existing at the present time. This fact imbued the Congress with a perceptible spirit of ardour from the very hour when it assembled, and aroused in us all a deep sense of responsibility.

During the past ten years, almost everywhere throughout the missions, there has been a marked and auspicious increase of interest in catechetics. But at the same time this was to a certain extent inhibited by anxieties about the future. For everywhere there was a lamentable shortage of well informed and well trained specialists in the subject. This is why the most thoughtful and zealous leaders of the catechetical apostolate in the missions ardently desired a congress on missionary catechetics; at this congress the very best authorities on the subject should be asked to collaborate, and to work out a clear plan of campaign for that catechetical renewal which seemed imminent. The need for such a congress was all the greater because, in spite of uncertainty about details, one conviction had won an ever increasing acceptance in recent years; it was that no mere increase in catechetical activity would suffice to solve current problems. It was not a question just of promoting more catechetics; what was needed would be a profound renewal of catechetics, which, however, would have to fulfil two requirements. It would have to adopt for mission countries all that was best in the wonderfully fruitful renewal of catechetics which has recently taken place in the home countries; yet at the same time it must also take into account the special exigencies of missionary catechetics and preaching. Such problems, it seemed, could best be studied by a large-scale international conference convened for the express purpose of seeking their solution. Here the greatest experts from the home countries, and missionaries with the widest experience in catechetics would be able to confer together fruitfully.

Another point which had also become increasingly clear in recent years was the failure of catechesis to adapt the Christian message to the people whom we have to instruct. We are, indeed, only just beginning to cope with this problem. Yet this is not where our greatest weakness lies. This is to be found rather in a failure to grasp the universally valid basic laws of missionary catechesis. Indeed one can go a step further without hesitation, and say that the most serious problems which we have in the mission fields are basically the very same as those which formerly troubled – and to some extent still trouble – those who have brought about the catechetical renewal in the home countries. Now if the fundamental problems facing both are in essence the same, it is manifestly a sensible and a promising plan to bring together the most able representatives from each sphere – from the missions and from the home countries – so they may take counsel together about their common problems.

The prospect of such an opportunity for discussion in common was attractive also because of the urgent need for compiling better textbooks of religious instruction. Anyone who really understands the special nature and value of the catechetical renewal cannot possibly be content with catechisms of the old style, written perhaps twenty years before even the first tentative stirrings of the catechetical movement, and left unchanged in fundamentals ever since. In recent years excellent new catechisms have been worked out for use in the home countries; naturally those who work in mission lands want to profit by all this experience. And how better could it be passed on to them than at a congress which would bring together the leading authorities in this sphere?

This brings us to the second reason pointing to the success of the Congress, namely, the unique concord between episcopal leadership on the one hand, and the conclusions of both specialized science and missionary experience on the other. A coincidence of favourable circumstances made it possible to bring together at the Congress an astonishingly numerous and representative proportion of the missionary hierarchy. In spite of the disturbances in Africa, which broke out only a short while before the Congress, and did in fact prevent not a few bishops from attending, there came to Eichstätt more than sixty missionary bishops who took an extremely lively part in the discussion throughout the week. Quite a large proportion of the lectures, especially of those dealing with delicate subjects, were given by bishops. We are convinced that no feature of the Eichstätt Study Week will have more effective results in Rome and throughout the mission fields than this widespread and lively participation of the missionary bishops. And that, after all, is what matters most of all.

Besides the missionary bishops there were many leading specialists in the catechetical apostolate. Each was personally invited, and they assembled from all parts of the world, in many cases at considerable financial sacrifice. Specialists from the home countries and leading personalities from the catechetical apostolate in the mission lands were present in numbers approximately equal. It was carefully arranged that, both in the general assemblies and in the restricted discussions groups, those with personal experience of the missionary apostolate should preponderate. Yet the organizers considered it of the highest importance to draw on the very best learning available in the home countries. They did in fact succeed in obtaining for the Study Week the collaboration of practically every specialist of international fame. It is safe to say that no previous catechetical congress excelled this one as regards the quality of those who took part in it. The missionary bishops were enabled thus to meet intimately the most outstanding leaders of the modern catechetical renewal; they were able to learn at first hand everything they wanted to know about the aims, principles and practice of modern catechetics, and to discuss the application of all these to the missionary apostolate.

All of us who were at Eichstätt were deeply impressed by the utterly devoted collaboration of catechists drawn from every continent. A special cause of satisfaction was the complete absence of any kind of nationalistic factiousness. Every group was honourably eager to learn from any other. We have abundant reason to be most grateful to the *Institut Supérieur Catéchétique* of Paris, and to its able Director, Canon Brien, for the truly admirable way in which the leading experts worked harmoniously together. As a result of this fraternal collaboration there emerged a unity of outlook which filled us with wonder. Again and again we noted how each lecturer, in dealing with his own subject, kept on referring back to the same basic principles of the catechetical renewal which he held in common with other speakers. This means, of course, that there was a certain amount of repetition; but, in view of the wide field that was covered by the various lecturers, this was seen by the participants as confirmation and evidence of agreement. For this reason we have thought it wise to eliminate repetitious material from the published proceedings only in a few exceptional cases. Thus it is made impressively clear that there does exist among the experts a unanimity held with conviction – something of great importance for the modern catechetical movement.

Everyone who reads this book will be easily convinced, for example, that the kerygmatic ideal consistently inspires all the papers, from the opening speech of the Cardinal-President to the very important concluding paper by Archbishop Hurley on the role of the bishop in the catechetical renewal. It is pleasing, too, to observe how that same kerygmatic ideal can be discerned in the Conclusions of the Study Week, and in the programme, worked out in common, for the future of the catechetical apostolate. The Proceedings of the Eichstätt Congress should make it abundantly clear also that we were not concerned with this or that novel Greek word, but simply and solely with the very heart of the matter. Our study was of the basic ideal; it is for us to communicate to the generation of mankind living today the message of salvation which has been entrusted to us as Christ's heralds – to pass it on without any distortion, in the organic unity given to it by God himself, and in all its unparalleled inner beauty and life-building power.

From the consistent, well thought out, kerygmatic direction given to our proclamation of the faith there will follow naturally that religious instruction close to real life, to the Bible and to the liturgy which has been so often demanded. Also the repeatedly emphasized adaptation of our teaching to the people to whom we are sent as Christ's heralds will derive equally and immediately from this kerygmatic attitude. The most learned and illustrious representatives of the modern catechetical movement have never before spoken so clearly and unanimously as they did at Eichstätt. Anyone who seriously studies the papers read and the conclusions reached at Eichstätt will not be able to entertain the slightest doubt that the kerygmatic viewpoint is, for modern catechetics, both characteristic and basic.

The purpose of this book should now be sufficiently clear. It is intended to point the way in our future work, and not merely to preserve happy memories of a particular congress. It should help us to map out our catechetical apostolate both in the missions and at home. This avowed purpose will explain the omission of everything which would serve only to bring back memories. We have included in the book only those elements of the Eichstätt Study Week which are of permanent value. But, in order to make it in some way resemble a handbook of missionary catechesis we have given something over and above the papers which were in fact publicly read at Eichstätt; we have included some papers which, though not publicly read, were communicated to all the participants in typescript form, and thereby had some influence upon the discussion. These papers can be identified by the asterisk printed by their titles in the Table of Contents. The Index at the end of the book digests all the rich material to be found in it, thus rendering it more accessible.

We rejoice exceedingly that this congress did actually take place, that it was possible to assemble for it so many prominent personalities from all parts of the world, and that it subserved so universal an aim. The credit for these achievements must go above all to the unselfish collaboration of those jointly responsible for organization, to the whole-hearted generosity of many benefactors in the home-countries, and to the unbounded hospitality of our distinguished hosts, Monsignor Josef Schröffer, Bishop of Eichstätt, and the Oberbürgermeister, Dr. Hans Hutter. May the publication of this book serve as an expression of our deep and lasting gratitude to them all.

The great sacrifices made by our friends in the home countries to render possible the Eichstätt Congress will be fully recompensed only if this Congress becomes a prelude to a fundamental and far-reaching renewal of catechetics throughout the missions. The many and powerful impulses which the Eichstätt Congress was able to give by reason of its unusually favourable concentration of the best resources and exemplary collaboration must now be applied in the several mission fields, and there made to produce their due effect as the result of hard work. Eichstätt will foster real progress in the missions only if the riches of its ideas are now exploited by the missionary periodicals, suitably digested for the missionaries, adapted to local circumstances, further discussed and made familiar to all. The same task should be undertaken at numerous meetings held for missionaries and catechists, and at further catechetical congresses held on a regional basis. Such regional congresses, well organized and thoroughly suited to local circumstances, would seem to be of prime importance especially in the near future. Regional catechetical centres have a vital role to play in this connection.

But above all we must hope that the ideals of Eichstätt will penetrate ever more thoroughly into those institutions engaged in training the missionary priests and lay catechists of the future. The same thing holds good both in the home countries and in the missions: a complete renewal of catechetics can never be brought about solely by some kind of after-care or help offered to missionaries and catechists already trained in other ways. It can come as a result only of an entirely suitable catechetical training given to the futuure generations of those commissioned to spread the Good News of our faith.

(Tr. C.H., S.J.)

JOHANNES HOFINGER, S.J.
East Asian Pastoral Institute,
Manila.

# THE KERYGMATIC RENEWAL OF CATECHESIS IN THE MISSIONS

# Catechetics as a Task for our Age

CANON ANDRÉ BRIEN
Director of the *Institut Supérieur Catéchétique,* Paris

THE demand for social and political maturity is the external expression of an historical phenomenon comparable to that occasioned by the barbarian invasions of the Roman Empire in the fifth century of our era. The expansion of the working classes in the West, and the emergence in Asia und Africa of new nations freed from colonial rule exemplify, in fact, a social revolution just as important as that which took place in the fifth century. People have become conscious of their solidarity and their collective power. They have progressed from a traditional existence, devoted to the preservation of the group and fidelity to ancestors, to a passionate desire to make other men take notice of them, and to build up a new world. The immense forces generated by these social and political movements and the radical changes which they impose on individuals are facts just as impressive as the victorious might of the fifth-century barbarian conquerors.

We know, however, that in spite of the far-reaching disturbances occasioned in the Christian mind by these sudden changes (St. Augustine's *Civitas Dei* suffices as proof for these), the Church of that time never had the least doubt of her mission; with unshakeable confidence she addressed herself to the task – which at first must have been frightening – of christianizing the new human world then emerging. The fruits of her work and her dauntless courage were to be seen in the magnificent cultural achievements of twelfth and thirteenth-century Western civilization.

We are faced with a similar task. We have no more lost faith in the promises of our Lord than did the men of St. Augustine's day; we know that he will be with us till the end of time. That is why we devote ourselves without fear to solving the problems of teaching the Faith which this age, at once so terrifying and so wonderful, presents to us.

Your presence here, the long journeys which most of you have undertaken in order to be in this town, are proofs of your unity, not only in your work, but also in your hopes. Let us, therefore, try at the beginning of the work which we have before us in the coming week, to choose from the eternal stipulations of the Church some basic rules which apply to the catechesis of our time, because our earth has become so open and so small.

I would like particularly to emphasize three points, namely, that our catechesis should be personal in its approach, should be comprehensive, and should throw light on the meaning of our human occupations.

### *Our Catechesis Should Be of a Personal Nature*

First and most important, our catechesis should be personal in its approach. One of the fundamental characteristics of the technical age in which we live is its impersonal attitude, imposed not only on individuals, but upon entire communities. By drawing men to the great industrial centres, and by imposing on them new methods of work, technocracy is breaking down the traditional framework of family and village life. It throws masses of men together in new towns, often hurriedly built, and filled with a mixture of people from differing races, provinces and nations. For these people everything which formerly preserved the balance of human life, the maintenance of morality and the direction of religious ideals has suddenly disappeared. The individual man has found himself delivered over helpless to the physical exhaustion induced by industrial labour, and to the elemental urges of his lower instincts. Materialism has weighed down upon him with all its power and has completely enslaved him.

Technical work leads man more and more to a mental life which ignores unseen forces and the divine mystery. Technology leads inevitably to a rationalization of effort, that is, to the reduction of all the phases of production to simple rules whose application results in a strict carrying-out of scientific laws. In the organization of such an effort, no attention is paid to factors which do not allow themselves to be reduced to simple formulas, but which are governed by the human intelligence.

Such an attitude towards work, valid and even necessary if the prime object is the methodical use of all sources of material energy, exerts a profound influence on the minds of those who subscribe to it. It makes them unaccustomed to take any notice of things which cannot be reduced to an organized scheme and, above all, of factors interfering with human liberty.

Hence they are often led to ignore the infinite worth of human persons, as well as that of divine Persons. For them the free being becomes a mere source of energy to be utilized, like other sources, according to the laws governing maximum efficiency, but without any respect for personality. That is why our age is one of spectacular inventions – but it is also an era of the bodily uprooting of whole populations, of secret police organizations, of the use of torture and of the terrible loneliness of the man without roots.

The outlook which sustains this technical *habitus* presents special problems for our catechesis. If we want to save our fellow men, and to make known to them the life of happiness to which our Saviour calls us, we must help them to recognize the grandeur of their freedom. The way to do this is not just to go on repeating that they are free, or to give theoretical disquisitions about the dignity of the individual, but to awaken in them everything that is capable of attaining eternal life and love, and to illustrate it from the teaching of Christ.

That is why our catechesis must be directed, in the first instance, to the individual. What does that imply? It means that our teaching must bring out, with all possible prominence, everything in Christianity which confirms the mutual relationship of persons. For our faith does in fact introduce us to a "world" which is eminently personal; it brings to our knowledge the only personal "world" which can hold out against the forces of standardization and dehumanization which are characteristic of our industrial "world". That is why it alone can bring salvation to mankind. Our God is in very truth a living God;

it was by his own free will that he created the world and invited Abraham and his descendants to make a covenant with him; and it was by an equally free decision of his love that he allowed us to have amongst ourselves his living and eternal Word.

Thus it is through fidelity to his personal gift that Christ has rescued us from that separation from God which is sin, and through his resurrection, has led us to his Father in the community of grace. Lastly, it was of his own free will that he established the Church and permitted us to become members of his body through our personal capacity to be faithful to him. Thus everything in Christianity – dogmas, sacraments, institutions of the Church – points out to man this personal mystery and offers him the joy of having part in it. The whole Christian religion, then, demonstrates not only the worth of men, but also the love which God has shown towards them, and the great dignity which he has bestowed upon them through his grace.

All our catechetical teaching must bring out this personal reality. We have no need to hide the fact that in former days, when the Church's teaching was communicated to men by different pastoral methods, catechesis was not concerned to place any emphasis on this personal aspect of the faith. Before the onset of the industrial civilization and the uprootings which it brought about, there were many things in a Christian civilization which emphasized the worth of the individual and the joy in the gifts of God, such as the family, with its tradition of piety, the parish, closely bound as it was to local life because parish feasts were at the same time community feasts, and, lastly, the nation, whose organs of government were based upon human relations constantly renewed by faith.

Catechesis at that time had but one fundamental task to perform: to pass on the teaching of the Church accurately, to assure precise teaching about morals, to instruct each one as to what he might do and what he must avoid; to explain the correct meaning of the liturgical rites and the sacraments, drawing attention to the dispositions required for these. That was sufficient in those days when the conditions of everyday life were a constant reminder of the mystery of God, of the humanity and the love of Jesus Christ, and of the intercession of the saints. But it is not enough now that an impersonal civilization has banished from places of work and of public life almost every reminder of the invisible presence of our Lord.

And so, without failing in its duty to teach the Church's defined doctrine with accuracy and rigour, catechesis must now rediscover the biblical and patristic sources of our faith; working through dogmatic formulations, moral commandments and liturgical signs, it has to make the personal mysteries of the God of love felt in the world again. It is only in this way that catechesis will be able to lead back those who are being smothered by an impersonal world to a knowledge of that happiness to which they are called.

### *Our Catechesis Must Be Comprehensive*

Another characteristic of the religious instruction demanded by our own times is that it must be comprehensive – that is, it must be addressed to the whole man. We must never forget that our technical civilization is itself the product of rationalism, and that rationalism is something which disrupts man's internal unity. For the rationalist, nothing matters except the act of thought and its logical coherence; that a thought should be rooted in an expectation of happiness and fulness of life, that it should be developed by means of sensible images, expressed not merely in language but also in bodily attitudes, and related to communal life, seems to the rationalist of no importance whatever, and without any bearing on the discovery of truth. For rationalist philosophers and pedagogues the ideal of knowledge is like that which is expressed in a mathematical equation.

The spread of technology has caused the diffusion of this mental attitude to many. That is why, for a great many of our contemporaries, truth does not seem to have any influence on the shaping of their lives. They regard scientific truth as an instrument enabling them to take increasing possession of this world, and not as a sustenance for their hopes. And so they are powerless to control the recurrent impulses of their own desires or the conflicting urges aroused by the variety of their emotions. And so, by way of a paradox, our technical and rationalist age is at the same time an age of frenzied desires, longings, passions and irrational emotions constantly whipped up by the stimuli of neon-lighted advertisments, glossy magazines, films, television and the unceasing blare of the radio.

To man thus divided within himself, catechesis has to bring a new unity, for its task is to make known Christ who unites and who creates peace. We must never forget that the truth to which we bear witness is not a mere certitude which forces itself upon the mind; it is also a salvation which frees and directs the will, and a "power of resurrection" which brings new life to the body as well as to the soul. The proclamation of the Christian message cannot, therefore, be addressed solely to the intelligence; it has got to appeal to the innermost desires, to the will, and even to the body. It must be for men a cause of their reunion into new communities, those which constitute the Mystical Body of Christ. That is why the catechesis by which we are to hand this message on to mankind must be all-embracing; that is, in the very mode of its proclamation it must take into account all man's spiritual faculties, his social nature, and even his bodily powers.

That does not mean that catechesis has to ignore the enlightening of man's intellect, or that it should not pass on to mankind any exact formulation of the Church's doctrine. But it does mean that in our era we cannot be content with merely didactic instruction which presents to the intellect nothing but clear formulae easily memorized and which fails to introduce the whole man into the new life of God's kingdom. And so we must be on our guard lest we ourselves fall into rationalistic ways of thought, and teach Christianity as if it were only truth brought to man, and not also the personal presence of God and of his love.

### *Our Catechesis Must Present a Correct Evaluation of Temporal Things*

In conclusion let us look at a third quality which our catechesis must possess nowadays. It must teach men to assess properly the value of temporal things. Nothing is a greater obstacle to the implantation and growth of a living faith than an existence divided between two worlds which have nothing to do with each other. "No one can serve two masters", said Christ our Lord. Now it is certain that the fashioning of a new world, to which modern technology invites this generation, is an undertaking which arouses vivid hopes in their minds. They can see for themselves how the conditions of man's existence and the very face of the world have already and speedily been transformed; and they visualize still further progress in the same direction and are captivated by the worldly hopes aroused by these ideas. For a long time they have thought that the future would be similar to the past; but now they think it can be quite different and filled with all kinds of attractive things. For them the word "progress" has become charged with meaning.

On the other hand, if they are Christians, they still have a desire and hope for eternal life, and they know that for man God alone is the absolute good. But these two hopes, relating to the temporal world and the eternal world, exist side by side and have no connection with one another. To modern man it seems very often that his Christian faith has nothing whatever to do with the progress of the world, and that, conversely, this progress has no bearing on his Christian life. This is the reason why so many of our contemporaries lead a sort of split existence, living in two worlds completely sealed off from each other. This way of living reduces the Christian faith to an individualistic and discarnate hope, not in the least interested in that restoration of the Kingdom of God which the Gospel proclaims.

A catechesis worthy of the name can never accept such a dichotomy; it must restore life to a man's hope, and must bring into proper relationship with supernatural goods those material goods which technology renders ever more and more available. Clearly there can be no question of justifying a feverish pursuit of money, luxury or power to which technology can lead. This originates in sin, and can only worsen man's blindness and render him even less susceptible to divine revelation. But it should be emphasized that man is to co-operate with God the Creator, and that creation cannot reach its due perfection without the co-operation of human labour. We must prevent people from mentally separating things done by God from things done by men: as if God's work were merely to create the world of nature, and man's work was to improve on what God had done by applying to nature his inventiveness and industry. An attitude like this would represent work as a kind of disdain for and destruction of God's work, and hence something intrinsically sacrilegious or atheistic. As long as a man entertains any ideas of this kind, the result will be that every time he achieves something new he feels that he is cutting himself off from God.

Such a view of man's relationship with his creator vitiates both the respect with which the Christian ought to treat material things and also the reverence which he should have towards God. For God does not only transcend man – he dwells within him. Hence nobody can render to God due homage unless he understands that all his mental powers derive from God. Nothing whatever is exclusively human except sin, which is rejection of God. Proper instruction concerning the meaning and value of material things is therefore indispensable to men of today if they are to don the civilization they are even now creating and to renew their faith.

### *Conclusion*

The forces which emanate from the present-day diffusion of technical culture are enormous. At first sight they appear absolutely alien to the faith and, in those parts of the world dominated by Marxism, opposed to it. Yet we should no more allow ourselves to be shattered by the unleashing of such forces than did the fifth century bishops faced with the barbarian hordes. Forms of civilization which look utterly inhuman and incompatible with the faith can be conquered from within by a catechesis absolutely in accordance with the life-giving truth it is intended to transmit.

And so, in the light of the problems which this new civilization presents to the Christian conscience, we must reconsider this traditional work of religious instruction. We must transmit Christ's message of freedom and enlightenment to the children, adolescents and adults of our time in an authentic manner, that is, without changing either its dogmatic precision or its redemptive force. Only Christ can save our world from finally succumbing to the inhumanity consequent upon the forces it has unleashed.

(Tr. C.H., S.J.)

# Modern Catechetical Renewal and the Missions

VALERIAN CARDINAL GRACIAS
Archbishop of Bombay, India

BOTH at the Nijmegen Study Week on liturgy, last year, and at this study week on mission catechetics, it has been my privilege to participate actively in the sessions, responding on both occasions to the pressing invitation of Father Hofinger. But, at the very outset, I must confess that both in the sphere of liturgy and catechetics, I have neither any particular competence nor experience of appreciable value. Having striven, however, over the years in the cause of enlightened Catholicism among university students, and subsequently among the educated laity of the city of Bombay, and since first things must come first, I feel that what I hope to learn from this conference on catechetics, as I did last year on liturgy, will exceed by far whatever little contribution I may make to its success.

Speaking of enlightened Catholicism, there seems to be no more crying need, all the world over, including the missions (I will not say particularly the missions, because I am wondering if the need is not as great among the de-Christianized masses in Europe), than that our laity should know better the riches and treasures to which they are heir as Catholics. Relevant indeed is the observation made by Dr. Frank Sheed in *Theology and Sanity*: "When we look at the universe, we see pretty well what people see, plus certain extra features taught us by our religion. For the most part, the same influences that form other people's minds form ours – the same habits of thought, inclinations, bodily senses, indolences, worked upon by the same newspapers, periodicals, best-sellers, films, radio-programmes. So that we have not so much Catholic minds as worldly minds with Catholic patches. Intellectually, we wear our Catholicism like a badge on the same kind of suit that everyone else is wearing." And the message of Cardinal Newman is as actual today as it was in his own days: "I want a laity, not arrogant, not rash in speech, not disputatious, but men who know their religion, who enter into it, who know just where they stand, who know what they hold and what they do not, who know their creed so well that they can give an account of it."

Of course, the foundations of an enlightened Catholicism are to be laid in our educational institutions and in our parochial apostolate; hence the value of this study week.

Reviewing the past sixty years of this century, we may note a continuous renewal and much progress in the field of catechetics. This indeed is gratifying; it augurs well for the catechetical movement in the mission lands. Moreover, it is singularly appropriate that this study week on mission catechetics, should be held in the very cradle, so to speak, of the modern catechetical renewal.

## *The Modern Catechetical Renewal*

### THE PSYCHOLOGICAL STAGE

It was about 1900 that the "Society of Catechists" of Munich, with Dr. Stieglitz as its head and chief exponent, began the present catechetical renewal. Being dissatisfied, on the one hand, with the superficial procedure adopted by catechists in general, as evidenced by the abstract language employed in most catechisms, and a faulty order of presentation; and profiting, on the other hand, by the findings of secular pedagogy (Pestalozzi and Herbart), and by the attempts of Hirscher, with regard to "Biblical Narration", they put forward the Munich or Psychological Method. This method became the basis for a score of other similar catechetical methods, such as the Eucharistic Method of Dr. Edward Poppe in Belgium; Dr. Shields' Primary Methods in North America; the Sower Scheme of Canon F. H. Drinkwater in England; the *Fulda Lehrplan* or curriculum of the Fulda Bishops' Conference; Canon Quinet's active method in France; Dr. Maria Montessori's catechetical games and *Atrium* for children at a kindergarten.

The principal postulates of these methods may be summarized as follows. In the first place, religious instruction must adapt itself to the child's psychology; and, therefore, it must begin with the visual and concrete. Secondly, religious instruction at the school level should not only communicate religious knowledge, but also, and above all, it should establish dispositions and convictions.

### THE THEOLOGICAL STAGE

The light thrown on the educative side of catechesis by the above method led the promoters of the renewal to a better understanding of the fundamental problems of material catechesis. They shifted their attention from the externals of the methods to the interior structure or contents of our catechesis. Father Josef Jungmann's book, (The Glad Tidings and Our Proclamation of the Faith), *Die Frohbotschaft und unsere Glaubensverkündigung,* inaugurated this new stage of the present catechetical renewal. Since the publication of this book in 1936, catechesis has been directed towards this central theme. Our religion is an organic unit, in which we must discern a fundamental core which we have to proclaim emphatically (kerysso – to proclaim). This core is the message of Christ, "the mystery which hath been hidden from ages and generations but now is manifested to his saints". (Col. 1:26) Our way back to the Father is in union with Christ, through the working of the Holy Spirit. All the other truths of our religion have to be explained from this standpoint and with this perspective. What we have to teach is the gospel – the good news that Christ is among us.

### THE INSTITUTIONAL STAGE

With the establishment of the International Catechetical Organizations – like *Lumen Vitae,* in 1946, in Belgium; the *Deutscher Katechetenverein* in Munich; and, most recently, the East Asian Pastoral Institute in Manila – the present catechetical renewal entered the institutional stage. Catechesis is now studied as an organized task in relation to the various social entities and other aspects of pastoral theology.

A glance at the titles of the different issues of *Lumen Vitae* is an indication of this new development. To mention but a few, we have issues devoted to training religious educators, catechesis in the technical world, the human community and religious education, etc. This present study week is a clear example of international co-operation, rendering possible a better exchange of views, with every hope for further progress in thought and action.

## *Present Missionary Catechesis*

### CHINA

As a result of the National Council in Shanghai in 1924, the Committee, to whom it was entrusted, published, in 1933, one catechism for all the Chinese missions in three different editions – small, medium and large. The Synodal Commission created after the Peking Council, dealt with questions of catechesis in *Collectanea Commissionis Synodalis.*

In 1940–41 the catechetical movement emanating from the District of Tatung published a periodical *Ut vitam habeant – Periodicum pedagogico-catecheticum,* which gave promise of a real catechetical revival, and actually reached the stage of practical conclusions; but this was ruined by the Communist revolution.

In 1954, however, thanks to the former Jesuit missionaries in China, and under the direction of Father Hofinger, the East Asian Pastoral Institute was founded in Manila. Its aim is to keep the missionaries of the far east, especially in China, in touch with the latest developments in missionary and pastoral science in Christian countries. It is not only concerned with catechesis, but with all matters connected with the Christian message.[1]

### TAIWAN

The Catechist System in Taiwan was founded by Monsignor William F. Kupfer, M.M., for the Prefecture of Taiching; it started in 1951 with 6; it now embraces 83 men and 51 women catechists, spread out in 26 different parishes. Candidates

[1] J. Beckmann, S.M.B., *Lumen Vitae,* 1957, pp. 116–7.

selected by the missionaries from their parishes are required to have a minimum of three years of lower middle school, and submit to an entrance examination and a three days' retreat. There is a daily routine similar to seminary life with mental prayer and classes in Church history, liturgy, apologetics, scripture, and a careful study of the prevalent superstitions practised by the non-Christians of Taiwan. Besides theory, they have practical pedagogy in the neighbouring school; they are responsible for the pre- and post-confirmation classes and the parish middle school. Though they are paid catechists, the idea of a vocation is instilled into them. This has proved to be relatively successful with 19,000 baptisms in eight years.[2]

### JAPAN

Before the last World War the magazine, *Actio Missionaria,* promoted progress in the sphere of catechesis. Father Hogolin Noll, O.F.M., created the method called "pedagogical" in his efforts to adapt catechetical instruction to the Japanese temperament.

In 1945 the National Catholic Committee founded a catechetical sub-section of the Missionary Department. It is entrusted with the task of furnishing Japanese and foreign missionaries with practical means for action; the *Missionary Bulletin* follows in the steps of *Actio Missionaria,* and is at the service of the catechetical movement sponsored by the Scheut missionaries.[3]

Father George Gemeinder, S.V.D., founded the Catechist Training Centre of Nagoya, in 1950, for women and in 1957 for men. According to him, " a catechist in Japan must deal with people who have a high standard of education". A catechist who makes the apostolate his life's work must have adequate general education, a good training as a catechist, and a sound, healthy, religious life.

All candidates are from high school or college. The Fathers in charge insist on a high spiritual and intellectual standard with special emphasis on leadership and faith. They follow a two-

[2] Mission Bulletin, March 1959, pp. 222–8.
[3] J. Beckmann, *Lumen Vitae,* 1957, pp. 117–8.

years intensive and extensive course designed to prepare the catechist for the active apostolate in heavily populated industrial and rural areas. This course includes dogmatic, moral and ascetical theology, together with scripture, ethics, psychology, education, music, literature and missiology. To qualify for a catechist's diploma, students must pass an examination and receive a character recommendation from the Director.[4]

The Secular Institute of the Catechists of Mary, Virgin and Mother, was founded by the same Father, and approved by the Sacred Congregation of *Propaganda Fide* in January 1954. While the Institute does not establish educational or charitable institutions, it strives to penetrate the world and exercise the apostolate through personal influence in missionary, professional or domestic circles. The missionary section comprises those catechists working in mission stations, all the training centre's graduates holding a first class diploma. The professional members work as teachers, nurses, office workers, etc. They infiltrate into secular institutions as employees, and spread the spirit of Christianity in their daily contact with the pagan world. Members of the domestic section are trained to cook and keep house in families and mission stations. Membership is restricted to young women, who after a one-year noviciate, take the three canonical vows and an oath to dedicate themselves to the performance of apostolic work. The perpetual vows are taken only after seven years. They are not tied down to any religious habit, and their spiritual life is provided for by their constitutions.[5]

### INDIA

The Plenary Council of India (1950) recognized catechesis "among the most important duties of those who have charge of souls". As a result, a Section of Catechetics was established by the Standing Committee of the Catholic Bishops' Conference of India.

In 1955 the following instructions were issued. The professors in seminaries were recommended to be familiar with the progress

[4] See *Mission Bulletin,* May 1959, pp. 454–5.
[5] *Mission Bulletin,* May 1959, pp. 456–8.

of modern pedagogy and catechesis; the need was felt for a catechetical manual embodying the latest results in this sphere and adapting them to Indian conditions; and, since these conditions differ because of the various linguistic groups in the country, it was suggested that group catechetical centres (catechetical documentation centres) be established with the purpose of systematizing the work of each particular mission and helping missionaries with advice.[6]

In 1956 the annual report lamented the fact that although there are seventeen Catholic training colleges for men and twenty for women, very few have provided religious training for the students. As a result of this report, De Nobili College, Poona, was approached by the catechetical section of the Catholic Bishops' Conference of India to open a catechetical centre on the lines laid down in the recommendations of 1955. Refresher courses for the training of Catholic teachers were also recommended.

Catechetical exhibitions, as practical efforts to foster the catechetical movement, became regular features in some educational centres. Worthy of mention are those held by the Holy Family Convent, Trimulgherry (Deccan); the Sacred Heart Training School, Srivilliputtur (Ramanathpuram Dt.); The Pontifical Atheneum, Poona; and the one prepared by the combined efforts of all Catholic Schools of Bombay in October 1957 on the history of the Catholic Church.

The Catechetical Congress (March 11–15, 1956) organized by the Sacred Heart Seminary, Poonamalee (Chingleput Dt.) was entrusted to the Salesians of Don Bosco. It had five sections, namely, Catechism and Catechists, Methods and Aims, Catechism and non-Catholics, Catechism and the Sacraments, and Catechism after First Communion. There was also an exhibition.[7]

[6] Since 1940 Bombay has two catechetical institutes for the training of religion teachers in schools. After a course of one (St. Xavier's C.I.) or two (St. Margaret's C.I.) years, and a successful examination in the different catechetical and pedagogical subjects, they receive a Religious Instruction Diploma from the Archbishop.

[7] (J. Beckmann, *Lumen Vitae,* 1957, p. 118; Archambeaud, *Lumen Vitae,* 1957, pp. 537–44).

In 1959, Bombay launched a scheme of religious instruction compulsory in all the Catholic schools of the Archdiocese. It was prepared with the generous collaboration of the Catechetical Centre of De Nobili College. In formulating this scheme, the following key points were kept in mind; kerygmatic syllabus with textbooks adapted to India; a gradual initiation into the Christian message through bible history, liturgy and catechism; an initiation into the liturgical life of the Church during the last school year; the psychological approach of learning by doing and an adequate stress on Christian values.

Tindivanam Catechist Training Centre, the training centre for catechists in South India, founded by the late Father Thomas Gavan Duffy, has become famous for its results and methods. Though originally meant to train full-time catechists, its object now is to train teachers possessing the outlook of catechists. It has already trained 2000, among whom over a thousand are Catholic teachers and catechists. It gives the candidates a double formation – personal and catechetical. Their personal formation is built on human nature. It is intended to exploit all the resources of rational human nature, tilling the natural ground to make it ready for the supernatural seed. It is based on personal qualities such as trustworthiness, activity, cleanliness and generosity. Catechetical formation is inspired by the catechetical formation received in a Christian home, which is not reduced to merely few hours a week. It consists primarily in living with the boys and then instructing them. Father Duffy's motto was "Everything helps". Study, sport, exhortation, and religious practices, are all tools with which to mould children to the form of Christ.[8]

A catechist school in Tongo (Chota Nagpur) was established in 1922. The candidates are required to be married, to have a primary education and teaching experience for two years as assistant catechists. Since 1933 it is a two years' course. The catechists stay with their wives, who do the cooking, washing, cleaning and receive instructions so as to be model Christian wives and mothers in the villages. They may help the catechists in the preparation of children for the sacraments, and hence

[8] See *Mission Bulletin,* February 1959, pp. 126–31.

they also receive spiritual formation. The catechist begins his training with an explanation of the Mystical Body of Christ for a better understanding of and participation in the daily Mass. The whole catechism is explained and notes are given as to how they should conduct the three catechumenates (before baptism, before confirmation, before marriage). They study the four Gospels, Church history, practical apologetics, pastoral theology. Great importance is given to the practical training in the school and the villages, as well as in the way of conducting a *Panchayat*. For their spiritual training, they have meditation, examination of conscience and particular examen; they all join the Third Order of St. Francis and take the pledge. The follow-up work is kept up by regular letter writing and refresher courses.[9]

### AFRICA

Africa is a model of great fields of missionary activity among primitive peoples. Though handicapped by the division of the country into many races and languages, the lack of the most elementary means of action, and isolation by colonial barriers, much work has been realized with the production of large numbers of catechisms and the ensuing multiplication of catechetical didactical aids in various languages. In contrast with missions among educated nations, the African missionaries have had to work for decades in the compilation of a vocabulary; this work has led many missions to revise their catechisms. Father Gaston's catechism is the latest suggested for common use and is being translated into different languages. The White Fathers and the Holy Ghost Fathers have given standard regulations and practical methods for the teaching of Christian doctrine.

Recently, Africa has been in touch with the catechetical progress of Christian countries. *Le Centre Documentaire Catéchétique* in the Congo started the *Revue du Clergé Africain,* affiliated to *Lumen Vitae* and edited by Father Denis, S.J. In 1955 the International Week of Studies in Religious Formation was held at Léopoldville with an attendance of 500 delegates.[10]

[9] See *Mission Bulletin,* May 1958, pp. 425–30.
[10] J. Beckmann, *Lumen Vitae,* 1957, pp. 118–9.

*Adaptation of the Modern Catechetical Renewal to the Needs of Mission Lands*

The Encyclical *Princeps Pastorum* on the missions was issued on 28th November 1959. Its occasion was the fortieth anniversary of *Maximum Illud* of Benedict XV, "which had given a fresh impetus to missionary activity in the Church". Its purpose was to treat the inner problems of the missions and of the means to bring them to their full stature.

The inner problems of the mission countries cover a very vast range indeed; the problems which concern us at present are limited to the field of missionary catechesis only; yet a glance at some of the headings of the encyclical and comparison with the programme of this study week shows that we can find in the former the right directives to adapt the modern catechetical renewal to the needs of mission lands.

The motivating force of the present catechetical renewal is to adapt the message of Christianity to the present de-Christianized world, not to compromise with the principles and currents of the world, but with the object of presenting the message from such an angle, and under such a light, as to produce in the modern man an interior and supernatural experience, and create a new man.

For this reason it demands a radical re-orientation of the contents of our catechism. No more the traditional scheme, according to which the truths of our religion were classified into what I have to believe, to do, to receive, something like a "must" imposed on us from without. It demands the presentation of the contents of our catechism as an organic unit which springs from within; the nature of the relations between God and man. The central and essential theme is our way to the Father in union with Jesus Christ brought about objectively by the infusion of grace, subjectively by the imitation of Christ, and all this through the workings of the Holy Spirit. All the other truths of our faith have to be exposed and explained under this God-centred, Christ-centred perspective.

The result will be that our preaching will be the announcing of the gospel – the Good Tidings. It will satisfy the present quest for peace, rest and security; it will produce a supernatural experience – "Christ among you, your hope of glory" (Col. 1:27) – it will establish a new life with Christ, to be developed within us, to be spread outside us.

The same is the triple role of missionary catechesis: To break the charms of paganism, to lay the foundations of a new life in Christ in the new Christian, to plant Christianity in every member so as to serve as a solid basis for future generations.

Such also are the directives given by the Holy Father in his encyclical. Our missionary catechesis must produce a supernatural experience in the catechumen, for "a Christian instruction and education which concerns itself only with teaching the formulae of the catechism and the fundamental precepts of Christian morality, illustrated by a few examples or cases, if it does not inspire the hearts and wills for the effective practice of a Christian life, runs the risk of providing the Church with a passive flock". The result of our missionary preaching should be a new life in Christ in the new Christian. "Even in new Christian communities, it is not enough to multiply conversions and to inscribe long lists of names in the baptismal register. The number of Christians will mean little if they are wanting in quality, if they are not staunch in the profession of their faith, if their spiritual life lacks depth and fails to produce visible fruits, if, after having been born to the life of grace, they give no evidence of that vigorous youth which is ever ready for right and fruitful action. The profession of the Christian faith is not merely a matter of statistics, it must create a 'new man' (Eph. 4:24), it must give a supernatural energy to all his actions stimulating and directing them." Our preaching should be such as to awaken in the new Christian the urge of duty to witness to the truth. "Christians, being members of one living body, may not remain turned in upon themselves and think that they will discharge their whole duty if they provide for their own spiritual needs. Everyone must contribute his part for the growth and the spread of the Kingdom of God on earth. All should, therefore, give assiduous testimony of their zeal for the spiritual welfare of their neighbour, defending their faith and making it known to those who are ignorant of it. This sacred duty must be inculcated in all from infancy and adolescence, by the clergy, the family and the various apostolic organizations, even in communities where Christianity is new. A particularly favourable occasion for this education is the time of preparation for confirmation. Another favourable opportunity exists in those places where there are ceremonies of initiation for youths at the time of their official entry into their social group."

### *Adaptation of our Preaching to Traditional Culture*

Christianity is always looked upon at the beginning as an "intrusion" into the sacred beliefs of a race or nation, something "foreign" to the traditions of a people. Adaptation does not mean that the Church "acts like one who recklessly cuts down and uproots a thriving forest; no, she grafts a good scion upon the wild stock that it may bear a crop of more delicious fruit".[11] Adaptation is like endowing the organic unit of the catechism with flesh and blood and the features of the people to be evangelized.

In missionary catechesis the positive teaching of Christian doctrine, and not apologetics, should come first; yet in our evangelization of the people to whom we are sent, we must take into account whether there are some remains of the primitive revelation among the religious beliefs of the people, because the revealed truth and moral law add to the natural law greater precision and a supernatural character; whether and how far the philosophical and religious thought of this non-Christian people can help us to understand and express Christian truths, for thus we present the unchanged and unchangeable Christian doctrine in another vesture which will make it better understood; whether there are customs, religious practices and festivals deeply rooted in this people which can be Christianized and transformed into Christian feasts and practices.

In *Princeps Pastorum* the Holy Father emphasizes the Church's regard for all authentic values, and quotes *Evangelii praecones:* "The Catholic Church does not despise nor reject pagan teachings, but she rather completes and perfects them with Christian

[11] Pius XII in *Evangelii praecones*.

wisdom once they have been freed of error or defect. Thus she has welcomed progress in arts and sciences . . . and in a certain manner she has consecrated the customs and ancient traditions of peoples; she has taken their pagan feasts and transformed them into memorials of martyrs and of sacred mysteries." He repeats his own address to the World Congress of African writers and artists: "We Ourselves have already expressed Our thoughts on this subject. Wherever there are authentic values of art and science that can enrich the human family, the Church is ready to favour such efforts of the spirit. Her mission belongs to the order of the religious salvation of man. Rich in her youthfulness which is constantly renewed by the breath of the Holy Spirit, the Church is ever ready to recognize, to welcome, and indeed to encourage all things that honour the human mind and heart."

The Pope goes further still; he wants his missionaries, and in particular the native clergy, to lead the cultured classes to Christ and to establish centres for special studies and for the diffusion of Christian doctrine. "Native priests who are trained in this difficult and important field will, under the direction of their bishops, be able to give life to movements of penetration among the cultured classes. In this respect it will suffice to cite, for all, the example of Father Matteo Ricci. It is also the native clergy that must 'bring every mind into captivity to the obedience of Christ' (2 Cor. 10:5). Thus they will enjoy 'the esteem of the elite and the learned in their own countries'. *(Rerum Ecclesiae)* Following their own judgements, bishops will, at the opportune time, establish centres of culture, according to the need in some particular region, or in several, where priests, both native and foreign, will be able to put their knowledge and experience at the service of the nation in which they were born or to which they have given themselves by choice."

### *The Role of Liturgy in Missionary Catechesis*

Liturgy is "education in faith". It is catechesis in that it concentrates our attention on the essence of Christianity, namely Christ, our way to the Father through the Holy Spirit. This is the undeniable message of all eucharistic celebration during the whole of the liturgical year. Liturgy is a means of initiating new converts into the Christian way of life, and of educating and perfecting them in it without the help of Christian surroundings. The external celebration of worship is a constitutive element of interior faith, which, like sorrow, is not really deep unless we have to weep. St. Ambrose affirms: *Fides tua pleno fulgeat sacramento,* while St. Thomas calls the sacraments *protestationes fidei* because faith finds in the visibility of the sacrament its body, so to speak, and its human dimension. In this sense, the celebration of worship is the constitutive factor of a faith come to maturity. If the community does not come together "for the breaking of bread and prayer" the faith in its spiritual community remains incomplete.

The Holy Father recognizes these values of the liturgy and insists on union in prayer and active participation in the divine mysteries. "The testimony of individuals must be confirmed and amplified by that of the entire Christian community after the manner of what took place in the infant Church, when the close union of all the faithful who were 'persevering in the doctrine of the apostles and in the communion of the breaking of the bread and in prayer', as well as the generous exercise of charity, was a motive of profound satisfaction and mutual edification; 'for they were praising God and were in favour with all the people. And day by day the Lord added to their company such as were to be saved' (Acts 2:47). Union in prayer and active participation in the divine mysteries of the liturgy contributes most efficaciously to the fulness and richness of Christian life among individuals and the community."

In our missionary preaching we must not lose sight of those problems which are cropping up on all sides at full speed, in mission countries much faster than even, perhaps, in the Christian countries. In this connection, the encyclical *Princeps Pastorum* opens out new avenues for the missionary apostolate for all Catholics, those native to the soil, and those born in Christian countries.

The Holy Father first clearly indicates the actuality of the problem. "Today in every part of the world there exist various problems the solution of which is sought by appeal to merely human wisdom and by principles that are not always in conformity with the demands of the Christian faith. 'Most mission territories are going through a phase of social, economic and political evolution that is pregnant with consequences for their future.' *(Fidei Donum)* Problems which in some countries are already solved or find elements of solution in tradition, confront other nations with an urgency that demands a quick solution; this urgency is not without danger, in so far as it might lead to hasty decisions and to the incautious acceptance of doctrines that ignore or contradict the religious interests of individuals and nations. For their own good and for the good of the Church, Catholics may not ignore these problems nor wait till they are given harmful solutions which it will afterwards take much greater effort to correct."

Next, the Holy Father points out the function of the indigenous laity in various fields. "It is in the various sectors of public life that the laity in mission countries can exercise their most appropriate and most important activity. It is, therefore, a matter of utmost urgency that the Christian communities be able to offer to their earthly homelands, for their common good, men who will honour the office and the tasks committed to them and at the same time will be a credit to the Church which has given them the life of grace."

Finally, the Pope appeals to international organizations and to lay catholics who in any part of the world are in any eminent position. This is a unique appeal. "It is easy to see how international Catholic organizations can offer valuable help to the lay apostolate in mission countries, either on the scientific level by the study of the Christian solution to be given to the problems (especially social) of the young nations, or in the directly apostolic field, especially for the organization of an active Christian laity. We know what has been done already and what is being done by lay missionaries who have chosen to leave their own countries, temporarily or definitively, in order to make a contribution by various activities towards the social and religious welfare of mission countries; and We pray the Lord to increase the number of these generous souls and to sustain them in the trials and difficulties they have to face."

"We address Our appeal also to all those lay Catholics who, in any part of the world, are in eminent positions by reason of their profession or public office: let them seriously consider how they can, even without leaving their own countries, come to the aid of their newly acquired brothers. Their advice, their experience, their technical assistance may at times, without excessive inconvenience, be a decisive contribution. Men endowed with the spirit of initiative will find means to put this desire of Ours into practice."

## *Concluding Recommendation*

### THE ESTABLISHMENT OF CATECHETICAL CENTRES

This is the task we are undertaking by our active participation in this study week on missionary catechetics, and these are the Holy Father's directives which must guide us in our meetings and work-shop discussions.

These are also the problems and directives the missionaries in their own mission regions will have to study and adapt; because we must not forget the fundamental principle of all missionary catechesis. "Preach the Christian message to the people to whom you are sent to evangelize", and every region has its own milieu; hence, the need of catechetical centres scattered all over the mission world, and erected at real central places, with the purpose of systematizing with the direction and approval of the hierarchy the work of each particular mission, keep constant contact with the catechetical movement in Christian countries, and help missionaries with guidance and literature.

# Characteristics of Missionary Catechesis

MANUEL LARRAIN
Bishop of Talca, Chile

## *Biblical Foundations*

IN order to discover the fundamental meaning of the concepts "catechesis" and "mission" we must follow them back to their sources. In the light of divine revelation we shall see what riches these two words contain. Even brief reference to the sources will show us their deep significance and will provide us with guiding principles for our work.

The announcement and preparation of the divine commission is the predominant theme of Old Testament revelation. Everything is directed towards the founding of the Messianic Kingdom, in expectation of him "who is to come", in anticipation of "the Lord's Day". When Christ is sent by God, eminent proof that with his mission "the fullness of time" has come is seen in the fact that "the gospel is proclaimed to the poor". Thus Christ's life can be summed up in two words: Evangelion – Kerygma, the proclaiming of joyful tidings.

Jesus *is* himself the Good News; in him the prophecies are fulfilled, with him the era of types is concluded, and the Kingdom of God actually begins. He announced this himself in his first sermon: "Today hath this scripture been fulfilled" (Luke 4:21). Today, in the synagogue of Nazareth, the prophecy of Isaiah has come true.

Christ's public life begins, and with it the founding of God's kingdom. The primary vocation of the Twelve is that of "envoys" commissioned to proclaim the message of salvation. After Christ's resurrection the apostles receive their final vocation, which is a consecration of the original one. But these final orders have a new character of universality, embracing the message itself, all time, and all history. As the early Church is pervaded by this consciousness of an all-embracing mission, she is predominantly characterized as a community by a spirit of vibrant hope.

The apostles' first preaching is like a "glorious manifestation" of the Kingdom of God. The task of proclaiming the message of God's kingdom finds its response among those who hear the word – the response of faith. Faith means dedicating oneself wholly to Christ. Faith is the living water drunk by the just. This faith forms the foundation of the original community. The *Ecclesia* is the assembly of the faithful.

After kerygma has transmitted faith, there begins the work of *catechesis,* which is to confirm this faith. The believer becomes a catechumen. As it has traditionally been understood for sixteen centuries, catechesis is a supernatural form of religious education. Thus catechesis and mission are two concepts whose biblical and historical origins are so intertwined that mention of one necessarily evokes the thought of the other. It is in conjunction and correlation with the missionary spirit that catechesis acquires its dynamic significance and its true dimensions within the Church.

Missionary catechesis is thus written on the very heart of the Church's life. It represents, now as in the past, the encounter of Christianity with each generation and with each historical epoch, and is the chief means by which each period of history is enabled to play its part in the advancement of the kingdom of God. Through it are fulfilled in a special way our Lord's words: "God sent his Son into the world not to judge the world but in order that the world should be saved by him." (John 3:17)

### *Characteristics*

In the light of the Bible and of history let us examine the characteristics of missionary catechesis. These can be summarized under three headings, namely, concentration on the essential, dynamic vitality, and method.

## CONCENTRATION ON THE ESSENTIAL

The purpose of missionary catechesis is to lay the foundations of a new life. This is the thought which reappears constantly in the preaching of Saint Paul. "My little children, for whom I am again in travail until Christ be formed in you" (Gal. 4:19). This *donec formetur Christus in vobis* is the goal of the apostle's supernatural teaching. It is certainly the ultimate goal of catechesis: that Christ should take shape in man.

According to the encyclical *Divini Illius Magistri* "the true Christian, the product of Christian education, is a man of supernatural motives, who constantly and consistently thinks, judges and acts according to right reason illuminated by the supernatural light of Christ's example and teaching".

The manner of introducing Christianity determines the attitude of the catechumen as well as how deeply the gospel takes root on the spot and in the surroundings where it is preached. Initial instruction in Christianity should be of a wealth and solidity that assure the preservation of its initial vitality and enable it to overcome the adversities it encounters during its expansion and development. This presupposes a very clear view of the task of evangelization, one which distinguishes the essential from the accidental, throwing the basic truths into relief and pointing out the intimate connection among them.

It is disheartening to see how often those to be instructed are presented with a mixture of fundamental biblical truths and private revelation, without any discrimination in the hierarchy of values; essential Christian practices mixed with devotions laudable in themselves but not of decisive importance for the Christian life; the great Christological significance of the liturgical seasons drowned in a deluge of private devotions; bible stories of secondary importance placed on the same level as the miraculous drama of the mystery of redemption. More than once I have had to reflect how well the proverb about not seeing the wood for the trees applies to much of our catechesis. Our catechumens' perseverence in the faith and the vitality or decadence of many Christian observances depend very much on whether the catechist was able to present the essentials during the initial instruction.

To accomplish this task it is equally important to make a distinction between controversial points and matters of faith, and, as the encyclical *Divino Afflante Spiritu* reminds and recommends us to do, when interpreting the Bible to distinguish among the various literary genres. How well it has been put by Father Colomb: "Our teaching should be progressive, but homogeneous and theologically accurate, distinguishing the certain from the uncertain, the essential from the accessory. Respect for the word of God must keep us from presenting as divine thoughts what are only human interpretations."[1]

From what has been said it follows that the initial instruction should be less a matter of quantity than of quality, that is, it should concentrate on the essentials of religion. This requires an ability to present the great facts of the faith, not as a collection of elaborate theological formulas, but as an entirety consisting of persons and events through which the divine plan of salvation is gradually realized. The God whom we must make known to the catechumens is the God of Abraham, the God of the Prophets, the Father of our Lord Jesus Christ, the God who accomplishes his plan of salvation in time. This presentation of the essential truths should be historical in nature. It is not a metaphysical disquisition. It is the account of happenings to which the whole Bible bears witness. Divine revelation, from Genesis to the Apocalypse, is the story of God's great deeds for humanity: *magnalia Dei*.

This initial teaching, precisely because it insists on the essential, should possess in very vivid form the character of revealed religion. That is, it should show that God intervened in human history, that he took the initiative in redeeming man, that his infinite love has destined man to possess God eternally. At the centre of this plan of salvation there must stand out the figure of Christ, the Alpha and Omega of the life and history of humanity. It is imperative to avoid making the mistake of many counter-Reformation catechisms, which are pronouncedly anthropocentric in character and whose vision of Christianity presents the aspect of a natural religion with a strong moralistic accent.

[1] J. Colomb, *Aux sources du Catéchisme*.

Sometimes we turn catechesis into a course of philosophical or sociological lectures, forgetting that, although we are not forbidden to make use of such argumentation, the ultimate purpose of catechesis is a higher and transcendental one. The pagan world was never converted in the past, nor will it be converted in the present, by philosophical wisdom or scientific erudition; the only thing which will ever convert it is the authentic and enthusiastic proclamation of the mystery of Christ: "The Jews ask for signs and the Greeks seek after wisdom: but we preach Christ crucified" (1 Cor. 1:22–3).

Finally, the initial catechesis, together with concentrating on the essential, should impart a profound sense of the unity of the gospel.

Genuine catechesis consists in teaching not disconnected truths but truths integrated into a harmonious central plan. This unified plan should be constructed on the basis of historical rather than logical order, and of progress from one event or personage of the story of redemption to the next. The unifying centre of this plan should be the figure of Christ and especially the mysteries of his death and resurrection. Christ is the heart of the gospel.

Catechesis in general, and especially missionary catechesis, is increasingly concentrating its attention on the selection, interconnection, and relative value of the truths it has to teach.[2]

Centering catechesis on Christ will give the catechumen the marvellous vision of the divine grace of the message working in his own heart. It will make him aware of the old ferment of wickedness making way for the new leaven, and will let him experience in all its intensity the paschal mystery of the new life to which he is reborn. This confident and joyous paschal certitude will give him the strength to confront his pagan surroundings with his Christianity, and the enthusiasm to live a full and genuine Christian life.

The missionary movement based on a catechesis which concentrates on the essentials is assured of vitality and the impetus necessary for expansion. Past history and present experience teach us the doleful consequences that follow for the

[2] See the article by J. Hofinger in *Lumen Vitae,* 1950.

Church when this primary characteristic of missionary catechesis is neglected.

### DYNAMIC VITALITY

The second characteristic of missionary catechesis is its dynamic vitality. A concept of central importance in the Bible is the "conversion of the heart", that is, of the personality to its very depths. This conversion – μετάνοια – consists in man's placing his confidence in Christ, his Lord and Saviour. It is St. Paul's *scio cui credidi* – "I know in whom I have placed my faith" (2 Tim. 1:12). This requires that our teaching appears as an aggregate of *values,* not as a catalogue of duties. This is the basis of the sense of dynamic vitality that the message should convey.

A merely apologetic or predominantly moralizing form of catechesis cannot have the necessary dynamic effect. The dynamic approach shows all history as culminating in Christ. It makes it felt that "the Kingdom of God is among us", but that it is up to us to enlarge and extend it. It conveys a dynamic sense of the Church as God's people advancing among the vicissitudes of history.

Christianity must be presented not as man's "duty", but as a loving response to the initiative taken by God. It should appear not as a doctrinal system but as communion with the living God, a religious life in which the word of God meets the response of man. Thus Christianity is seen as dialogue in which God summons man and man responds, obeys, freely decides: a dialogue which is a reflection of another, profounder one that has been going on for all eternity within the central mystery of the Trinity.

From what has been said it follows that the instruction should not appeal exclusively to the intelligence but should present Christianity as an object of love, appealing to and capturing the heart. Because Christianity is love, knowledge of it should arouse love in us. No one has provided us with a greater wealth of fine examples of this than St. Paul. Because he "lives his faith in the Son of God", "his life is Christ"; and it is the goal of Christian life as he presents it that "speaking truth in love, we may in all things grow up into him who is the Head"

(Eph. 4:15). Therefore he lends terrible force to his demand that his catechumens and neophytes practise the love of Christ which he preaches to them, not hesitating to say: "If any man loveth not the Lord, let him be anathema" (1 Cor. 16:22).

Catechesis must maintain close contact with life. Christianity is not an esoteric religion of initiates. It is the realization in time of the mystery of the incarnation: God incarnate, who has taken on the whole reality of our human existence, with the exception of sin. Through catechesis the Christian should be brought to contemplate the double dynamism of creation and of grace, and to realize that the same God who creates is the God who saves. This doubly dynamic aspect should make him love human life and understand that it is there that he accomplishes his own perfection. One must beware of the Manichaeism latent in many Christian educators, who present the religious as opposed to the human, the temporal over against the eternal, the natural versus the supernatural. But this is a disavowal of the profoundest mystery of Christianity and deprives redemption of its dynamic potency.

The liturgy of the Christmas season speaks of the *admirabile commercium,* describing with all the pathos of the liturgy the double action of God, who, "having assumed a living body, deigned to be born of a Virgin and 'in exchange' enriched us with his divinity". Only through the twofold dynamism of creation and grace can the tension which frequently appears between religion and life be converted into harmony.

This dynamic vitality should concentrate on living the mystery of the Church in all its intensity. Christ came to bring us new life, which the Church bestows. This vital conception of the Church is what engenders in the faithful the expectation of salvation and inflames in them the desire of apostolic charity. Missionary catechesis should awaken a consciousness of belonging to a growing Church, to a dynamic community, to the people of God moving towards their ultimate goal. It must convey a vision of the world and of the Church, and show that Christ has entrusted to the Christians the evolution of the Church, that the work of the apostles has not yet been completed, and that the modern world, shaken to its foundations by profound convulsions, must be faced in a missionary and apostolic spirit. A Christian community in non-Christian surroundings which lacks the apostolic impulse is the living accusation of a deficient and impotent religious education.

The dynamic vitality of the Church is expressed in a special way in her liturgy. This is "the voice of the Bride", "the assembly of the people of God", in which the Christian people relives the mystery of Christ, its teacher and Redeemer. "The most effective form of evangelization", wrote Father Jungmann, "is the celebration of a Church feast." "The Christian feasts are a profession of faith of the community, celebrating specifically Christian values."[3]

Applying to the liturgy the axiom of Catholic teaching on the sacraments, *dant quod significant,* the liturgy makes us participants in the mystery celebrated by it. The public prayer of the Church is the most lavish expression of her vitality, and active participation in it is "the primary and indispensable source of the true Christian spirit" *(Inter Pastorales)*. Do we understand now why much of our catechesis succeeds only in forming "ex-alumni" and not men "reborn in the Spirit", living the wonderful adventure of their Christian vocation?

It is chiefly in his liturgical life that the Christian experiences the dynamic vitality of the Church and her message. Under the aspect of this dynamic vitality, missionary catechesis gives history its Christian sense. The great ideological danger of the present, to which our rising generations are insensibly falling prey, is a materialistic conception of history. Missionary catechesis must gradually show, in the course of its development, that God is not absent from history. Since the advent of Christ, his presence runs through history like an invisible stream. Christ is present – one must only learn to discover his presence in all that happens. Christ will come. History must be given its eschatological significance, the wide horizons of the heavenly Jerusalem must be open before the catechumens and awaken in their hearts the supreme desire for Christ's final coming. *Veni, Domine Jesu – Marana-tha.* Such is the dynamic vitality which should characterize missionary catechesis.

[3] J. Hofinger in *Lumen Vitae,* Vol. X.

## METHOD

The third characteristic of missionary catechesis must be a method adapted and attractive to the catechumens. Cardinal Mercier said that "the two sciences most useful to the priest are theology and sociology: the science of God and the science of man". While revelation provides us with the content of the message, religious sociology in its turn gives us a knowledge of the mentality, the religious state, the ideological tensions, the material conditions of life of those for whom the message is intended. Adapting catechesis to the catechumens means giving it an incarnation in their lives. That is, it must respond to their problems, desires, worries, and so on. It must be adapted to the circumstances – whether among workers or in the country. It must be psychological, that is, it must correspond to the mentality of those to whom it appeals. This accommodation of catechesis to the catechumens constitutes its realism. There is a sort of realism in catechesis to which can be applied what Father Congar said of preaching: "It should treat real problems and give real nourishment to souls, should proceed in a manner understood by a real audience composed of men with concrete responsibilities in the world of men, should be capable of producing fruit in the consciences and hearts of those who hear it."

This requires a knowledge and appreciation of the non-Christian values encountered in pagan or materialistic surroundings. As Father Hofinger says: "The absolute superiority of Christianity by no means requires us to consider everything in paganism as absurd and superstitious." St. Paul speaks of creation groaning in expectation of its liberation, and St. Augustine reminds us of the *anima naturaliter christiana*. In the midst of natural realities, hidden beneath materialistic appearances, there exist Christian roots, apostolical opportunities, open furrows awaiting the seed of the gospel.

Paul dreamt of the Macedonian saying to him "Come to our assistance!" and he left without delay for this unknown land. In pagan disguise and in an unfamiliar language of the spirit there are calls of souls which the catechist should learn to hear. Wholesale condemnation of all the values of a culture for not being apparently Christian is a serious mistake which may be made by the catechist in his work of preaching the gospel. Upon penetrating more deeply into this culture, he may then exclaim with Jacob: "This place is sacred, and I knew it not." There are many stones which may turn into a "Bethel".

The God who became man two thousand years ago is present in our twentieth century, and on all continents. The form of his presence is of course now of a different nature. One must have a profound respect for his hidden presence and remember that, etymologically, the profane – *pro-fanum* – is that which stands before the sanctuary.

Missionary catechesis must take the form of a *dialogue* instead of polemics. On the Areopagus Paul mentioned – without condemning them – the statues of false divinities which decorated the public squares of Athens, and took this opportunity of preaching to the people of Athens on the unknown God: "*Quod ergo ignorantes colitis, hoc ergo annuntio vobis*" (Acts 17: 23).

Adopting the attitude of a dialogue is productive of respect for the opposite side. This is the other indispensable condition of missionary catechesis: respect for the various civilizations, cultures, and types of character. Again St. Paul teaches us: "What is my reward then? That preaching the gospel, I may deliver the gospel without charge, that I abuse not my power in the gospel. For whereas I was free as to all, I made myself the servant of all, that I might gain the more. And I became to the Jews, a Jew, that I might gain the Jews: to them that are under the law, as if I were under the law (whereas myself was not under the law), that I might gain them that were under the law. To them that were without the law, as if I were without the law (whereas I was not without the law of God, but was in the law of Christ), that I might gain them that were without the law. To the weak I became weak, that I might gain the weak. I became all things to all men, that I might save all. And I do all things for the gospel's sake: that I may be made partaker thereof" (1 Cor. 9:18–23).

The catechist must not appear to be teaching a lesson which he has brought out of cold storage for the occasion, but to be speaking in testimony of something which he knows and loves. He is not the representative of a people, a race, a civilization, or a class, but a man proclaiming the One in whom he believes and whom he loves. "And we have known, and have believed the charity, which God hath to us. God is charity: and he that abideth in charity, abideth in God, and God in him" (1 John 4:16). Because he has a sense of his mission, his language will be simple (1 Cor. 2: 4–5), simple language using words suited to the mentality of the hearers and carefully avoiding philosophical or theological terminology. But simplicity should characterize not only the language but also the attitude we adopt. Full of humility because we have been deemed worthy to announce the gospel, of respect because we are exercising the sublime ministry of transmitting the word of God, of love because we are begetting in faith new children of the Church. The simplicity of our attitude should be like that of a mother speaking to her child, or brothers and sisters to one another, and should express the supernatural meaning of the mission we are fulfilling. This spirit of simplicity will open to missionary catechesis the wide field of souls.

### *The Church Encounters an Emergent Civilization*

No civilization is born Christian. The Church's mission is to baptize each one. This requires of us fidelity in transmitting integrally the message, whose permanent structure we may not alter. The characteristics of missionary catechesis are the expression of this structure. In speaking of them: concentration on the essential, dynamic vitality, and a method adapted and attractive to the catechumens, we have attempted not merely to give a description or to make an arbitrary classification, but to point out the basic line of thought that must guide us in our task. The three characteristics indicated lay down the conditions which our catechesis must accept if we wish it to be profound and effective. In fulfilling these conditions we follow both the course of tradition and the path of reform. Thus we make the response which the world demands of us und confront the new civilization that is arising with a vision of Christianity.

If the modern world is losing its Christian character, this fact of itself requires us to concentrate on the essentials and the substance of our message. If the world born of technology is quivering with the dynamic force that transports man to the stars, that is one imperious reason for us to demonstrate the dynamic force of redemption: "God who became man that man might become God."

Modern man professes his lack of receptivity for the Christian message. Our catechesis should demonstrate that, without sacrificing its transcendency, it is capable of adapting itself to the contemporary mind and of responding to the worries and anxieties of the modern soul. The faithful fulfilment of these three conditions will make visible the beauty and the appeal of the message conveyed by missionary catechesis. "Beauty consists in the lustre of truth."

The world changes, but the essential problems remain. The first generation of the Church understood and experienced the close relationship of the two realities: catechesis and mission. The fruit this bore was the expansion of Christianity in a pagan world. The present generation must experience the same realities and establish the same connection between mission and catechesis. This will also bear fruit in the presence of Christianity in the world of the future.

In conclusion, let us remember the sublime vocation of which Saint Paul reminds us and which appears to-day in all its tragic and imperious urgency. *Opus fac evangelistae.* "Accomplish the task of evangelization."

# The Core of Missionary Preaching

DOMENICO GRASSO, S.J.
Gregorian University, Rome

BY "missionary preaching" we understand the first stage in the communication of the Christian message to non-Christians. It is also called κήρυγμα (KERYGMA: the proclamation, the announcement) or "kerygmatic preaching"[1]. It differs from catechesis, which initiates to membership in the Christian community converts who have already accepted the kerygma; as likewise from homily, or liturgical preaching, which is reserved to full-fledged Christians. Whereas the kerygma looks simply to conversion, with a broad and inclusive acceptance of Christianity, catechesis aims to make conversion more thorough, by means of a deeper and more detailed appreciation of its doctrinal and moral implications, in those who are preparing for baptism or for the renewal of their baptismal promises. We may observe in passing that the re-discovery of the kerygma as a form of preaching distinct from catechesis and sermon is a by-product of modern exegesis, which has made it plain that the Gospels and Epistles took shape from a nucleus of primitive preaching common to all the apostles, including Saint Paul. The kerygma is precisely this original nucleus of the Christian message, as presented to non-Christians by the apostles, and afterwards developed for converts in the course of catechetical instruction. It is found throughout the New

[1] C. H. Dodd, *The Apostolic Preaching* (second ed., New York and London, 1951), p. 7; A. M. Hunter, *Un Seigneur, une Église, un Salut* (Neuchâtel-Paris, 1950); A. Rétif, *Foi au Christ et Mission* (Paris, 1953), p. 8 and elsewhere. Conversely by *kerygma* the German authors understand the Gospel message taken as the object of preaching. See Jungmann, *Handing on the Faith* (New York and London), Appendix II.

Testament, and indeed serves as its unifying element. "Like a tune which follows us wherever we go", writes Hunter, "we catch this characteristic melody of the kerygma again and again in Gospel, Epistle, and homily."[2] It runs through "the multi-colored tapestry of the New Testament like a golden thread".[3]

The title of this paper, which deals strictly with missionary preaching, would call for treatment of the core of the kerygma, namely of that truth or that fact which occupies the central place in the Christian message, the focal point of departure and of reference for all the other truths and facts. Since preaching, however, is not confined to the kerygma, but must of necessity pass on to catechesis, we shall treat of this latter also, showing how the heart of the kerygma is also the heart of New Testament catechesis. This basic unity will be further apparent from a brief analysis of the professions of faith in the apostolic community, of the Apostles' Creed and of the catechesis of the Fathers of the Church. The determination of the central element of missionary preaching will enable us to arrive at a synthesis assembling all aspects of the Christian reality under a single light, and to assign to each of them its proper place in the general design.

## *Christ in the Kerygma*

The kerygma, we have said, is the initial presentation of Christianity to non-Christians. As recent studies have brought out,[4] this was accomplished by all the apostles in the same way, in more or less stereotyped fashion. "That is our preaching", says St. Paul, "mine or theirs as you will; that is the faith which has come to you" (1 Cor. 15:11). In the New Testament, however, we have the catechesis or development of the kerygma, where its moral and doctrinal implications are made explicit in the light of theological reflection, the method varying according to the temperament of the author and the needs of the intended readers. St. Paul is alluding to catechesis when he speaks of

[2] Hunter, *op. cit.*, p. 32. [3] Hunter, *op. cit.*, p. 38.

[4] In addition to the works of Dodd and Hunter cited above, see J. R. Geiselmann, *Jesus der Christus* (Stuttgart, 1951).

"that gospel which I preach" (Rom. 16:25), of "a wisdom which we make known among those who are fully grounded" (1 Cor. 2:6), of "a superstructure to be built upon the foundation already laid" (1 Cor. 3:10). In the Pauline Epistles nevertheless, and in other books of the New Testament[5], we repeatedly hear echoes of the original kerygma, which enable us to piece it together accurately enough.

Especially inviting in this respect are the Acts of the Apostles, the book of books for missionary preaching. The discourses of Peter reported in the first ten chapters, more particularly the two delivered on the day of Pentecost (2:14–36; 3:17–26) and the one addressed to Cornelius (10:34–43), embody, in the judgement of scholars, the kerygma of the Church in Jerusalem. Its content may be outlined as follows.

It begins with the outright assertion that "the happenings of these days were foretold by the Prophets (2:16; 3:18; 3:24) and that the Messianic age, in consequence, is now inaugurated. This inauguration has come to pass through the life, death and resurrection of Christ, whose story is told in brief summary, notably in chapter 10. In virtue of the resurrection, Jesus is exalted at the right hand of God as Lord and Christ (2:33–6). The bestowal of the Holy Ghost foretold by the Prophets as a proof of the glory and exaltation of Christ (2:33). The second coming of Christ as Judge and Saviour (3:20–1; 10:42). An invitation to repentance and forgiveness in the name of Jesus Christ (2:38).[6]

The same plan is also followed by St. Paul for his discourse at Antioch in Pisidia (Acts 13:16–41). Such, then, is the kerygma of Jerusalem[7].

Substantially identical is the scheme to be gathered from the kerygmatic fragments found in the Epistles of St. Paul[8]. Suffice it to recall the familiar passage of the first epistle to the Corinthians, chapter fifteen, verses three to nine: "The chief message I handed on to you, as it was handed on to me, was that Christ,

[5] For these texts, see Hunter, *op. cit.*, p. 28 et seq. See also P. Hitz, *L'Annonce missionnaire de L'Évangile* (Paris, 1951), p. 72 et seq.

[6] Dodd, *op. cit.*, pp. 21–4.

[7] Dodd, *op. cit.*, p. 21.

[8] Dodd, *op. cit.*, p. 17.

as the scriptures had foretold, died for our sins; that he was buried, and then, as the scriptures had foretold, rose again on the third day. That he was seen by Cephas, then by the eleven apostles", and so forth, to the conclusion: "this is my preaching as well as theirs; this is the faith you have made your own."

These fundamental themes we find developed in the Gospels, in the Epistles of St. Paul and St. Peter, in the Epistle to the Hebrews. It is the kerygma, we repeat, which accounts for the unity of the New Testament.[9]

We are not here concerned directly with the whole of the kerygma, only with its core. But a mere reading of these schemes is enough to warrant the conclusion that the heart of the kerygma is a person, the Person of Christ. Say rather that he is the one and only object of which the kerygma treats. If messianic prophecies are mentioned, it is because they point to him; if there is question of the Holy Spirit, it is because the bestowal is a sign of his glorification. If reference is made to God, it is because he has raised up Christ. Very often the kerygma is called simply the preaching of Christ, of Jesus, of the Lord, of the Word of Jesus. Thus when the apostles are given their freedom by the Sanhedrin "every day, both in the temple and from house to house, their preaching (is) continually of Jesus Christ" (Acts 5:42). The deacon Philip "preaches Christ" in Samaria (Acts 8:5), and when by the Angel's command he goes to meet the chamberlain of Queen Candace, he "preaches to him about Jesus" (Acts 8:35). Paul has just been converted, when he "preaches that Jesus is the Son of God" (Acts 9:20). At Antioch Paul and Barnabas "preach the Word of the Lord" (Acts 15:36). They also say that they are "preaching Jesus Christ" (Acts 17:3), "bearing witness in the name of the Lord Jesus" (Acts 18:4–5) and so forth. Summing up his preaching before the Jews and pagans St. Paul affirms that he has been "preaching repentance before God, and faith in our Lord Jesus Christ" (Acts 20:21). The book of the Acts is brought to a close with the statement that Paul has been teaching all along "the truths which concern our Lord Jesus Christ" (Acts 28:31).

[9] Hunter, *op. cit.,* p. 32 et seq.

There is more of the same in the Epistles. Here also the apostles are pictured, though not exclusively, as preaching Christ (Phil. 1:15, 17, 18; Col. 1:28), or Jesus the Son of God (2 Cor. 1:19), or Christ crucified (1 Cor. 1:23), or the gospel of the cross of Christ (1 Cor. 9:12; 2 Cor. 2:12; 9:13; 10:14; Gal. 1:7; Phil. 1:27; 1 Thess. 3:2; 2 Tim. 2:8), or the glorious gospel of Christ (2 Cor. 4:4), or the gospel of the Son of God (Gal. 1:16), or the gospel of our Lord Jesus Christ (2 Thess. 1:8).

Our first conclusion is, therefore, obvious: the core of the kerygma is Christ. But missionary preaching makes Jesus Christ the chief character in a story, which is told in three phases: a prologue, a narrative proper and an epilogue.

Christ in his *prologue*. Before he appears in the world, the coming of Christ has been announced by the Prophets. They have foretold his royal descent from David (Acts 2:30; 13:34); his prophetic mission (Acts 3:22–3); his sufferings (Acts 3:18); his rejection by the Jews (Acts 4:11); his resurrection (Acts 2:25–31); his ascent to glory (Acts 2:34–5); the coming of the Holy Ghost (Acts 2:17–21). For St. Paul also, as we learn from the kerygmatic texts, Christ is of the seed of David (Rom. 1:3), was marked out in the holy Scriptures as the Son of God by his resurrection from the dead (Rom. 1:4), died and was buried as the scriptures had foretold (1 Cor. 15:4–5). This is the prehistory of Christ.

Christ in his *narrative*. Of the story of Christ, of his life on earth, the kerygma gives a brief sketch, which includes the following episodes. His baptism by John, his activity in Galilee, his miracles, what happened in Jerusalem, his passion, death and resurrection, his apparitions, the mandate to his missioners, his ascent into heaven. When preaching to Cornelius, Peter sums up the life of Jesus in these words: "You have heard the story, the story which ran through the whole of Judaea, though it began in Galilee, after the baptism which John proclaimed; about Jesus of Nazareth, how God anointed him with the Holy Spirit and with power, so that he went about doing good, and curing all those who were under the devil's tyranny, with God at his side" (Acts 10:37–9). Among the events in the life of

Christ there are two which occupy the central place, namely, his death and resurrection. Both facts are combined (Acts 2:23–24; 3:14–25. Cf. 4:10; 10:39–40; 13:27–30). But the more important of the two is the resurrection. Indeed it is so central that it is sometimes called the single event to which the apostles bear witness (Acts 1:21–2; 4:33). For St. Paul the resurrection is so plainly the cardinal factor in the message as to warrant the statement that if Christ is not risen, his own preaching is groundless (1 Cor. 15:14).

The *epilogue*. After his ascent into heaven, Christ sits at the right hand of his Father. Here he will abide "until the time when all is restored anew, the time which God has spoken of by his holy prophets from the beginning" (Acts 3:21). In the meantime, the gospel is preached to everyone, even to the pagans (Acts 3:25). He alone is the salvation of men (Acts 4:12). All that remains is to repent of one's sins and to be baptized in his name (Acts 2:38; 3:19–26).

Accordingly, we may now derive our second conclusion: the core of the kerygma is not Christ alone, but Christ seen in the story of salvation. This story comprehends three phases: first, a preparatory in the Old Testament; then a phase of achievement through the death and resurrection of Christ; and a final phase of consummation, the return of Christ in his glory.

### *Christ in the Catechesis*

Thus far we have been considering the person of Christ as the core of the apostolic kerygma. In the New Testament, however, as noted at the outset of our discussion, special emphasis is laid on the catechesis, which is a development of the kerygma. But it goes without saying that if one is a development of the other, both should have an identical centre. The fact is that Christ also occupies the central place in the catechesis of the apostles, in what St. Paul calls "his gospel" or, more usually, "the mystery". On the apprehension of this mystery the whole impressive body of St. Paul's teaching takes form and shape. Here lies his originality as compared with the other apostles.

We shall examine his concept briefly to see how far it may be said to be dominated by the person of Christ.

It is a matter of common knowledge that the word "mystery" recurs twenty times in the Epistles of St. Paul. In six instances the apostle speaks of a great mystery, revealed by God to him, which he has been deputed to announce to men (Rom. 16:25–26; 1 Cor. 2:7–10; Col. 1:26–27; Eph. 1:8–10; 3:3–7; 3:8–12, etc.). He identifies this mystery with the gospel explicitly (Rom. 16:25; Eph. 6:19) and implicitly (Col. 1:25–26; Eph. 1:9–13; 3:2–6). In the wake of great waves of controversy raised by the works of Odo Casel, most authorities are today agreed that the mystery of which St. Paul speaks is a design worked out by God for our salvation. In the apostle's eyes it is made up of three distinct phases: one of preparation, one of revelation, one of communication.

In the first phase God *conceives* a plan for our salvation, and while keeping it hidden from men and angels, disposes all the happenings of history so that he can disclose it when the times are ripe (Eph. 1:10). In the fulness of time God *reveals* his plan, obscurely first in the Old Testament, clearly afterwards in the New. The revelation is accomplished both by making clear the meaning of scripture (Rom. 16:26), and directly by Christ. It is then transmitted to the apostles and to the prophets who are its intermediaries among the Christian people (Eph. 3:10). St. Paul himself has had a particular revelation of the plan with regard to the call of the Gentiles to the faith (Eph. 3:8–9). In the third phase the mystery is *communicated* to men by means of the preaching of the Church. They have knowledge of the mystery. This knowledge is a gift of God (1 Cor. 1:5–6), and can increase if man is faithful (Phil. 1:9–11; Eph. 3:14–19).

To describe the content, the centre, of the mystery St. Paul makes use of various formulas. Now it consists in the divine blessings God has prepared for our glory (1 Cor. 2:7–10), now in the vocation of the Gentiles to the faith (Rom. 16:26). Again it is to be found in the winning back of all things in a single head (Eph. 1:9–10). Elsewhere it is claimed that the content of the mystery is Christ, in whom are hidden all the treasures of wisdom and knowledge (Col. 2:2–3), or more clearly that the mystery is Christ, our hope of glory (Col. 1:27).

All these expressions, as Deden remarks[10] say the same thing: the sum and substance of the mystery is Christ. They vary in describing his role in the divine plan. It is Christ who by his passion and death has merited for us the divine gifts of sanctifying grace, or restored men to friendship with God, or established once more the cosmic unity that sin had destroyed.

The Pauline concept of mystery lays the groundwork for an authentic theology of history. In the apostle's view history is a thread of events directed by God first to the revelation, then to the dispensation of Christ. In consequence our Lord is the centre of history, the term towards which all that occured before the incarnation is ordained, and the point from which all that happens after the incarnation derives. Christ gives history its meaning. Precisely because it is designed to communicate the gifts of God, to bring about the union of God with men, history is a *sacred* story, a story of salvation, the story of Christ in whom God saves us. Christ is the centre of the Old Testament (Rom. 4:24; Cor. 9:10; 10:11) and of the era which begins with the New Testament, the "age of the Church", whose aim it is to round out the number of the brothers of Christ (Apoc. 6:11).[11]

In the light of this doctrine St. Paul in his catechesis sees everything centred in Christ. Each aspect of Christian life is an element or part of the mystery of Christ. God is the Father of our Lord Jesus Christ (2 Cor. 1:3; 3:31; Eph. 1:3); the Church is the body of Christ (Eph. 1:22 et seq.); the life of grace is living with Christ (Rom. 8:10); to be baptized is to die and rise again with Christ (Rom. 6:3); marriage is a great mystery in Christ and in the Church (Eph. 5:22). Christian morality is nothing more nor less than the conduct of a member of Christ. Fornication must be avoided because our bodies belong to the body of Christ, and what belongs to Christ cannot be made one with a harlot (1 Cor. 6:15, 19, 20). We are not to scandalize our brothers because Christ died for them (1 Cor. 8:11). We must flee sin because Christ dwells in us (Rom. 8:3 et seq.).

[10] D. Deden, "Le mystère paulinien" in *Ephemerides Theol. Lov.,* xiii (1936), p. 408.

[11] For these concepts see the interesting book of O. Cullmann, *Le Christ et le temps* (Neuchâtel-Paris, 1952).

The whole of reality, then, is seen by St. Paul in the light of Christ, as part of his mystery. Everything for him is "in Christ", an expression which recurs one hundred and sixty-four times in his letters. Christ is the fulness of the word of God (Col. 1, 25–29). He it is whom God gave us to be all our wisdom, our justification, our sanctification and our atonement (1 Cor. 1:30). He is the true likeness of the God we cannot see. In him and through him all things were created (Col. 1:15–21).

The notion of Christ as centre of all creation is also to be found, although the perspective is different, in other writings of the New Testament. Let it suffice to recall the prologue of the Gospel of St. John: "Through him all things came into being, and without him came nothing that has come to be. In him there was life, and that life was the light of men.... And we had sight of his glory, full of grace and truth.... We have all received something out of his abundance, grace answering to grace" (John 1, 3, 14, 16). Similarly also the opening verses of the Epistle to the Hebrews (1:1–3). The book of the Acts contains a text attributed to St. Paul in which we see reflected his all-inclusive conception of Christ, the whole of God's plan (Acts 20:20–26). Even morality is looked upon as man's answer to the love of God: "Yes, we must love God: he gave us his love first" (1 John 4:7 et seq.).

This brings us to our third conclusion. Christ is the heart not merely of the kerygma, but of New Testament catechesis as well.

### *Christ in the Professions of Faith*

The central place of Christ in the preaching of the apostles is confirmed for us by the professions of faith drawn up under various circumstances within the early Church. They are to be found both in the New Testament and in subsequent documents. Cullman reduces the occasions for which they were prescribed to these five: baptism with the catechumenate, divine worship, exorcism, persecutions and disputations with heretics.[12] In these circumstances the Christian was called upon to sum up his faith

[12] O. Cullmann, *Les premières confessions de foi chrétienne* (Paris, 1948). p. 1.

in a short formula. Of necessity, therefore, he had to select the essential points in the doctrine taught by the apostles. Examination discloses that Christ holds the central position in these formulas.

In the apostolic Epistles, especially in those of St. Paul, we have several of these summaries, which represent a sort of quotation. The apostle inserts in the context of the letter, without saying so, a profession of faith already familiar to the Christians for whom he is writing. Here are a few examples. Baptism was beyond doubt an occasion when the candidate had to make his faith manifest. Hence the need to create formulas for use in answering to the priest. Perhaps the most ancient of these is the one that served for the baptism of the eunuch: "I believe that Jesus Christ is the Son of God" (Acts 8:37)[13]. Baptism itself was conferred in the name of Christ. With the simple exception of the tripartite text in Matthew (28:19), the New Testament formulas mention only Christ by name (Eph. 3:27; 1 Cor. 1:13; Acts 2:38; 8:16; 10:48; 19:5). A liturgical profession of faith is exemplified in the second chapter of the Epistle to the Philippians (vv. 6:11). Its culminating point is reached with the following words: "Jesus Christ is the Lord, dwelling in the glory of God the Father." The phrase of St. John affirming that "Jesus Christ has come to us in human flesh" probably forms part of a confession of faith as a challenge to certain heretics (1 John 4, 2). Still another from St. Paul aims to confute the pagans in periods of persecution or controversy: "There is only one God, the Father who is the origin of all things and the end of our being; only one Lord, Jesus Christ" (1 Cor. 8:6). Most popular of all is the declaration that "Jesus is the Lord" (1 Cor. 12:3; Rom. 10:9). This expression, connected in all likelihood with the persecutions, assumes a variety of forms in other passages of the New Testament where there is a question of the faith or its preaching. We note for instance such equivalents as these: "Our Lord Jesus Christ" (Col. 2:26); "Jesus Christ and Master (Acts 2:36); "the Lord Jesus" (Acts 16:31). Another variant reads: "Jesus is the Christ" (1 John 2:22), or "Jesus is the Son of God" (Acts

[13] Cullmann believes it to be the oldest of them all. See *op. cit.*, p. 14.

8:36–38; Heb. 4:14), to which must be added the expression *Maranatha* (1 Cor. 15:22; Phil. 4:5; Apoc. 22:20) which means "the Lord is coming", or "Come, Lord", considering it alternatively as an indicative or an imperative.

It is clear from Cullman's study that these formulae of faith consist for the most part in a single article bringing Jesus Christ to the fore.[14] A few are made up of two articles, featuring God and Christ. Only a stray one here and there includes three articles, one for each of the three divine Persons.[15] A given formula, therefore, may fail to name the Father or the Holy Ghost, but none omits mention of Christ. This is positive proof that the proclamation of Christ is the point of departure for every public profession of the Christian faith.[16] Though it would be an exaggeration to argue from this fact to a Christocentric belief which excludes theocentricity,[17] none can deny that Christ is accorded a predominant place in the Church of Apostolic times.[18]

## *The Apostles' Creed*

The central place of Christ in the preaching and catechesis of the infant Church finds further confirmation in a document of very first importance: the Apostle's Creed. Several interesting studies of its origin and structure have been made during the past few years, with the result that its Christocentric character is now established. In the Creed we are presented with a synthesis of the story of salvation. Each of the divine Persons, actually, is considered not in himself, but in the part he plays in that story. The Father is the Creator, the Son the Redeemer and the Holy Ghost is the Sanctifier of the Church, in view of the second coming and life everlasting. In the Creed we have a popular edition of the Pauline "mystery". From all eternity God

[14] Cullmann, *op. cit.,* p. 16.
[15] Cullmann, *op. cit.,* pp. 28–9.
[16] Cullmann, *op. cit.,* pp. 30–1.
[17] P. Benoit, "Les origines du Symbole des Apôtres dans le Nouveau Testament." in *Lumière et Vie,* 2 (1952), p. 56.
[18] The demonstration would be more complete were the traces of primitive prayers in the New Testament to be examined. See J. Schmitt, *Jésus ressuscité dans la prédication apostolique* (Paris, 1949), pp. 85–99.

conceives the plan of salvation. To bring it about he creates the world. Creation is the introduction to the story of salvation. When the time is mature, he carries out his plan by means of the death and resurrection of his Son. Then follows the communication of his great design, thanks to the labour of the Church, sanctified by the Holy Ghost. And the story ends with a final chapter on the second coming and life eternal.

The composition is Christocentric through and through. It is for Christ that the world was created, to make it possible for him to accomplish the divine project. It is Christ who reunites us with the Father through his death and resurrection. Christ it is, again, who sends the Holy Spirit to continue his work in the Church. And it is Christ who will bring the history of the world to its close with the Last Judgement. As Monsignor Garrone has well said, "the Creed is no straight line, but a circle with Christ at its centre".[19]

To bring home the difference between the Christocentric structure of the Apostles' Creed and one which is Trinitarian, a glance at the Athanasian Creed may suffice. This latter dates from the fifth century, and owes its origin to the disputes occasioned by the Trinitarian and Christological heresies. It embodies a description of the Three Persons according to their nature and mutual relationships. The persons of the Blessed Trinity are considered in themselves, rather than in their relation to us, as in the case of the Apostles' Creed. Hence our fourth conclusion. Christ in the story of salvation is the centre of the preaching and liturgy of the primitive Church in their entirety.

### *Saint Augustine*

The story of salvation, which is altogether Christocentric is found also in the Fathers of the Church, whose catechesis amounts to an explanation of the Creed. St. Augustine has reduced this scheme to a set of rules, in his famous work *De catechizandis rudibus* (Catechism for Beginners), written in the

[19] "Simples Réflexions sur l'unité du Symbole" in *Lumière et Vie,* 2 (1952), p. 8.

form of an answer to the deacon Deogratias, who has asked him how he could make his own catechetical instruction attractive. The great Doctor seizes the opportunity to set forth for us the general principles of catechesis which, in addition to the light they throw on common practice among the Fathers, were also destined to provide guidance for the catechetics of later years, and to remain standard in fact, until the time of the Scholastics.

For Augustine catechesis is a narration, an account of the great things God has done to stir up the love of our hearts. If the whole tale is to be told, it must extend from the very first verse of Scripture up to the present age of the Church. "The story *(narratio)* is complete", he writes "when you start to catechize from the words: 'in the beginning God made heaven and earth', and then carry through to the Church of today".[20] "That does not mean", he is quick to add, "that you have to repeat from the whole of the Pentateuch, the books of Judges, Kings and Esther, the Gospels and the Acts of Apostles. You are not even required to record and expound in your own words what these writings contain. For that there is neither time nor need." And here Augustine lays down the rule of selection: "Choose, therefore, out of the whole story a few of the highlights *(quaedam mirabiliora)* which you think likely to be listened to with greater interest, and are the most essential; then arrange them in a certain order, so that it will not be necessary to go back and forth confusedly, thus jumbling the plot of the story previously told in outline".[21] The task is therefore to dwell on the more impressive topics at some length, and to fit the rest into the context with rapid strokes.

In the eyes of Augustine all the deeds of God are marvels; but there is a gradation among them. Since, then, for lack of time not all can be treated, one must limit oneself to the most striking, to the *mirabiliora,* which he calls the "junctures of time" *(articuli temporis)*. These are the great chapters of the story of salvation, which he reduces to five: the first runs from Adam to Noah and the Flood; the second from Noah to Abraham; the third from Abraham to David; the fourth from David to the Babylonian

[20] *De catechizandis rudibus,* 5. [21] *Op. cit.,* 5.

captivity; and the fifth from Babylon to the incarnation of the Word. At this stage begins the sixth or present age, which will last until the Second Coming, and be brought to a close with the resurrection and life everlasting. During this period, the *tempus Ecclesiae* or era of the Church, all nations are called to redemption.

For St. Augustine, consequently, catechesis must cover the whole story of salvation, from creation to the final resurrection. But of what kind of narrative is he speaking? Is it a simple account such as might be given by a historian, whose purpose is to inform? Or has this story a particular aim of its own? Augustine makes it quite clear: the account of the *mirabilia Dei* is not an end in itself. It must acquaint man with the works of God in such fashion that love may be kindled from them. If the Word took flesh, he did so for love of us, and to impel us to love him in return. "With the coming of the Lord" says Augustine, "God had no other desire to convince us of his immense love, and to make us appreciate it. We were still his enemies, and Christ died for us."[22] This divine way of acting is understandable. It is deeds which convince us. Even if we derive no pleasure in loving others, it is hard to resist one who takes it on himself to love us first. "If we have been reluctant to love, let us at least not be slow to love back. For there is no better invitation to love than to begin loving, and less hard is the heart that refuses love than one that will not respond to it."[23] If this is true of unholy loves, how much truer must it be of real friendship!

Augustine's criterion in presenting the facts of the story of salvation is not, then, to impart knowledge or to instruct, but to arouse love by telling what God has done for us. This is valid for the facts of the New Testament, for the coming of the Son of God, as well as for those of the Old Testament, which prefigure the New. God is a wise pedagogue. It may well be that we are unprepared to accept the extraordinary and unusual; hence God arranged a gradually unfolding plan by way of preparation for the greatest of all proofs of his love, the coming of his Son: this was the long prelude of the Old Testament

[22] *Op. cit.*, 7. [23] *Op. cit.*, 7.

which does but foretell the coming of the Lord. "All that was written before in sacred scripture", declares Augustine, "and everything afterwards set down and sealed by divine authority, tells of Christ and moves us to love him. The Old Testament thus hides the New, as the New reveals the Old."[24]

If love is the objective at which catechesis must aim, that is far from saying that it cannot also envisage the speculative and apologetic aspects of the *mirabilia Dei*. It can and it must do so, provided this will serve to bring love into bolder relief.[25] "The explanations ought to string the gems neatly together like a golden thread, and not break the line of the jewel with their exuberance."[26] In this way the catechist's words will succeed in making his listener "believe in what he hears, hope in what he believes, and love what he hopes for."[27] Up to the twelfth and thirteenth centuries, as Vagaggini observes, the ideas of St. Augustine served as a text for the catechesis of the Fathers and of theology itself.[28] Only when Scholasticism appeared, with the Aristotelian concept of science, did the "reasons" *(rationes)* begin to get the better of the "narrative". The advent of Protestantism, although it did not prevent the compilers of the *Catechismus ad Parochos* (Catechism for Parish Priests) from finding their inspiration in the views of St. Augustine, led to the composition of catechisms based largely on sectarian controversy with theological formulas which were rigidly precise, but abstract and often difficult to grasp. The excessive development of certain topics, at the expense of others perhaps more important, resulted in the loss of that perfect integration which catechetical instruction had maintained throughout the early epoch.

Now that the period of counter-reform may be said to be closed, the story of salvation can and must once more endow all of our modern preaching with its perspective. The ideas of St. Augustine, expressing as they do in principle the entire content of the New Testament and the Apostles' Creed, are basic for preaching. Concentrate preaching wholly on the story of salvation, and the result will be that synthesis and unity which

[24] *Op. cit.*, 8. [25] *Op. cit.*, 10. [26] *Op. cit.*, 10. [27] *Op. cit.*, 8.
[28] *Il senso teologico della liturgia* (Roma, 1958), p. 625.

modern catechesis aims to achieve. The centre of the story of salvation is Christ. With reference to his Person all the various components of Christianity can be merged into one: the Church, Holy Scripture, dogma, morals and liturgy. Christ is the centre of the Church of which he is the head: of the scriptures which owe to him the unity of their design; of morals, which is the answer of man to God's invitation to share in his life; of the liturgy, which is a representation of his mystery through the symbols of sense.

Christ not only enables us to see the several elements of Christianity in a single light. He also makes it possible to establish a hierarchy among them. A dogma, for example, should occupy a place of greater or lesser consequence in the measure that it expresses a more or less significant aspect of the mystery of Christ. In catechesis, therefore, grace will have more importance than sin; sanctifying grace more than actual grace; the Holy Spirit more than Our Lady; the resurrection of Christ more than his childhood; the mystical aspect of the Church more than the juridical; baptism more than penance; the Eucharist more than extreme unction. The greater or less distance from Christ furnishes the genetic principle on which to assemble our preaching material.[29]

### *Christ-centred or God-centred*

Setting Christ again at the heart of our preaching, within the perspective of the story of salvation leads also to the solution of a problem which is always raised when there is question of Christocentrism. Would it not be nearer to the truth to say that the centre of natural and supernatural reality is *God,* rather than Christ? How then can we focus everything on Christ?

Let us note, first of all, that the issue between God-centredness and Christ-centredness must not be minimized, after the manner of certain authors. The problem really exists. Though scripture does in fact often point to Christ as the object of

[29] A. Liège, "Pour une catéchèse vraiment chrétienne" in *La Vie Spirituelle* (suppl.), 42 (1957), p. 289.

apostolic preaching, instances where the object indicated is God, or the Word of God, are less frequent, but by no means negligible. The terms most commonly employed in the New Testament to describe the act of preaching are εὐαγγελίζεσθαι (with its many derivatives), κηρύσσειν, παραδιδόναι, διδάσκειν on the one hand, and μαρτυρεῖν on the other. But according to a statistical table compiled by Father Hayward, the first four verbs have "Christ" for their complementary object twice in the Gospels, and forty seven times in the remainder of the New Testament. They have "God" for their object twenty times in the Gospels and twenty-four times in the other books. In the same books seven times "Christ" and "God" are mentioned together. For the verb μαρτυρεῖν we have the following figures: in the Gospels, sixteen times for "Christ", none for "God"; in the rest of the New Testament: "Christ" twenty-eight times, with four for "God", and eight for "God" and "Christ" together. In the Gospel, therefore, "Christ" is the object of preaching for a total of eighteen times, "God" for a total of twenty, and both together, not at all. In the rest of the New Testament "Christ" is featured seventy-four times, "God" twenty-eight times, and both together fifteen. From these calculations it is plain that Christ-centredness though undoubtedly to be found, is by no means exclusive.[30]

Now let us examine the second purpose of preaching, which is to arouse faith in the hearers. The objects governed by the verbs πιστεύειν, γιγνώσκειν and ἀκούειν can be classified as follows. In the Gospels "Christ" is the object of faith one hundred and thirteen times, "God" eighteen times, and both together twenty-three; in the other writings of the New Testament, "Christ" is the object ninety-two times, "God" seventy-nine, both together sixteen.

If these statistics have any meaning, they show that the Christ-centredness of the New Testament is not so exclusive as some authors would have us believe; and that the issue of Christ-centredness and God-centredness is a real one. It involves

[30] Reference is made to a doctoral dissertation defended by the Rev. Curtis Hayward at the Pontifical Gregorian University, Rome, and as yet unpublished.

a problem of biblical theology, to which we need here refer only in passing.

First let us remark that the answer to this question, whatever it may be, cannot affect our conclusions. We have asserted, as a matter of fact, that Christ is the centre of the preaching and catechesis of the New Testament and of the early Christian centuries as well. But we have added that he is always seen in the setting of the story of salvation. The divine plan of salvation, however, is at once theocentric and Christocentric. Theocentric, because it was conceived by God from all eternity, was adapted and prepared by him for its full realization, and tends finally to his glory. But it is Christocentric, too, because the plan has Christ at its centre. Towards him the course of history moves before the incarnation. After the incarnation all history derives from him. Christ gives history its direction.

In revelation God has not told us, at least directly, what he is in himself but what he means to us. The God of the Bible is not, before all else, the Supreme Being on whom everything depends, but the God of the covenant, the God stretching forth to those of his creatures who are capable of knowing and loving him. If he has spoken, it is because he wanted to make manifest his plan of salvation in their regard. But this plan of God for us is Christ, as St. Paul declares in the Acts of the Apostles (Acts 20:20–28). For Paul it is one and the same thing to preach conversion to God and faith in our Lord Jesus Christ; to bear witness to the gospel of the grace of God and to proclaim in its entirety the plan of God. The apostle's assignment is to preach the Word of God, and this Word is identical with Christ (Col. 1:25–29).

It is Christ, then, who makes us know God, who reveals to us what he is and what are our relationships to him. Penetrating to the heart of the mystery, the Epistle to the Hebrews tells us why it is that in Christ we know God. The fact is that Christ is "the radiance of his Father's splendour, and the full expression of his being" (Heb. 1:3). When we gaze upon the Son, we are looking at the Father whose Son he is. When Philip asks to see the Father, Jesus answers him: "Philip, whoever has seen me, has seen the Father" (John 14:9). The reason is clear: "Christ and the Father are one and the same" (see John 10:31). Life eternal will consist in "knowing thee, who art the only true God, and Jesus Christ, whom thou hast sent" (John 17:3). Christ speaks as he does because of the things he has seen and heard from the Father (John 3:31–36). At his baptism, then the Father can say: "This is my beloved Son in whom I am well pleased" (Matt. 3:17). God "has given him a name which is greater than any other name, so that everything in heaven and on earth and under the earth must bend the knee before the name of Jesus, and every tongue must confess Jesus Christ as the Lord dwelling in the glory of God the Father" (Phil. 2:10–11).

In the light of these texts we can say that God-centredness and Christ-centredness cannot be separated from each other. Natural and supernatural reality is theocentric because it was created by God for his glory, and Christocentric because God obtains this glory only in Christ. If we must please God in order to be saved (Heb. 11:6), we can please him only in Christ, in whom he is well pleased (Matt. 3:17). He who is with Christ, he who accepts him as the centre of his life, by that very fact submits himself to God. This necessary subordination is expressed by St. Paul as follows: "the reign of Christ must continue until he has put all his enemies under his feet . . . . God has put all things in subjection under his feet. . . . And when that subjection is complete, then the Son himself will become subject to the power which made all things his subjects, so that God may be all in all" (1 Cor. 15:25–28). It is in yielding ourselves to Christ that we surrender ourselves to God. "Everything is for you", writes the apostle earlier in the same epistle, "whether it be Paul, or Apollo, or Cephas, or the world, or life, or death, or the present, or the future, it is all for you, and you for Christ, and Christ for God." (1 Cor. 3:22–23).

Understood in this way, Christocentrism is inseparable from theocentrism.

### *Conclusion*

When we have made Christ, as he now lives on in the Church, the very core of our missionary preaching and catechesis, we shall have solved one of the most urgent problems of our contemporary pastoral ministry, namely, that of restoring to the gospel message the quality of joy which is proper to it.

The movement for renewal in the field of preaching started precisely from the evident anaemia in the spiritual life of so many Christians, for whom Christianity means merely a series of moral precepts that must be observed if one would escape hell. When we have come round once more, in the preaching of our faith, to emphasizing the aspect that renders it an encounter with Christ living in the Church, it will have acquired again the distinctive quality of Good News which was so vivid in the early centuries of Christianity, and which belongs to its very nature.

# Adapting Catechesis to Missionary Conditions

WALBERT BÜHLMANN, O.F.M.CAP.
Catholic University, Fribourg, Switzerland

WE all know of the dangers besetting the Church in the missions today. Nationalism and Communism have dealt her serious blows, and it is with anxiety that we await the coming years. But our greatest anxiety is caused by the question: "Have Christians received the preparation, the spiritual nourishment, which would enable them to withstand these dangers?" Outward attacks are not what is most to be feared. They can even be a channel of grace, if the persecuted persevere in the spirit of Christ. Churches and mission schools may be closed down, the Christians may be placed in chains, yet they can rejoice at heart, and benefit from their tribulations.

But are Christians sufficiently animated by the spirit of Christ and do they have sufficient hope? Among missionaries and the native clergy the fear is increasingly expressed that, just as European clothing and standards were adopted, so also Christianity has been applied too much in the manner of an outer garment, like a varnish to wood, pounded in and memorized, but not experienced and lived.

Without wishing to subscribe to these generalizations, it is clear that such misgivings are not entirely unfounded. At the first Asiatic congress of laymen in Manila in 1955 it was affirmed that catechism instruction was too much a mechanical procedure, having only a thin connection with Christian life.[1] To be sure, Father Paul Foster, O.P., student chaplain at Makerere University in Uganda, was able to report that eighty per cent of the Catholic students attend Sunday Mass and that forty-five per

[1] W. Gardini, *Asien für Christus* (Frankfurt, 1958), p. 225.

cent also come to occasional evening Masses on weekdays. But he observed that when taking part in religious discussion their questions were always of a purely formal nature, for example: "How far away from a church must one be in order to be dispensed from attending Mass?" "If the Church forbids eating meat on Friday, how can she permit us on that day to consume the body of Christ at communion?" "Can a priest declare a dance to be a sin?" and so on. Answers to questions put by the student chaplain, such as: "What is religion? What is grace? What is the effect of baptism?" showed a staggering lack of understanding.[2] When we observe facts like these, we cannot possibly be complacent about them, and would do well to examine critically the real value of our missionary catechetics. The question we must discuss in this lecture is how we can adapt catechesis in missionary countries so as best to ensure that it ceases to be a mere outward drill, and becomes instead a true fountain of life and of grace.

There is no need to prove the necessity of adaptation in the whole field of missionary work. Yet we do wish to emphasize that outward accommodation, whether in church art and architecture, in liturgical rites and vestments, or in the missionary's way of living, is of secondary importance. The most important thing is the way in which spiritual values are presented and, correspondingly, organically assimilated by the hearers. Once the core of a person's heart has become Christian, the outward forms of expression for his new life will come of themselves.

As regards catechetics one has the happy feeling that the catechist enjoys complete freedom of movement. Unlike the liturgy, the celebration of which is prescribed in minute detail, catechetics leaves him free to adopt different approaches depending on the audience, which may consist of children or adults, Africans or Asiatics. But is enough advantage taken of this freedom? Do not many, perhaps, among those who inveigh against the liturgical rubrics, tread well-beaten catechetical paths and with few objections use ready-made European catechisms in Africa or Asia?

[2] "Catholicism at Makerere" in *African Ecclesiastical Review,* Oct. 1959, pp. 162 et seq.

We do not doubt that many missionaries, members of the native clergy, and catechists are able to give wonderful religious instruction even when using a little catechism whose one hundred questions and answers betray not the slightest trace of prior adaptation for the missions. But there is so little written record of their work that one is at a loss to make practical suggestions for the accommodation of catechetics to the missions. I asked an African priest who, in Rome, had written an excellent dissertation on this question, and since then had spent a few more years in Africa, whether he had followed these principles in practice and what his experience with them had been. His answer ran: "When I consider the problem of adaptation, I increasingly realize that the ideas developed in my thesis are only a few basic principles. One *ought* to attempt to develop an entirely new catechetical approach for Africa. The whole of dogmatic, moral and liturgical instructions *ought* to be reconsidered in the light of the Bible and the true African situation. The instructions given to our neophytes are so permeated with European elements that Christianity is all too easily confused with European civilization. It *would be* so easy to africanize religious instructions. . . ." But on the subject of how to do so in practice, in the concrete, the dissertation had little to offer.

## *Method*

The following statement, paradoxical though it may sound, is my earnest belief. The first and most important step in accommodating catechetics to the situation in the Missions is to fulfil the basic requirements of the European catechetical revival. This is so because these basic requirements are founded, on the one hand, on a deepened theological insight, which is of universal validity, and, on the other hand, on a thorough study of the learning process, which starts from the concrete and absorbs the meaning of a truth for life less by means of theoretical instruction than by *doing*. If this is true of humanity in general, it is still more true of those in missionary countries, as the following remarks, considering Africa alone, are intended briefly to show.

The principle of action in religious instruction is learning by doing. Africans have rites of initiation, lasting for weeks, which consist not of lessons but of exercises. They do not "learn about" good behaviour, about respect for elders, about bravery. They practise these things. They practise helping one another, undergo tests of courage, "hear" the voices of their ancestors when a wooden rattle is whirled nearby or the voices of the departed are imitated for them. Could not we, too, give our instructions in the form of mystery plays, if only very simple ones? Here is a little example of the effectiveness of acting. A missionary had done his best to teach the children the Angelus, but with only a limited degree of success. A native catechist arrived on the scene, assigned to one of the girls the role of Mary and to one of the boys that of Gabriel, and in a twinkling both actors and spectators alike had mastered the words.

What is the place of the Bible in religious instruction? How strongly does the Bible appeal to Africans? Many usages, many biblical turns of phrase which we Europeans must have explained to us are perfectly clear to the Africans because they are customary in their language and culture. It is not surprising that missionaries say they have in many respects acquired a greater appreciation of the Bible while in Africa.

How can we present the story of redemption in religious instruction? To be sure, Africans have a good memory, and have no trouble in learning catechism questions and answers by heart. But do they understand them? Are their hearts warmed by them? Does what they have memorized make any great difference in their lives? They are more impressed by their own myths of creation, the story of their ancient forbears and the history of the tribe. Why should we not present revelation, which did not take place by means of theories and definitions but by what God did to his people, to our Africans as a living process?

African religion does not consist of a collection of doctrines, but of religious practices. Their beliefs are expressed and experienced by the celebration of joint sacrifices, by being buried and resurrected, by receiving a new name and a new garment at the initiation rites. That is why there have been no "non-practising heathens" in Africa. Neither is Christianity mere doctrine: it is life belonging not merely to the past but also to the present. The divine process of salvation continues even now and will be completed by the second coming of Christ. That is why religious instruction must always keep the liturgy in mind and even be accomplished as far as possible by means of the liturgy, thus obviating as far as possible that fatal gap between theory and practice, unknown in African religion but so widespread in European Christianity.

All these things will be more thoroughly treated in the following lectures, but I have had to make some references to them here because they are essential to the African mentality and constitute basic requirements for the adaptation of catechetics for the missions.

### *Language*

Beyond these common basic requirements there is also the possibility and, indeed, the urgent necessity of specific adaptation, first of all in terms of language. Christ intuitively realized this and gave an example for the missionaries of all time. He did not speak in general, abstract or timeless terms. Rather, as he "was sent to the lost sheep of the house of Israel", he clothed his message entirely in the language of Israel. In emphasis, choice of words, sentence construction, proverbs, images, and comparisons he was thoroughly the man of his people and spoke so that everyone could understand him. And just as Christ preached to the Jews in Jewish style, so we must clothe the message to the Africans in African fashion.

But if the foreign missionary is to succeed with his speaking of African, it does not suffice that he should merely be present on the continent of Africa, having learnt the language from a manual. He must acquire a deeper contact with the people, become one of their equals. He must experience, as it were, an African rebirth, an incarnation in African flesh. Then he will, like a child growing up in this milieu, begin to express himself in its images and comparisons, adduce proofs in their fashion, and gradually come to speak like one of them.

In my first years in Africa I took advantage of opportunities here and there to attend court sessions, in order to become familiar with African speech and the administration of justice. Once, a man who had been away at Dar-es-Salaam for seven years, prosecuted his wife because she had in the meantime had a child by another man. When he had finished speaking, a relative of the defendent arose and spoke a single sentence: "If you leave a hoe in the field during the rainy season, need you wonder that it gets rusty?" Once I was trying to bring together again Anna and Paul, who had been separated for months, and, after lengthy persuasion, asked Anna whether she would agree. She was silent for a while and then answered, "Who will eat again what he has vomited up?" In the Legion of Mary we once planned a project for getting new members. At the following meeting the various members gave an account of their activities. Most of them had asked several people, who had not yet made up their minds. So they planned to ask other people. Someone remarked, "No, don't ask others, but keep working on the same ones. You don't begin hoeing a field here a little and there a little, you dig in at one spot." The others answered, "That's all right, but when you're hungry you don't insist on bananas, you take what you can get. . . ."[3]

Proverbs deserve special attention. Missionaries say that the sermons of native priests make the most telling use of them. One proverb proves more to Africans than a dozen syllogisms. They grasp it immediately, for it is part of their mental heritage. A proverb expresses a time-honoured experience of life, silencing discussion. Most of them have nothing to do with religion as such. But it would be worth making a study of P. G. Hulstaert's collection[4] to show how such proverbs can be applied. For example, proverbs on generosity.

"When a child begs for Mbimbo seeds, give him a whole handful." Application in connection with prayers of supplication: You say, "When a child . . .". Don't you think God will give you what you ask him for and more, though perhaps in another way?

[3] See my further exposition of the subject, with bibliographical notes, in my article "Die Predigtweise in Afrika" in *Neue Zeitschrift für Missionswissenschaft,* pp. 204 and 251–65.

[4] *Proverbes Mongo* (Tervuren, 1958), 828 pages.

"He who eats no meat goes hunting." Meaning: It is the sign of a magnanimous man that he goes hunting to get meat not only for himself, but for his wife and children. Application in connection with the Christmas and Passion stories: Christ was with the Father in glory. He needed nothing for himself, but came to earth for our sakes. If you praise the man who eats no meat and yet goes hunting, then how much more should we admire and thank Christ!

"The heart is generous, but the hand is poor." Meaning: One would like to help, but cannot. Application in connection with the miracles of our Lord: Christ always has power to help. How glad we should be to belong to him!

"A mother economizes only with the children of others." Meaning: Everybody is generous to his own children. Application, for example, in connection with the chance to go to confession and communion again and again: God is so generous to us because we have become his children through baptism.

## *Content*

Linguistic accommodation is both important and difficult; but even more so is accommodation of the content of catechetical instruction. The message brought by the missionary originated in heaven and not on earth. Yet it is not to be proclaimed to the empty air, but to men and women of flesh and blood, with their own history and culture and a personality that has hitherto been at home in a particular spiritual and mental climate. It is to this individual personality that the missionary's message is addressed: in it that the message must find its reception and realization. This calls for a change of attitude on the part of him who hears the message, but also for consideration on the part of the message-bearer for that personality. It is only in this way that "the two" can become "one" (Eph. 2:14).

The missionary's attitude towards "paganism" may be, to various degrees, either negative or positive. The negative attitude may be rooted in the most holy zeal. One is imbued with a sense of "the novelty of Christianity", one feels like a herald bearing fabulous tidings, and besides, one looks upon paganism as idolatry, as a work of the devil, as the incarnation of vice, and thus the only possibility is a radical renunciation of it. There are those with whom it may have been less a matter of zeal than of ignorance, for which, to be sure, they are not personally to blame. They were children of their times. The pagan spirit was believed to be a *tabula rasa*. Paganism was not considered worth "studying". It was simply ignored. Missionaries shared the opinion of all Europeans that only the white man is cultured, and that the coloured peoples are barbarians and savages.[5]

The peoples of Asiatic culture remained rather reserved in the face of this attitude. Primitive peoples shifted ground comparatively easily; they were impressed by western civilization and adopted western religion as well. Of course they gained a deeper understanding of religion during the catechumenate. But the wholesale condemnation of paganism caused the young Christians much unnecessary tension. An African priest, in his dissertation on the Ngoni religion viewed in the light of Christianity, writes: "In this respect I can speak from personal experience. How it weighs on the heart of a young Christian Ngoni, when he does not know how to behave in this or that pagan environment. In every pagan ceremony he sees an occasion of sin. He is caught between two great opposing forces: the authority of his parents on the one hand, the authority of the Church on the other. The Church, it seems to him, offers him nothing but the command "Thou shalt not". If, for instance, his elders serve a ceremonial meal, he feels obliged to eat it. He eats it against his conscience and repents of having eaten it. Thus he forms in his mind a world which is nothing but a source of vexations. He ends up thinking that Christianity has nothing positive, no happiness to offer."[6]

This negative attitude has destroyed much that was of value in pagan culture and thus given rise to the reproaches of the awakening nationalists and the ethnologists, which, however,

[5] See our article "Die Rechte der Person und ihre Bedeutung für die Mission" in *Neue Zeitschrift für Missionswissenschaft,* 1957, pp. 196–207.

[6] J. J. Komba, *God and Man, Religious Elements of the Ngoni of South-West Tanganyika, viewed in the Light of Christian Faith* (Pontif. Urbanian Univ. de Prop. Fide, 1959), p. 264.

very often shoot far beyond the mark, as do the dreadful remarks of the cynic R. Wright. The opinions of this writer, which have unfortunately received ill-deserved publicity in R. Italiaander's book *Der ruhelose Kontinent,*[7] are exemplified in the following passage: "The longer I thought about the work of the missionaries, the stranger it seemed to me. These men, driven by neurotic impulses, destroyed a people's whole philosophy of life without having another one to put in its place – indeed, without even knowing what they were doing..." The reply to this is that after all it was not the missionaries but the secularized western world that dealt religious Africa such severe blows; that many missionaries were eager to accommodate even at a time when the Africans no longer stood up for themselves; and that the missionaries were everywhere the first to record the language and culture of the people among whom they worked, and thus achieved something which really made the African renaissance possible.

The second attitude, the positive one, seeks to establish a relationship with paganism in religious instruction. At the very least, certain "heathen" tribal customs are accepted as in some way meaningful and are used as parallels in explaining Christian truths. In speaking of the *character indelebilis* of three of the sacraments it may be pointed out that the pagans, too, have their indelible tribal tatoos, which immediately identify a member of the tribe anywhere. In order to illustrate the effect of baptism and confirmation, one may compare them with the initiation rites which make the young men fully fledged members of the tribe. But such illustrations alone do not accomplish much that is essential.

The essential thing is to Christianize paganism as far as possible and desirable – not to uproot people only to replant them spiritually, at great pains, in a foreign climate, but instead to let their old roots drink the new water of salvation. It is not our task to make Christians "out of pagans", but to convert the pagans as such to Christ!

Christ himself showed us in his attitude towards the Old Testament what is meant by this. He bore a message far surpass-

[7] Econ-Verlag, Düsseldorf, 1958, p. 624.

ing that of the Old Testament, but he anchored it in the Old Testament. He taught in the synagogues like any other teacher, though with astonishing power. He unrolled the book of the prophet and read from it. But then he said: "This scripture . . . is today fulfilled!" (Luke 4:21). This was the newness of it, that in him all the expectations of the chosen people were fulfilled and surpassed. He came, not "to set aside the law and the prophets . . . but to bring them to perfection" (Matt. 5:17). This did not keep him from saying quite clearly: "It was said to the men of old . . . but I tell you . . ." (Matt. 5:21 et seq.), nor from dying for the newness of his doctrine. But to repeat: he did not set aside the Old Testament, but fulfilled it.

"The great new message brought to the Jews by the New Testament is simply the following: All that was prepared, announced, and foreshadowed by the Old Testament has now been fulfilled in the person of Christ and in the Christians. The New Testament manifests this belief throughout. St. Paul expressly teaches it in speaking of the appointed time (Gal. 4:4; Eph. 1:10); of the law as a tutor bringing us to Christ, who has superseded the law (Gal. 3:24; Rom. 10:4); of the Christians, in whom history has reached its fulfillment (1 Cor. 10:11); of the true Israel, which God had in mind in his covenant with the ancient Israel (Gal. 6:18); of the true children of Abraham, in whom the promises made to Abraham are fulfilled (Rom. 9:7 et seq.), of the law as a shadow of those blessings which were still to come (Heb. 10:1)."[8]

Of course paganism is not παιδαγωγός εἰς Χριστόν in the same sense as the Old Testament, and yet it does fulfil this function in some way. The great Clement of Alexandria, the first Christian scholar, who knew the holy scriptures, but also the whole of Greek philosophy and classical literature, expressed this thought clearly. According to him – and his reasoning is convincing – all true knowledge bears a relation to Christian revelation, and just as the law trained the Jewish spirit, so philosophy *trained* the pagan spirit towards Christ.[9]

[8] C. Vagaggini, *Theologie der Liturgie* (Einsiedeln, 1959), p. 279.

[9] *Stromata* 1, 28 et seq.; see also H. Rahner, *Griechische Mythen in christlicher Deutung* (Zürich, 1945).

Thus the question of whether to absorb paganism into Christianity is not merely one of tactics which may achieve better results: this absorption has been planned and desired by God's providence. Although in the Old Testament God "chose" only one people to be an immediate preparation for Christ, he continually had his eye upon all peoples, to whom the promise was made through their common ancestor in paradise. God has preserved in these peoples much that is good and destined to ornament the royal robe of Christ. Only recently have the positive values of pagan religion been more thoroughly recognized, and now many are falling into the other extreme, taking these values as absolute, and denying that Christianity should be brought to these people. By idolizing these religions they rob them of their real meaning. "Only in the light of revelation can the myth be properly seen and evaluated as religion, faith, and experience: as a reminiscence, distorted by sin, of original revelation, and as a partial expression of natural revelation, which is not set aside but conquered, fulfilled, and redeemed by Christ, the end and fulfilment of the myth."[10]

In the light of New Testament revelation, therefore, paganism – like the Old Testament itself – can be reconstrued and reevaluated. At the same time it follows from this parallel that paganism, as a foreshadowing, must give way to the light; that it is now invalid, because fulfilled. But if paganism refuses to accept this glorious offer and to be absorbed into Christianity, it may lose its character as a religion of advent and become apostate and anti-Christian. From then on it is of negative value. It has condemned itself. We must ask ourselves whether our previous negative attitude was not sometimes partially responsible for the hardening of the pagan heart, whether we did not wish to deal paganism a deathly blow to begin with instead of showing it the path of life.

The positive attitude requires that we do not simply sermonize and force Christianity upon people, "or else", but that we become conversant with paganism and learn to appreciate

[10] H. Fries, "Mythos und Offenbarung" in *Fragen der Theologie Heute* (Einsiedeln, 1958), p. 36.

its positive values; that we confidently believe that – like sinful man – much of what is "heathen" can be baptized and thus freed of poison and filled with truth and life. Our hearers must have the impression that we take their religion as seriously as they do, that we are interpreting it in a great new way. Then they will follow us and suddenly discover in the gospel the solution of all their problems and the fulfilment of all their vague hopes. Whatever in paganism cannot be brought into agreement with the law of the gospel will then die out of itself.[11]

We must really ask ourselves whether the widespread contention is correct, that in the first stages of missionary work a *choc surnaturel,* as it were, must be given and a very clear line be drawn between paganism and Christianity, and that in the later stages the native community can then establish some sort of positive relationship between paganism and Christianity.[12] As an emergency solution – because at first the foreign missionary generally had too little knowledge of paganism – this was, alas, quite probably the usual procedure. But as a matter of principle we really do not believe that people first have to be entirely uprooted from their tribal religion, only to be later replanted, at great pains, and with only partial success. We believe that there is no chasm between paganism and Christianity, but that there is a path leading from the one to the other. But this path is not at all easy to find.

It must be counted a great tragedy that the doctrine of vital energy characterizing the whole Bantu philosophy of life was not discovered in its whole structure and significance until the middle of the twentieth century.[13] Not only is this philosophy of life fit to be guided along the path to Christianity, but the *mysterium Christi,* the central doctrine of the Mystical Body of Christ, is much more easily and surely grasped by

[11] For an elucidation of this attitude see the excellent article by Father Tempels, O.F.M., "Les bases de notre catéchèse en Afrique" in *Orientations pastorales* (Léopoldville, Oct. 1959), pp. 59–68.

[12] See A. M. Henri, O.P., *Esquisse d'une théologie de la Mission* (Paris, 1959).

[13] Father Tempels, *La philosophie bantoue* (Elisabethville, 1945); *Bantu-Philosophie* (Heidelberg, 1956).

taking this philosophy as a starting-point than by using the intellectual, typically western catechism method.[14]

Unfortunately too little advantage has been taken of this by catechetics. And so it happens that J. J. Komba (in his book mentioned above) must conclude: "The Bantu religion governed the economy, society, politics. But now comes the puzzle: The same people whose pagan faith was second nature to them begin, once they have turned Christian, to separate religion and life. They never made statements like: 'I must not do that on account of my faith' as long as they were servants of the spirits. To be freed from the spirits would have meant a loss of vital energy to them then. But now it is the opposite: emancipation from Christian faith would mean an increased *joie de vivre*. What is the cause of this way of thinking which is contrary to their whole mental attitude? That is a problem to be solved by the missionaries!"

We do not believe that the transition from paganism to Christianity without any break necessarily entails any greater danger of syncretism than if Christianity is simply implanted as something quite new in the consciousness of the hearers, any more than if a foreign word is adopted; on the contrary. In the first case one is obliged to learn something about paganism, whereas in the other case the danger exists that the new will be driven into but not grafted onto the old and that the two of them will go on living side by side, without any relationship to each other.[15]

Of course the confrontation of paganism and Christianity takes a different form depending on whether the hearers are pagan children, adult catechumens, or Christians. Thus there is by no means a guarantee that education to Christianity will be easily accomplished. Christ himself had much difficulty in directing the earthly thoughts of the Jews towards the spiritual and heavenly kingdom of the Messiah, and several times he

[14] Tempels, *Catéchèse bantoue* (Saint-André, 1949), and especially V. Mulago, *L'union vitale bantoue face à l'union vitale ecclésiale* (Doctoral Dissertation, Rome, 1954). See our exposition of this in *Neue Zeitschrift für Missionswissenschaft,* 1956, pp. 296–314.

[15] See my exposition of the subject in my book *Die christliche Terminologie als missions-methodisches Problem* (Schoeneck, 1950), pp. 64–70.

sighed: "Are you still without wits? How long must I be with you, how long must I bear with you?" (Matt. 15:16; Mark 9:18). But that has nothing to do with the basic considerations. The right way must be seen, even though some difficulties along it still remain.

The individual missionary cannot be expected to blaze his own trail from paganism by way of the Old Testament (the Old Testament should not be replaced by paganism as if the latter were its equal, but paganism should be regarded as an earlier stage in the history of salvation) to Christian revelation. But there is still no trace of a handbook to help him. We have not advanced beyond theoretical requirements. There are many catechisms in use in Africa today, among them good ones – for example, the new *Katholischer Katechismus Deutschlands* is at present being translated into Swahili – but none of them embodies the spirit of adaptation, the positive attitude towards paganism which I have described. Might not Father Tempels and Abbé Mulago, both of whom work in the Congo and have the necessary qualifications, on the basis of their publications and their whole attitude, be asked to attempt such a pagan-Christian mystagogy? It would only help to deepen the roots of Christianity in Africa and to perfect African paganism in Christianity.

## *Catechesis should suit the Missions

DONAT MÜLLER, O.F.M.CAP.

IMAGINE my surprise when some time ago I first read *Mungu na Wanadamu,* the religious instruction textbook used in our mission. I expected to find a translation of some European catechism of the type used in my youth. Instead, I was amazed to discover that our missionaries had produced a book of religious instruction for the Africans that is not constructed according to the logic of our western thought. The Christian truths based upon the "story of salvation" quite certainly make a greater impression on the African than does that presentation which, to be sure, is systematic, but which has developed from Aristotelian thought. Right from the beginning this book was an indispensable textbook for me in instruction and preaching.

And the more opportunity I had to pursue practical instruction in school, the more I became conscious of the fact that a catechesis in Africa is simply different from the one at home, especially when it is taught by an African teacher. Of course it is explained and taught, but in general, the teachers are much more lively when teaching, and know how to illumine the truths according to the African way of life; imperceptibly, the lessons can break into singing.

And then the *children* in the classes! They are very receptive to religious truths, more indeed than the children at home. They really join in and are interested. This is shown by their questions, too. I have to marvel at how they are always full of religious questions. I could turn almost every class in religious affairs in the Middle School into a question and answer period.

In spite of these positive aspects, our catechism in the missions still shows some weak points. Despite certain spontaneous adaptations already mentioned, it is more or less the same catechesis which missionaries learned at home that is transplanted to Africa. What the revision of the catechism in Europe confirmed holds true to an even greater degree in Africa: our religious instruction is too school-oriented, too intellectual. The reasons are as follows.

The missions leave the entire religious training to the schools. Even in those cases where the parents are already Christian, they have not been instructed enough to give religious training to their children. Religious instruction is too much a mediation of intellectual knowledge. The teachers have to work through a prescribed programme; when the priest comes, the children have to be able to show this prescribed knowledge. The instruction does not turn into prayer often enough. At the beginning and end there is generally mechanical recitation of a prayer: it is not the listening to God's message which should flow quite naturally into a thanks to God. In those cases where the book really attempts to be the "catechism", the questions and answers are too much a simplification of our scholastic dogmatics. Its contents develop too little out of the biblical passages; they are too abstract and bear too little relation to life. Baptismal instruction for children and adults is purely scholastic. Where is the liturgical admission into the catechumenate, the adjuration, the delivery of the gospels and the Lord's Prayer? Such liturgical celebrations would take hold of and slowly consecrate the entire man.

This western intellectualism in religious instruction has more devastating consequences in the Missions, because there is nothing to supplement it in the way of a Christian family life or public opinion, completely apart from the fact that the African who has not yet lost his natural feeling wants to be addressed as a man with body and soul, intellect and emotion.

Besides this all too one-sided intellectualism, I should like briefly to touch upon yet other aspects which show that catechesis in the Missions is *too little adapted* to African conditions. To begin with, in *Mungu na Wanadamu,* where biblical pictures are concerned, the persons are always represented as Europeans. In the other pictures about Christian life, the priest and guide is always a European (the Guardian Angel, too), while those being led, kneeling and receiving the blessing are Africans. The children ask me again and again why it is represented in this way. Understandably, the Africans are very sensitive with regard to these things today. This observation also points to the wholly questionable nature of our all too realistic religious art. If we do not yet possess an African Christian art, would it not be better to use the more symbolical, spiritual art of early Christian history which has meaning for all races and continents? See the universally valid pictures in "A Catholic Catechism".

In its contents, the religious instruction does not preach the glad tidings enough. Often the teachers do not get beyond the Ten Commandments. And then, at that point where the Christian message should reach its peak, in the message of the resurrection of Christ, the foreground is given over to the sacrament of confession and the aid to an examination of conscience. But the African was made for rejoicing. Would not the African, who is so often persecuted by fear, hate, hunger and disease, be most thankful for the *eu-angelion?*

In addition, we often pay too little attention to an African method — that of repetition. The African is not so harassed as we are; he does not always want to see and hear something new. He is happy with the same tunes and rhythms, and always sings the same refrains.

In the instruction, we take too little notice of these characteristics. We think that we always have to bring in something new instead of repeating the same things in a different way.

A good catechist must know the conditions in Africa. African life and feelings are the starting point for every fruitful catechetical teaching that has appeal. When, for example, I draw a house on the blackboard, I do not draw a European house with a tiled roof and windows on the second floor, but a straw-roofed hut. Or if I want to represent graphically the parable of Christ about the gathering of the good corn into the barn, I cannot portray an ancestral barn; rather I must draw a simple shed of branches standing on piles. I stress the fact that on the flight to Egypt, Christ really came to Africa and blessed this continent; that in antiquity, North Africa, all the way to Abyssinia, experienced a flourishing Christianity. The religious instruction has to make our children conscious of the fact that the Church is not the faith of Europeans alone; that Christ does not distinguish among the races.

The most suitable catechesis for the African is probably the story of salvation. In the great deeds of the God of the Old and New Testaments, the African learns not only to know God, but to wonder at him and to be thankful to him for his acts. Even the less educated man is moved by the biblical events. In the Middle School I carry out the following programme of religious instruction. Grade 5: Abraham to Christ (Books of the Old Testament). Grade 6: Christ, the central part of the story of salvation (The Gospels). Grade 7: Beginnings of Church history (The Acts of the Apostles and the Epistles). Grade 8: Church history (Apocalypse).

The children participate with interest. The central point of the lesson is always a reading from that book of the holy scriptures under discussion. In this way I should like to guide them to a direct witness of the word of God. And the lesson becomes a service to the word of God. Through this I hope to prepare the children for a religious service in its genuine form.

Catechesis must be liturgical. The lessons should not be allowed to remain merely intellectually understood. It is, of course, the unsophisticated person who learns by doing. Therefore the instruction must prepare for an active participation in the service. Together with untiring references to the Church Year and the liturgical life, the lessons themselves should lead entirely spontaneously to common prayer; and because the prayer is in common, it is bound to be stamped with the principles of the liturgy. It is for this reason that I usually choose as a closing prayer a psalm with a corresponding antiphonal variation which is then always repeated by the children.

In this way I prepare the children gradually for that time when in the service the faithful will again sing psalms. I was honestly astonished how quickly my school-children grasped this form of worship by responding to the psalms. Altogether, it seems to me that our missionary catechesis can only succeed if we learn more of the characteristic features of the liturgy, for example participation of the whole person, even with gestures animating the whole body; symbolism; repetitions in the responses. As the goal to strive for, I always keep in mind a rhythmic singing of the psalms with symbolic gestures. To learn through rhythm, and to praise God through rhythm: would that not be the catechetic ideal in Africa?

Our religious instruction will always be different from that at home just because it must be missionary. We must never forget that our school-children and catechumens to a great extent still originate from a heathen or Islamic environment, and invariably live in it. All the more, then, do we have to seek to understand them in their entire human condition. And when there is finally a nucleus of Christian parents, they have to be trained to contribute their share to the Christian upbringing of their children. They should not be allowed simply to leave this part of the education to the school and to the missionary. And it is just in this regard that there is still something lacking in the missions.

For above all, missionary catechesis must be a message of something new, a joyous, indeed the long yearned-for salvation. To be sure, the catechesis has to embrace the entire Christian message of salvation, but it must not be allowed to become lost in devotions and private revelations. The catechist must lose no time over explanations of liturgical trivialities, over doubtful stories of the saints, and certainly not over though pious theologically not well-founded views. Christ, crucified and risen, must continually come before the minds' eye of the catechumens as our salvation and our only salvation for whom we must decide. Then missionary catechesis has to demand something: the catechist must not be afraid to make demands of the children. I would rather set a candidate for a baptism back if he is not willing to achieve something for Christ. It is just in the missions that we dare not have too much consideration for the single weak man, whether it concerns admission to baptism or to the sacraments. Otherwise, from weak religious teaching a rather lame Christian faith will develop. It seems to me that the best catechesis for baptized and unbaptized alike is a living, strongly Church-centred community, where doctrine and life merge into one another.

# THE RENEWAL OF CATECHETICAL METHODS IN THE MISSIONS

# Origin and Development of Modern Catechetical Methods

KLEMENS TILMANN
The Oratory, Munich

AT a moment of world history fraught with decisive consequences for the missions as well as for the countries supporting them, we cannot be content to go on preaching the gospel and teaching catechism in the old familiar way: we must, rather, make the best possible use of all that tradition and the present day have to offer. Therefore let us review the development of catechetical method, with special attention to its missionary aspect.

Jesus' method of teaching reveals the essence of missionary preaching. He begins his "catechism instructions" with the words: "The Kingdom of God is near at hand; repent, and believe the gospel" (Mark 1:15). Thus he heralds the advent of something new and unheard of, something producing a revolutionary effect on the whole human situation, compelling men to repent, to make a decision, to reform, and to live and act in a new way. Through the preaching of the gospel the whole man is stirred to the roots of his being by God's majesty, transformed, saved from sin, and finally reborn as a child of God. That is why St. Paul says of his own preaching and teaching: "It was I that begot you . . . when I preached the gospel to you" (1 Cor. 4:15).

Thus those attending religious preaching or instructions hear the word of God. Through the preacher or catechist whom he has sent, God speaks to man – in the words he uses, but also by means of the inner grace with which he "opens" (Acts 16:14) hearts. It is not primarily a matter of imparting factual knowledge, which the listener afterwards possesses as his property. It is a matter of calling the listener into God's kingdom, of imparting a message that arrests him and through which God takes possession of him. Such preaching and teaching give catechetics its missionary character.

Of course catechetical instruction is also doctrine in which the gospel is explained, elucidated, and defined so as to prevent error, as is the case with the Church's teaching. But this is a second stage, which necessarily presupposes the first. Otherwise divine truth would be deprived of its character as the "gospel which is your salvation" (Eph. 1:13). Besides, proper catechetical instruction retains its missionary character even while explaining doctrine, for it has its source in the mission of Christ and the Church; it is a testimony of faith, presupposes a lively faith in the catechist, enriches faith in the hearers and deepens their love. And the result even of doctrinal instruction is not primarily the possession of knowledge, but rather the praise of God, thanksgiving, faith, love, joy, submission to God and his commandments, and life with him. The value of religious instruction, therefore, depends above all upon the extent to which the word of God, his truth and grace, quickens within the hearer, so that he responds to it and turns towards God; upon the extent to which his Christian character is formed. This is what gives catechetics its missionary character. Only in the second place does this value depend on how much detailed and verifiable knowledge has been acquired by the intellect or committed to memory.

The development of catechetics can be considered in several stages.

## *Early Christian Catechetics*

In the early centuries of the Christian era the chief catechetical activities were the preparation of catechumens for baptism and the formation of a liturgy close to the hearts of the people. Both had a missionary purpose. The main purpose of the preparation for baptism was not the imparting of knowledge but the formation of Christians. Care was taken to provide solid instruction, in the course of which, however, the catechumens were required to do but very little memorization. The chief means of educating baptized Christians was the joint celebration of the divine liturgy, in which the faithful participated comprehendingly, actively, and in common. The liturgical forms were immediately comprehensible, and the language was the vernacular. The Mass of Catechumens had a continual catechetical and missionary effect on the people through the reading of the divine word, the sermon, and the various forms of prayer – spoken by the celebrant, responded to by the people, or meditatively sung. In the Eucharist the central mystery of the faith was proclaimed to the congregation, became present in the rites, and was celebrated with the active participation of all present; at the same time it was an act of thanksgiving and surrender to God, and of union with Christ and with one another. The whole celebration took place in an atmosphere of neighbourly love. The liturgy was an expression of religious vitality and at the same time a form of religious instruction powerful in the lives of the assembled parishioners. Thus the early centuries of Christianity were a peak in the catechetical work of the Church.

### *Catechetics in the Middle Ages*

From this peak catechetics had declined sharply by the Middle Ages. The old form of baptismal instruction was no longer practised. The catechetical force inherent in the liturgy was greatly hindered by the increasing unfamiliarity of the ritual and especially by the incomprehensibility of the language. The liturgy became the affair of the clergy and the congregation observed the holy rites from afar, understanding but little of what went on. There were no special religious instructions for children, whose preparation for confession and holy communion was left to their parents. The Sunday sermon, the learning of the Lord's Prayer, the Apostles' Creed, and later of other catechetical formulas, Christian art above all, and at the end of the Middle Ages books of devotion, including those on preparing for confession, served as religious instruction for the faithful. Of decisive importance was the communal life, which was steeped in faith. Faith was acquired like one's native language – as a part of life, without special instruction. It was found on every hand: at divine service (scarcely comprehended though this was), on feast days, and in the extraordinary wealth of religious usages. It was more a process of becoming familiar with the faith than a knowledge of or an insight into divine revelation. When the Reformation broke out, the results of neglect in the fields of liturgy, the preaching of the Bible, and catechetics became evident. An understanding of important truths of faith was lacking. People had practical faith but lacked spiritual insight and clarity about important questions and religious truths.

### *After the Council of Trent*

Catechetics was substantially furthered by the Council of Trent. Sunday school in the parish church was made obligatory for children; this practice was, however, not at all generally adopted. There appeared catechisms briefly summarizing the doctrines of the Church, presenting the Catholic faith and defining it against the innovators. The book became all-important in catechetics. But the religious spirit of mutual participation became less important – a retrogression which had serious disadvantages. The method was unskilful; it consisted merely of explaining the text. Questions and answers were first recited or read out by the catechist, who then analyzed the text, expressed its meaning in other words, if possible illustrated it by examples, and concluded with an admonition or a practical application. The stress was laid on memorization and recitation, which unavoidably became somewhat mechanical. This sort of religious instruction had but little missionary force.

### *Religious Instruction in Schools*

At the end of the eighteenth century the state made attendance at its elementary schools compulsory, and religious instruction became a school subject. Thus all children could now be reached with the regularity provided by the school surroundings, and there was now time for religious instruction. But along with these advantages came serious disadvantages: faith was taught in the secular setting of a compulsory state school. Religion was a school subject. The emphasis shifted from faith and life to doctrines and knowledge. This secularization has influenced catechetics down to the present day. Religious instruction was affected by the historical errors of rationalism and the Enlightenment, in which an attempt was made to replace the truths of revelation by a religion of reason and to turn religion into a handmaid of morality. There was, however, some attempt to adapt the teaching to the special requirements of children, and to cover the ground in a methodical manner by the aid of questions; these features were pedagogically of some value.

### *Deharbe's Catechism*

As opposed to the textbooks of the Enlightenment, which generally gave a watered-down naturalistic version of the faith, Deharbe's catechism, published in 1847, was characterized by a return to tradition and a theologically correct, clear, and complete presentation of Catholic doctrine. It became the prevalent catechism in Germany and had a world-wide effect. Its disadvantage, which has influenced catechetics down to the present, was that of being a textbook of theological science in miniature. It appeals one-sidedly to the intellect and the memory, neither considering the psychology of the child, nor making faith appear worth loving and living, and it has led generations of catechists all over the world to adopt a non-missionary method of dry explanations of text and tedious memorization – a mistake subsequently often committed in religious instruction in the missions as well. The Bible was considered to be of use in catechesis only as a handmaid of moral teaching.

### *The Munich Method*

At the turn of the century Heinrich Stieglitz, a catechist in Giesing (a suburb of Munich), found that the old method of explaining texts was no great success with the children of his working-class suburb, where faith was easily endangered. He recognized the general lack of missionary spirit in religious instruction. At the same time, in seeking a solution, he noted the strides which had been made in secular education towards instruction suited to the mental faculties of the child. He called the old method – first teaching the catechism text and then explaining it – an "outrage upon the human faculty of perception". *Omnis cognitio incipit a sensu* is the scholastic teaching. "Observation, thought, action" are the three steps (known as early as Aristotle) indispensable to the acquisition of all true knowledge, and thus to teaching. Therefore Stieglitz and the new method of religious instruction originating in Munich required that each doctrine treated be introduced by a story illustrating the truth in question. Starting with the story, the truth itself is arrived at by a process of thought and explanation. And finally the way from this truth to action must be pointed out. With two steps added to the three major ones, the teaching of any particular doctrine should normally run according to the following psychological scheme.

INTRODUCTION. The threads of the last lesson are taken up or the right mood is created in some other way; the purpose is to focus the children's attention on the object of the lesson.

PRESENTATION of an illustrative story.

EXPLANATION. The object of the lesson is developed from the story.

SUMMARY. The truth that has been learnt is stated briefly.

APPLICATION to life of what has been learned.

The treatment of each doctrine should be based, if possible, on one illustrative story only, thus forming a unit.

This scheme should not, of course, function as a straight-jacket.

Elasticity of treatment, depending on the subject and the situation, is also possible in religious instruction. The illustrative story may itself serve as the introduction. The story may be told in parts, and each part discussed separately. Occasionally, when the subject is such that it needs no illustration, it will be sufficient to start off with nothing more than a question which arouses interest, passing on from that directly to the explanation. Sometimes the explanation will be immediately followed by the application, and the summary left till the end. In lessons on ethical questions, explanation and application are often but a single process. But the three steps: observation, thought, action, should always be kept in mind.

In lessons on the Bible the subject often is itself a story, in which case no other story need be told. The presentation of the bible story is followed by the explanation of what is revealed in it and of its meaning for our lives; God's actions and man's response are contemplated more deeply and then made fruitful in the application. Here, too, we see the three stages: observation, thought, action, which form the basis of all religious instruction, whether for children or for adults.

### *The Activities Method*

As unbelief became increasingly widespread, affecting families, the catechists found themselves confronted more and more with a missionary task. With ever greater urgency they asked themselves what would capture the imagination of the children? How can we give them lessons that will help to form their lives? A new solution of this missionary problem, which has given constant impetus to the development of religious instruction down to the present day, was found in the activities method that had already been developed in secular education. Children learn not only through hearing and speaking but, especially, by doing. Words must be supplemented by deeds, passivity superseded by activity, for in this way a more lasting impression results. Activity appeals to children at a much deeper level. For they love to investigate things and make their own discoveries, so as to acquire knowledge by themselves. That is why we should not attempt to suppress or to side-track their itch to be up and doing, as teachers of a bygone generation thought they ought to do. In our catechism lessons we should, instead, make use of this characteristic of children, encouraging it and turning it to our purpose.

On this principle teachers began letting the children contribute as much as possible of their own knowledge and observations to the class instruction. The children were also encouraged to make sketches and to keep a workbook in which they compiled what they had learnt, often in a creative way.

The catechism, too, began to allow for the activity of the children. Thus there appeared, at first in France, questions without answers, requiring the children to tell in their own words what they had learnt from the lesson. There appeared exercises which encouraged activity of various kinds: reflecting on, collecting, looking for, investigating, observing, or forming an opinion about something; other exercises encouraged creative activity: drawing, handicraft work, writing descriptions, and composing prayers. These activities were carried out at school or at home, to prepare for or to conclude a lesson, by the pupils individually, in couples, and in groups. All these activities fit into the framework of the Munich Method and can serve as an introduction, as a means of presenting or explaining the material, as a summary, or as a practical application. Thus the Munich Method was greatly enlivened by means of activities.

### *The Religious Formation of Life as a Whole*

Children's activities were encouraged not only as a method of learning. The children were not merely to acquire positive knowledge – they were to become Christians, were to be shown how to live a moral and religious life. What they learnt they were to put into practice, here and now.

Thus education to action was more clearly seen to be an important goal of religious instruction. The children were encouraged to aim at the good not only while in catechism class but also in their everyday lives. A mutual resolution would be formed and renewed at frequent intervals during the period for which it had been taken. A project would be carried out, for example collecting money for a child about to be baptized in one of the foreign missions. As part of moral training and the formation of conscience, problems calling for a decision in which not only a permissible but rather the best possible Christian solution was sought – orally, as written work, and in playlets. Indeed, the class itself or the school became the place for the realization of ideals, for the practice of charity, for acting jointly in the spirit of Christ. Thus Christian teachers created together with the children the sort of Christian milieu that was more and more lacking at home and in the world about them. This formation of character by means of milieu was particularly important in France, where on Thursday, there being no school on that day, the children attending state schools spent the whole morning at church, learning, praying, playing and singing, celebrating occasional festivals, doing charity work, and attending Mass – all the time having a feeling of living in religious surroundings, by which they were formed. In France also, catechisms were published which were suited to the various social environments of the children.

As in the moral, so also in the religious sphere, catechism class was the scene of action and practical realization. The teacher sought to awaken the response of the children and to maintain religious depth by his very manner of presenting the doctrines and in class discussion. In addition, beginning with an experience leading to prayer, then developing the various forms of prayer, he trained the children to pray – at catechism instructions and in their everyday lives.

Once again religious instruction underwent a development, this time in the direction of personal as well as of religious depth. Children are capable of being deeply moved; thus it has become the catechist's task now to guide children towards meditation, towards contemplation of the truth they have heard, towards sympathy and prayerful response – whether by listening to the moving story told by their teacher, contemplating a picture, imagining something with their eyes shut, performing children's devotions, or acting out a playlet. Children are capable of working for the Kingdom of God; thus catechetics began to include education for the apostolate and guidance in speaking with people of another persuasion, which calls for personal insight into the truths of faith, not just a stock of catechism phrases. Children are capable of advance in holiness; thus religious instruction aids children in leading an ascetic life, a life of divine love and of rejoicing in God, in fact, a life of sainthood, which is God's vocation for all of us.

All the developments of the last sixty years in the religious instruction of children are, *mutatis mutandis,* of equal value for the instruction of adults in the missions. These developments represent no mere refinement of method but rather the consideration of what is suitable for and natural to the child – one of the considerations forced upon us by the crossroads of history at which we stand. The modern approach appeals to the whole wide range of the children's God-given talents and to the spiritual depth which they possess, and it awakens religious life and awareness in them. Thus modern catechetics has made use of all the best elements found in the instruction of early Christian catechumens, in the all-pervading faith of the Middle Ages, and in the methods of more recent times.

In the course of this development the science of catechetics has made a double discovery. On the one hand it has recognized its own limitations, those posed by the classroom environment. On the other hand it has discovered that it had as a partner not only the Christian family but also another potent force for spiritual formation – newly discovered and yet ancient: the liturgy. In the liturgy modern catechetics found itself confirmed, indeed surpassed in many ways and therefore most happily supplemented. The liturgy is not classroom instruction but a sacred celebration, not theory but life and practice, not only the work of human hands but above all the work of God. If the catechist takes care to arrange the celebration of Mass according to its full meaning, Mass will be impressive for the eye, will have variety and spiritual impact, and the congregation will be taken into the most sacred rites. Such a manner of celebrating Mass is suited to the psychological requirements of children and of adults. The increasing discovery of the Mass as a catechetical masterpiece, especially in its most ancient form, has been a joyful process. It is, therefore, with longing that countless teachers of religion look forward to the reinvestment of the liturgy with its original full catechetical force.

## *The Material and Kerygmatic Renewal*

The harder catechists tried to fulfill their pastoral and missionary task on children and young people, the clearer it became to them that the most important thing in religious instruction is not the method but the *content*, the joyful tidings, the kerygma. Thus religious instruction was caught up in another great revival movement, which had arisen independently of catechetics, and which is also of the greatest importance for the religious instruction of adults in the missions. In the years following the first World War there was an awakening of interest in the holy scriptures. As soon as we young students began reading the New Testament we discovered in it a whole new world of expressions, statements, and challenges which we had never encountered in the course of our religious instructions. What riches seemed to lie concealed in words like: the joyful tidings, the Kingdom of God, reborn, a new creature, begotten by the Word of Truth! The Bible spoke of a comprehensive design, to be fulfilled by God (Eph. 1:10), of the mystery kept hidden from the beginning of time but now made manifest in the Church (Eph. 3:9). It declared that the whole treasury of wisdom and knowledge is stored up in Christ (Col. 2:3); that those who follow the leading of God's Spirit are all God's sons (Rom. 8:14); that the Spirit of God's Son cries out in us Abba, Father (Gal. 4:6); that we are to become transfigured into the likeness of Christ, borrowing glory from his glory (2 Cor. 3:18); that deliverance will not be complete until the Day of Judgment (Luke 21:28); that there will be a new heaven, and a new earth (Apoc. 21:1). What vitality, what strength were manifest in these tidings! What glories were yet to be discovered therein! From what deep emotion arise the words of St. Paul: "I do not count my life precious compared with my work, which is to finish the course I run, the task of preaching which the Lord Jesus has given me, in proclaiming the good news of God's grace" (Acts 20:24). The language of the old catechism had been clear and objective, but dry, dispassionate, serving to define concepts. That which, in life, belongs together, was separated by the arrangement according to concepts. Through the old catechism we had not come face to face with living reality and all its power to stir, inspire, and exalt.

The interest in holy scripture and the liturgy after the first World War led to a significant theological and religious revival movement. While the power of faith decreased among the great majority of the people, in the heart of the Church the sources of faith broke forth anew. This process necessarily had an effect on religious instruction. When, for example, exegesis and biblical theology came to the conclusion that "New Testament teaching stresses above all the coming of the Kingdom of God", of which the old catechism made no mention, an attempt had to be made on the part of catechetics and the catechism to do justice to these new insights. Shaken into awareness by the oppression and persecution of the Nazis, confronted with a new missionary situation, exposed to the horrors of war, to nights spent in air-raid shelters, and to the devastation of the post-war period, we felt our task to be that of cultivating for the benefit of religious instruction the tremendous reserves contained in the divine word of the Bible. Our basic insights concerning catechetics were as follows.

Religious instruction consists in imparting to the children not primarily formulas but the consciousness of a sacred reality.

This reality is not a collection of individual facts but a living organism, whose centre is Christ. All the individual truths are vitally related to him and to one another, and only thus can they properly be presented.

This organism is not only something statically present but above all something in process of happening; something set into motion by God, and having its living centre in the life, death, and glorification of Christ; an event which includes us in its course and which, according to the dynamic process inherent in it, is hastening to its overwhelming conclusion.

This event is not only worth knowing about, it is the event on which our salvation depends. It is a matter of salvation or perdition, eternal life or eternal death.

As the form of revelation God did not, therefore, choose universally valid dogmas, but a clear, gripping event, one which he allowed to take place and then caused to be proclaimed. The centre of the mystery of salvation is Christ, in whom the whole treasury of wisdom and knowledge is stored up (Col. 2:3). Religious instruction must join hands with revelation by proclaiming the fact of salvation. Upon the story of salvation must be based what the children are taught about the doctrine of salvation and what it requires of us. Catechetical method must correspond with God's method. God is the best of catechists.

Outwardly, religious instruction appears to be like other instruction. But religious instruction is infinitely superior in kind to all other instruction; for while the catechist is speaking, Christ is acting. He, the sublime Lord of his Church, stirs the hearts of the children with his Holy Spirit, so that they come to believe and to love (see Acts 16:14) and be saved.

The story of salvation could now be treated in Bible lessons as concrete historical events. But catechetical instruction, although now much more closely related to the Bible, stood in need of a careful theological evaluation in the light of the order which is inherent in its material. The theme of primary importance, requiring the strongest emphasis, is that of the Kingdom of God. Christ our Lord stands at the centre and is mediator of this kingdom; its living space is the Church. The chief activity by which it imparts salvation is the celebration of the Eucharist. Its spirit and permanent fruit is love. The whole structure must rest upon the events by which salvation is accomplished – as they first took place in the life, death and resurrection and glorification of Christ, as they are presented to the world in the Church, and as they must penetrate our own lives.

The individual subjects also had to be reconsidered. The teaching on God, for example, no longer begins with the concept of God, nor does it proceed from the abstract to the concrete in treating the divine attributes. God has revealed himself chiefly through his actions. Therefore we must begin with the actions by which he has revealed himself in order to introduce the children to the fact of his being. In the teaching on Christ, our Lord must be seen in his rôle as the preacher of the gospel, and as our teacher, an example to us, and our master. The significance for our salvation of his resurrection and his active presence enthroned in heaven, prepared to return to us again, must also be stressed in a way befitting their importance. Christian life is a response to the action of God. Therefore it must not be treated primarily under the heading of the Ten Commandments, but must be considered in connection with all the truths of faith and, when it is treated as a subject by itself, be shown in its full scope as the life of redeemed children of God.

Thus religious instruction can expand its full, God-given dynamic, stirring, missionary vigour. The living God, his way of revealing himself, his plans of salvation, even his active redeeming presence are presented. This renewal of the subject matter has constantly joined forces with the renewal of method, so that the two have become an inseparable whole – that whole which we have experienced as the catechetical revival of the last few decades.

The catechetical method of our day has brought in the harvest of nearly two thousand years. From contemporary times it borrowed a theological view centred on salvation, and the advances made in educational practice and in child psychology; from the beginning of the century its methodical care; from the post-Tridentine period the religious instruction of all children, and the book, the catechism; from the Middle Ages a recognition of the importance of a religious milieu, and of catechetical formulas; from the early centuries of the Church the spirit of the catechumenate and that of a vital liturgy. But from the very beginning it has been inspired by God's work and God's word, bestowed on us in the Catechist of catechists, in Jesus Christ, our Lord.

# Advantages and Difficulties of Modern Methods in Mission Catechesis

LÉOPOLD DENIS, S.J.
Director of the *Centre Documentaire Catéchétique*, Mayidi, Congo

LET me begin by recalling briefly the essential characteristics of present-day catechetics, as a framework for the subject I have been asked to treat.

The task of the catechist presents itself today as that of initiating the catechumens into the mystery of Christ. We do well to call it initiation and not mere instruction. It is intended to impart not a theoretical but a practical knowledge of religion, one which seizes the whole man, engages the entire personality. Christian doctrine is not merely something to be learnt and committed to memory. It is something to be assented to and lived. We must cling to it with our whole souls. We must make it the centre of our lives.

This process of initiation is concerned with the mystery of Christ, that is, with the divine plan of redemption of which our Lord was the bearer. This plan did not take the form of a philosophical system but that of a series of historical events making gloriously manifest God's incredible love of man. It is revealed to us in the form of joyful tidings, the Good News brought by Christ, which we should receive with alacrity through faith and which we should respond to with love.

What concrete ways are there of accomplishing this initiation? Today everyone agrees that it should be done by means of the Bible, the liturgy, systematic exposition, and by means of life itself. The story of the Bible presents the simplest, most suitable, and inherently effective means of establishing contact with the Christian religion. Thanks to the liturgy our catechesis not only reaches the mind but enters into and becomes part of life.

A systematic exposition of doctrine, centred around our Father in Heaven and the living person of Christ, our brother, is nevertheless necessary to satisfy the requirements of logical and psychological unity. Finally, as the message transmitted by the catechist concerns not a mere abstraction possessing reality only in the mind that conceives it, but a life existing independently of any formulas that express it, religious initiation must of course have its beginning, middle, and end in life.

Another point emphasized by today's experienced religious educators is that the initiation into Christianity involves the entire person: the sensibilities, the intelligence, the will. Therefore it should take advantage of all modern educational techniques: the intuitive process, the inductive method, activities, teaching by experience, the teaching of values. It should advance along with the personality and thus differ according to the age group. It should be directed towards the person in his social context and always take account of the environment. A last point stressed by modern catechetics is the necessity for the catechist to fulfil his task of initiation with ardent conviction, and to support it with the testimony of his life. He should be aware that grace works with him in the souls of his hearers.

### *Advantages of the Modern Methods in Mission Countries*

The application of these ideas and methods in the foreign missions has proved most fruitful and opportune. The members of the dynamic East Asian Pastoral Institute of Manila have well demonstrated this in their books and articles especially concerning Asiatic countries. I wish to point it out especially in relation to Central Africa where I have lived for twenty-seven years. As it would take too long to do so in detail, I shall limit myself to showing the beneficial effect on catechesis in Africa of having recourse to the Bible and to the liturgy.

### *Initiation*

Africans in our part of the country do not acquire their native religion in a theoretical way. It is through the rites celebrated in the family circle or clan that the children are initiated into the ancestral beliefs; through the vivid stories told and the conversations heard around the fire in the evening, they come to know of the God "who made us with our fingernails and fingers" (a Bakongo proverb), of the spirits who so frequently intervene in human affairs, of the "ancestors' village" which will welcome them at their death .... At the feasts held to celebrate births and marriages, in the course of the long funeral ceremonies, during the interminable palavers, they learn from the "elders" the religious and moral maxims of their people. They know very early what it is to be initiated into "mysteries", "to pass from life to death", to take a new name as the symbol and evidence of a new existence. Therefore they are much less astonished than the pagans of Europe to hear of a baptism which confers divine life, the baptized dying and being brought to life again with Jesus Christ, receiving a new name and entering a fraternal community united by mysterious bonds.

Thus we see how wise it is to present Christianity to Africans not in the form of instruction given only at school – like a course in mathematics or geography – but as a religious initiation, as the entrance into a group, as participation in a new, higher life shared with others. It is therefore desirable – to use a concrete example – not to separate the religious instruction of our catechumens from the liturgy and from life. As in the early days of the Church, this instruction should be closely united to communal prayer, to the chants, genuflections, fasts, vigils, and exorcisms. It should follow certain definite stages, each one marked, as formerly, by its own ceremony: the imposition of the sign of the cross, the abjuration of pagan errors, the solemn renunciation of superstitious rites, the recitation of the creed, and so on.

## *Into the Mystery of Christ*

Christian initiation, we have said, is an initiation into the mystery of Christ; it is the joyful acceptance of the glad tidings that once resounded at Bethlehem: "Behold, I bring you tidings of great joy . . . This day is born to you a Saviour, who is Christ the Lord" (Luke 2:10–11).

Nothing appears more in harmony with the mentality of many pagan peoples in the under-developed countries than this concrete and optimistic presentation of Christianity. The idea of a miraculous redeemer awakens a profound response in their beings. They have an immense desire to be "saved", to be delivered from the terrors of magic, to enter a marvellous Golden Age.[1] The success of the sects which promise the Africans deliverance from "sorcery", which proclaim to them the "resurrection of their ancestors", is an evident manifestation of this. Thus, the person of our Lord Jesus Christ, the world's Saviour, master of the elements, of sickness, and of death, holding forth the promise of a new life, strongly attracts them when presented vividly, enthusiastically, in a spirit of admiration and love.

### *By Means of the Bible*

There is general agreement today, as we have said, that the Bible, as the story of salvation, is one of the best introductions to the Christian religion. If this is true for western countries, then how much more so for the countries of Africa! It has been said that biblical man has "the gift of assimilation, the faculty of story-telling, a sense of the past and of continuity, a need to instruct, and to communicate his thoughts, a feeling of responsibility for the community, a taste for symbols and mystery".[2] The same can be said of the African.

He too evidences a true genius for assimilation. In less than a century he has learnt from Europeans a multitude of things in every domain of life and has adopted much of western civilization. He also loves to tell stories. In the evening, around the fire, he recounts with grand gestures and expressive mimicry the fables and legends of his tribe or the events of the day. He too is interested in the history and traditions of his people: he guards them jealously and transmits them faithfully in tales or proverbs which pass from father to son, from uncle to nephew,

[1] On this subject see the studies of ethnologists on the initiation ceremonies in certain secret African sects.

[2] See Gelin, *L'âme d'Israël dans le Livre,* p. 110 et seq.

from the old to the young, in all of which he recognizes with pleasure the psychology of the members of his tribe. He loves expressions which appeal to the imagination and lively images which evoke ideas dear to him. He loves mystery, as is shown by his taste for secret sects with their complicated ritual.

Like biblical man, the African has a natural sense of the sacred. His whole life is steeped in religion. He senses his dependence on the invisible even in his very least actions. He does not seek, like the European, to determine precisely what we call "secondary causes". He instinctively looks deeper, for the profound, hidden causes situated in the beyond. Just as biblical man attributes Sara's sterility to Yahweh, so will the African attribute a woman's barrenness to the inauspicious influence of the spirits, before thinking of natural medical causes.

His conception of life is the fruit of concrete experiences handed down by his ancestors; it is not the result of systematic intellectual research. It is expressed – as also with biblical man – in often savoury proverbs, in moral fables concerning traditional personages, in legal rules and customs peculiar to the tribe.

Like Old Testament man, the African knows – even before Christ's message has been officially transmitted to him – that God is the master of life and death, that he is the creator of all things, that he sees all, that he knows all. "You, O sun into whose face we cannot gaze, you life force to whom our chieftains give glory"[3], say the Baluba addressing themselves to God in times of distress. "O thou who hast created heaven and earth, come to the aid of thy servant"[4], cries the Bubi of Fernando Poo. "O thou who surveyest the life of men", prays the Wafito of the Tanganyika Territory, "thou knowest all things. I am but a creeping worm who moves by thy grace."[5] "God is my witness", swears the Mukongo, raising his right hand in testimony to divine omniscience.

[3] See Van Caeneghem, *La notion de Dieu chez les Baluba du Kasai* (Brussels, 1956).

[4] Martin del Molino, "L'idée de Dieu chez les Bubis de Fernando Poo" in *R.C.A.*, 1956, p. 34.

[5] Robert, *Croyances et coutumes magico-religieuses des Wafita païens* (Kipalapala), p. 38.

The prayers of our Africans – addressed more frequently to their ancestors than to God himself – are reminiscent of the prayers in the Book of Psalms. They bear, on the contrary, absolutely no likeness to those in our manuals of piety[6], which – for example our acts of faith, hope, and charity – are often masterpieces of logical composition, analysis, and lucidity, and contain a whole summary of abstract theology but do not appeal to the imagination and can scarcely be said to quicken our sensibilities. The prayers of the Semite and of the African, on the other hand, start off a whole gamut of complex feelings that mingle and interlock: anger, indignation, distress, humility, joy, admiration, gratitude, regret. They are cast in form of passionate entreaties, often bordering on violence, of impassioned curses called down upon enemies and evildoers, as cries of joy, gratitude, or admiration, in soothing formulas of humility, regret, or happiness. They suggest ideas by means of some evocative formula rather than expressing them in precise terms. They develop more by a process of association of images or concepts than by logical deduction. They are concrete, vivid, spontaneous. They are instinctively translated into chants supported by the sound of instruments. They are set to pantomime and declaimed aloud with gestures animating the whole body.

"Life", it has been said, "is what most impressed the minds of the Israelites."[7] It is what impresses Africans too. They "believe in the direct intervention of God in the mystery of the transmission of life."[8] They believe above all in the intervention of the powers of the beyond, especially their ancestors, in all their vital activities. They can scarcely be called contemplatives, but they live in close union with the rhythms of nature. The sights of the outer world do not interest them as such but captivate them in so far as they are felt to have a bearing on their lives, constituting an aid or a danger – and also in their capacity to serve as symbols in fable and story. Just as he loves to recount tales, the African loves to listen to fables and stories

[6] See Paul Brunner, "La place des Psaumes dans le Culte en missions" in *Pastorale liturgique et chrétienté,* pp. 117–40 (especially pp. 126–32).

[7] Pautrell, S.J., *L'homme de la Bible.*

[8] X. Seumois, P.B., *L'adaptation dans le culte,* I, p. 70.

which are new to him, especially if they bring to life before his eyes straightforward personages whose psychology he has no trouble in grasping. Thus he will listen with passionate interest to the exploits of Abraham, Isaac, and Jacob, the story of Joseph, the epic of the Hebrew people in the desert, the account of Job's misfortunes, the mishaps of the prophet Jonas, the marvellous journey of the young Tobias, the parable of the prodigal son or of the pharisee and the publican, the curing of the man born blind, the resurrection of Lazarus – particularly if these narratives and moralities are enhanced by images, songs, and acting.

Moreover, the negroes of Africa, "just like the Hebrews, are peoples of farmers and shepherds"[9]. Many passages of the Old Testament, numerous customs, images, and expressions remind them of the world in which they live and which, while lacking neither wisdom nor moral values, stands in great need of the complement and correction provided only by the doctrine of charity, humility, and purity preached by our Lord. Let me indicate at random some traits characteristic of both peoples. In the Bible as in many African tribes, circumcision is held in honour and the term "uncircumcised" is a term of contempt. Consanguineous marriage is practised in certain African tribes and is met with in the Bible, where it plays a primordial rôle (the Covenant). Among many African tribes there is – or was – such a thing as trial by ordeal, as there is occasionally in the Old Testament (Cf. Num. 5:27–8). Biblical parleys and commercial transactions resemble those of the Africans in atmosphere and in several of their characteristic features.[10] Polygamy exists in the Old Testament as it does in Africa, where it has the same essential characteristics. In both cultures it is a sign of wealth and the wish to make sure of numerous progeny, rather than a manifestation of carnal passion. It often betrays the same deficiencies in African as in Hebrew life, and calls for a return to primeval monogamy, as taught by Christ. Old Testament man and the African are similar in their conception of

[9] Seumois, *op. cit.*, p. 67.

[10] See M. De Cocker, CICM., "Essai de parallélisme biblico-congolais" in *Zaire,* 1950, pp. 277–98.

guilt – in which the material aspect plays too great a part – in their connection of guilt with misfortune (infirmities, illness . . .), in their manner of viewing justice. Both cultures greatly needed the perfecting and deepening of their religious mentality urged by the preaching of the prophets and above all by the gospel of our Lord Jesus Christ.

## *The Liturgy*

But the Bible – as the story of salvation – is not the only way of leading the African to Christianity, of making it pervade his senses and his mind. The liturgy, which makes abundant use of the Bible, is also an excellent – and necessary – means of initiating the African into the religion of Christ.

By the aid of the liturgy the Christian religion can do more than merely enter the mind of a convert; the liturgy enables Christianity to penetrate and envelop his whole life. The liturgical rites of baptism, confirmation and the Eucharist are what makes him a full member of the Mystical Body of Christ.

Moreover, the liturgy makes natural use of all the techniques commended by modern educators: the intuitive process, activity, teaching by experience, the teaching of values. It appeals to the entire person: the sensibilities, the intelligence, the will . . . . It is a form of teaching highly suited to the African. It appeals to all his senses, to his mind, to his heart. The rites of the Church catch his eye, strike his ear, and charm his imagination, which loves symbols and signs.

The Church invites him to take part in the ceremonies as they unfold, to be active, to live his Christian life in gestures, words, and songs. Now the African delights in pantomime. He loves "music passionately. The ceremonies surrounding marriage, birth, death, hunting, and war are composed of songs – songs of joy, of combat, or of mourning – assisted by the sound of instruments. The palavers themselves are accompanied by chants which repeat and enhance the arguments of the speakers."[11]

[11] Ignace Mbambu, "Le catéchisme par le chant" in *R.C.A.*, 1953, p. 542.

Therefore the African loves High Mass, the paschal liturgy, the Christian burial service, the conferring of confirmation by the bishop. He takes pleasure in chanting the psalms, whose melody by its very simplicity recalls to him one of the characteristics of African music. Thus he may be said to pray the very doctrine which he is taught. The cycle of the liturgical year will make perceptible to him the mystery of Christ and the divine dispensation whose bearer Christ is. It will awaken feelings of gratitude and love in his heart.

By contrast with the catechism, which is taught for a few years only, the liturgy will accompany him his whole life long and remind him, in the prayers and readings of the Proper of the Mass, of all that he has been taught.

### *Difficulties*

After sketching thus briefly – and imperfectly – some of the advantages afforded by using modern methods of catechesis in mission countries and especially in Africa, I have still to mention the difficulties which the modern catechist has to meet there.

Our catechesis, we have affirmed, should be based on the Bible. "Catechesis in the form of historical narration is the simplest, most suitable, and most effective introduction to Christianity."[12]

Very well. Unfortunately, we are reminded with very good reason by priests working in Central Africa, that there are many languages (or dialects) spoken here. We have been here for only seventy-five years. It takes time to learn even one of them well. Besides, the Bible is not easy to translate, and the Book of books should not, moreover, be translated indifferently.

Even when we succeed in translating a few parts of it satisfactorily, we have difficulty in obtaining permission to publish them, because these editions, being so limited, are expensive. One doesn't cover one's expenses, and money is lacking.

Furthermore, they point out, contact with and reading of the Bible are not without their dangers for our catechumens

[12] Hofinger, *Formation Religieuse en Afrique Noire,* p. 110.

and neophytes. The Old Testament in particular, read with a still half-pagan heart, may easily become the source of fatal illusions and gross errors. The neophyte may easily imagine that it seems to justify sentiments, customs, and ways of life condemned by Christianity: polygamy, superstitious practices, cruelty towards enemies, duplicity. . . . Moreover, everyone knows that indiscriminate reading of the prophetic books has favoured the growth of fanatic sects, which, like the Gnostics of former times, concoct an abominable mixture of pagan and Christian elements. These are real difficulties and cannot be ignored. Nevertheless, we believe it possible to make extensive use of the Bible for catechesis in Central Africa.

Let us begin by translating the Bible into the principal African languages which cover the widest areas and which seem to us to have the most future promise. Let us have recourse to specialized European charitable institutions to assist us in meeting the expense of our editions. Let us not translate the whole Bible at once, but first the most meaningful parts, the clearest ones and those which do the most good. Let us make a biblical anthology of the kind edited by Grelot[13]. Let us have it illustrated simply and well. Let us be careful to indicate the historical and geographical context of the selections. Let us explain what needs explaining. Never let us neglect to throw the light of the New Testament upon the Old. Let us keep especially to the former.

It should be the major seminaries of Africa that set to work on this project. The collaboration of European teaching and African pupils in this task may produce wonderful fruit.

And let us not be content to place the biblical texts into the hands of the Christian school-children, catechumens and adult Christians. Let us explain them aloud in the light of the teaching of the Church. Let us make use of them to enliven our sermons and catechism lessons, in which we set forth the story of salvation and endeavour to deepen the faith of our Christians and to inspire in them faith in, and love for, the fatherly providence of God.

The liturgy as a means of initiating Africans into the Christian religion also presents certain difficulties. In order that the liturgy

[13] Grelot, *Pages Bibliques,* Paris, Berlin.

may effectively play its part in Christian initiation, it must come alive to the faithful and be *understood* and lived by them.

Now it must be admitted that the Roman liturgy is not in full harmony with the African spontaneity. Its character is almost always reserved and sober, having little in common with the exuberance of the natives, with their love of rhythm and of dancing. Moreover it is in Latin. The faithful do not understand the words spoken and are in danger of considering them as magic formulas instead of recognizing in them the prayer of Mother Church and learning and living from it. The adaptation of the liturgy to Africa is a delicate task, which must take account of several factors. Firstly, the liturgical forms contain certain essential and universal elements which may not be altered because they are instituted by God himself. Nor can it be ignored that for two or three generations the Roman liturgy has obtained in most of Africa and that many Christians have got used to it and seem attached to it.[14]

In our opinion a wise and effective adaptation can, nevertheless, be carried out by using the language of the country extensively in administering the sacraments and sacramentals as well as in certain parts of the Mass. The Roman authorities have already granted permissions for many changes; the priests have yet to take the fullest possible advantage of them for the actual participation of the faithful in the liturgy. Other ways in which it can be carried out are by adopting music close to the African soul, which emphasizes rhythm, and by introducing – after obtaining the necessary permission – new sacramentals, and by creating paraliturgies drawing their inspiration from African customs and traditional narratives.

There remains a final difficulty, a most serious one. The clergy working in the missions are not yet familiar enough with modern methods. The lay catechists rarely have the qualities necessary for the application of these methods: ardent faith, disinterested zeal, profound knowledge of Christian doctrine, advanced pedagogical training.

[14] See the article by Tharcisse Tshibangu, "Une Liturgie Africaine" in *L'Église vivante,* 1960, pp. 116–24.

Moreover in many countries in Africa the function of the catechist is tending to disappear: religion is learnt more and more at school, where religious instruction is far from taking its due place, either in the time or in the care devoted to it. The teacher is poorly prepared to give it. At the normal school he has probably been taught no religious methodology. On the other hand, the prestige of the catechist who instructs adults has greatly diminished. He is poorly paid and often insufficiently prepared for his work. How can these difficulties be eliminated?

To acquaint the priests who some day will be working in the missions with modern methods, there is one more obvious way, that of organizing, in the scholasticates of the Missionary Institutes and in the regional seminaries, a substantial course in catechetics, to be given by a professor familiar with contemporary religious methodology and with some practical experience in teaching catechism. And it would be helpful to send an occasional scholastic or seminarist to take part in the courses of the Catechetical Year of *Lumen Vitae* or other similar institutions.

As for putting the missionary priest already in the field in touch with modern methods, the most effective immediate step to take appears to us to be that of organizing catechetical, biblical and liturgical conferences in the various ecclesiastical territories. Experienced theologians will set forth the basic principles there: the priests participating will discuss, subject to the authority of the Ordinary, the concrete application of these principles to existing conditions. The creation of pastoral centres in the dioceses, and catechetical reports in the reviews would also be useful.

There remains the thorny problem of lay catechists. As religious instruction is often given in the schools, we believe it would be worth the trouble to bring in lay teachers of religion. They would need definite qualifications: they would have been given an advanced religious training; they would possess a diploma recognized by the bishop, which would be evidence of a cultural standard equal to that possessed by teachers of other subjects. They would, in fact, be "specialists" in religious instruction.

More attention must be paid at normal school to training the future teachers in the spirit of Christianity, in zeal, and in piety, to insisting on their duty to give the pupils the good example of a sincerely Christian life.

With respect to the lay catechists who instruct adult catechumens not attending schools, instead of making a sort of business of their functions, could these functions not be entrusted to unpaid volunteers who would offer to fulfil them out of pure generosity and zeal for the cause? We could apply to the militants of Catholic Action, to the members of the Legion of Mary, of the Sodality of Our Lady, etc., who had received careful pedagogical and doctrinal preparation. Many more considerations would be in place on the advantages and difficulties of applying modern methods of catechesis in mission countries. The little I have said will, I hope, suffice to arouse reflection and provoke a fruitful exchange of views.

# Catechetical Method as Handmaid of Kerygma

JOSEF GOLDBRUNNER
University of West Berlin

CATECHETICAL method and *kerygma* are like two sisters whose relationship reveals all the different possibilities of sisterly contact. They can live together harmoniously – they can quarrel – one can dominate the other – they can go their separate ways. And yet they need each other, and should try to find their proper relationship. The one sister, Method, must serve the other sister, Kerygma. The conditions for this service and the effect which it in turn will have on Method are the subject of this paper.

## *Method without Kerygma*

The relationship of the two sisters already has a history. They are not of the same age. If we consider only the catechetical climate of our own era, the twentieth century, we see that Method is the older of the two. She was born at the hour when psychology demanded its rights in every form of human guidance including teaching and religious instruction. This was the time of the first catechetical awakening, the concern for method. Until then, religious instruction had often been only the more or less compulsory memorization of catechism answers.

While it is true that the child or the young adult can be drilled in religious knowledge, this will lead merely to external habits. Those things which man learns by heart through drill and compulsion remain unrelated to his interior life. The result will be empty knowledge, not genuine faith. Such a person would be merely a conformist in his spiritual life, motivated perhaps by pragmatism but lacking conviction. His religion would be lived much in the same way as one wears a dress. The dress is not identical with the one wearing it; the person who wears it is distinct from it and can lay it aside without any difficulty, should circumstances make it advisable.

Catechetical method seeks to reach the human person and to make him religious, so that his religion will not be a mere form but his very life. That is why method must do more than instruct, it must address man personally. It must have insight into man if it is to succeed in awakening his interest, so that he will become personally involved in what he is learning, will come to understand it, relate it to his life, will say Yes to it, will even change his life in accordance with it.

Such a method is more worthy of man than drill, because it awakens all his faculties and makes possible his free consent. It is also closer to the life of the spirit and better adapted to it. That is why catechesis seized upon this method, which made its entrance into the history of religious education under the name of the "Munich Method".

The Munich Method is a psychological method. It teaches us to address man by preparing and structuring the material according to certain psychological laws in five "normal steps": Preparation – Presentation – Explanation – Recapitulation – Application. As a result, the subject matter is not only learned but contemplated, assimilated, and understood; only then does the Application follow naturally. Through this method the child comes into contact with the substance of what is taught, learns to work with it and to make it his own. From the viewpoint of method, the trend which came into the forefront more and more strongly was this: if I do something with the material taught, if I am active, I grasp it better than if I only hear it. The principle of "learning by doing" was now combined with the Munich Method.

Catechesis applied to its own domain this method which originated in secular education and was stimulated by psychology and, still using the old-style question and answer catechism, achieved a much greater vitality in religious instruction. In many countries this constituted a first flowering of catechetical life. Method came to be considered as the key to the children's hearts. It flourished, and was refined and developed, especially along the lines of various resources such as discussion, dramatization, drawing, films, slides, etc.

Automatically, however, it was also applied to all religious themes, and it was considered sufficient if only the children were kept busy. In this way activities, which constitute only a part, overran the whole. We feel like calling out to this Gargantuan Method, to this older and now adult sister: "Martha, Martha, you are busy with many things."

What led to such mechanization, to such a shallow use of catechetical method? What caused it to degenerate into merely external activities? The method was psychologically correct – was there perhaps something lacking in the subject matter, in the catechism? And now, the very people who had hitherto been concerned with method began to analyze the structure and content of the catechism. They found that it was adapted neither to children, i. e., it neglected the demands of psychology, nor – and this was the decisive point – to the teaching and the method of Christ. It was written not as a message, but as a systematic textbook. A message seeks to awaken life, to invite, to call. A system on the other hand, attempts to provide a survey for people who already believe. The children who sit in our classrooms are more easily reached by a message than by a system. Accordingly, in several countries the concern for method developed quite naturally into a re-evaluation of the content of religious instruction. The catechetical renewal continued to gain momentum and developed into the kerygmatic renewal. The one sister, Method, spontaneously called for her younger sister, Kerygma.

## *Kerygma*

After Christ had said to the sister who was absorbed in external activities: "Martha, Martha, you are busy with many things" – he continued: "Only one thing is necessary." He was referring to the very thing to which Mary, the younger sister, was listening intently: to the message of the "Kingdom of God". In this biblical concept the whole kerygma is summed up.

The "one thing necessary" is lacking to method, and it is here that its limitations become apparent. Through method, it is true, we reach the interest, the participation, even the enthusiasm of the children; but all this can degenerate into external mechanism. It is as though the human interest which has been aroused through method now cries out for more than the formulations of the traditional catechism, even if these are transmitted by the best method. Man's heart cries out for life, for a message from God, for a living Person. Method alone is like a vessel calling out to be filled with a new content, kerygma.

Let us explain the role of kerygma in religious education through a comparison. A young girl is doing her housework reluctantly, slowly and wearily. Her mother who lies sick in bed sadly watches the joyless activities of her daughter. Suddenly the door bell rings and the postman delivers a letter for the young girl, which she opens and reads. The mother witnesses in amazement the sudden transformation which now comes over her daughter. She returns to her work singing and refreshed with keen interest and joy, and swiftly accomplishes all her duties. She is like a different person, like one reborn. What news did the letter bring? Her fiancé will be here in a week! This news, this message of a future event, makes its effect felt in the present. The message has the power to change the existence of the young girl.

This comparison reveals the situation, "transmitting a message", as a complex of different elements: the messenger – the message itself as news – the recipient – the effect – the sender. All these together form a whole, and show in a comparison what religious instruction is meant to achieve when Method and Kerygma work together hand in hand, when the older sister serves the younger, when Method is in the service of Kerygma.

Faith, the fruit for which we strive in religious instruction, is according to this comparison the acceptance of a message and its effect on one's whole life. The message is not drilled and memorized, but takes possession of the whole man, gradually transforming him into a "new man". The message becomes real, is realized. This constitutes conversion, a long process which will be furthered by religious instruction only if kerygma and method find each other. Let us examine this process more closely by considering each of the elements which have been mentioned above, namely, the message, the recipient, the effect, the messenger, and the sender.

In each of these elements both God and man, grace and nature, are at work. While grace is the decisive factor, it does not replace human co-operation, in catechesis no more than elsewhere. We shall demonstrate this by showing the effect of the material taught – kerygma – on the "normal steps" of catechetical method.

### *Kerygma and Method*

THE MESSAGE. The heart of catechesis is the message which we as catechists are to transmit. Now let us suppose that method takes possession of the message; books are distributed in which the students are to look up scriptural references and discover their meaning – for after all, their initiative and independent work are to be encouraged. Such a method may be correct in secular subjects, for example, in geography, where we may ask students to make a list of the rivers and cities of a given country with the aid of an atlas. By carrying this method blindly over into catechesis, however, Method, the older sister, does violence to Kerygma, the younger. A message cannot be discovered by itself. It will lose its very character as message if Method does not become subservient to Kerygma. Man cannot discover the message of salvation, which is a divine revelation, on his own. It must be announced, proclaimed, transmitted as Word of God, under his mandate.

The form in which this is done may vary. It can be the account of an event from salvation-history. The ability to narrate well, in the spirit of scripture and if possible in its words, without getting lost in the details, is the most genuine and important form of Presentation in catechetical method. It can be very helpful if, at the height of the story, a picture is shown which pin-points the heart of the message and makes possible a visual contemplation. (It should be added that one picture is more valuable than several pictures.)

An example. The catechist tells of the trial of Jesus, and how the Lord was scourged, mocked and crowned with thorns. No one could see that he was the Son of God, he seemed to be only a suffering man like unto us. And yet he said, I am the Son of God, I am a king. What if we could see him thus? (Here the 'Ecce homo' of Richard Seewald is shown. Pictures which are artistically good, biblically correct, and catechetically expressive are urgently needed for catechesis.)

Another way of approach would be through an account of the words of Jesus, or of one of his parables or discourses. Or it may be something that the Church teaches about Christian life; or, a presentation from the liturgy.

Whatever the form, however, it is essential to the method that the message be transmitted with authority. It cannot be found by itself, it cannot be grasped through the "learning by doing" principle. It must be proclaimed and heard. This can be achieved in the Presentation and the Explanation.

THE RECIPIENT. The message which is transmitted with authority is addressed to the recipient, to people of all ages. Let us here single out the children who sit in our classrooms – children of men, not yet in full possession of their freedom of choice, but who, nevertheless, may not be considered and treated as children who are receiving an order which they must memorize without further ado. A divine message, especially if it is directed to children, must be transmitted in a manner worthy of human beings.

The messenger must do more yet. The message is waiting for the soul to turn towards it with all its powers. Consequently, the right method must try to unlock the door to the children's souls, to woo their hearts and to warm them, to awaken their interest in the message. We cannot simply barge into a house like the postman, who merely delivers the letter. For it is by no means certain that the children of men will be interested in a message from God – not even our school children. We know that we touch here on the mysteries of original sin and grace.

As messengers of God we have the duty to woo the recipients. This we do through the step of Preparation. The Preparation seeks to make a link with some familiar experience in the children's lives, and to prepare their souls to receive the message. Let us illustrate this through a sample lesson, the lesson about the Victory of Christ.

PREPARATION. You all know what enmity is. Two men are enemies and carry on a feud, sometimes over a long period of time. In what different ways can this enmity end? One man is victorious, the other is killed. Or? Reconciliation. Or? Truce. (This is the Preparation. It is built on a typical human situation known to everyone, a general experience which is of interest to all.)

PRESENTATION. Now look at this picture (the teacher shows a picture of Christ suffering on the Cross). Here too there is a fight. One of the two who are doing battle (Satan) is invisible; the other (Christ) we see in this picture. Does it look like a truce? Or like a reconciliation? No, it looks like a defeat. (The teacher draws a diagram as follows on the blackboard.)

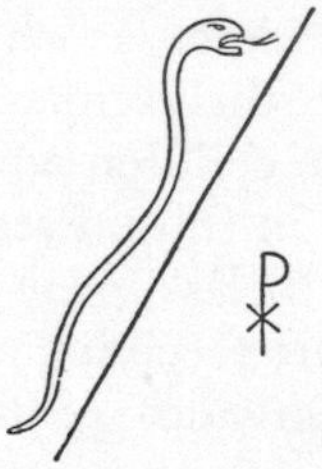

EXPLANATION. When did this enmity begin? When God the Father said to the serpent: "I will put enmity between you and the woman, between your seed and her seed." Ever since then the feud continued, and when Christ came it reached its climax. Who will win – Christ, or his enemy, the "murderer of men from the beginning"? We can see all the weapons with which Satan is fighting: pain, mockery, dishonour, finally the cross and death. After three hours Christ dies on the cross! Who has won? Satan. He has destroyed Christ. Christ can no longer do his work, he can no longer teach or work miracles, no one will henceforth believe him.

God the Father, however, predicted another outcome to this enmity: he will crush the head of the serpent, of Satan. That means that Satan will be conquered. Is it not this that we expected of Christ? But how can he now be victorious?

Now let us look at a second picture (the teacher shows a picture of Christ appearing to his apostles). He is alive again – with new life – risen – with new possibilities – an undreamt-of "invention" of God: he is glorified! (The teacher draws a diagram as follows on the blackboard.)

Let us pause here and consider the method. The starting point is a human situation which all can experience and understand – enmity. Through this the interest of the children is awakened. The life of Christ is judged in the light of this situation, according to natural, human standards, up to its hopeless ending. Into this situation is spoken the message of the victory and resurrection – a supernatural message, a divine revelation.

The Preparation has made ready that room in the soul in which the new possibility, the Christian message of joy, can be received – provided that grace and free consent find each other.

The normal steps of Preparation, Presentation, and Explanation have the task to unlock man's powers and depths in order to bring them face to face with divine revelation. The child's whole human nature is activated as it takes sides in the situation, "enmity against Jesus". The intellect has a share in this, but it is only one faculty among others which turn, questioningly, toward the fact of the resurrection.

What has been gained by this? Is it not enough to present in a lively manner the "articles of faith" and to make the children learn them by heart? Could method not rest content with this? Here we come to the heart of the question concerning kerygma and method. Message is more than teaching. True, message must also be understood and committed to memory. But it aims beyond, at the encounter of human reality with the reality of the divine message. Both these must "mingle" if the message is to be realized in daily life. It is the task of method to serve this realization, in which kerygma and method are combined. Method helps to make kerygma real, to "realize" it, as Cardinal Newman said. Hand in hand the two sisters, Kerygma and Method, make possible the realization of the message in daily life, in a life grounded in faith.

In only one respect does Method have a determining influence on her sister Kerygma: in her concern that the recipient, the child, may not yet be sufficiently mature for the message. It is indeed possible to overwhelm a child with the entire catechism; if he is obedient, he will learn all of it. But perhaps the child is unable to grasp the relationship between individual doctrines because he does not yet have any sense of time and space, nor of history, and so he can only put side by side unconnected details, like stones in a mosaic. Or perhaps we may describe suffering in such a way as to ask too much of the children's emotions. Or, in teaching children who have no concept of even the external events of death, we compare baptism to our being taken into "the death and the resurrection of Christ" (Rom. 6:4–5), rather than to a new birth. Or, we teach them the Sermon on the Mount, which far exceeds the human experience of a child; or the doctrine of the Trinity, as it is presented in certain catechisms. In short, we may be transmitting to the child a message which is too powerful for him, just as the engine of an airplane is too powerful for a car; or worse still, we may give him an entire world order, while his world consists only of the domains of family, school and parish. In all such cases Method must cautiously interpose a filter for Kerygma in the form of a syllabus which will take into account the degree of maturity of the children. This would be the case when we teach, in the lower grades, through sacred history and the Church year as it is lived in the liturgy, rather than through the catechism.

THE EFFECT OF THE MESSAGE. We have spoken of the collaboration of kerygma and method in connection with the message and the recipient. Now we shall consider method in the next element of religious instruction, that is, the effect which the message has on the recipient. The message is meant to change man, to bring about a μετανοεῖν, a "putting off the old man" and a "putting on the new man". Because this is a life-long process known as conversion, which brings forth genuine faith as its fruit, religious instruction does not end with school but continues throughout the whole of life.

The lesson in the classroom has as its purpose to serve this process of conversion with the step called Application. This step stands in the same relation to the Explanation as the word to the concept. Therefore, it must be organically linked with the theme of the Explanation, and should be the direct outgrowth of the message, rather than simply some pious or moralistic practical application.

Let us suppose, for example, that the theme of a lesson is the "grace life" (sanctifying grace) and its aim, a joyful awareness of what Christ has given to us in our baptism; but that the application would be: "Now let us call forth perfect contrition, in case we have already lost the grace life." Through such a moralistic application the message is destroyed, sinks to the level of a formula which must be memorized and which obliges us to be good.

If, on the other hand, method serves kerygma, the application will correspond to the message and will help to make it effective. Examples of such an application would be: listening to one's own heart in which this wonderful life which we call "grace life" lives; or meditating on a beautiful picture of the risen Christ, in whom the grace life has already become visible; or visiting a baptismal font; or drawing a baptismal robe and a beautifully decorated baptismal candle.

Whatever the application – whether prayer, drawing, resolutions, or homework – it will become mere external activity unless it is the expression of the message. One great danger is to have a purely moralistic application at all costs; the other is to lose oneself automatically in various tasks which have only a very remote connection with the message. Method serves kerygma best when all the normal steps are penetrated and united by kerygma into one whole. The application, therefore, should be intimately related to the theme of the lesson, and should serve with great delicacy the realization of the kerygma in the life of the young catechumen. This makes certain demands, it is true, on the messenger, the catechist. He must achieve the realization of the kerygma in his own life; he must be conscious, from his own experience, of the very tender and fragile growth of the life of faith, so that he can protect his students from having demands made on them which they are incapable of fulfilling, especially in the moral realm. This constitutes the problem of the catechist.

THE MESSENGER. If the catechist is to transmit the message faithfully, the Sender expects him not only to know and love the message and him from whom he receives it (God the Father and his Son), and to be penetrated as a prism with the joy of the message, but also that he fulfills his commission by transmitting the message through a flawless method. Two things must fuse in him: his own faith – not only his knowledge, but a life of faith born from the kerygma – and a catechetical skill which will do justice to method. Once this has happened he will find that his believing word is filled with power to beget a new life of faith; he will be an instrument of grace. The life of faith cannot be bought, nor taught, nor learned, it must be begotten, by the Holy Spirit and water, by God and the Church. These are living events during which the Sender is personally present.

THE SENDER. We receive our commission directly from the Church, in the person of the bishop; but behind him stands the divine Person of our Lord Jesus Christ. He is present in his message at all times. This means not only that the method must present Christ as the focal point of the kerygma, but that the message be orientated toward Christ in every single aspect. Catechetical language, if it is truly kerygmatic, will not stop at a natural doctrine, but will always bring about living contact with Christ.

## *An Example*

Let us, in closing, sum up the relationship between kerygma and method in a sample lesson which has as its theme the difficult concept of grace life, a concept which we have already touched upon. We shall try to communicate it clearly and in living relation to Christ. It is obvious that only some points of the theme "grace-life" can be touched, but these are clear, graphic and easily understood by children.

PREPARATION. You all know about the varieties and different forms of life: a plant has its life, the fish lives, so do the bird and the dog. We human beings have a higher life than all these, but is this life the highest of all? Don't we often dream of an even higher life? For our present life has terrible limitations: it is beset by pain and danger, and at the end stands death. Many doctors try to improve our life, but it is prolonged only to be conquered in the end by death. Is there a better, a higher and more perfect life? What would such a life be like? The two pictures which we have already looked at will help us find the answer.

PRESENTATION. (The two pictures, the 'Ecco homo' and the apparition of the risen Christ are shown.) Both pictures show what actually happened: Jesus shortly before his death, and Jesus three days after his death. He is once again alive. He is the same as before, but now he has another kind of life. Look how amazed the apostles are upon seeing this life in him!

EXPLANATION. 1. Let us compare the two kinds of life, and make a list of the characteristics of each:

| | |
|---|---|
| sorrow | joy |
| weakness | glory |
| danger | safety |
| death | immortality |
| human life | risen life = grace life |
| he became like us | he is a new creation |

2. This risen life is a higher life than the one we have. It contains wonderful life powers which no man has ever possessed. If only we could acquire this life! And now, here comes a message. Christ does indeed give us this life! He has said: "I came into this world that they may have life, and may have it more abundantly" (John 10:10). He takes a spark from his own wonderful risen life, like a ray of light, full of the life powers

which we see in him, and implants them in the hearts of his Christians. This is a wonderful gift, a grace, and that is why we call it the grace life. This ray of light, these resurrection forces, this new life, this grace life, is the most precious thing we have in our hearts. It works in us imperceptibly, it grows and grows until, on the Last Day, it will break forth in all its power as it did in Christ, the Risen One, and will transform us.

APPLICATION. 1. For the time being this wonderful life is still invisibly in us. But the Church, to help us believe in it, each year enacts a holy play in which we can see it. Who can tell me what this play is? The Easter Vigil! When we celebrate Christ's resurrection the paschal candle is brought into the dark church. Then we sing, "Lumen Christi", – "Deo gratias!", and we all light our small candles from the paschal candle. First the pastor, then the servers, then, at the third time, all of us. Each of us now holds a candle in his hand and knows: this flame, this light, comes from the paschal candle which represents the Risen One. In just the same way the grace life with its resurrection forces came to me from Christ. And so we belong together, Christ and the Christian. – I hope that all of you will go to the next Easter Vigil!

2. We will now draw the paschal candle and many other small candles, and will recall the characteristics of the grace life.

3. What shall we pray today at the end of our class? Let us look at the picture of the risen Christ: "Dear Lord Jesus Christ, you have in you the highest life of all, and you give me a spark of this life. Now I know what a Christian is – someone who has this grace life. I will protect it and live in such a way as to be worthy of it. Amen."

Permit me a concluding comment. Method serves kerygma, but kerygma penetrates method with its content. The message of the grace life is seen as life, as the highest possible life, as the life of the risen Christ. That is why the Preparation speaks of the different degrees of life. The Presentation juxtaposes in two already familiar pictures human life and the Christ-life. The Explanation describes the grace life, the risen life, and draws from it the content for what is dogmatically defined as "sanctifying grace". This life is given us as a free gift, as a grace, hence we call it "grace life". The Application is liturgical, and shows how the liturgy represents graphically the relation between Christ and the grace life, in order to help us to have faith in the invisible grace life. Thus are given both an understanding of the Easter night, and an invitation to participate in it.

Method fulfills its role of servant if all the normal steps are penetrated by kerygma. Then human nature, which has been prepared psychologically, will receive kerygma not as an alien element, but as the revealed fulfilment of its own nature.

Kerygma and Method have now fused into one. The sisters walk along hand in hand, each attentive to the other. For they have, after all, the same origin. Kerygma is Word of God, while Method corresponds to the nature of man, God's creature, who is open to the message as the ear is open to the word.

# * The Missionary Role of European Schools in Missionary Countries

SISTER M. HERMINE, O.P.
Salisbury, N. Rhodesia

EUROPEAN schools as such have no future in missionary countries! Amongst young missionaries today there is a definite bias against working for the Europeans in a missionary country. The price of "home and country" was paid primarily in order to help save the souls of the indigenous people of the mission land. Cannot the Christianized European fend for himself? Let him save his own soul if he wants to. To think thus is to know but superficially. The history of colonization by the western powers is, in the main, responsible for the presence of Europeans in almost every mission country, excepting those lands where an established material culture already exists (for example, Japan, China). This accounts also for the subsequent establishment of schools for the offspring of those European settlers or colonists. Those facts can be altered as little as the natural physiognomy of a country. What, however, is often forgotten, is that a European school in a missionary country must differ from its parallel in the home country in that it must be prepared to base its policy on a system worked out for that specific country and not to perpetuate that of the mother-country. The educational products of these schools must be so formed that, when the children leave school, they have a certain open-mindedness and adaptability to changing circumstances which stands them in good stead when the time is ripe for their becoming an integral part of the country of their adoption.

The missionary role of the teachers in the European schools is, then, to remould the western European outlook in such a way that Christianity founded on indigenous culture shall be acceptable to both sides, this culture being eventually a composite of both: the indigenous and the European. As grace builds on nature, so the Church builds strongest on an indigenous culture, freed, of course, from what would be purely pagan.

European children of other religious denominations attend these schools quite frequently. Catholic influence, exercised by staff and pupils alike, though in an indirect way, has not infrequently led to conversion to Catholicism; and it has always led to a lessening of prejudice against the Catholic Church and Catholic missions. Catholics and non-Catholics alike in these schools have, in my experience of such schools in Southern Rhodesia, a far more tolerant and sympathetic outlook upon racial questions than their fellow-students in undenominational schools. And where a number of these non-Catholic pupils have passed in later years into prominent positions in civic life, or, in the case of girls, married potential leaders of the country, the influence received at the missionary European school has in many cases been a marked one, and priests and religious alike have been helped by them in their work. The goodwill and assistance of the whites as a whole is not to be despised by the missionaries as a source furnishing means with which to carry on missionary work.

However, the main task, confronting the Catholic educators in such schools is nothing less than a spiritual transformation of the pupils into "other Christs", who think Christ's thoughts, cherish his values, and are concerned to promote God's interests and the good of the souls, especially of those of their indigenous fellow-beings in the particular mission land they inhabit. What a scope there is today in mission lands for these "other Christs" to "go about doing good"! Examples may be seen in our own mission-land here in Rhodesia, where the prominent races are Bantus, the Asians, the Europeans, and, the in-betweens, the Eurafricans and Eurasians. The Europeans in the country for the great part hold fast to the old-fashioned idea that the coloured races in the country are only second-grade human beings, and need for ever to be kept in order by a kind of master-servant policy. What else but outward indications of that inner attitude are the many pin-prick regulations that deny the person of the coloured or black race, even if he is well-educated, the same rights as a European enjoys in the same circumstances? Repercussions of conflicts of thought, or emotion, or ideals figure prominently in the daily newspapers. An enlighted section of Europeans advocates integrated education, another section decries it as leading to a lowering of white standards and views it as "harnessing a donkey to a horse". African townships are advocated so as to enable the African to live with his family within easy distance of his work; then there follows an uproar from the European side against it. Eurafricans, being a minor body, resent the discriminatory social and economic differences that operate in their regard. As one of them writes: "Unfortunately, the system of classification of persons by skin-colour which pertains in this country, rules out all hopes of complete understanding because the colour-bar is such that while the European can impose and enforce it, he is himself immune to it. It is necessary to have experience of the colour-bar in order to know its profound impact upon the people on whom it is imposed."

In my dealings with coloured children at school and boarding hostels I have personally felt with them the inferiority complex that haunts them because of their colour, and the deep-seated feeling of frustration and bitterness engendered because of differences made in regard to them. Few, if any, can join European Youth Clubs: certain places are labelled strictly: "For Europeans only"; skilled jobs, excepting for the teaching and nursing professions, are, in the main, for whites only. A boy or girl may get a stop-gap job, or one in which the European hopes to save himself a few pounds each month by underpaying his coloured employee. Where a European girl may get paid £30 as a starting salary, a coloured girl gets for the same job £15–20, with no increase to follow.

In this same society Africans are emerging who are ready to take their place by the side of the European in civic and professional work. In African mission lands (save the Congo) emergent Africans and those of mixed race have no opportunity to do so.

These are only a few examples which show how tensions can arise in such a society, and what need there is for a change of outlook in the rising European generation. We need to educate courageous men and women who dare to go against accepted custom and public opinion where the rights due to the essential human dignity of man are violated or disregarded. This will only come to pass in fullest measure – for even today there are exceptional cases – when European schools are one in training educated, disinterested, zealous apostles, who not only hold as knowledge but feel as a burning responsibility what faith teaches: "What you have done to the least of my brethren, you have done unto me."

Fortunately, the religious doctrine lesson, vivified, made palatable and dynamic by the new approach the catechetical revival has brought into prominence, has shed its former drabness, and assumed the freshness of a new springtide in presenting the old spiritual truths. Hence faith, in its presentation to the children and in its possession by them, can fill their minds with a supernatural splendour that outshines the attractiveness of purely natural truths, thus colouring all their thoughts. In the light of this supernatural illumination we can make the children become aware of the universal fatherhood of God and the brotherhood of men, not in a vague or remote sense, but as operative in the indigenous neighbour who may rank bottom on the list of general adult European estimation. Faith, thus illumined, will throw light upon the truth of the essential dignity of man and will bring conviction that the soul of the coloured "native" has fundamentally the same value as that of the European settler or colonist, since both have been redeemed by the Precious Blood of Christ. Faith, handed on as a treasure beyond compare, vitalized and made practical by participation in the liturgy of the Church, and channelled into Catholic action, will thus become the first transforming power, capable of generating a missionary outlook in the children of European schools in missionary countries.

But the supernaturally enlightened mind must be reinforced by the virtuous qualities of the heart, and that implies formation of the will and character. Spiritual values, as opposed to material ones, supernatural desires in contrast to worldly ones must become the driving powers from within the heart. For, as someone wrote: "How could a Catholic, who, by the very fact of his baptism, is pledged to be an apostle and who holds at his disposal the spiritual strength and riches of the Mystical Body, fail to work with all his might for the extension of the Church?" In a missionary country, where the implanting and spreading of the faith is the Church's primary function, European youth trained in Catholic schools must not only hold the faith, but be proud of it, eager to share it, and incarnate it by living example.

As all these points are fundamental to Christianity and not furnished by any particular culture, they can be utilized on a broad basis as a preparation for the growth of an indigenous church, which should be the eventual fruit of racial integration.

Theory and practice, however, must go together. No use regarding one's fellowman as equal in dignity before God, if in the human relationship actions belie ideas held, and words uttered. I do not suggest that "equality in dignity before God" is the same as social equality judged by the standards of attainment of cultural and moral values, of mode of European living, of rank of birth and seniority. Even without European society there are shades of discrimination: the stable-boy does not expect to be invited to dinner by his employer; no ordinary person would shake hands with royalty, without having been encouraged to do so. Equality in dignity before God applies universally and equally to each member of the human race. In consequence of this, it is the same, therefore, in the boy and girl topping classes in academic subjects, and the African servant sweeping the class-rooms of those same students. It is the same in the European shop-keeper and the African buyer: the same in the mistress of the home and her coloured maid-servant. Relations, therefore, should be based upon mutual deference for one another as brethren in Christ. Courtesy, consideration, fairness and justice are virtues to which every human being has a personal claim. This calls for a training that rules out snobbishness, rudeness, and mean dealing in the small and big transactions between black and white or whatever colour may come into question. Opportunities for this self-training will arise in the home, at school, in public places, and bear witness to the Church of Christ they are helping to implant in indigenous soil.

All in all, there is a demand for a genuine, solidly Christian European population, zealous in working for the interests of God's kingdom on earth. The missionary task of European schools in missionary countries is to aim at these ideals, to direct the school's policy along these channels, and to avail themselves of the many opportunities for moulding the conduct and missionary outlook of the young in accordance with these principles.

The type of young people sent to the European schools is by no means ideal from a missionary point of view. Some 95 per cent are baptized Christians, it is true, but a deep Christianity implanted in the home is rare. Few know any prayers or have any previous religious knowledge. In schools where the staff is itself uninterested in religion, this state of affairs is often prolonged into adolescence and maturity, if not remedied by the service of catechists, who have right of entry once a week or so in British Government Schools. Only what is barely necessary can be taught in these short half-hour periods, and much of what has been taught one week is forgotten by the next, home-conditions in most of these cases not being favourable. To evolve a solid Christian out of such material in such circumstances is more than can be attempted.

Of those parents who bring their children to a Catholic school some do so because of their Catholic obligation, many because they are morally of a higher standard, and most because these schools have generally a higher reputation for achieving academic results. What parents expect of the school is that their children should pass State examinations successfully, shine on the sports-field, and acquire social graces and accomplishments within their cultural milieu. Religion as such is not objected to in most cases, but is given the lowest place in the scale of values among the subjects taken. This engenders in the children a religious indifference and apathy that is difficult to fan into flame. Where pupils come from broken homes, non-practising Catholic families, and non-Catholic circles there is often nothing to build on, for a long time; for what is built up in the classroom, is torn down in the home afterwards. "My father does not believe this rubbish", said a nine year-old when questioned about attending Sunday Mass. Very often, even the best of parents are imbued with racial prejudices that colour the very conversations in the home, and the relationship between the members of the family and the indigenous servants. Brought up in this atmosphere, even small children take it for granted that the "coloured" servant is his underling, and dares to defy and ill-treat him. Children imbibe these notions from their parents' attitudes in speech and conduct, and so the vicious cycle of race prejudices is propagated. Older ones in addition absorb these prejudiced ideas from newspapers and from anti-racial propaganda. To weed out such deep-rooted, unchristian notions, nourished daily in the home, at business, in society at large, requires patience, tact and ingenuity, and light from above. Hardest of all is it to convince the "white", whose superiority has until recently never been challenged, that merit and not colour is the decisive factor of promotion within all the spheres of social and political life. Only the implanting of a strong, nourishing and enlightening faith can deal successfully with this problem.

Yet the gift of faith and an increase of it exercises but little attraction upon materialistically bent minds and pleasure-filled hearts. Many times the rubble of material gain in prospect, good position, high salaries, plenty of leisure, wealthy marriage, an easy life, has buried the love for spiritual values; and sensual pleasures offered by cinemas, dances, and parties cloy the appetite for the things of the spirit.

Then the fact that most Europeans in missionary countries employ servants taken from the indigenous people, has produced a type of European that is used to be served rather than to serve, and has little idea of the dignity of work. To train such people to become active members of the Mystical Body of Christ, zealous apostles with burning souls, mission-minded Catholics preaching Christ's message by their example and relationship with members of the non-European race, would be a superhuman task were it not for the all-powerful grace of God sustaining educators' efforts, and powerfully drawing souls to God. Missionary vocations coming from the ranks of these Europeans in the past prove that there is good material for the grace of God to work upon – only, there is not enough.

If the European schools in mission countries take their duty of training apostles seriously, apostles who are deeply conscious of their spiritual responsibility in regard to the eternal happiness of others, apostles who cheerfully and generously sacrifice themselves for the missions, then it is paramount that teachers who undertake this training should be conversant with the best that the new catechetical revival has to offer and should apply it in their religious teaching.

What has the new catechetical movement to offer us to fulfil more effectively our missionary role in European schools in missionary countries? In the first place it has made religious teaching Christo- and theocentric. With Christ as the focal point of our teaching, religious truths become charged with the magnetism of Christ's own personality. Where the God of the Old and the New Testament, and his only begotten Son the Christ of the gospels, have become living and loveable personalities for the young, there is only one step more to the surrender of their minds and hearts to him and his teaching. Our first duty must therefore be to get children in touch with the gospel stories where his utter goodness, mercy, power, and loveableness are portrayed, and his actions and words stir to admiration and imitation. Parallels should be drawn in those incidents and parables of Christ that throw light on, and offer a Christian solution to, the problems existing specifically in mission lands, for example, the good Samaritan, one of the despised race, acting against racial prejudice; the publicans and Christ's attitude, choosing one of these, despised by the superior class of Jews, for a post in the apostolic college, etc. If we succeed in this we equip ourselves with an educational means of the first rank. Children are drawn to persons rather than to abstract ideas, and for the sake of a loved person will do even what is difficult. In this way the contents of the religious doctrine lesson can be converted to spiritual nourishment for their souls, and this in turn will generate the spiritual energy to apply in their daily lives what has been inculcated in the lesson. In that way some degree of spiritual transformation into "other Christs" will take place from day to day, so that ever more clearly and fully they may think Christlike thoughts, entertain Christlike sentiments, hold Christlike attitudes, profess Christlike principles, and perform Christlike deeds.

But, as always, this kind of teaching must go hand in hand with practice, individually and collectively, in private life as well as in social life.

For instance, after the lesson on the fatherhood of God and the adoption in Christ of all men (irrespective of colour and race) as his children, there follows a series of practical applications, one of which will be to recognize that "all men are children of God" and equal before him. This should lead to respect for and appreciation of all one's fellow human beings, in particular those we meet.

Some practical experiments tried out in schools in this part of the world come to my mind when viewing this problem of race-relations, so unpalatable to Europeans in missionlands in general. Naturally, there is a decided difference between Catholic Action in Europe and in mission lands where it must take the form of "contact" between members of different races. Here, in Rhodesia, where colour prejudice is still strong among adults, children from European and from mission schools have met on friendly and mutually respectful terms in the course of visits to each other's schools. On the sportsfield, in game-contests, at concerts, where integration has temporarily existed, prejudice and mistrust have given way to spontaneity and mutual confidence. The Girl Guides, and particularly the Catholic Guides, are prominent in demonstrating a happy racial relationship within their ranks. Experience has shown that all that is needed on the part of the European is the generosity to help and the readiness to accept the less privileged. Youth is willing enough, but the obstacles come from the elders. But the practical lesson is not learned with one application; opportunities must be provided, where the issue involved is of essential importance because of the Christian value given to it by God. Thus the Christian idea of the dignity and brotherhood of men must not remain something notional, touched off with an isolated act of charity towards a member of a despised race, but by repeatedly bringing the light of faith and Christ's own example to bear upon it, to create an attitude and prompt acts that finally lead to a Christian habit of charity free from racial or social prejudice.

Only if we succeed in harnessing spiritual notions to practical action can we hope for a Christian transformation of character, the best foundation for apostolic activity.

After teaching the pupils how to "put on Christ" by learning and living the faith in all its implications, we must show them the coherence of all the various truths as part of God's loving plan for our redemption. This will stimulate appreciation for what God has done for them personally and for all of mankind collectively and incite them to show gratitude for favours received. With a mind steeped in the knowledge of God's ways to man, and inflamed in heart by the redemptive love of Christ, the young are ready to be formed into apostles, lay apostles, or religious workers in the vineyard of the Lord. A start can be made at school by means of the Mission Notice Board for which children themselves collect pictures and cuttings and write the captions. Not only does this divert them from preoccupation with the affairs of their own race exclusively, but, at a subconscious level, it breaks down the European child's inhibition against having anything to do with races he has been taught to regard as inferior to his own. In this way, from early years, not only can racial prejudices be weakened or altogether undermined, but it is possible even to build up some appreciation of the indigenous children of other mission-lands. The Mission Notice Board activity helps to open their minds to an understanding of the weal and woe of Mother Church in other parts of the world. Then the monthly missionary intention is brought to the childrens' notice, some research work is done in connection with it, and the information gained, is channelled into "missionary talks" for the class by the pupils themselves. Mission literature is made available; membership of the missionary associations, such as the Holy Childhood and the Propagation of the Faith, is actively encouraged, and the duty of helping to spread the faith is taught in connection with the sacrament of confirmation. Mission-minded, missionary-sensitive, missionary-active; the European pupil is initiated into a missionary role, he is to continue in other ways besides these on leaving school. The Gospel Enquiry with its see-judge-act method is also an excellent means of training young apostles. Experience shows that "the Gospel teaches self-responsibility, brings the message of Christ into the tangible world of the pupil, brings home the personality of Christ, and finally is distinctly apostolic in its approach". And, if such enquiries are carried out by interracial groups, then this coming together for the common purpose of getting to know Christ better is one of the finest acts of Catholic action in a missionary country. Where devotion to Christ and to Our Lady are solidly grounded in guilds and sodalities, these become a further means of exercising a missionary influence, in that they absorb into their ranks or bring together at rallies all the racial elements of the Church in a mission country and unite them by a spiritual bond. Opportunities thus arise for social contacts by arranged sodality parties, sodality fêtes, sodality debates, sports, contests, etc. Experiments of this kind have reaped a rich reward in bettering race-relations in our part of Africa, S. Rhodesia, where Europeans of the professional and university level interchange ideas with Africans and people of mixed race within these groups without the slightest trace of artificiality to remind one of the colour-bar. The basic uniting forces to start with were Christian principles brought alive in a religious teaching that radiated Christ.

The more this "contact" spreads as leaven into the mass of indigenous people, the quicker there is hope of forming an integrated Christian society that can act as a bulwark against extreme nationalistic and racial onslaughts; but unfortunately, in Africa at least, we are beginning to build the dykes while the storm-waves already are beating against the shore.

The Church once again, through the catechetical revival, offers the world, and the missions in particular, the most effective means of teaching the consolidarity in Christ of all nations and races: through revival of the liturgy the Mystical Body of Christ is, so to speak, rejuvenated. Now that the ritual words in the administration of some of the sacraments and parts of the Mass are presented in the vernacular, understanding for them is deepened, and the oneness of the Church's sacrifice, sacraments and faith, irrespective of where the Church is acting, becomes more apparent. A training for appreciation of, and participation in the Mass, as the offering of the one Mystical Body to the one God, would be a most powerful incentive in emphasizing that, just as the multiplicity of cells, organically separate but constitutionally one, form nevertheless one physical body, so the Church of Christ is one, though the members constituting it vary in colour and culture.

It is by thus letting the leaven of vitalized Catholic teaching penetrate the scholastic programme and the lives of the pupils, that European schools in missionary countries fulfil their missionary role and can apply to themselves the words of St. John Chrysostom: "Christ left us on earth that we might become the lighthouses that illuminate, the masters that teach the seed bearing much fruit."

# THE CATECHISM AND RELIGIOUS INSTRUCTION BOOKS IN THE MISSIONS

# The Bible and Catechesis

LÉON ARTHUR ELCHINGER
Coadjutor Bishop of Strasbourg

BEFORE we examine the influence which the Bible ought to have in catechesis, we should look first of all at the place which it occupies in the lives of those whom we have to teach. This we might perhaps do by considering a few, possibly indiscreet, questions. Firstly, if we were to enter the libraries of our missionary schools, where would we be likely to discover the Bible or the New Testament? Would they be in a place of honour, among the books most frequently used, or would they be somewhere at the back of a dusty cupboard?

No doubt most of our catechumens, having received their instruction, say their prayers before some statue surrounded with flowers and candles. But what would be thought of a missionary who – even without abolishing the statue – erected in the room a beautiful lectern and placed a large Bible on it? Still more, what would be thought of him if he maintained that this Bible would enable us to recollect ourselves before a sort of "tabernacle" containing the Word of God, and that the proclamation of this Word would put us, in a certain way, into the presence of God? Would not some voices be raised to question the orthodoxy of this missionary?

Suppose one day you were to announce to your catechism class: "God will speak to you this evening, at such a time, in such a place so many miles from here." Would not a whole crowd of impatient folk make their way along the road, heedless of fatigue and discomfort, in order to get to the place where God would speak to them . . . oblivious or ignorant of the fact that God's word is at our disposal any time, even in the humblest of our dwellings?

If, one day, a pagan were to ask our young people, to whom we have taught the faith, what they knew with certainty about God, and why they were certain about these things, what would they answer? In searching their memories for what they should reply, would they drag up a lot of catechism answers which they had learned by heart, or would they try to remember what the Bible says? Which of the two books, catechism and Bible, would they think more valuable as a source of direct and sure knowledge of God?

These and similar tests, based on real life, help us to assess what place the Bible really occupies in the minds and hearts of our mission Christians. And the place which it occupies in their life depends, without doubt, very largely on the place which was given to it in their catechism classes.

And let us see what role the Bible does in fact play in catechesis; how is it used? What importance is assigned to it in the catechetical training given to the children and the youth in our countries?

It is often said that the use of the Bible in catechesis carries with it more disadvantages than advantages. Some of the arguments advanced for this view are as follows. The Bible was not written for children. Some of its passages refer to matters or events so coarse and crude that the reading of them would injure the susceptibilities of children. Moreover, the reading of the Bible sometimes raises difficulties or objections which become stumbling-blocks, not merely for the young, but also for adults.

Again, there are important dogmas which find no explicit mention in the Bible. Hence, one cannot make the Bible the essential foundation for catechetical instruction.

These arguments explain why it is that, in many countries and for long periods, the Bible has been used for catechetical purposes in limited ways only. It has been drawn on as a rich mine of pious and instructive stories used to illustrate catechism lessons. The Bible has become the equivalent of a picture book. Or else the biblical texts have been used as confirmatory proofs of the harmony which exists between scripture and theological reasoning. The Bible has become a sort of check, like the answers in the back of an arithmetic book. If a quotation can be adduced in support of something that has been taught, then this must be correct.

Again, Bible history may have been taught, indeed, but only as a subject quite separate from the catechism. Such teaching has been a sort of archaeological investigation into the origins of revelation. The history of the Jews, the life of our Lord and some early Church history were taught; but instruction of this kind did not necessarily lead to education in the faith. In mission countries a great many non-Christians have learned about the history of Israel or the events of Christ's life, but have not thereby been drawn into becoming Christians. What they heard was, for them, just cultural enrichment.

There is, however, a completely different way of regarding the relationship between the Bible and catechesis. According to this view the Bible is no mere accessory: it is not just a book of illustrations or a complimentary proof of doctrine or the historical background of revelation. All these ways of using the Bible reduce it to the level of an aid to study, when, in truth, the Bible is "the Book". It cannot be put on the same level as other books. It is the privileged vehicle of the Church's tradition; it is the very source of doctrinal instruction.

This is why certain recently produced religious instruction books have not relegated scripture quotations to the end; instead they have been used within the text as points of departure for the development of doctrine.[1]

In some dioceses the traditional handbook of Bible history has been radically altered, and now provides material for the religious instruction to be given in the first school years. In some cases a collection of biblical extracts has completely supplanted the textbook of Bible history used in classes of children over eleven.[2]

Does all this indicate a mere passing phase? Or is it a dangerous imitation of what the Protestants do? Or are we, on the other hand, witnessing a healthy re-orientation of catechesis?

[1] This applies, for instance, to the new German Catechism, which in France has been given the title *Catéchisme Biblique*.

[2] This is so, for example, in the case of the book *Lectures Bibliques*, used in the Strasbourg Diocese.

In any case we cannot ignore the fact that, during the early centuries of the Church's history, both the instruction of catechumens and also the more complete education of the faithful were solidly based on holy scripture. Up till the middle of the thirteenth century the Bible was always held to be the book on which all religious teaching had to be based; and throughout all this time the teaching even of theology consisted essentially in giving commentaries on scripture.

What, then, ought we really to think about the idea of biblical catechesis? Far from being an innovation, would it not rather be a return to the most authentic Christian tradition?

## *The Advantages and Necessity of a Catechesis Based on the Bible*

### DOCTRINAL ADVANTAGES

Our task is to proclaim the "Good News" with the purpose of introducing our pupils to the reality and the mystery of salvation. But salvation does not consist, in the first instance, of a plenitude of concepts or a plexus of obligations, nor even in any reality divorced from time. It is through and in a series of salvific historical events that God has willed to save us. If we are to bring salvation to our faithful we must, then, make them participate in these historic events and become integrated into them. But where can we find this design of God traced out if not in the Bible, from Genesis to the Apocalypse? And how can we make our young Christians more clearly realize God's intervention in human history and the effects of this for us all, except by familiarizing them, in one way or another, with the book which recounts the "deeds" and intentions of God? We must take account also of sacramental initiation and moral education. Now the purpose of the sacraments is to lead us into and keep us in sacred history (the train of historic events); and it is because our Christian vocation involves us in these historic events that we must regulate our moral conduct accordingly.

It is, therefore, the Bible which reveals to us the fundamental outlines of the Christian mystery. It is the Bible which makes known to us the course of the economy of salvation. So how can we neglect, in our work of religious education, that which is its fundamental element, and of which all the rest is but a development, an explanation or a corollary?

True enough, it is the Church which, by the aid of the Holy Spirit, teaches us revealed truth. But that does not mean that holy scripture, which is the authentic expression of God's word in terms willed by God himself, has therefore but a secondary importance in the economy of salvation. The Church is the authorized interpreter of scripture, but scripture remains the only divinely inspired expression of doctrine. The doctrinal primacy of the Bible is thus evident, even though the doctrine which the Bible teaches is explained by theology and expressed in liturgy. It is impossible, therefore, to give a solid spiritual education to any Christian without giving him a biblical education. (And why should it be a privilege of Protestants to do this?)

## EDUCATIONAL ADVANTAGES

Consider what a difference there can be between knowing somebody through a description or definition of him, and knowing him through experience, through personal contact. Take an example. To know how best to behave towards a new superior it is not sufficient to have been told that "he is a very good man, but rather exacting". You need to have been with him for some time, to have experienced how he reacts to this or that situation; only then are you in a position to approach him with any confidence about matters of difficulty or delicacy; only then have you any idea what you may prudently ask of him, and what you can expect from him, particularly if you have a guilty conscience.

In like manner we need to have some experience of God if we are to know how we should behave towards him, how to deal with him. But this is possible for us only with the aid of the Bible. It alone enables us to study his way of acting and reacting towards men.

Take another example. What do we know about God when we say that he is merciful? How merciful is he? Within what limits and under what conditions may we expect his mercy? What does all this mean in practice?

To discover in what God's mercy consists we shall not get far with definitions and incomplete principles. There are undeniable advantages in a different way of going about it.

Let us study a certain number of specific instances of God's mercy as we find them in the history of salvation and in the inspired accounts. From the dialogue between God and Abraham about Sodom and Gomorrha we can deduce the conditions in which God is ready to forgive sin, and the reasons which move him to mercy. From the story of Jonas we learn how ardently God desires to pardon sinners. We see other aspects of God's mercy in the parables of the Prodigal Son and the Lost Sheep, and the promotion to authority of St. Peter in spite of his denials, in the way in which Christ will judge men at the end of the world, and so on.

Now we cannot possibly condense into a catechism answer all the knowledge and experience of God's mercy which we can derive from biblical accounts. But we can let ourselves be impregnated with this knowledge and experience, so that a living image of divine mercy becomes engraved, as it were, upon our hearts and we become able to recognize whether this or that attitude on the part of a Christian does or does not really correspond with God's ways of acting.

This is something like the way in which we can come to know an author or a painter from his style. No mere definition about the style of some composer or poet would enable us to recognize his work when we hear it among others. It is only when we have come to know this musician or poet through his works, when we are familiar with his musical or poetic idiosyncracies, that we can say with confidence "that is surely by Bach! Shelley must have written those lines!" It is in just the same way that we become familiar with the ways of Almighty God and of his kingdom.

Consider how a lesson about God and his demands and his "psychology" can become alive and real if, instead of producing abstract arguments, we adduce certain passages from the story of salvation to give us a complete picture of the way in which God behaves towards us. The world described by the Bible is not, after all, so very different from our own world. In both of them we find the same sort of people, those who are faithful and unfaithful, those who attain to purity and simplicity of heart, but who abandon God from time to time only to seek him once more and ask his forgiveness.

From the Bible we thus learn what we might call the "divine pedagogy"; we see the way in which God teaches man about himself; how God approaches man when he is a mere pagan, leads him out into the desert to extract the poison from his heart and let new desires take root there; how he uses even the sins of his people to make them grow in their understanding of his loving design for them.

God, desiring to "teach us our catechism", has produced a story. To give himself to us he put himself into that story. And so is not the Bible itself the prototype of all religious instruction? There is nothing better calculated to rescue catechists from rationalism — the great danger threatening religious instruction – than the very concrete character of the relationship between God and man which we learn from the Bible, and which derogates neither from the mystery of the calling of God's chosen people, nor from those of the incarnation and of the redemption.

## PASTORAL ADVANTAGES

The mere acquisition of knowledge is not faith. There must also be adherence to the revealed truth. One's trust must be given to God, to Christ. There has to be a choice, an engagement, the assumption of an attitude towards God.

Hence the need for making known an invitation from God, an invitation which is intended to call forth a personal response. But summarizing or describing God's intervention in human history is not of itself an invitation. If God has issued his invitation through the medium of words and events, why not let our catechumens hear these words for themselves? Why must we interpose a screen between God and men?

If man comes face to face personally with God's word, he feels himself invited by God much more directly than if catechists come along to interpose their own intellectual interpretations. That, of course, does not cut out commentary on God's word as made by the Church. On the contrary: it is the

Church which makes God present to man; it is the Church which actually confronts man with God's word.

Christian faith does not consist only in choosing Christ. Such an individualistic attitude would be hardly Catholic. We have to introduce our catechumens into a community. But the Bible is precisely the book of that community which is the "people of God". It is their charter. It is their code. It is from this book that we know the sacred ties which bind us to the innumerable generations whom God has gathered together before our own time. It is this book which shows us the path to be followed by the people of God on their way. The Bible is like a family history that enables us to know our ancestors, the wonders worked for them by God in the past, and the promises he has made for the future.

To acquire a family spirit one must live in the family. To belong truly to any country, it is not enough to have studied the grammar of the language spoken there and the laws which are in force there. Anyone who immigrates into a country continues to be a stranger until he has lived there long enough to have become acclimatized. In the same way, to acquire the spirit of the people of God one must live among them as one of themselves – in the atmosphere derived from prolonged familiarity with the Bible.

An atmosphere is not completely absorbed as the result of explanations; it penetrates by a kind of osmosis.

Having accepted the doctrinal, pedagogical and pastoral advantages of a catechesis based on the Bible, what practical steps should we take to link up the Bible with catechesis?

### *How to Achieve a Catechesis Based on the Bible*

The Bible is more than just history. Bible history textbooks are wont to lay too much stress on the historical nature of the events recounted (in the sense that they belong to the past) and not enough stress on the permanence of their meaning and consequences. However important it may be not to underestimate the historical character of revelation, the history of salvation must never be reduced to a mere series of past events.

The most important aspect of these past events is the connection between them, and the intentions of their invisible agent, God, who continues to intervene unceasingly even now. A mere historical account does not bring out this aspect at all. Our pupils have to learn not just the history of salvation, but the economy of salvation.

On the other hand, in Bible history books such as we have had up till now, there is no room for all sorts of wonderful biblical passages which would contribute greatly to education in the faith. Think, for instance, of those chapters of Jeremias wherein the prophet inveighs energetically and poignantly against merely exterior and insincere worship. What a powerful antidote they would be against the formalism of many Christians. And why not let our young folk know about those astonishing passages of the prophet Osee, in which God, in words of unexpected tenderness, reveals to us his incomparable love for men? And there are some chapters of Isaias whose poetic inspiration alone puts them among the most exquisite pages from world literature. And those verses from Proverbs and from Wisdom filled at the same time with solid common sense and generous idealism! So many treasures will be for ever closed to our catechumens if we deprive them of direct contact with the text of sacred Scripture.

Not everything in the Bible is history. Our books of Bible history distort the Bible because they do not make any distinction between the various literary *genres*. The story of Abraham, of Joseph in Egypt, the fall of Jericho, the history of David, of Jeremias, the didactic stories of Jonas, Tobias and Job – all these are put on the same level. Consequently there is danger lest we deceive our pupils by making them take all these things literally, as if they were all verbatim reports by contemporary eye-witnesses.

Those who want to reduce biblical education to mere history should not forget that children, especially those less than about twelve years of age, have no sense of history whatever. They find great difficulty in situating any past event with relation to any other past event. They are just incapable of any synthetic view – this view of events from a distance – which is needed for grasping the progress of the economy of salvation, the plan of God concerning this world, which is recounted in the Bible.

On the other hand, from the time children reach about the age of ten, it is necessary to emphasize for them the incarnational aspect – the situation in place and time – of biblical events and persons. This is so in order that biblical persons – even Christ himself – may not be left in a kind of unreal atmosphere of fairy story and legend which would be an impossible basis and preparation for the certainties of faith.

So we see that the kind of Bible history book we have used so far offers no solution – at least not by itself – to the problems of the biblical education to be given to children.

## FIDELITY TO THE SACRED TEXT

God becomes present among us not only under the species of bread and wine but also – as the Fathers of the Church used to say – "under the species of scripture". To nourish us God not only made himself man; he made himself book and word. And God made himself word in order to be read, just as he made himself bread and wine to be eaten and drunk.

Now why should we neglect this form of God's presence, this kind of divine nourishment, and replace it by substitutes of our own making? Why should we prefer Bible stories – even be they more complete and written by some famous historian or renowned educationalist – to extracts from the sacred text guaranteed by inspiration and filled with the breath of the Holy Spirit? Do such writers deserve more esteem than the authors who were chosen by God himself to tell us his secrets?

If God has thought it well to make himself known to us through writings guaranteed by himself, what business have we to conceal these writings from our children? Are we to leave them under the impression that some book written by a catechetical expert is more authoritative than the books written at the behest and under the inspiration of God? Are we to let them think that the catechism is the very source of our faith? It is as if we wanted them to believe that the origin of water is the tap; or that tap water, because it comes through long pipes, is better than spring water. No doubt the formulae of the catechism are very important: they are a protection, a breastplate for the truth; they are a vehicle, a basket in which the truth can be safely handed on. But what use would the basket be if it contained nothing but indigestible food, that is, if its contents were only abstractions which the children could not grasp?

So we must give to our children something beyond the *history* of salvation. They must be given also the *economy* of salvation; and they must get it, wherever and whenever possible, in the words of the Bible itself.

Certainly, until they have grown up, they can be given only carefully chosen extracts; for the Bible is like a great forest through which large avenues must be made to prevent inexperienced explorers from losing their way.

## APPLICATIONS

In order to make it clear that the economy of salvation is something operative here and now, and to show that the sacred history of the past is prolonged into the present, we must ally the study of Bible history to the course of the liturgical cycles. Liturgical feasts provide catechists with a pedagogical and spiritual climate of incomparable value. The story of our Lord's birth, for instance, makes a totally different impact according as it is told at just any time of the year, or by leafing through the pages of a picture book, or at Christmas when the event is lived by the child within the Christian community that is celebrating the feast. The same holds good for each of the mysteries professed in the creed; for these are not only commemorated, but actually made present in the course of the liturgical year. In this way sacred history becomes a reality going on all the time, full of personal meaning for each one and for the entire community of God's people.

## OFFICIAL PRAYER AND REVELATION

If we were to sum up the way God taught man in Old Testament times we could well do it by saying: "God taught the world to pray." So why not employ for the children the manner of prayer which God himself inspired and which is set down in the sacred books? Why not imitate the dispositions suggested to men or demanded of them by God's messengers? Why invent and put together model prayers when God himself has gone to the trouble of providing some for us? The Church gave us chiefly God's prayers when she composed her divine Office.

Can one imagine any training for prayer more theocentric than biblical piety? It takes a man into its grasp and puts him straight into God's presence. It curbs his tendency to withdraw into himself and to spend too much time on lamenting his own human miseries. Such things seem of no account before the majesty and sovereignty of God. The sacred writers draw us along irresistibly to great and wide views which extend far beyond the mere incidents of life and let us see ourselves in true proportions before God and understand the only values which he regards as important.

Like extracts from the Bible, prayer based on the Bible should form the first stage in all training for prayer and sacramental life.

### CHRISTIAN LIFE AND THE BIBLE

Essential Christian dispositions are founded, not on our own reasonings and logical deductions, but on God's word – what God has revealed to us and what God wants of us. The education of a child in morals should be directed to making him feel responsible for his actions before God, rather than before his parents or teachers. But how can we impart this sense of responsibility if the commandments seem to the child to come from us, to be our own inventions, because we fail to refer the laws of Christian life to God's will as revealed to man? It is in the Bible that God has made his will known to us. And it is through that converse with God rendered possible by the Bible that moral life can be seen as a positive way of reacting to God, instead of being a mere submission to a set of principles of conduct, or to the articles of a code of behaviour.

Moreover the Bible guarantees to us an authentic understanding of Christian dispositions. Let us take, for example, the difficult virtue of humility. What a lot of woolly thinking there is on this subject! How many wrong ideas! Is a man really expected to pretend that he has not got the talents which God has given to him – or else to despise them? The true idea of humility comes to light from study of the parable of the Pharisee and the Publican, or of the Guests at the Banquet, and so on. From these a man learns that he must not push himself forward, and that we are all sinners. On the other hand the parable of the Ten Talents shows him his duty in justice not to neglect the talents God gave him precisely in order that he might make good use of them. Beyond doubt the Bible helps us to arrive at the truth in such matters.

You may have realized that what we have just discussed corresponds to the three sections of the traditional catechism, – creed, cult and code. We have shown how each of them has its roots in the Bible.

## *Educational Conditions Needed for a Catechesis Based on the Bible*

### PROGRESSIVE USE OF BIBLICAL TEXTS

Although education in the faith is governed by laws of its own, it cannot afford to neglect the general principles of child psychology, since grace does not destroy nature.

Hence catechists must choose Bible passages within the capacities of the children, according to the progress they may have made towards intellectual and spiritual maturity.

It is important to avoid cramming. Telling small children almost every story that can be found in the Gospels is no way to train them to faith, for then it will be difficult to hold their interest later on. They will have the idea that they know it all already, and will not spontaneously deepen their knowledge. Yet it is just this kind of personal reflection, or meditation, which best arouses in them dispositions of faith and love.

On the other hand, apart from certain scripture passages which are fundamental and inexhaustible, there must be a good deal of variation in the biblical passages used during the years of formation. This is necessary so as to avoid blunting the sense of curiosity natural to children, and to avoid also the impression of offering them a dish of food which they think they have already emptied.

## CHOICE OF TEXTS WHICH HAVE A REAL EDUCATIONAL VALUE

Each time we choose biblical passages for use in our catechism classes there is one question which we should always consider beforehand, namely, in what way will this particular passage nourish the faith and piety of our children or adolescents? Do not let us confuse sacred history with pious stories; under the pretext of wanting to keep them interested we must not fall into an attitude of pedagogical demagogy, which would consist in using the Bible as a mere source of anecdotes. To interest the children is not necessarily to educate them. There must be a great many children who have heard the story of Samson but do not remember anything except that his hair was cut off! Was it worth telling the story if that is all they learned from it?

It would be possible to illustrate the various phases of the economy of salvation by biographies: Abraham, Moses, David, Jeremias, and so on. But we must not just take the easy way. It is not the picturesque features in the lives of these heroes in the Bible which matter; what we have to bring out is the attitude of their souls, the ideals they cherished, their converse with God – in other words the religious import of their life stories.

The educational value of a biblical passage depends not solely on its content but also on the way in which it is presented. The story of the Flood is certainly a wonderful religious story which reveals to us both God's demands and also his mercy. But, told in the way it is sometimes given to children, it might just as well be used in the natural history class under the title "Different kinds of Animals found upon the Earth". And what about the story of Jonas? There are teachers who tell their children all about the whale, but say nothing about the moral which the story is intended to convey.

A catechist – that is a witness of God working among the children of our own day – ought not to waste his time telling bible stories from which he is incapable of extracting the religious meaning.

## STUDY OF BIBLE TEXTS IN A DEVOTIONAL SPIRIT

This brings us face to face with a pedagogical problem. How to reconcile the presentation and scholarly analysis of a biblical passage with the requirements of reverence for the sacred text? For passages from the Old or New Testament should not be studied as if they were just pages in a textbook.

All biblical instruction should be invested with a quality or ambience of sacredness. It cannot be a merely intellectual study. The passages we have to expound to our children were not written just by men; they have God for their author, and hence bring us into direct contact with God.

In planning our catechism lessons, therefore, we must make provision for such things as a formal reading of extracts from the Bible, or a few moments of interior recollection, which would foster a transition from intellectual study to a more profound attitude filled with faith, longing and receptivity towards God's word.

It is in vain that we give to our children the most complete and precise explanations; if we have not also taught them to "listen" to God's word we have failed to induce in them proper religious dispositions. The most important thing of all is an attitude of receptivity at a deep level. They must give the attention of their very hearts to the word of God. That is the atmosphere we have to produce by our religious instruction.

## MEMORIZING BIBLICAL TEXTS

School age is the age of memory, and we do right to make the children learn catechetical texts by heart. Moreover a precise text to be memorized gives a certain sense of security at this age. But why should we not also – perhaps especially – make the children learn some biblical texts by heart? After all, these are the words of God and are more precious than the words of any theologian. It is essential that certain biblical passages of special significance should be learned by heart. By means of these the children will store up in their subconscious minds considerable active reserves of power and light. Far more than catechism texts, biblical texts – our Lord's own words – can sustain the children throughout their lives both at school and afterwards.

All this, of course, presupposes that we should have at our

disposal collections of biblical texts in a sound translation and suited for public reading.

## *Conclusion*

It only remains for us now to consider how these principles can be applied in drawing up books intended for use in religious instruction. I refuse to admit that these principles are valid only for the catechesis of children. They hold good equally for the instruction of adolescents and of adults. And what is essential for catechesis in the home countries is equally essential for catechesis in the missions.

We are living at a time when far reaching changes are taking place. We are experiencing an astounding revolution everywhere in the spheres of science, economics and politics. We are involved in a whirlwind which is tearing away the very roots that bind us to the past. How can faith remain firm among such confusion of values? How can the man of today remain open to the Christian mystery when in the grip of habits of mind, increasingly dominated by technology, which render him insensible and even indifferent to the transcendental world, to the invisible God?

We must keep immersing our young people continually in a biblical atmosphere so as to familiarize them with an order of values that is becoming ever more and more depreciated. If we do not, then soon they will be beyond the reach of God's message; they will be able neither to understand it nor to appreciate it.

To separate catechesis from the Bible is like separating a plant from its roots. It is to render survival impossible. We must save the very roots of catechesis. And the precious roots of catechesis are the Bible.

(Tr. C.H., S.J.)

# Experiences in Compiling a New Catechism

HUBERT FISCHER
President of the *Deutscher Katechetenverein,* Munich

IN nearly all mission countries work is being done on the drawing up of new and better textbooks for catechism instruction. The new German catechism has attracted much notice and provided a stimulus and many suggestions for this work. And as the headquarters of the German association of catechists in Munich have been carrying on a lively exchange of ideas for years with leading catechists in the foreign missions, I agreed at once when Father Hofinger asked me to report to this congress on the practical experience we in Germany have acquired in the course of writing our catechetical textbooks.

My report is limited in two ways. First, it deals with only two religion textbooks – the new catechism for eleven to thirteen-year-olds, and a smaller catechism for six to ten-year-olds, which is still in preparation. Religion textbooks for apprentices, for pupils in intermediate schools, professional schools, and the upper forms of secondary schools are not considered. Its primary purpose is to explain how work on the two books was organized and what practical experience has been acquired, not to discuss in detail the content and structure of the books themselves and their arrangement in the form of lessons. This has been done in my book, *An Introduction to A Catholic Catechism.*

## *From the Mönnichs Catechism to the New Catechism*

In 1925 Father Mönnichs compiled a new catechism for Germany which was adopted by all the dioceses except Freiburg and Rottenburg. Its superiority over the previous catechism by

Father Deharbe, with its neo-scholastic tone, consisted above all in that the questions were considerably shortened, the question technique improved, the material clearly organized, and more emphasis placed on Christian life. Thus it may certainly be termed one of the best of the old-style catechisms such as were in use everywhere at that time and still are in some places today – not only in the missions, but also in America. In spite of its undoubted adventages, the Mönnichs catechism was soon subjected to vehement criticism as a result of the emergence of new and powerful currents in pedagogical and didactical thinking and in theological thinking as well.

The following objections were made to the form of the catechism: the appearance of the pages was bewildering, the subject matter too tersely presented, and the correspondence between question and answer often only of the slightest, which made understanding and, even more, learning very difficult. The whole plan and arrangement of the catechism was more like that of a theological textbook than that of a schoolbook for children. It looked dry and dismal compared with the other schoolbooks. And it laid too much stress on thinking and memorization and too little on Christian life.

But the theological objections and misgivings were of an even more serious nature: the catechism was still too much influenced by the controversial theology of the Counter-Reformation. The faith was thus presented mostly from the point of view of abstract theology and apologetics rather than from that of the story of salvation. The lack of biblical orientation made the mystery of our faith disappear. The abstract presentation of the great mysteries of salvation deprived them of their splendour and religious force. One felt the absence of the living, dominant centre of our faith: Jesus Christ and his eschatological tidings of the Kingdom of God. Particularly severe criticism was directed at the treatment of ethics, which, being based entirely on the Ten Commandments, lacked a peculiarly Christian stamp and thus was scarcely able to instil the decisive awareness of the Christian's attitude and behaviour as that of an *alter Christus*. The German Bishops joined in the criticism of the catechism then in use and at Fulda in 1935 resolved to reform it.

The criticism of the old catechism already gave some conception of what the new catechism should be like. What was to be expected of it? Bishop Berning of Osnabrück, the bishop then in charge of school affairs, in a pamphlet about the catechism summarized the requirements for the new catechism in the following six points, quoted here in somewhat abbreviated form.

The new catechism should be God-centred. Its purpose is not the imparting of dry facts, as if it were an abridged compendium of theology; the whole book must appear to be the word of God spoken to the children.

The catechism should be Christ-centred; Christ must be the focal point of all religious instruction. He is "the way, the truth, and the life". To serve and follow him lovingly and faithfully must appear to the children as the shining goal of Christian life. Then the catechism will fulfil its purpose: to be a "tutor unto Christ" (Gal. 3:24).

The catechism should be Church-centred. The sources of the Church's doctrine are scripture and tradition, and it is from these sources that the catechism teaching on the Church is to be drawn. If the catechism gives a true conception of the meaning of the ecclesiastical *magisterium,* the children will be proud to belong to such a Church and feel bound to the Church in cheerful obedience and absolute devotion.

The catechism should be child-centred; its language should be adapted to the children's understanding. The catechism's teaching of the faith should imitate Christ's preaching to the people. Christ's words are much better remembered by the children than scholastic definitions; definitions should be restricted to the barest essentials. The children should be required to memorize only those doctrines whose formulation must be preserved from distortion or is in itself of constructive value.

The catechism should be centred on living. It is not just one school-book among others, since its primary purpose is a spiritual one: not that of teaching theological facts but that of leading the children to God by teaching them the truths of faith.

The catechism should be centred on our times. Christ's truth undergoes no change with time, but the form in which it is proclaimed must take account of the times, the spiritual needs of the children, and of the advances made in teaching methods and in child psychology. All our previous catechism have born the stamp of their times. Since the publication of the catechism now in general use, conditions for the religious instruction of young people have very much altered, and the young people themselves have changed.

While the bishops' conference of 1935 at first had planned only a modification of the old catechism, it soon became clear to all concerned that the constructive criticism which had been made showed the need for a new type of catechism. As the proposals made for the reform or modification of the catechism also tended towards incisive changes in the nature of the catechism, the bishops' conference of 1938 in Fulda resolved to create a completely new catechism, one "as perfect as possible", for all the dioceses of Germany. The task of writing it was entrusted to the German catechists' association, in which the new catechetical movement had been at home for years, and which had won the particular confidence of the bishops. Monsignor Götzel, then the president of the association and a collaborator of Professor Göttler's, was responsible for the organization of work on the new catechism, which developed as follows.

In 1938 a conference of diocesan representatives outlined the basic procedure. They determined that the new catechism, unlike the old one, should be the work of one author, not that of a commission voting on each point. They also decided not to set up a competition with a prize for the best catechism submitted, as it was felt that such a book could only be produced by an author working in close collaboration with a team of catechists.

Towards the end of 1939 a small group of catechetical experts came together in Munich for the purpose of discussing the basic theological aims and structure of the new catechism. Klemens Tilmann was asked to sketch out a plan for it and to submit this to Bishop Berning for preliminary examination.

Following his approval of the plan, it was, together with the first specimen texts, submitted for examination to a group of about twenty catechetical experts in 1940. The result of their deliberations was published in the pamphlet *Auf dem Weg zu einem neuen Katechismus*.[1]

[1] Herder, Freiburg, 1943.

Meanwhile Doctor Tilmann, who had been called up into the armed forces, had been writing a preliminary, broadly conceived running text presenting all the material of the catechism in children's language. This text was sent to a group of experts and discussed during their holidays.

During and after the war the material and the structure of the catechism were worked over by Franz Schreibmayr and Klemens Tilmann. They gathered and sifted material, especially scriptural material, illustrative of the various themes, and took great pains with the preparation of a text, in the form of readings and some material for memorization, which was centred on the Bible yet indebted to the classical tradition, and which they discussed thoroughly with the team of collaborators in Munich. In 1946 the publishing house of Herder was able to print a sample run of the first part of the catechism, which, together with a guide to its use, was sent for trial and examination to all German Diocesan Administrative Offices and to numerous catechists and teachers of catechetics, and was discussed at a series of conferences.

The booklet *Taufe und Gnade*[2] presented the final form of the text, which was based on the model of Quinet-Boyer's French catechism. Each lesson begins with an expository text (mostly taken from the Bible) and is illustrated by a picture. After the expository text comes a lesson-text, followed by questions without answers, then questions and answers to be memorized, and supplementary texts entitled "For my Life", "From Holy Scripture", "From the Life of the Church", "The Teaching of the Saints", "What would you say?", "Things to do", and so on, varying according to the theme.

In 1948 and 1949 catechetical and theological problems of decisive importance for further work on the catechism were discussed at two large conferences of catechetical experts. Meanwhile, in collaboration with Jan Wiggers, the text of the catechism was written up in the new form and sent to about seventy experts. After their criticisms and suggestions had been worked into the text, a large printing was carried out by Herder and the book was tried out in practice in the schools.

[2] Herder, Freiburg, 1948.

Early in 1952 all parts of the catechism had been printed. The bishops' conference had meanwhile appointed a committee of examiners consisting of one representative from each diocese and an editorial committee responsible for the concrete realization of the examiners' proposals. At Whitsuntide the committee of examiners met in Würzburg. They gave their basic approval to the proposed text but wished the size to be reduced by one-fifth and the number of lessons increased from 101 to 136. About 15,000 changes in all were proposed.

Following the instructions of the editorial committee, and maintaining continual contact with them, the authors and their collaborators worked over the entire text, and the results of their labours were approved at a final meeting of the editorial committee. At Whitsuntide, 1953, it was submitted to the Bishops' Conference at Fulda.

The Bishops' Conference of 1953 put the Bishop of Eichstätt in charge of preparing the final version together with collaborators appointed by him. In 1954 the book was finally adopted and in 1955 put into use in the schools. The *Deutscher Katechetenverein* (German association of catechists) was given the responsibility for working out the syllabus and for giving courses of introduction to the new book for catechists.

Here are some facts which contributed particularly to the success of our work. The work was organized by the *Deutscher Katechetenverein,* which permitted great freedom in the choice of authors and in procedure. The close cooperation between the authors and numerous experts and interested groups aroused widespread interest in the work, enabled us to profit by the experience and suggestions of well known catechists before publication, and thus assured the production of a catechism which would meet with general approval. By means of combining teamwork with the work of individual authors, agreement could be reached on almost every point without having to take a vote. Trying out the catechism in the classroom on a large scale before publication enabled us to make many practical corrections and considerably facilitated its final adoption, so many catechists being familiar with it by then.

In retrospect we do not regret having spent so much time writing the catechism, the quality of the book seeming to us to justify the time and pains taken. The new catechism has also won many friends in other countries and has already been adopted by several dioceses outside of Germany. And it has been translated so far into more than twenty languages. One reason why *A Catholic Catechism* has been so well received in foreign countries is that, although we already had numerous expert collaborators here at home, we continually kept an eye on catechetical advances in other countries and were glad to consider and make use of any valuable suggestions we received, whether they came from home or from abroad.

### *The New Religion Textbook for Younger Children*

After finishing the new Catechism, we turned to another task which had also been urging itself upon us for many years: drawing up a new catechism for the lower classes of the primary schools. There were two main reasons for writing a new one. Firstly, the material and the form of presentation of the old smaller catechism no longer met the requirements of modern material and formal kerygmatic instruction, and it also had to be made more like other contemporary schoolbooks. Secondly, as the smaller catechism lays the foundations for the major catechism, it must, while retaining its independence and its own approach, build up to the latter organically. The new catechism made a change in the smaller catechism necessary.

Catechism instruction at the primary level is so important because it is many children's first encounter with the world of faith, at a particularly receptive age. First impressions are known to be lasting, and they generally form the mind for a lifetime. It is at this age, too, that the children must be prepared to receive the sacrament of penance and the holy Eucharist, and they should also be taught to fulfil, in a childlike way, some of their duties as members of the ecclesiastical community.

### *Organization of the Work on the New Smaller Catechism*

The task of organizing the work on the new smaller catechism was entrusted by the German bishops, just as in the case of the major catechism, to the president of the *Deutscher Katechetenverein*. After agreement had been reached on basic points at a preliminary conference of diocesan representatives at Würzburg on March 5th and 6th, 1958, a working committee appointed by them established general principles for the structure, form, and content of the new smaller catechism at a conference on April 25th and 26th. Groups of catechists were put in charge of working out the various parts of the book: one in the Diocese of Aachen doing the first part (for the second year of school), one in Munich that for the third year, and one from the Hegge (Paderborn) that for the fourth year.

These three teams kept in close touch with one another and met regularly to confer upon the progress of the work. As the individual parts of the new catechism for younger children are likewise being tried out on a large scale in the classroom, the final edition will also be able to make use of the practical experience thus acquired. We hope that the book can soon be submitted to the German bishops.

### *Form and Content of the Religion Textbook for Younger Children*

For psychological reasons the book will consist of two units: one for the first two years and one for the third and fourth year. The book for the first two years is intended primarily for children as they reach the age of reason. Therefore it emphasizes the instruction given during the second year of school, in the course of which the children reach the age of seven. The first year is also included in the plan, because none of the children are too young to acquire some basic religious attitudes, and during the first year, not earlier, many of them reach the age of reason defined by the Church as a condition of receiving the Blessed Sacrament.

For these reasons the small textbook must contain everything children of this age group need for living a Christian life: an interpretation of the world around them based on faith, an introduction to prayer, and a first preparation for the sacraments of penance and the holy Eucharist corresponding to the children's needs at this stage of development. But in order that more and more children may receive the sacraments as early as they can, the small textbook must contain no more than what is prescribed by the Church for the receiving of the sacraments and what the children are capable of understanding. The textbook for the third and fourth year provides for thorough instruction on confession and communion. A special prayerbook for children is a practical aid to them in receiving the sacraments of penance and participating in the Mass.

The structure of the book is based on the liturgical year. The facts and the truths of salvation are culled chiefly from the Masses throughout the year; this establishes the intimate and necessary connection between faith, liturgy, and Christian life. Thus the children learn to know and love God as their heavenly Father and to fulfil their duties as children of God, and they develop a close yet respectful relationship to Jesus Christ. The material is divided into lessons, the form of which varies with the subject matter. They may contain pictures and readings taken from holy scripture, the Mass, the lives of the saints, or everyday Christian life; furthermore short doctrinal texts, material for memorization expressed in childlike form, prayers, songs, sayings and so on. Thus the separation of a special children's Bible from a children's catechism, a separation unsuited to the child but still existing in some dioceses, will be abolished, as was already urged, with convincing arguments, by such men as Stieglitz and Pichler. The pictures are meant not only to illustrate the text but to fulfil a kerygmatic function and to complete the text in their own way.

The book for the third and fourth year is divided into three parts: the Old Testament, the New Testament, and sacramental life. The children become aquainted with the most important events in the Old and New Testament history of salvation. Thus they gain access to the world of the Bible, experience more strongly the basic religious and ethical attitudes of Christian life, and acquire a deeper understanding of the basic concepts of faith and salvation from the point of view of scripture. Thus catechism instruction at this stage serves as a preparation for work with the larger catechism, yet does not anticipate anything.

The biblical texts should keep as close as possible to the word of scripture and contain no amplifications or interpretations beyond an occasional simplification of expression. Each biblical text is followed by a doctrinal text emphasizing the point or points of kerygmatic significance in the excerpts and, where this suggests itself, relating the text to the liturgy and to the life of the child. After the doctrinal text come questions in the form of review questions, which make certain that the biblical or doctrinal text has been understood. There are also supplementary questions relating the lesson to other lessons from the Bible or to the child's life or the life of worship; and questions encouraging independent thinking and activity in order to deepen the children's comprehension of the process of salvation begun in the Bible, their participation in divine service, and their realization of Christian doctrine in daily life.

The book will also contain material for memorization sufficient and suitable for a smaller catechism and a large collection of prayers and hymns. The various supplementary texts (for example "Things to do") are drawn up not according to a fixed scheme but rather as suggested by the individual excerpts from the Bible.

The third part deals with the seven sacraments in a form suited to the children's age. The most space is devoted to the sacraments of penance and the holy Eucharist, because the children who receive these sacraments for the first time during their third year of school must receive a thorough and fundamental preparation for their first confession and communion, while all the others must be helped to deepen and develop their knowledge of these first two sacraments. The instructions on confession are preceeded by a section on Christian life for children. The section on the sacraments is also in the form of lessons.

In conclusion let it be repeated that the instruction should keep in mind the children's spiritual, mental, and linguistic development when introducing them to the mysteries of faith; the textbook must develop the material in an organic way. Therefore we disapprove of using the major catechism in primary school, for the following reasons. Primary school children think in very concrete terms and only gradually become capable of abstract and conceptual thinking. Linguistic development, a mirror of spiritual development, also necessitates a very careful and gradual introduction to the language of the major catechism, which bears the mark of abstract thinking. It is tiresome to have the same book years on end. Children love variety and enjoy marking their progress in the knowledge and life of faith by a change of catechisms.

All our work on the new catechisms has aimed at appealing to and forming the whole child in a religious sense, not only at imparting religious knowledge. As a reflection of catechetical method, the religious textbook must also appeal to the whole person and not only to his intellect or power of memorization, and this in a way suited to the various ages and stages of development. Only thus will the children grow stronger in their love of the faith, which alone is the source of knowledge and Christian life.

# * Katekisimu

GERALD RUPPER, O.S.B.
Ndanda Mission Press, Ndanda, Tanganyika

## *Before the Open Door*

IN the missions one cannot just introduce new books simply because they are better; the catechisms already in use have first got to be used up! Thus in East Africa, particularly in Tanganyika, we had to wait for the right moment before attempting to introduce the German Catechism into our schools. After the war Pichler's little religious instruction book, greatly enlarged by the incorporation of the entire Austrian Catechism, was brought out in a large and rather expensive edition. The aim was to provide one religious instruction book which would do for all the classes in the schools we then had, as well as for catechumens and for adult Christians. This book is in general use at present right up as far as the Congo.

But in the meantime a new type of school has come into existence – the so-called "middle school". The Catholic missions were unprepared for the task of undertaking religious instruction in these schools. So a Conference of Catholic Seminary Directors was called in 1953; they decided to suggest to the bishops that a religion book should be drawn up for use in the middle schools, and that a competent committee should be appointed to deal with it. Both requests were immediately granted.

The committee went to work in June 1954, and consisted of two Dutchmen, one American and two Swiss. This fact was of considerable importance, though in other ways nationality does not affect the issue at all in Tanganyika. One of the Swiss had already obtained a copy of the new German Catechism, and he was determined to do everything he possibly could to recommend it. But the secretary of the Catholic Bishop's Conference was an Irishman, and he opposed it on the grounds that public opinion was not ripe for it, and such a suggestion might wreck the whole plan. So nothing could be done beyond recommending the framework or approach embodied in the German Catechism, without betraying its origin.

American religious instruction books were very popular about that time, and one of the seminary professors who was enthusiastic about them had planned a four-year course of instruction, each of the first three years being concerned with one of the Persons of the Trinity: God the Father, God the Son, God the Holy Ghost, and a finishing course for the fourth year! It was worked out on practical lines, with suggestions for reading, for projects, and detailed teaching hints.

The Swiss members of the committee worked hard and loyally on this scheme, but in their heart of hearts they were not in favour of it and never really gave up their original idea. This four-year course did not meet with much success. One reason was that it had not been made known widely enough, and there were new schools which had not even heard of it. Another reason was that the books required were not easy to obtain from America; some schools never got them at all. There was no system for religious inspection in the middle schools; a few young priests had been appointed to do the job, but they had not been given any particular catechetical training before being sent out to the missions. Another contributary cause of the failure was the fact that in several dioceses it was still an obligation to work through the catechism question by question, day by day, learning the questions by heart; and the catechism prescribed for this was the one in use in the primary schools. Any middle school which, in addition, got so far as to work through the Gospels and the Acts of the Apostles (which the syllabus included) were exceptional and deserving of much praise.

Meanwhile the final edition of the German Catechism came on the market in Germany, and the monasteries at home sent copies to all their Fathers and many of their Brothers in the missions. So now the wheels began to turn. The Benedictines of Peramiho, through their Education Secretary, Father Mathias Tremel, beginning in December 1956, brought out a plan for catechetical instruction throughout the year – and this plan was intended to correspond with that of the German Catechism. There were some delays through lack of any precedent for such an undertaking; but it transpired later, when the Bavarian syllabus was sent from Munich, that the shot had by no means been wide of the mark. At the same time a suggestion was made to Father Alcuin Bundschuh that he should undertake a translation of the German Catechism, even if this could be used only in the missions run by the Benedictines. Everybody was very helpful about the whole idea, but other more urgent tasks slowed down its execution.

So the door still stood open, and hopes were by no means abandoned. On the contrary, they rose high when the English version of the German Catechism (called *A Catholic Catechism*) was published, even though it came out at a price that put it utterly beyond the reach of the missions (thirty shillings for the edition with coloured drawings). In addition there came some very constructive criticism from Canon Drinkwater, in his periodical *The Sower*. He makes no claim to fluency in German; yet he published in English all the questions and answers from *A Catholic Catechism* before the full edition appeared. After a while the popular edition, at ten shillings and sixpence, was made available. The Benedictine missions immediately ordered it in large numbers for their Teachers' Training College and Technical School.

And thereby hangs a tale! One of the religion teachers left a copy of it lying open on a desk, and the boys were looking at it with delighted astonishment. For a while the teacher let their interest mount; then he asked them, "Wouldn't you like to have a copy of this book?" "What sort of book is it?" they replied. "One of you, come up and read out its title." *A Catholic Catechism,* read the boy. "Catechism?" they all cried, "Katekisimu? Hapana – *No,* we don't want a *catechism*!"

That was absolutely typical. However, they were told that anybody who wanted a copy could take one. Very few of them did at first – probably through human respect. But those who did take copies became enthusiastic about the book.

A similar situation arose when *A Catholic Catechism* was introduced to a teaching community as the basis for further religious instruction. It won its way chiefly because one teacher, who had already been using it in his own catechism classes, spoke about it with much enthusiasm and made the rest understand that it was not by any means the sort of book they were imagining from its title of "Catechism".

Meanwhile the Teachers' Training College for the middle schools came under new direction. An energetic young Dutchman took over the teaching of religion, and set himself to carry through the plan which had been earlier decided on – the four-year plan based on the Holy Trinity. But he could not find material for some parts of this syllabus, and wrote for help to the Education Secretary in Peramiho who was delighted to know that a new wind was filling the sails, but saw at once that the wind was blowing in the wrong direction. He did indeed send the old plans back with the information asked for, but he also sent the new (Catholic Catechism) plans. The result was a real disappointment! But about the same time the Bishops' Conference and the Conference of Headmasters from all the missions were about to meet. So the points were quickly set; a memorandum was drawn up to show that *A Catholic Catechism* was being introduced in places all over the world. The bishops of Ndanda and Mwanza vigorously supported the proposal, and the religion teacher at the Training College had ruefully to admit that he had lost the battle. Now it was time to set strong hands to work.

## *An Insight into the Workshop*

Father Alcuin Bundschuh, mentioned above, managed to finish his translation of Part One, for which he had already done some preliminary work. He sent it to the Director of the Teachers' Training College, asking him to work through it with a certain missionary. But this missionary was frequently away in his bush stations to teach and hold services, and only came home when he was sick! In consequence Father Alcuin got his manuscript back with long lists of questions unanswered. Meanwhile he had translated Part Two, and this also was corrected but only under great climatic difficulties in extreme cold up by Lake Nyasa, some six thousand feet above sea level.

It was up here that a lonely missionary, being shown *A Catholic Catechism* for the first time, frankly admitted: "I never knew before that this world would continue to exist in the new creation! Nobody ever told us anything about that when we were being trained." One need hardly investigate or embroider upon the background of this remark to get a picture of past missionary training. Yet this zealous man, in the course of five or six years, had succeeded in creating a Christian community of about 1600 souls out of nothing! There were pictures by Fugel hanging all round the walls of his little corrugated-iron roofed church, to keep the work of redemption before the minds of his flock; but among them was no picture of the "great restoration"!

Meanwhile it had become clear to Father Alcuin that he must call a meeting to settle all outstanding questions. The priest who had helped him by correcting Part Two asked his superior for the aid of an African priest; and this African turned out to be highly suited for the work to be done. Apart from his natural gifts he was fluent in Swahili because he had been sub-editor of a Catholic paper, and had been trained by his chief editor to do careful and accurate work. Also he had been in charge of a school for catechists for a whole year, and at the time was the diocesan secretary for trained catechists. So now the translations could be subjected to really careful and informed examination; it was a long business, and the fearful heat prevailing at this time of the year did nothing to make it shorter. Some of the problems which came to light in these discussions will now be described.

## THE PRESENTATION TEXT

At the time there was no generally accepted translation of the Bible in Tanganyika; a committee is at present working to produce one. One of its members has himself brought out two translations of the Gospels within the last fifteen years, but they are completely different. The texts of the original German Catechism were based on the Greek; our African colleague strongly opposed this, for he and his brethren were brought up on the Vulgate. Fortunately he does know a little Greek for, by way of exception, he learned some in our seminary. But he maintained that the text, thus directly translated, left something out, and insisted that all these places should be indicated by the inclusion of three dots. This almost hypercritical attitude exemplifies the mood of all the collaborators. In some places it proved possible to adopt the text used in the missal; in such cases nothing was changed so as to accustom the reader to one version. The translator of the English edition, by comparison, was in a fortunate position though he, too, had to complain of difficulty in choosing which version he should use. The checking of biblical quotations for the Swahili edition took up an unconscionable amount of time, and the room in which we worked was strewn with different Swahili versions of the Bible.

## THE EXPLANATORY TEXT

Here the concentration of style and the use of adjectives raised many difficulties. In Kiswahili, for instance, it is not possible to attach two adjectives to a single noun, and there is no scope whatever for the construction of sentences with dependent clauses and the like. We were very tempted to depart widely from the text, and have recourse to African ways of speech. As is well known, an idea very familiar to the Bantu people is that of "vital force"; the Franciscan, Father Tempel, in his book *Bantu Philosophy* maintains that the Good Tidings can be expressed in terms of it. But we felt it would be a mistake to take too much notice of African circumstances; we did make two attempts to do so, but both were failures, and we concluded that the idea was too idealistic and not practicable. After all, we are told that the Christian truths are the same for all nations; it is up to the catechist to impart them in a way which suits each of the peoples. Moreover the history of the origin and development of the German Catechism induced in us a certain feeling of awe and a hesitation to do much tampering with it.

It may be still more surprising to hear that even the concept "Church" came in for much discussion. The Swahili language does not have genders for its nouns but divides them into eight classes. In the Benedictine missions, under the influence of the seminary, it had become customary to use two different forms for the word "Church" according as it referred to the building or to the community. This is possible grammatically because certain other words are treated in a similar way. But other translators had decided to stick exclusively to the one form which, in our convention, meant "Church building"; they had managed to get their terminology adopted into the generally accepted Ritual. And so, for the sake of uniformity, the catechism just had to do the same.

The expression "sanctifying grace" had been a subject of dispute and confusion for twenty-five years. Many said that the word formerly used for this could not be justified grammatically, although the Office for East African Languages had indeed accepted into the language certain words of ecclesiastical origin when these had already passed into common usage. But owing to this objection on the grounds of grammar some preferred to use a different term for "sanctifying grace"; this, however, was opposed by yet others on the grounds that it originated from the Protestants and had Protestant connotations. In everyday speech it meant "purifying". As "purifying grace" it was not opposed, but it quite failed to express the positive aspect of sanctification, referring, as it did, only to the negative aspect of the removal of the stain of sin. A welcome opportunity, therefore, existed for introducing a new expression meaning "life of grace" or "grace-life".

Up till now, one and the same word had been used for "spirit" and "soul". So by saying "God is a pure spirit" one could be understood as saying "God is a pure soul". So for the sentence "God is a spirit", occuring in Lesson 15, Section 3, we wrote "God is a spirit, but he has no body like a mortal man". And when we came to Lesson 18 we combined the word for "soul" with another meaning "seat of life". It is a word not often used in Swahili, yet it is in fact found in all dialects of Bantu even beyond the borders of Tanganyika. The African priest was extremely glad that a solution had been found to distinguish thus between "spirit" and "soul".

In the teaching about the Church we had to be careful to use the expression "Mother Church" only when it referred to some activity of the Church. And so, for example, in Lesson 46, Section 2, we doubted whether it would be good to adopt from the English the phrase "our holy Mother the Church" because in that place the reference was primarily to the unity of head and members within the body. For the same reason it might be better to introduce the expression "Mother Church" more formally in Lesson 49, Section 1.

In Lesson 81 (about Mortal Sin) the translators were reminded of an old missionary who had died three years previously at the age of eighty-six. Throughout his entire life he had protested against the definition of mortal sin in current use. How is one to judge the case in which a drunken man kills someone, or leads him into a sin against the sixth commandment? Here, much more than in Europe, one has to take into account the sophistry of the Bantus. It should be mentioned also that, in connection with the effects of perfect contrition, our Christians always want to argue away the necessity for confession before the reception of holy communion even when mortal sin has been committed. Such a thorny problem cannot possibly be treated adequately in a mere paragraph of a catechism; it has to be handled *per longum et latum* in the course of the catechetical instructions themselves.

In Lesson 85, on confession, the shade of the venerable Hirscher came over the threshold to ask whether Christ had not been somewhat forgotten? When a Christian confessed his sins, did he not repent, resolve and do penance in Christ and with Christ (Hirscher Catechism, p. 598)?

## QUESTIONS AND ANSWERS

A desire for uniformity in the wording of Questions and Answers had long been felt in all the dioceses, because in Tanganyika many Christians spend half their lives wandering from one place to another or working away from home. In *A Catholic Catechism* it was in the Questions and Answers more than anywhere else that the compilers did their best to adhere to traditional formulations wherever possible. We therefore tried to do the same, and in our translations found it harder to reach agreement here than in any other section of the book. The task was rendered the more difficult because quite recently a commission of four priests in one diocese had made a revision of the catechism questions then in use, and had obtained an *Imprimatur* for it. However, in spite of everything, we did manage to reach agreement thanks to a simple policy. Whenever we could not agree to the adoption of any of the existing formulations we set them all aside and took over the form given in *A Catholic Catechism*. In some instances, where the answer seemed a bit long, running into two or three sentences, we were particularly careful to translate it into words which the children would find it easy to say.

There was one very well-known catechism answer which we simply had to abolish completely! The African priest told us that the expression used in it was quite common among the people, but only as a vilification! If a man really wanted to "tear strips off" somebody he cast aspersions upon him in terms of powers of generation, saying that none such had been operative in producing him and that he himself possessed none! And the customary phrase for expressing these uncomplimentary asseverations was "You have no beginning and no end!" Obviously, therefore, we could not possibly give, as a catechism answer, the statement that "God has no beginning and no end"! Fortunately we were able to arrive at another way of imparting the truth to be conveyed.

#### FOR MY LIFE

Here we felt that matters concerning the missions would have to be brought out with greater emphasis; also that the versions given were somewhat too individualistic. The Good News must not be kept to oneself, but passed on to others.

### *And the Future?*

The "Katekisimu" will first be published in three parts. The reasons are mainly technical. We shall print it here in our own small press at Ndanda, and it will have to be set by hand. The schools are waiting for it, for they plan to work through Part One after the end of 1960. We are hoping to let them have the copies by March or April of next year, though we fear some difficulties may arise. As regards the illustrations we have laid down the principle that everything specifically European must be eliminated (except, of course, where the pictures concern historical events). Unfortunately we find it impossible to fulfil this ideal in every instance, but Professor Burkart has made a number of new drawings for us. When Part One appears the pictures will doubtless cause many hackles to rise, but they will probably subside by the time Parts Two and Three come out!

The type of reaction we expect to meet most frequently was that expressed by a young teacher. "We teach religion from one catechism in the primary schools; why should we have a different text for the middle grades? Has our religion been changed?" Only the future can show to what extent "Katekisimu" will be able to find acceptance, by reason of its quality, among catechists, priests and bishops.

(Tr. C. H., S.J.)

# A Good Mission Catechism

MARTIN RAMSAUER, S.J.
East Asian Pastoral Institute, Manila, Philippines

## *Needs and Aims*

ONE of the greatest needs felt in the mission today is that of a good mission catechism. We would like to get a catechism which would be as useful for the missionary catechesis as the newly developed catechism proved useful for the instruction of our Catholic youth at home. In this paper we shall try to determine the qualities which a mission catechism should have. This will lead us to the second question, how we should go about achieving it, which we will take up in the discussion. A good mission catechism must meet demands regarding the content, regarding the methodical presentation and regarding the proper adaptation to the mission people.

### WHAT IT SHOULD CONTAIN

These demands are substantially the same as the catechetical movement requires from any good catechism. But in view of the task of a mission catechism these demands gain much greater urgency. What is the core of our demands regarding the content?

Our teaching as presented in the catechism shall become again the proclamation of the "glad tidings", the message of our salvation in Christ (see Eph. 1:13) and shall be regarded again as the divine invitation calling for our answer.

Whatever is part of this divine message is certainly included in our present catechisms, but that the sum of all these details constitutes a divine invitation for our salvation does not appear with the clarity we would wish. This is also the reason why our catechisms frequently seem to be dry and very unattractive. What is the cause?

### EXCESSIVE PREOCCUPATION WITH APOLOGETICS

The message of our salvation as coming from God contains many details about the destiny God has given us, the means offered by him and the way leading there, in other words, our salvation. About all these details the catechism must inform us. It must also consider the difficulties which could hinder a true understanding of God's message or block our way to God. For this purpose questions of apologetics had and have to be treated in the catechism. But here we observe that at times we have got lost in the details of apologetics. Now since the apologetical consideration did not usually proceed from the context that a particular truth has in the whole of the Christian faith, the truth in question was not always sufficiently realized as part of the message of our salvation.[1]

Furthermore we observe that apologetical considerations, required perhaps in that detailed accuracy to protect the Catholic faith in one country from distortions and misunderstandings, were transferred into other countries – so to say for the sake of "completeness" – where the points of controversy were at most of historical or scientific interest, but of no particular pastoral importance, that is, influencing Catholic life. Those considerations entered even the mission territories where a necessity for a similar apologetical completeness did not exist. This not only diverted the attention from the core of the Christian faith, but made it difficult to realize the heart of our message.

Even the question-answer form served an apologetical purpose. But dividing the content into short statements hindered a synthesis and obscured the fact that we bring the "message of salvation".

[1] This can be seen very clearly in the doctrinal expositions on the Church found in the catechisms of the last few centuries; cf: my article "Die Kirche in den Katechismen" in *Zeitschrift für Kath. Theologie* (Innsbruck) 73 (1951) pp. 129–169; 313–46.

## CURTAILMENT OF THE GOOD TIDINGS

Our teaching gave exhaustive "information", but it was not always conveyed as it came to us from God through Christ: as an "invitation". Following thus the apologetical trend we not only lost a deeper understanding of the inner unity of God's message and at the same time a source of powerful inspiration – but the message itself received an unintentional curtailment – despite the growing amount of information contained in the catechism.

As a result of the apologetical trend aggravated by the question – answer form, what we finally find in our catechisms is a list of truths which have to be believed, of commandments imposed under pain of eternal condemnation, and of means indispensable for gaining heaven. In consequence our Christian religion is perceived as a burden which we have to carry. But what has happened to the character of the Good Tidings – the characteristic quality of Christ's teaching (see Mark 1:14)?

The reason for this is the fact that the individual points of our religious instructions have been separated from a greater and inner context in which they were revealed by God, and have been made to stand independent of one another and of the whole. The realization of the context, the understanding of the whole plan for our salvation, not the study of individual parts and details, reveals the full meaning an individual truth has and shows without distortion God's infinite love who so much desires our salvation "that he gave his only-begotten Son" (see John 3:16; Rom. 8:32).

The loss of this vivid insight into the whole of God's plan for our salvation brought about what we just called the "curtailment" of our teaching. What remains of God's "invitation" is a great heap of mere "information". And this is the reason why Christian teaching is experienced rather as a burden than as the glad tidings of our salvation (Eph. 1:13). How can we eliminate these shortcomings?

## ARRANGEMENT OF CONTENTS

That God's invitation contains a number of revealed truths is evident if we consider the supernatural character of our end.

But the accurate transmission of God's message, the faithfulness which Saint Paul demands in our ministry (1 Cor. 4:2), requires from us that we should not be content with a complete enumeration and explanation of all the individual parts and details, but that we show with all possible clarity and conviction that the sum and the core of our teaching is God's invitation into his Kingdom and thus to our salvation. This has to be stressed and put at the beginning as Christ himself did (see the Beatitudes at the beginning of Christ's sermon on the Mount) and as the new German Catechism does (see Lesson Three).

Only after such a first understanding of God's call and plan can we go into details which will now reveal their full significance, explaining further our message and serving its accomplishment. This approach makes us realize that the core of our teaching is a message of Glad Tidings; and this mark of joyfulness flows over into all details making our teaching in all its parts the proclamation of the Good News.

These considerations lead to clear demands for a mission catechism which, with much greater urgency than a catechism in Catholic regions, has to present the Christian message in its characteristic features. The mission catechism should not only affirm that the Christian religion is the message of salvation . . . but it should convey the Christian religion in such a way that it makes us realize that it is the message of salvation. This truth must be the central truth dominating the whole catechism, and be found in every truth of our faith and every demand of a Christian life, since all these details reveal their full meaning, and gain that motivating power which is required for a Christian life, only in the light of their significance for our salvation. The Christian message contains a two-fold element: the invitation on the part of God – calling for a response on our part. This two-fold element has to determine the whole plan of the catechism and show it forth in all parts so that we never enter a detail without realizing immediately its relationship with and significance in the whole of our message of salvation. The character of our message as invitation, demanding our cooperation for its realization, has to be felt in the catechism by a spontaneous dynamic element. Our message from God is a challenging, promising, inspiring proclamation, demanding our decision.

As soon as our teaching is realized as the message of our salvation, our teaching becomes necessarily the proclamation of the Good News, the *Evangelion*. This effect shall be at the same time the proof that we have transmitted God's message faithfully. Saint Augustine already has demanded *"hilaritas"* for the catechumenate. But certainly not as a mere pedagogical help which would facilitate the teaching, but as the fruit of the instruction, as proof that Christ's message of our salvation has been handed on faithfully and has been understood by the catechumen properly. For apostolic reasons missionaries have a special esteem for this *hilaritas,* the joy of catechumens and Christians, that springs forth from the knowledge of the Christian message. This *hilaritas* penetrates deeply the life of catechumens and Christians, and changes it completely. Thus it draws the attention of the pagans and becomes a most powerful motive for them also to become Christians.

The demand regarding the content of a mission catechism does not require, as we have seen, a still greater scholastic exactness, nor a more detailed presentation and explanation of the mysteries of our faith, nor a more popular and simplified presentation of God's revelation. What it does require is a realization that what we are dealing with is a message coming from God, that this message comes to us in the form of an invitation to a joyful sharing in divine life, and that it calls for a magnanimous and enthusiastic response from us.

## THE AIM OF CATECHESIS AND THE LESSON FORM

The form of methodical presentation has to be in conformity with the content and serve its aim. Since it is not so much our task to present a great number of individual truths, as to communicate God's whole plan from which all the details can be developed organically and into which they merge harmoniously, we have to reject the exclusive question-answer form since it hinders the understanding of God's plan in its entirety and coherence. The form which best suits our task is presentation in the form of exposition. Just as this form of exposition – developed by the modern catechetical movement – has determined the shape of the new French and German catechism, it will also determine the external appearance of the mission catechism.

Furthermore it is our task to present the plan in such a way that God's intention of leading us to salvation (see 1 Tim. 2:4) is shown clearly, in an inspiring and challenging manner, so that not only man's intellect is informed, but his will and appetitive power is challenged, that man does not only know the revealed truth but follows God's call with determination and generosity.

In this point, too, the catechetical movement has rendered excellent service from which the mission will profit. In order to influence man's appetitive power a methodical procedure has been developed based on the laws that govern human actions and prepare decisions. This methodical procedure aims at winning man's will for God – the aim of religious education – by a three-fold step: the "presentation", the "explanation", and the "application".

The oral instruction in the missions generally makes use of these methodical steps, but there is still hardly any trace of them in the mission catechisms. In most cases it is therefore entirely up to the catechist to develop those steps and find a sound psychological approach.

## THE RELIGIOUS PURPOSE OF THE CATECHISM

Since the religious-pedagogical, or educational aim (namely winning man's will for God) is essential for our teaching of religion (since not knowledge, and not even faith alone, but deeds will save us: see James 2:24), it is only consequent that this aim be explicitly included in the catechism which shall serve the oral instruction.

To include this educational aim in the catechism – so that the catechism would not only explain the truth (and serve thus the Christian life) – was found necessary even in Christian countries, in order to replace the influence which in previous times the Christian society had contributed to the development and continuation of the Catholic life – but which our present time (somehow de-Christianized) is not able to exert, at least not to the desired extent.

Under real missionary conditions there is no educational influence from a Christian society – or it is still too little. Therefore there is an even greater urgency to include the educational element also in the mission catechism.

A further reason to include the educational aim explicitly is the objective difficulty of showing properly the value contained in the doctrinal element for attaining the educational aim. But this "evaluation" by which the truth becomes a motive is precisely the point which distinguishes true religious instruction from any mere theoretical instruction and which makes teaching religion difficult.

If therefore the religious-pedagogical element (which gives to the doctrinal element the orientation towards the Catholic life) is not sufficiently taken into consideration in the catechism itself, we have to fear that in the oral instruction this educational element is either dropped out entirely (because of its difficulty), or left to the spur of the moment or imparted by some kind of general application which will prove futile. Furthermore we should not forget that the education and formation of the catechist in the mission are usually far behind what Christian countries require from lay-teachers.

The catechists in the mission therefore depend much more on the text of the catechism. They consider it generally as their task to explain what they find there. Therefore if the catechism contains only the doctrinal element we have to fear that the proclamation of the message of salvation – for which we are sent by Christ –shrinks to a mere communication of information on the Catholic religion. As a result their teaching is without the proper dynamic, arousing and challenging orientation.

Since the "catechism of exposition" and the inclusion of the religious-educational aim (as it is done by the psychological steps) means quite a radical change and also some enlargement of the catechism, it is only natural that although missionaries accept the aims of the catechetical movement, they evince a certain hesitation.

In our dilemma we might learn perhaps from the experience of the catechetical movement at home. There it was still more difficult since there was no model that had proved successful and could be imitated. First of all we have to acknowledge that missionaries everywhere have done their best not only to explain the content of our faith but also to lead the catechumens to a Christian life. And we must not overlook their attempts to show Christians and catechumens the inner coherence and relation between the many truths. If therefore the missionaries can be shown how the intended reform of the catechism will help their aims, a basic acceptance seems to be certain. But above all things we should remember one thing. The catechism is intended for the catechumen, and should offer him not only a summary of those questions he has to learn by heart, but should be a help to him to find his way into the world of our faith, which is so new to him, to understand God's call, and to answer it wholeheartedly. The catechism, in one word, has to be not only a book for study, but still more a book for life.

Since in the mission we have not the beneficial influence of a Catholic tradition and Christian environment, it is much more important that the mission-catechism shows that orientation towards the Christian life as it is contained in the "catechism of exposition".

## EXPLANATION AS EXPOSITION

The greatest care in the catechism has to be given to the second step, to the explanation. In the explanation we should never be satisfied with giving only clear concepts and distinctions. The explanation has to serve the Christian life and has therefore not only to state the plain truths, but has to show the significance those truths bear on our salvation, has to lead to a personal realization and appreciation of the fact that with this revealed truth we are given a most precious pearl whose value goes beyond any comparison with earthly values since it means eternal life and participation in the Divine Life. It is evident that such a full explanation cannot be given in brief questions and answers only; consequently we need a "catechism of exposition".

In order to show more clearly the meaning a certain truth has for our salvation, we frequently have to go back to the context and connection which this particular truth has with the whole message of our salvation. This shows again the necessity of a "catechism of exposition" which offers the possibility for such a completeness.

If the explanation has made clear the significance which a truth bears on our salvation, we have gained a motive for our religious-pedagogical aim. And by this we have built a bridge from knowledge to action. Our human service cannot go further. In order to prepare man's decision we can (and have to) show the motives contained in God's message – but the conversion, the answer to God's call, the Christian life remains the free and responsible decision of the individual. But it is our task and responsibility as God's messengers to prepare and facilitate the decision of the individual as far as we can and may influence and persuade (see 2 Cor. 5:20 et seq., 6:1 et seq.). Therefore a proper development of motives has to be included in the catechesis and the catechism. This is done primarily by showing the significance of the truth for our salvation and the coherence of it with the whole work of our salvation.

Here it becomes also clear that the catechetical method which aims at a proper motivation to promote Christian life is not a mere "technical" procedure, but is ultimately founded in the content and aim of God's message itself. Knowledge of human psychology is necessary and likewise the mastery of catechetical method. But the motive which is necessary to stimulate the free will to the work of salvation is not produced by mere psychological skill, but has to be gained from the content of the message.

From this it becomes also evident why we have to insist on the spiritual formation of our catechists. How could they otherwise unfold and unearth for their catechumens the values of God's revelation which are hidden in the truth like the treasure in the field?

While discussing all these demands on a good mission catechism, by which we want to serve the message of our salvation in the most effective manner, we have to remember that the catechism, that relatively small book – and it shall remain small and handy – will not be able to answer all our demands with all the desirable completeness; if this were done, the catechism would turn into a handbook or commentary. But the catechism shall be a real help for a proper catechesis and recall the instruction received before, and revive our Christian spirit and determination. To fulfil this task, the catechism has to contain in some way the component parts.

### HOW IT SHOULD BE ADAPTED TO THE MISSION PEOPLE

The demands discussed so far are in substantial agreement with the demands we have on any good catechism. Still, it would be of only limited value to translate a good catechism written for Catholic countries and use it as a catechism for the missions. Wherever this has been attempted (with some minor modifications perhaps), missionaries have not been completely satisfied. There are peculiar circumstances in the missions which demand special consideration and a different pastoral approach. Perhaps we could summarize the peculiarities a mission catechism has to meet in this manner. The mission catechism has to be apt for first-instruction; must appeal to adult or mature people, who come frequently from a specific (i. e., non-Christian) cultural milieu, and who have to fulfil a special mission in their pagan environment.

### THE FIRST-INSTRUCTION

The systematic religious instruction a catechumen receives (as outlined in the mission catechism) supposes in the catechumen a certain "readiness" which is the result of a spiritual-religious preparation towards the Christian religion. Without a certain religious desire, without the "religious question", man is not ready to receive a systematic presentation of God's message since there is not the right kind of soil, that is, a man who "grasps the message and bears fruit" (see Matt. 13:8, 23).

How this preparation or approach proceeds in the individual is subject to God's providence (see Rom. 9:16) which frequently uses external means some of which we can, and are expected to supply. A special paper by Joseph Spae will discuss these possibilities.

Only when this "religious question" is aroused has the disposition for a fruitful instruction been obtained. This disposition may be shown in many ways. It is certainly indicated, if the prospective catechumen has a longing for light on religious questions, for true happiness, for a worthwhile aim to live for, if he feels a disturbing emptiness in his heart, or desires the acquittal of his guilt before God. If we find this disposition, we may judge the ground prepared for God's word.

As we stated above, the content of our message has to be realized from the very outset of our instruction as a joyful message, as the proclamation of our salvation. It must be recognized as something which provides light for the dark and tormenting problems of the intellect which searches for clarity, meaning, direction; as the answer to the longing for true happiness which the pagans miss in the emptiness of their lives but observe with a strong desire in the peaceful-happy life of the catechumens and Christians. But how can we give to the catechumen something of the light and happiness of the Christian message so that, even though it be impossible as yet to give him the whole answer, he will be able to assure himself: "here I shall find what I am seeking"?

A theoretical, syllogistic argumentation would certainly not serve our purpose. This way is much too abstract and difficult for many of our catechumens, and besides would not answer their problems. The answer must be concrete, clear, personal.

Let us ask it this way. What is the core of Christianity? What is, in brief, our message of salvation? Where and whence do we expect the salvation which we proclaim to the world? Is it a sum of doctrines and rules – or is it not Christ, God's Son, who became man, in whom "the grace of God has made its appearance" (Tit. 2:11) who could say about himself: "I am the light of the world, he who follows me will not walk in the dark, but have the light of life" (John 8:12). "I am the way, and the truth, and the life" (John 14:6). "Come to me, all you who are weary and over-burdened, and I will refresh you" (Matt. 11:28)?

And who could state: "Absolute authority in heaven and on earth has been conferred upon me" (Matt. 28:18) and therefore declare: "Your sins are now forgiven" (Matt. 9:2) and promise: "I assure you this very day you will be with me in paradise" (Luke 23:43).

The contents of our message is simply Christ. And our task as God's messengers is the same as St. Paul's who says "I strive to bring consolation to their hearts, and by strengthening their love, to enrich them with the fulness of understanding, and to bring them to the deep knowledge for the divine mystery, Christ. In him are to be found hidden all the treasures of wisdom and knowledge" (Col. 2:2 et seq.).

Therefore Christ, the historical person of Christ, is the answer we give to the catechumen. From Christ we hear God's invitation; from him we hear what happiness is waiting for us; he shows us the way that leads there. By him we are told how near God is to us already, embracing us with his love and care. He teaches us how to speak to him: in praise, in thanksgiving and confident prayer.

Just like the contemporaries of Christ we listen to the powerful teaching of our Lord as handed down to us in historically trustworthy documents, we marvel at his miracles, we begin to admire and to love him. Thus we grow towards the day on which the catechumens will perceive the inevitable question: "Who do you say that I am?" (Matt. 16:15) If the heart has been won for Christ, the will will give without hesitation what is required from its side to the act of faith in Christ.

Once we have professed faith in Christ's divinity we have reached the culmination of the catechumenate. From now on Christ's word is divine revelation, his Church is divine institution and God's plan and way leading to our salvation is the beginning of our share in the eternal life and blissful love that fills the heart of God.

While we communicate to our catechumens Christ's message we have to be careful not to make any suppositions as to their knowledge about the Catholic faith. Christ's message is new to them. The catechism has therefore to progress in an organic, unfolding manner. We should avoid as much as possible anticipating facts which can be understood and proved only at a later stage of the instruction. Otherwise we might cause uncertainty, confusion and perhaps even suspicion in some of our listeners, which would be detrimental to the progress of our catechumenate.

This condition of "newness" must be considered in the catechism and will necessarily imply a marked difference between the catechism for the missions and the catechism for Catholic regions. The latter can presuppose a certain knowledge and familiarity with the Catholic faith: and therefore does presuppose it. But the mission catechism has to begin without such suppositions; and this is the reason why a mere translation of a catechism written for Catholics is only of little help for mission conditions which demand a first-instruction.

Would it not be the best approach to start with fundamental theological and apologetical questions? This procedure might be recommended for the theological science. Perhaps also for special cases among the catechumens. But since it cannot be considered the best and most effective way for achieving the aim of the catechumenate, it cannot be considered as the norm for the catechism and a possibility for its order and arrangement. The catechumen comes to the Church in a seeking attitude; he hungers and worries, feels his failures and shortcomings – and searches therefore for an answer and fulfillment, not for theoretical reflections and abstract considerations. He wants first to experience in his own life the inner riches of the Christian message (and where could he better find them than in Christ – see Eph. 3:8; Col. 2:3), and then only is he prepared and ready to enter into a reflection on what he has experienced and realized, and to understand the positive and enriching aspects of apologetical questions and not only their defensive task. Apologetic has a place in the catechism only if and as far as it helps the Christian life, but never for the sake of mere knowledge and information.

For similar reasons it might not be recommendable to begin – without any other "introduction" – with the creation of the world, the creation of angels and man. Does this part of God's revelation really contain the desired answer to those questions the catechumen bears in his mind when he comes for instruction? Does not this part in particular, especially in the beginning of the instruction, turn very easily into an unprofitable discussion about creation, origin of man, and the how and why of original sin?

*Creasti nos ad te,* St. Augustine begins one of his reflections, and he concludes from this fact, *inquietum est cor nostrum donec requiescat in te.* This *inquietudo* – one of the greatest gifts which God has given us for our journey through this life – has to be answered; and to arouse this *inquietudo,* if man should sleep in a state of false security, would be the first step in our work of conversion. The answer to man's restlessness is Christ. In him are all the unfathomable riches that can fill our heart and mind and bring joy and security. Christ is the centre of our teaching and its beginning. From him the way leads into the details which are fully understandable only if seen in their relation to Christ who is our salvation.

### THE INSTRUCTION OF ADULTS

The catechumens in the mission are frequently adults or people of a more mature age than those under instruction in Catholic countries. Since God's message requires the whole man and demands a complete service (see Matt. 22:37; 10:37 et seq.), our teaching has to meet man in the concrete, that is the adult; it has to consider his problems in order to convert the whole man to God – and not just to cover him with a Christian cloak.

A final personal adaptation, of course, which is necessary for this, has to be made by the missionary (catechist) himself. A catechism cannot go that far, since by too much consideration for a particular group of catechumens the catechism would lose its usefulness for many others. But the instruction of more educated catechumens can be supplemented without too much difficulty by guided reading which generally will have to be discussed in the periods of oral instruction. Thus there is no necessity for the catechism – destined for many and quite different catechumens – to enter into every possible detail and problem, as long as there is no detrimental "simplifying" of the problems found in an adult's life.

Our catechumens and Christians are exposed to a growing influence of materialistic ideas and have to remain faithful in a frequently a-religious milieu. The catechism has therefore to help the catechumen to recognize the act of faith, the assent to God's word, as reasonable – although the content is beyond a complete human understanding. And furthermore the catechism has to equip the catechumens and Christians sufficiently to answer – according to their ability – the difficulties coming up against the faith in their life and milieu.

We have also to remember that the justification of the adult is not achieved by a mere study and knowledge of our faith, but that it needs a "con-version". But this implies that the adult usually has to travel a long road, called and constantly helped by God's grace, to gain finally that disposition which is required for justification. As instrument of the religious instruction or better, of God calling to salvation, the catechism should not fail to foster in a becoming manner those dispositions which mark the way to justification and which are listed in a summary manner in the decrees of the Council of Trent: fear of God, hope, love, repentance, purpose of amendment. The greatest care will have to be given to the development of prayer.

## CULTURAL BACKGROUND

Our mission people frequently belong to an old culture in which we find precious elements of a natural religion. Sometimes we come upon sentences, mostly concerning their ethical life, which have a similarity in thought and expression to words in the scripture.

In the religious instruction of certain catechumens we will be faced with the question what attitude we should take. Could, or should we refer to such texts and customs? Or have we to fear to promote rather an attitude of indifference towards Catholic religion suggesting the conclusion: all religions are substantially the same and their own pagan religion is not inferior to the Catholic? Complete silence might be interpreted as ignorance of the religious culture of the mission people or even as contempt of a tradition highly esteemed by them. Or – at best – they might think that we do not dare to undertake a "comparison".

But then we must not limit our comparison to just one or very few points which show a certain similarity. We must widen the field of our comparison. Then it will become manifest how in the pagan religion, together with some dim light and some good beginnings, there is still much darkness, doubt, uncertitude and also error. At the same time we will realize the superiority of Christ in whom there is light without shadow, truth without any mistake, certitude without the slightest trace of doubt; and above all – and by this we get to the essential difference – who does not only teach ethical principles, but gives the strength to live them.

If the "comparison" is done in this way we often hear our catechumens say that none of our wise men has ever spoken thus.[2]

And we remember the word of scripture which reports what Christ's listeners felt: "Never has man spoken as this man speaks" (John 7:46) and "When Jesus had finished these discourses, the crowds were lost in admiration of his teaching; he certainly had a way of teaching them as one that has authority, and not as their Scribes and Pharisees" (Matt. 7:28 et seq.).

Such a comparison gives us at the same time an opportunity to make clear a fact which is most important for our missionary efficacy. By that transcendent superiority of Christ it becomes evident that he is not the culmination of a natural religious development and knowledge – as other founders of religions. If Christ had taken his wisdom "from below", from the human-natural cultural milieu in which he lived, he would not have reached an essentially higher level of religious knowledge than those others who, we may admit, came close to the limits the human mind can reach, especially in the state of our fallen nature.

Thus we come to understand that his teaching cannot be regarded as the product of a certain culture, that Christ's wisdom is "from above", that his message therefore is destined for all men; that he does not want to suppress the good to be found in any culture, but that he came to complete it and to bring it to new and greater perfection in a higher order (see Matt. 5:17).[3]

At the same time we answer very effectively the prejudice which identifies the Christian religion with the western culture

[2] This was the conviction of the seventy-five-year-old general Yang Tsin when he embraced the Catholic Faith: "I have read the four Gospels several times and . . . the Psalms twice, and I feel that nothing in our Confucian classics is comparable to the religious and moral doctrines contained therein." (Quoted in Dr. John C. H. Wu, *Beyond East and West,* pp. 320.)

[3] Dom Pierre-Celestin Lou, himself a convert, considers the treasures of the Catholic Church "the divine, marvellous and indispensable complement to all that I possessed, to all that I anticipated, sought and desired, and to the fundamental institutions of my people". (*Ways of Confucius and of Christ,* page 65.)

and therefore considers the conversion to the Christian religion as defection from and denial of one's own inherited culture.

If the comparison or reference to the culture of the mission people is made properly, only one conclusion seems reasonable. The Christian religion is not of human origin, but has been given to us from heaven. By our conversion we do not lose any natural values – but gain divine riches. "The truth is", says a leading Chinese convert, Dr. John C. H. Wu, "that only Christianity has satisfied all the aspirations of my heart and confirmed all the insights of my mind, and woven the two strains of my inborn nature into a perfect harmony, which is the music of the spheres rather than that of the earth or of man" . . . "By embracing the True Church of Christ, I have lost nothing, but gained all." (*Beyond East and West,* p. 30.)

## THE FORMATION OF APOSTLES

A great hindrance to the conversion of our mission people is a materialistic attitude which is spreading further and further, threatening the pagan religions as much as it threatens Christianity. How shall we bring to those men the Christian message of salvation with its spiritual values?

In answering this problem we must not overlook that this materialistic attitude implies a certain appreciation of realities that can be observed and experienced. And this applies also to religious questions. Our contemporaries do not just want to hear and to discuss arguments; they want to see and to experience the realities and values of our religion. But cannot the sanctity of life, the peace and joy of Christians, their contentment and assurance, and especially their love, which embraces even enemies, be experienced by the pagans and does this not impress them more than we sometimes think? This is the miracle by which they judge our Christian religion, the sign which God has given to the world to testify to the authenticity of the Christian message (see *Epist. ad Dogn.*).

Since this is probably the only way to reach a greater number of men and to lead them to salvation, it is our task (and obligation) to impel our Christians and also our catechumens to lead a holy and truly Christian life. They shall learn to strive for sanctity not only for the sake of their own salvation and greater happiness, but that their fellow-men may see their good example and praise the Father who is in heaven (see Matt. 5:16). The talent of our faith given to us from God must be multiplied (see Matt. 25:14 et seq.). Our Catholics, and even the catechumens, have to realize that growth and prosperity of God's kingdom also depends on them, and is part of their responsibility. As a consequence the mission catechism must not only be a catechism to be used in the missions, but to communicate a missionary spirit.

## CONCLUSION

These are the demands that a mission catechism must meet. For this achievement we need the co-operation of various experts, the exchange of experiences, and the pursuit of missiological studies. The execution which generally will consider a rather large and uniform territory, is done best under hierarchical guidance and authority. There will be time in the discussion to suggest details demanded by the peculiarities and various needs of the individual mission territories. Thus we may hope to obtain a useful instrument for the proclamation of the divine message of salvation in the missions.

# * Making a Catechism: A Personal Experience

CAMILO J. MARIVOET, C.I.C.M.
Rector of the Guadalupe Seminary, Makati, Rizal, Philippines

## *The National Catechism of the Philippines*

### PREHISTORY OF THE NEW INTERDIOCESAN CATECHISM

SINCE the end of Spanish rule in 1898, there has never been an official catechism in the Philippines, either on the national or the diocesan level. Hence the choice of catechisms was extremely erratic and chaotic. Usually schools bought whatever imported catechisms they could find in local bookstores, mainly the *Baltimore Catechism* and Cardinal Gasparri's, but their use was not consistent. In Catholic schools one could often witness a situation in which Bishop Jurgens' *Catechism in Pictures, I.* was used in Grades One and Two; in the next two grades, Morrow's *My Catechism, I;* in Grades Five and Six either Gasparri's *Catholic Catechism* or *Baltimore Catechism, II.* In the high school there was even more variety. In public schools the few children who attended the religion classes usually had no catechism text at all. Everybody can imagine the many inconveniences of such an unsystematic practice. Strongly sensing these difficulties because he himself was an outstanding catechist, Bishop Constancio Jurgens took the initiative in 1949 of calling together a group of priests who were either experienced religion teachers or specialists in catechetics. His purpose was to discuss the making of a new catechism and he wanted it to be a very good one, up-to-date in its method of presentation and its contents. In January 1950, at their annual meeting, the Ordinaries of the Philippines appointed Bishop Jurgens as the head of a special committee which was to prepare the first draft of an interdiocesan catechism for the Philippines. In the meantime his own *Catechism in Pictures, I* and *II,* would be used in public schools. He was given a free hand in selecting the members of the drafting committee. Some of those invited declined for various reasons; finally there were five members, but Bishop Jurgens himself fell seriously ill and died on June 3, 1952.

At the First Plenary Council of Manila, held in January 1953, the drafting committee was officially commissioned by the hierarchy to continue the work.

## DRAFTING COMMITTEE: MEMBERS AND WORK METHODS

After Bishop Jurgens' death, only four members remained. Two members had a very long experience in teaching religion to elementary school children. They had acquainted themselves thoroughly with the language – two different dialects – and with the mentality of these children. The third member is well versed in dogmatic and ascetic theology and at the same time an excellent catechist. The fourth member, secretary of the committee, is a specialist in catechetics. The committee, though limited to four by the force of circumstances, was intended from the beginning never to exceed six regular members. A big group goes on discussing endlessly and never satisfies all members; even our group of four had, at times, very animated and long discussions. To cite one example, the definition of the Church alone took us seven days of eight working hours. After three days we had finally agreed; when the whole chapter on the Church was finished, we checked it and found our definition still deficient; it took us another two and a half days to recast it, but subsequently we again clarified and shortened it.

Our work method was usually as follows. At the beginning one member prepared a draft, whereas the others read up on the matter to be discussed. This preparation took place during the school year. The actual full-day meetings took place during vacation: ten days each Christmas and about six weeks during each long summer vacation. The fact that all of us were engaged in educational and pastoral work necessitated such a procedure.

As the questions and answers are the framework of the catechism, in our meetings we took up the subject matter question by question, as outlined in the rough draft. We discussed each question as thoroughly as we could, changed the order, omitted or added as we saw fit. Later on we improved the system by preparing each of us his own preliminary draft before going to the meetings. This facilitated the work very much as it compelled each member to study the matter more thoroughly.

After finishing a chapter, a lesson, or any coherent part, we went over it again and revised it, for usually the discussions on later questions clarified earlier matters and forced us to make amendments in the earlier text. A similar revision was made after each major part, for example, when we had finished all the sacraments, we went through them again one by one.

When the whole first draft had been completed in this way, we submitted it to two professors of theology and to a few catechists: a religious sister known for her catechetical ability, a group of religious brothers, and an excellent lay catechist, though the latter failed to make any comments. When all these willing helpers had sent in their remarks, we revised once more the whole text on the basis of their notes. Their contribution was very valuable to our work.

We also had the draft sent out to several specialists abroad, in Austria, Belgium, France, Germany, and the Netherlands. Their replies and annotations came in after the revision just mentioned. Their excellent remarks forced us to make a few more alterations, particularly in the order of the catechism.

As the hierarchy had asked us to have the questions and answers examined and approved as soon as they were ready, we submitted the draft to the Ordinaries of the Philippines without first working out the planned expository catechism, in which the questions-and-answers would act only as the framework and as an accurate summary. The reactions of the hierarchy all dealt with minor points and necessitated few changes. The draft was finally approved for publication by the Ordinaries at their annual meeting of January 1956.

## PRINCIPLES UNDERLYING THE DRAFT

From the outset we wanted not merely to have a catechism for the Philippines; we were determined to make it a good and modern one in the five spheres of contents, order or sequence of the different parts, sociological adaptation, psychological adaptation, and form. In the light of the immense progress made in recent decades in the fields of theology, psychology, sociology, and education in general, and in the wake of strong catechetical, liturgical, and biblical movements, there was no more room or justification for a second-rate catechism; it simply had to be good or not exist at all.

Our first and foremost concern was the subject matter of the catechism. What was to be included and in what light was it to be presented? We wanted a good positive and synthetic view of the key points of our faith, particularly of those truths that are of vital importance for Christian living, and we desired to present these essentials in such a way that they would become the echo of God's appeal to man and values to live by, values which attach us to the person of Christ. In other words, our catechism was intended to be kerygmatic, whether one uses that term or not.

In this a catechism differs strongly from a theology manual for major seminarians. A theology handbook approaches the mysteries of our faith in an abstract and discursive manner and uses a highly technical language; the catechism views them from the angle of Christian living and avoids all technicalities when possible. In the past, too many catechisms were pocket-size digests of theology manuals, with a lot of definitions, distinctions, enumerations, and technical jargon. For example, even in its revised form, the *Baltimore Catechism* suffers from this evil. Even such an innocent-looking answer as the definition of a sacrament (already in the *Number One* edition for primary pupils) is too technical: "an outward sign, instituted by Christ to give grace". In this case one has to explain outward, sign, grace. Why not say directly holy actions and words (outward and sign) and divine life (grace)? This is also the reason why several such catechisms have to be supplied with a study guide for the difficult terms of each lesson.

We considered the apologetical approach, as still used in many catechisms, as outmoded; the catechism should directly lead to God, not directly disarm opponents. The great problem today is not to defend specific points under attack; in our times most people who fall away from the Church or refuse to enter her fold do so, not so much because of doctrinal objections or as individuals, but because of the materialism and indifference of their environment; and they gradually slip away with their whole group. In such cases a positive synthesis of our faith is the only adequate remedy and this, incidentally, proves also to be the best defense. A doubter cannot be but impressed by the beauty of a coherent and appealing whole.

We insist strongly on the idea of God. What our indifferent and earthly minded times need is a strong, exalted, and yet loving image of our heavenly Father. We do this best by presenting his attributes in themselves and in their relation to man and to the whole creation. We proceed from God and go back to him. Some call this the "theocentric" principle, but I prefer to avoid this term as it is confusing in the light of the following principles. More will be said about this when we discuss the arrangement of the catechism.

The catechism is strongly Christological or Christ-centred. Here we touch the heart and essence of our message. Our message can be summed up in one word: Christ, that is, Christ in his fulness. He is the centre of history, the fulfilment of the Old Testament; he lives on among God's new chosen people of the New Testament, in the Church, and communicates his redemption and life through her and leads her back to the achievement of his final return and the glory of heaven.

Christ, then, should become for the children not merely a great historical personality, but a contemporary, who speaks to them, lives and acts in them, for whom they become enthusiastic and to whom they commit themselves loyally and without reserve. Just look up how many times "Christ" appears in the text.

Also the Church occupies a very important place. It is through her prayers, sacrifices, and sacraments that Christ communicates his redemption and life to us, in her that he guides us through his Spirit, and in her fraternal community that we try to grow up in Christ. The sacraments appear not as means of grace, but as our participation in the mysteries and the life of Christ.

Our morality cannot be a doctrine of sin reduced to a literal "Thou shalt *not*". Christian morals are our response to our Father and our personal commitment to Christ. The commandments are closely linked to spirituality, for they must take their inspiration from theological and ecclesiological charity, from the other virtues, and from the beatitudes. That is why these are given before the commandments. Our morals must lead us to the achievement of our configuration with Christ at his second coming. Moral life does not consist in the juridical avoidance of sin but in the life of grace and virtue and even perfection; the counsels should inspire even laymen. Hence the attitude of the children should not be: "What is forbidden?" or "What must we do?" but: "What can and should we do for our loving Father?"

Our positive approach is also found in the wording of the commandments. Many will not agree with this and it is true that we should stick as closely as possible to the inspired words of scripture itself. Yet we found the reasons for effecting these changes very compelling. The negative phrasing of scripture was probably more striking for the primitive Hebrews than for us today. As the negative wording of the commandments is used to express the very positive laws of God, why not express them directly in a positive way? An additional reason was considered very important and clinched the case. English, though the language of the schools, is not the mother tongue of the Filipinos and it is almost impossible for Filipino children to understand the archaic terms of the biblical version of the commandments, however sacred they may be.

Much concerning the order of the catechism is easily understood in the light of our principles concerning the contents. We owe much inspiration to Father Hofinger's early article, "Die rechte Gliederung des katechetischen Lehrstoffes" in *Lumen Vitae*.[1]

The arrangement is very important, as it reflects the spirit of the catechism.

Here is a brief outline of the catechism.

Introduction: The Message of Christ

PART ONE: CHRIST'S MESSAGE: GOD LOVES US WITH AN IMMENSE LOVE

I. Christ reveals that God is our loving Father: the Creed.
   A. Who God is (our Father in heaven)

[1] II, 4 (1947), pp. 719–46.

B. God, the Creator
C. Jesus Christ, our Redeemer
D. The Holy Ghost and our sanctification (including the Church)

II. Christ gives us God's own life: grace and the sacraments.
A. Grace
B. The sacraments

PART TWO: WE ANSWER GOD'S LOVE FOR US BY LIVING AS CHILDREN

I. Our Answer in words: Praying with Christ.

II. Our Answer in deeds: Living like Christ.
A. Refusing to live like Christ: Sin
B. Living like Christ: Virtue
C. Living like Christ: the Ten Commandments
D. Living like Christ: Commandments of the Church
E. Perfect living in Christ
F. Triumphing with Christ

After this follow the ordinary prayers.

This outline gives already an idea of the principles that guided us in the selection and spirit of the contents.

We take God as our starting point. As said above, we proceed from God, go to Christ, and finally back to God. Imitating Deharbe, many catechisms, like the *Baltimore Catechism,* begin with the purpose of man's existence; in other words, their starting point is anthropocentric. Besides giving the impression that we go from man to God, with all this involves, such a departure entails the grave inconvenience that our religion easily appears as a system of duties rather than the glad tidings of God's redeeming love for man and our joyous answer to our Father in heaven. Indeed, if we begin by saying that man's purpose is to know, to love, and to serve God, then must follow what we must do to attain that end; we must believe in his truth; we must keep his commandments, and we must use the means of grace. This indicates also the arrangement of such catechisms: Creed, commandments, sacraments.

Another thing which cannot be brought to light in such a sequence, especially with the commandments placed in between the creed and the sacraments, is the intimate link between dogma (particularly the incarnation, redemption, and the Church guided by the Holy Spirit) and the sacraments. The sacraments should be placed after the creed and before the commandments. In this way it shows that the sacraments extend the meeting of the human and the divine elements in the person of Christ; they effect in us Christ's passion and resurrection and thus let us participate in his mysteries and give us his life; and that life of Christ we find in the Mystical Body of Christ, the Church.

When the commandments occupy the third place, it is much easier to see their connection with both the creed and the sacraments. Thus the commandments become an answer to our God-given faith and the example of Christ, and are easily put into practice with the help of the strength of Christ drawn from the sacraments. Also the sacraments and the cult surrounding them are sources of Christian living and spirituality.

To complete the creed, we also indicate briefly the eschatological part of it at the end of the creed, but we chose to explain this more thoroughly at the end of the catechism. Thus it appears both as God's crowning gift (at the end of the creed) and as the crowning achievement of our living with Christ (end of the catechism).

The arrangement gave us a lot of headaches. We were very sure about the order creed-sacraments-commandments, but we were not sure in what light we might best consider the eschatological part, hence where to place it. The same held true for prayer (as part of the first commandment or our answer in words?), Christian perfection (before or after the commandments?), the Blessed Trinity (at the beginning or after the Holy Ghost; showing the divine Persons at work first and then say who they are, or vice versa?), sin (before or after virtue: first negative or positive?) and a few other points. At the beginning we tried to delay clear-cut solutions by taking the sacraments first of all; but this dilly-dallying proved costly, as it later necessitated not only changes in the arrangement but many changes in the text as well.

## SOCIOLOGICAL ADAPTATION

The catechism is intended to bring the Good News of our salvation in Christ to school children who are members of the Mystical Body of Christ in the Philippines in the twentieth century. It must be adapted, then, to their milieu and mentality.

This means, first, that it is made for the faithful, not for theologians: while being theologically accurate and comprehensive, it must be kept simple; no theological terms should be used where they can be avoided, for the faithful do not understand them readily and an understanding of Christian doctrine is not only for the better educated but for all.

Made for members or members-to-be of the Church in the twentieth century, the catechism should, as said above, bring to the fore these truths and practices that lead best to Christian living in this age and this setting. Made for Filipinos, it should take cognizance of the existing religious and moral conditions in our country and adapt itself to them, as in the matter of delayed baptism, marriage practices, holidays of obligations, etc. To determine the type and level of school for which the catechism was destined was a tremendous problem for which there is no clear-cut solution. Educational situations are so varied in the Philippines, even within one city or school district, that we could directly aim at only one type of school, that in which conditions, though not the best perhaps, are average, that is, where religion is taught regularly as a part of the curriculum and not merely tolerated after school hours, where standards are normal or at least average, where the practice of religion is possible. These conditions are fulfilled in most Catholic schools. For other schools each pastor must decide according to the situation prevailing in his parish what can be given and in what class.

## PSYCHOLOGICAL ADAPTATION AND FORM

Both aspects will be treated together because they are intimately interwoven. The message taught in the catechism is to be adapted to the child, who is constantly growing and developing. This adaptation, however, does not mean that we aim our message or reduce it to the limitations of their experience; it does mean that we use a language that, while respecting the integrity of the revelation, remains within their grasp. In this way we open their minds and hearts to the mystery and help them to pass from stage to stage.

We use various means towards this end. First of all, the language is kept simple and clear and the style direct. We had the words of the catechism checked against the vocabulary lists for the class in which the particular text is to be taken up and we rarely went beyond it. Each question and note bears in the margin the number of the class for which it is destined. The present catechism will, as we shall see later, become a graded catechism, progressively more complete and difficult, though centred on the same key truths (concentric system); in this it follows the development of the child. When entirely worked out, it will consist of three catechisms for the elementary school alone. Firstly, a first communion catechism for Grades One and Two; secondly, the catechism for Grades Three and Four; and thirdly, the intermediate catechism for Grades Five and Six. For the secondary school we plan no formal catechism, but we will make the catechism the *basis* of a set of high school religion textbooks.

Another, though related, psychological principle is that the children take in later subject matter in terms of what they already know. This is why the answers which appear in the lower grades are expressed in the same terms for the higher years; and if they had by necessity to remain incomplete, they receive merely a complement in the later years. For example (one of the few definitions), "What is confirmation?" "Confirmation is the sacrament that gives us the Holy Ghost in a special way,* to make us strong and mature Christians, witnesses of Jesus Christ, and lay apostles of the Catholic Church."

This question up to the asterisk is destined for Grade 3 and will be printed up to that point only in Catechism Number Two. The complete answer will be given in Catechism Number Three and is to be studied in Grade 5.

We made the text rhythmic as much as we could. This facilitates understanding and memorization. Wherever we could, we divided the answer and the prayers in parallel thought-lines for the same reason, and to make the eye help the other faculties.

With the same end in view, we made the answers always repeat the question and we tried never to make any inversions or to make the answers exceed the bounds of the questions. If one asks "what?" he should not try to add also the reasons why.

The catechism is also what I should like call "personal" or "personalistic". In dealing with God, we do not ask what God is, as many catechisms do, but who God is – our Father in heaven – not a collection of abstract qualities. His attributes are stated later and always made concrete and related to man. Similarly, we dwell long on the Person of Christ. The Church is not merely the hierarchy but also we, with Christ in our midst, or rather, as our head. The creed is not our belief in something but in Someone. Also the child is always personally involved: when do *we* first receive the divine life? What is your dignity and *your* responsibility as a baptized Catholic? When do *we* have faith? What should death mean to *us*? In this way, incidentally, we avoid also many definitations, but most important is that we make our religion a personal appeal from God and a personal answer on our part. Yet notice that we do not say, "I, me," but "we, us". The personal invitation and answer take place in the Mystical Body and are, therefore, personal and communal at the same time.

One of the earliest memories of many of us is that the ugliest, cheapest, and least appealing of all books we ever used was the catechism. Does this fact not entail an unconscious depreciation of our religion itself? That is why we planned to publish the catechism in an attractive format and to illustrate it richly. The format is satisfactory, but unluckily the illustrations are far less successful. We had to use temporarily those of Bishop Jurgens' *Catechism in Pictures* and could not yet afford to replace them by new and better ones. We hope to do so gradually, beginning when *Number One* is published. Also the typography will differ according to the age level.

### WORK STILL TO BE DONE

Much remains to be done. The catechism as it stands now contains only the questions and answers, some notes that expand on the text, and a few texts from scripture. As stated earlier, the questions and answers are only the framework of the catechism. The catechism is to become an expository catechism (what the Germans call *Lehrstückkatechismus*), or rather a whole series of graded expository catechisms.

The first book of the series, destined for grades One and Two, is almost completed now. The first and second catechism (Grades One to Four) should be biblical and narrative, whereas the third should be more systematic.

Each lesson will generally appear as follows. A narrative, biblical whenever possible, containing the core of the doctrine exposed in the lesson; then a positive exposition of the doctrine; this is followed by the formal question and answer, which concisely and correctly sums up the main point or points of the exposition; this question and answer is usually to be memorized, although at present we have too many such questions for memorization. Future editions will indicate by their typography the questions not to be learned by heart, but to be known for their contents only. Even more of such questions may be added as review questions.

After this may follow, according to the nature of the subject matter, biblical texts – not as proofs but as the authentic word of God, whose living word is of more value than any human formulation – liturgical applications, occasionally striking sayings of the saints.

Then come assimilation exercises, practical applications for Christian living, perhaps directions for assignments and religious expression by means of suggested drawings, songs, prayers including psalms, activities, and other such means. Each lesson, particularly for the lower classes, should be illustrated by means of pictures that are both artistic and truly catechetical.

When thus planned, the lessons will naturally lead the catechist to use one form or the other of the text-developing or psychological method, like the Munich Method, and no longer stick to a method consisting merely in explaining a catechism text and then memorizing it, the so-called text-explanatory method. Another very important advantage of such a type of lesson is that our catechesis becomes liturgical and biblical, as any good catechesis should be, thus opening all registers for proclaiming our message: the historical, the liturgical, and the systematic. At the same time it integrates Christian living with the lessons.

The next task, of tremendous importance, is the preparation of a good set of teacher's manuals accompanying the textbooks. In these the catechists should find pointers for general methods and for work methods to be used in connection with each particular lesson, if possible also a short but penetrating study of the doctrine behind that lesson – the catechist should know much more than what he will teach the child –, then a model lesson on each specific topic, further materials, suggestions or activities, exercises, and assignments, and indications for the selection and use of audio-visual aids. Only then can our catechists give the best that is in them and bring out the best that is in the children.

We also plan to add at the end of the textbook a "little ritual" with, besides the prayers, the ceremonies of baptism, preparation and prayers for confession, prayers of the Mass, extreme unction, the liturgical year, etc.

Finally, when all this is finished, we should not rest satisfied with the work done. Our work will never be accomplished; we must constantly review and improve it.

# * The Syllabus for Religious Instruction in the Missions

J. VALLS, S.J.
St Mary's High School, Bombay

SOME years ago, the title of this paper would perhaps have sounded preposterous. Yet the era of pioneering improvization is gone, and missionaries all over the world are realizing more and more the need of a syllabus for religious instruction in their own dioceses, that is, an official, common, systematic and well-coordinated plan of religious education.

## *The Meaning of "Syllabus for Religious Instruction"*

It will certainly aid the study of this need if we explain briefly the meaning of "Syllabus for Religious Instruction". We take the word "syllabus" as an organic unit, that is, a systematic, well-coordinated plan of religious studies and practices which takes the student from the very start of his religious training and leads him on progressively, keeping in mind the different stages of intellectual development through which he passes, to a full growth in Christian knowledge and life.

Hence, the term "syllabus" comprises not only the index of heads or main subjects of the course of Christian teaching; it also points out the final goal or objective to be achieved by this training, as well as the intermediary objectives to be realized at every stage of development; it explains also the method to be followed and the different activities to be undertaken so as to secure the final aim we strive after.

From the above description of the term "syllabus" it is evident that by the word "instruction" we mean much more than mere teaching and learning. We mean "education", "formation of the Christian", "practical guidance", "exercise"; in short, the principle "learning by doing" fittingly applies here, but it means "doing" with personal conviction.

## IMPORTANCE OF THE SYLLABUS FOR RELIGIOUS INSTRUCTION IN MISSION COUNTRIES

### *Missionary Catechesis, Basic Religious Instruction*

Missionary catechesis is of fundamental importance for the individual to whom it is imparted, and for the whole community among whom that individual lives. St. Paul, speaking of his preaching among the Corinthians, says: "Yes, you may have ten thousand schoolmasters in Christ, but no more than one father; it was I who begot you in Jesus Christ, when I preached the gospel to you" (1 Cor. 4:15). This phrase indicates that St. Paul looked upon his missionary catechesis as the laying of the foundations of a new life in Christ. Being, as it is, the first religious instruction, it plays a preponderant role in the formation and perseverance of the new individual Christian. A preliminary teaching which has been done in an improvised manner, diffuse, superficial or not understood by the catechumen, is very difficult to remedy later on. Hence, although the initial instructions call for something very simple and easy, still the essential truths should be thoroughly explained; this explanation must at the same time make known the dogmas of our faith and help the catechumen to live them with ease. Only a well conceived syllabus will bring out the principal doctrinal idea and will place all the other truths in their right perspective.

Missionary catechesis is fundamental in a wider sense; for, while training new Christians individually, it at the same time sows Christianity in the midst of the whole population. Missionary apostolate aims less at multiplying the number of Christians than at firmly rooting Christianity in the first members of the mission. As the Holy Father says in the encyclical *Princeps Pastorum:* "The number of Christians will mean little if they are wanting in quality, if they are not staunch in the profession of their faith, if their spiritual life lacks depth and fails to produce visible fruits, if, after having been born to the life of grace, they give no evidence of that vigorous youth which is ever ready for right and fruitful action." Only a well-planned syllabus can achieve this. For it requires a very judicious choice of the subject matter and a solid catechesis which arranges, presents, clearly illustrates the fundamental truths, and then proceeds to build the life of believers on them.

### *Missionary Catechesis Adapted to Ancient Cultures and Modern Problems*

A second reason which points to the importance and consequent need of a syllabus is the question of the adaptation of the Christian message to the peoples we have to evangelize. It is enough to read the encyclicals *Evangelii praecones,* of Pius XII, and *Princeps Pastorum,* of John XXIII, to realize at once the importance the Church gives to the question of adaptation. But adaptation means that the Church has not only to adapt her message to ancient cultures, which are on the wane in spite of an apparent resurgence due often to emotional, and hence temporary, feelings; she has also to be much more ready for the problems which are cropping up on all sides at full speed, in mission countries perhaps much faster even than in the Christian countries. It is good to hear what the Holy Father says in this respect in *Princeps Pastorum*. Quoting *Donum Dei* he says: "Most mission territories are going through a phase of social, economic and political evolution that is pregnant with consequences for their future." The Holy Father continues: "Problems which, in some countries, are already solved or find elements of solution in tradition, confront other nations with an urgency that demands a quick solution; this urgency is not without danger, in so far as it might lead to hasty decisions and to incautious acceptance of doctrines that ignore or contradict the religious interests of individuals and nations. For their own good and for the good of the Church, Catholics may not ignore these problems nor wait till they are given harmful solutions which it will afterwards take much greater efforts to correct."

This adaptation to the problems of the modern world (either those common to the whole world, like science, technology, social upheaval, or those touching more directly the mission countries, like the resurgence of national ideas with its consequent dangers for the Catholic spirit, and the rush for economic as well as political progress and independence) must necessarily find an echo in the syllabus for religious instruction. These problems bring along new ideals and concepts, they enrich old terms with deeper and wider meanings, they make us look at things from different angles and give them different values, with the result that they finally influence our Christian, spiritual and supernatural lives; and it is the duty of the Church either in the teaching given, or in sermons, and on all occasions, to Christianize our new concepts, to raise and supernaturalize our values of things. All these things are the task of the syllabus for religious instruction.[1]

*The Role of the Syllabus in the Present Catechetical Movement*

We may add a third reason to indicate the importance of a systematic catechesis in the missions, namely, the part the syllabus proper plays in the modern renewal of catechetics. Three important factors influence every catechesis. The syllabus, the text-book, the catechist. Formerly, a capital importance was given to the text book. The work of the syllabus was to fix the number of pages and chapters of the text-book which had to be gone through each term and each year. The catechist was something of a mouth-piece whose duty was to go through the text of the answers, give a more or less clear explanation of the difficult words and make the children repeat the answers again and again until they were able to memorize them.

Nowadays, the roles have changed; whilst due importance has been given to the catechist and the syllabus, the role of the

[1] In this respect it might be useful to read the titles of the articles of Vol. XIII, 1958, No. 4 of *Lumen Vitae:* "Catechesis in a Technical World". (Technical Attitude and Approach to the Liturgical World – Technical Mentality and the Teaching of Religion – Planning Religious Instruction in a Vocational School, etc.)

text-book has become secondary. According to Klemens Tilmann the catechism is meant simply to be an aid; for the catechist it provides suggestion, and for the children, it provides matter for study and repetition.

"The most important factor in religious instruction", says Dr. Tilmann, "is you, yourself and what you teach." According to this statement, the catechist comes first in importance, the syllabus comes very close to him. The modern catechetical renewal is concerned with the contents of the teaching. We must see that the mystery of Christ, the good news of the gospel, comes first, that it is brought sharply into focus; that it permeates the explanation of all the other truths; that all these truths are presented in their proper perspective so that they clearly illustrate the fundamental Christian message.

Now as we have already said, this focussing and careful arrangement is the task of the syllabus; hence its importance. In mission lands this importance is more keenly felt because the missionary is not always the teacher; he has very frequently to confide this part of his apostolic ministry to lay catechists who need guidance, inspiration, and training in methods which they get from the syllabus.

## CHARACTERISTIC FEATURES OF THE SYLLABUS FOR RELIGIOUS INSTRUCTION IN THE MISSIONS

### *The Goal of the Mission Catechesis*

Having considered the importance and need of a syllabus for religious instruction in the Missions, let us now study the characteristic features of such a syllabus. We shall understand these better if we begin by saying just a few words on the goal or aim of our mission catechesis.

There is no doubt that every Christian has a twofold role to play in this world. Having been grafted by baptism into Christ, the divine vine, "we are to follow the truth in a spirit of charity, and so grow up in everything into a due proportion with Christ, who is our head" (Eph. 4:15). At the same time, in virtue of the "mandate" Christ gave to the whole infant

Church on the mount in Galilee after his resurrection, we have to be the "light of the world", "the seed of the harvest", "the leaven buried away in three measures of meal" (Matt. 13:33). This, though common to every Christian, applies in a very special manner to every Christian in mission lands. The chief characteristic feature of mission catechesis is not only to break the charm of paganism and unbelief and lay the foundations of a new life in Christ in the new Christians individually; it is also to plant Christianity securely in every member of the mission so that the faith and the life of those faithful Christians serve as a solid basis for future generations.

The Holy Father says: "Everyone who calls himself a Christian must realize that it is a fundamental and primary duty for him to be a witness of the truth in which he believes and of the grace by which he has been transformed. . .". It is easy to see how such a witness could bear special fruits in mission lands. Our Lord himself said: "So let your light shine before men that they will see your good works and glorify your Father who is in heaven." And St. Peter: "Your life amidst the Gentiles must be beyond reproach; decried as malefactors, you must let them see, from your honourable behaviour, what you are; they will praise God for you, when his time comes to have mercy on them." (1 Pet. 2:12)

### *A Well-orientated Teaching*

Given this decided dual purpose of mission catechesis, there is no doubt that the first characteristic feature of the syllabus in mission lands must be a perfect orientation in the teaching. The syllabus must present a perfectly focussed picture of the mystery of Christ: at every stage of its development (either at every stage corresponding to a new state of development in the mind of the child in school, or at every phase of progress in the case of the adult catechesis: baptismal catechumenate, first communion and confirmation catechumenate, marriage catechumenate, parochial catechesis), a thoroughly stressed teaching of our origin from the Father and our return to the Father in union with Christ brought about objectively by grace, subjectively by the imitation of his life, through the Holy Spirit must be clearly stressed. Secondly, a judicious selection of material is needed (particular doctrines considered necessary or very helpful to understand our Christian vocation and to live a truly Christian life, likewise theoretical doctrines of fundamental importance for Christian life, like the Blessed Trinity, creation, elevation, incarnation, etc.). Third, (in the case of the higher stages of development) a well thought-out arrangement of the remaining truths, placed in the right relation to the central core of our teaching rounds out the picture.

### *Personal Interest and Community Liturgical Life*

Theoretical religious instruction too little in touch with life would be particularly harmful in mission countries where souls have to be awakened to the Christian way of life, educated and perfected in it without the help of Christian surroundings. The formation of resolute and fervent Christians depends on enlightenment in knowledge and a great love of Christian values.

In order to attain this double end we must first create in the growing child, as well as in the progressing Christian adult, interest to advance and deepen his knowledge of religion; hence the syllabus should see that all those pedagogical means intended to create such interest are fostered and put into practice (home-made catechism, group research work, debating circles, study circles, Catholic Evidence Guild, etc).

Secondly, the syllabus should stress the need and importance of a Christian communal liturgical life. The Christians, particulary in the missions, must come together not only to take part in the liturgy as such whenever possible, but also to pray together.

Participation of the whole Christian community in the liturgical life as such may be difficult in some mission stations far distant from the mission centre. Yet we should remember that liturgy is the Church's worship and this means above all, prayer, the Church's prayer. To lead our Christians to the liturgy means, first of all, to lead them to liturgical prayer.

Now the purpose of the Sunday meetings without the priest should be to train our Christians in liturgical prayer. This means first of all to train them in the basic attitude of the Christian prayer in which the divine Father predominates; Christ is the elder brother with whom we go to the Father; the phrase "thank you", the prayer of praise and thanksgiving, is much more to be insisted upon and inculcated than the word – "please" or the prayer of petition. In fact, the simple prayers which form the common repertoire of the community should be repeated and memorized, and should express in an exemplary way the four aims of worship.

It means also to train them to pray *dogmatically* (which of course, does not mean dogmatic terminology but content). The explanation of the catechism by the catechist should end with an appropriate prayer recited by all. It means to train them in common prayer which should lead them finally to a more active participation in the liturgy proper, whenever possible.

By this participation, the Christian grows in communal Christian knowledge and feels himself to be a member of the universal community of the true servants of God, intimately united to the Church Triumphant even if he suffers through living in a pagan atmosphere. By a regular and, as far as possible, frequent participation in the sacrifice of the Mass the Christian will be encouraged to exercise himself bravely in the spirit of Christian dedication and sacrifice.

The Holy Father says: "Union in prayer and active participation in the divine mysteries of the liturgy contributes most efficaciously to the fulness and richness of Christian life in individuals and in the community."

### *Adapted to the People*

Missionary catechesis is to bring Christ to the people to whom we are sent; hence a third characteristic feature of the syllabus for religious instruction in the missions is that it should be adapted to the mentality and convictions of the people of the place.

Strictly speaking, missionary catechesis is addressed to pagans, to those who ask for baptism, who have another conception of God, the supernatural, and the world, and must be initiated into Christian ideas. Consequently, some truths of our Christian religion will be entirely alien to them, others will be different and even opposed to their conceptions, with the result that even the fundamental truth of the mystery of Christ may not be properly understood and fail to produce the religious experience it is called to arouse.

Now these conceptions will have to be taken into consideration in the setting of the syllabus; consequently, though the positive teaching of Christian doctrine should come first, and not apologetics and polemics, the Catholic teaching of certain truths will have to be emphasized more clearly and forcibly so that they may throw their full and perfect light on the core of our Christian message.

Besides, conceptions are accompanied by mental attitudes, practical dispositions, customs, practices and festivities, which will either have to be corrected and christianized or removed entirely from the Christian community; for, as we said at the beginning, the scope of the syllabus is not mere teaching and learning but also education, formation of the Christian, and practical guidance.

### *Simplicity of Method*

Up to now we have dealt with those distinctive characteristics of the syllabus which come from the very nature of the missionary transmission of the gospel message. As to the method, we may say, in general, that the syllabus for religious instruction in the missions must insist on Christian initiation through the bible story and community liturgical prayer carried along simultaneously.

The preaching of the gospel in mission lands today has not changed since the preaching of the gospel by our Lord among the Jews and since the preaching of the gospel to the Gentiles by the apostles – *Pauperes evangelizantur*. Except for individual cases, like the one of Nicodemus, which call for individual attention, missionary catechesis is often addressed to adolescents and adults who have not had any appreciable schooling. Hence, the bible story method seems to be the more advantageous, as it takes the bible story as the basis and body of the religion class, draws from it the revealed truth or the Christian moral principle to be taught, and brings the lesson home in a concrete, graphic and ideal way in order to provoke a supernatural experience in the soul of the catechumen.

The community liturgical prayer, as explained above, besides completing and confirming this supernatural experience, will bring the practice of a truly Christian family prayer to the new Christian home.

## PRACTICAL APPLICATION

After having considered the need and importance of a syllabus for religious instruction in the missions, and the fundamental principles which should characterize such a syllabus, it will not be beyond the scope of this paper to study the working principles of a particular syllabus, not in order to copy it mechanically but to draw suggestions for working out others along similar lines.

In May last year, Cardinal Gracias published and promulgated a scheme of religious instruction, under the significant title "The Message of Christianity", for all Catholic schools in the Archdiocese of Bombay. It is this syllabus we are going to study.

### *The Catechumen*

We take the term "catechumen" in its broadest sense, namely the person to be catechized. In our case it is the Catholic child attending any of the many Catholic schools of the Archdiocese of Bombay, the future Catholic youth of Bombay.

Bombay, though still a mission diocese with several flourishing mission centres, embraces a Catholic community which in its majority originates from longstanding Catholic ancestry. Practically all the children attend Catholic schools and come from deeply Christian and particularly pious homes. The Cardinal gave a very vivid picture of the Catholic youth of Bombay in his Inaugural Address under the auspices of the University Catholic Federation of Bombay. "When I take a general survey of Catholic life as lived and manifested in our parishes, I do find a notable increase in devotion and piety.... A strong devotional life will certainly keep our hearts warm; warm with the warmth of divine life; and shelter them against the chill blasts of modern materialism and neo-paganism. . . . But the main purpose of my address is that the mind has to be protected and developed on sound lines. If I know our youth they certainly have enquiring minds. . . . An enquiring mind can only be satisfied if the individual himself or herself is prepared to take to a positive and systematic study of the question involved. It would seem that for the most part our Catholics are content with perusing small publications.... What about the solid Catholic literature of which there is no dearth? Today reading is not any longer a luxury but a necessity – a necessity induced by the development of the intellect by education."

## *The Goal*

Having this true-to-life picture in mind, the Bombay syllabus takes the child as it comes from the warm atmosphere of a true Christian family where piety and devotion reign. Throughout the long eleven years of the school career, it sees to "the religious development of the entire child. In our case, this means developing the two lives in the child, the natural and the supernatural, blending them into a new creation, a Christian, a replica of Jesus Christ."[2] Throughout this same school career, "the teaching of religion is conducted in such a way as to create and develop in the child activity and personal interest in the subject. This personal activity will awake in him a desire to increase and perfect his religious knowledge during his youth and late maturity."[3]

"It creates, during the final year, in the grown-up child, a taste for spiritual life and the things of our faith . . . so that once he leaves school, and his religious instruction is reduced

[2] Bombay syllabus, p. 9. [3] Op. cit., p. 9.

to the essential practices of a Catholic, the services he attends, particularly the Mass, and the instructions he receives, may speak to him and be sustainers and strengtheners of his spiritual life."[4]

### *Intermediary Objectives and Methods*

In order to attain this final and lofty goal, the Bombay syllabus fixes a series of intermediary objectives along the long way, keeping in mind the successive mental development of the growing child.

It begins by leading the infant child to Jesus. "It is of capital importance that this (infant)-period of religious instruction should culminate in the child's first meeting with Jesus at holy communion."[5]

This leading of the child to Jesus is sought by awakening in the child the basic attitude of Christian prayer. Catechism is taught through the medium of prayers. "The chief objective is to have them (the children) understand the general idea of prayer and to have them know the prayers exactly."[6] God, the Creator, is presented to them as a loving Father who builds this wonderful world as a house for us to live in; in a child-like way our relations to God of praise, worship, repentance and petition are drawn from the fact of creation, and the common prayers are taught and explained according to these four ends of religion.[7]

Once the child has met Jesus, he is left with him under his tender care. The objective of the lower school period is "to cultivate, at the same time, a true spirit of piety and devotion, so that the experience felt at the first meeting of the child with Jesus, on the day of his first communion, may be lasting, and every further reception of the sacraments of penance and communion may be more sincere and fervent".[8] From this stage forward, the divine message which Christ came to announce from the Father is presented, explained and developed to the growing mind of the child, though through different media.

[4] Op. cit., p. 54. [5] Op. cit., p. 12. [6] Op. cit., p. 13.
[7] Op. cit., pp. 15–19. [8] Op. cit., p. 20.

"Our religion centres around Jesus Christ. Teaching religion means leading the children to Christ. Jesus, however, professed to be the way that leads to the Father. We become one with Jesus through the Holy Spirit whom Jesus sends into our hearts." "Consequently, in this present scheme, the teaching of Christian doctrine has been built at every stage in the religious instruction of the child round this central plan."[9]

In the lower school period it is God himself who, through the medium of the bible story, wished to manifest to us the mystery of Christ in a concrete and ideal-like way. "The objective is not so much the systematic explanation of the Christian faith which finds its confirmation in the stories of the Bible, but rather the unfolding of the chief truths of the catechism as God himself wished them to be manifested in actuality."[10]

In the middle and subsequent school periods, the child is given something definite to attain. In this middle school period he is to "memorize the catechetical formulae".[11] "All leading catechetical methods insist on this point: There must be a period in the long years of religious formation of a child, when he should be made to memorize the catechetical formulae."[12] *The Way and the Life,* the text book of this period, is intended to be a preparation for the German Catechism. In it the questions and answers have been taken from the German Catechism, yet a choice selection from them has been made.

During this same period, the child, practically initiated in previous periods into the basic attitude of Christian prayer, is now introduced into the liturgy proper, so that the activity which is bubbling within him may find an adequate outlet in Catholic faith, life, and action. This mystery of Christ is now explained to the child through the liturgy.

The high school period is the constructive period. "The objective in view during this period of religious instruction should be to take as a foundation the solid, concrete and clear teaching of the Church, as presented and memorized in the middle school period, to try now to construct the edifice of religious knowledge of our growing child as something of vital interest to him . . . .

[9] Op. cit., pp. 6–7. [10] Op. cit., p. 22. [11] Op. cit., p. 27.
[12] Op. cit., p. 26.

The catechetical formulae, learnt in the previous stage, have now to be ground down and, so to say, masticated, in order to be assimilated by the pupils and be turned into a source of supernatural and spiritual life for them."[13]

Naturally, the mystery of Christ is explained to them through the systematic medium of the catechism. Yet "we should not try to make our children little Catholic Encyclopedias, loading their minds with unnecessary details, but we must rather make them convinced Catholics who know their faith and the moral principles of Christ, and who understand the part this faith plays and how these principles bear on their spiritual as well as on their private and public lives . . . . The book is meant to be a pupil's book; yet it is not designed as a text book in the normal sense of that word."[14]

### *The Immediate Formation of the Catholic Youth*

The goal of the Bombay Syllabus is, as we said, to train the Catholic child of today to be the Catholic youth of tomorrow. Throughout the school career the syllabus strives after it in a remote way; but during the high school period and the school-leaving year, the syllabus works at this goal in a direct and immediate manner. The Bombay syllabus sends the grown-up child into the world equipped with three valuable books: the Catechism, the Bible, and the Missal. During these last two periods it trains him to use them and to read them intelligently.

We have seen how it trains the future youth to use the catechism. During the high school period the syllabus gives the pupil an introduction to a deeper and more serious study of this subject in later college years." In the school-leaving year "the main text book should be Stedman's *Sunday Missal* brought to life for the pupils by the use of the *Libica* method. They should keep a note book. From the text of the Sunday Masses the Christ of prophecy and of Gospel should arise to meet them; upon this text should be seen to rest the truths of the catechism and the life of the Mystical Body of Christ, the Church. The students

[13] Op. cit., pp. 38, 39 [14] Op. cit., p. 41.

must be taught to see and experience how the whole plan of God's love is accomplished by the glory of the Mass."[15] "With the goal still in mind, that is, preparing the child for life, a parallel course of lessons for life is given along with some fundamentals bearing on vocational guidance."

## *Conclusion*

These are the working principles of the Bombay syllabus. As Father Hofinger says in *Asia,*[16] "this pamphlet *(The Message of Christianity)* will encourage missionary bishops to direct their missionaries and catechists along similar lines". It was a real enterprise brought about by "an exemplary collaboration of local experts with leading catechetical institutes such as the Catechetical Centre of De Nobili College in Poona and the International Centre for Studies in Religious Education." It was an enterprise God has already blessed abundantly, for "a good number of teachers, in answer to a questionnaire circulated by his Eminence among the schools, positively thought that the present syllabus is a help to transform the children's life and is certainly conducive to their getting a better grasp of our faith, and coming to love it more."[17]

[15] Op. cit., p. 55. [16] May 1960, p. 478.
[17] Report of the Catholic Bishops' Conference of India Standing Committee, February 1960.

# THE CATECHETICAL IMPORTANCE OF DIVINE WORSHIP IN THE MISSIONS

# Basic Links between Liturgy and Catechesis

JOSEF BLOMJOUS, W.F.
Bishop of Mwanza, Tanganyika

IN late years the connection between liturgy and catechetics has been repeatedly discussed. Mostly, the discussion has turned on the practical aspects of the problem: a fact explained by the origin of the modern liturgical movement and its contemporary, the movement for catechetical revival (stimulated above all by the historical research in matters liturgical). But also the innovations in catechesis (prompted especially by studies of pedagogy and modern psychology) have aroused general interest.

The mainspring of this interest has been a preoccupation with problems of a pastoral and practical nature. This fact explains how it has come about that some have gone to exaggerated extremes; either through an excess of zeal, or through feelings of panic at the inadequacy of current religious teaching, the impotence of the liturgy to affect daily life or to attract non-Christians. These exaggerated reactions to long-standing practices which have shown their inadequacy are due to people not giving sufficient attention to the complexity of liturgical and catechetical problems, or to one or other of their many facets. Hence, for example, the tendency to look on the liturgy as the *only* adequate means of instruction for Christians, or the false idea that the liturgy has for its *principal* aim the inculcation of revealed truths; and in regard to catechetics to think of its object as not being instruction but solely the cultivation of Christian attitudes! All these exaggerations, instead of forwarding the cause of liturgical and catechetical revival, have been an obstacle to it. Only by keeping in mind every aspect of liturgy and catechetics can one see what is really their fundamental connection and what union there should be between them both in the Church's life and in pastoral practice.

In truth, the liturgy is not only a source of religious knowledge, but it is above all the *laus Dei* through and in Christ our Head. Nevertheless it is *laus Dei* that makes us live our faith and see its significance, and what should be its practical consequences; for liturgy is not merely a series of rites and prayers intended for the praise of God: one of its essential parts is the announcing of God's word through its scriptural texts and the interpretation of them; another is teaching the Christian community the main lines of the Christian mystery through the unfolding of the liturgical cycle and the ceremonies which accompany it. It is true also to say that the liturgy is not a mere human *opus Dei* in the sense that what we do is directed towards God; but still more it is *opus Dei* in the sense that it is a great *sacramentum* by means of which God works in us in the person of Christ. On the other hand we must say that the liturgy is not merely the official prayer of the Church producing its effects *ex opere operantis Ecclesiae;* it is also the prayer of the Christian community, and can have its full effect only through the active participation of the faithful. But such active participation is possible only if the liturgy is intelligible in itself and actually understood by the faithful.

Likewise, the teaching of the Christian faith has also two sides to it: catechesis ought to give not merely speculative knowledge . . . religion is not just another subject on the school curriculum; catechesis is especially religious education and must give formation in Christian living. From another angle we see that conscientious Christian living requires the inculcation of true and solid religious knowledge.

In order to avoid all misunderstandings, I would like to insist also on another aspect of this problem of the relationship between liturgy and catechesis. Very often when people talk about "catechesis" or "the catechism", especially in the home countries, they have in mind almost exclusively the instruction given to children and adolescents. But to understand the essential relationship between the two, it is absolutely necessary to bear in mind that religious instruction as such is concerned not only with children but also with adults. In mission countries the problem of a catechetical renewal is primarily that of how to deliver the gospel message to adults, whether they be catechumens or baptized Christians. This accounts for the extreme importance in missionary catechesis of the *milieu,* of the institution of the catechumenate, and of introduction into the economy of salvation by means of biblical instruction and participation in the cultural life of the Church, the liturgy.

Having reviewed the existing problem in this introduction, let us now move on to the subject of this paper, namely, the fundamental interrelation of missionary catechesis and missionary worship. The basis of the connection between liturgy and catechesis lies in the relationship between the Church's power of worship and her liturgical activity on the one hand, her teaching authority and work on the other. We know that Christ as priest, prophet, and king, gives being and continuity to the Church by the triple impact of his sanctifying influence, his life-giving teaching and his divine authority. From this threefold source comes to the Church, in the image of St. Paul, the system of joints and ligaments by which there flows from the head to the body an increase of charity and truth, that is to say an increase of divine love. But if it is true that we can and must distinguish in the work and role of Christ and his Church first the aspect of cult and salvation, then that of teaching and prophecy, and lastly that of sovereignty and jurisdiction, it is no less true that these are as inseparable and interdependent in the Church as they are in the person of Christ. The living unity of the Christian mystery and the life-giving unity of the Church's mystery mean that in the Church there is no division (and in our pastoral practice there should be none) between the teaching of dogma and the exercise of worship, between moral law and supernatural life, between ecclesiastical legislation and the inner influence of the Holy Spirit. It is because of this fundamental connection that the history of the Church shows how she constantly tends to re-establish unity and balance between these differing aspects, a unity and balance that our short-sightedness and our human inconsequences constantly tend to compromise. And it seems to me that one of the main duties of the hierarchy in these new countries of non-western culture, which are beginning to take their place in the universal

Catholic Church, will be to profit by these lessons drawn from the Church's history. The hierarchy must do all it can to give due weight to all of these aspects; bishops must use the positive riches to be found in all the ways pursued by pastoral work and catechesis in the course of the ages. Thus it is certain that the systematic instruction in the truths of faith, that is to say, catechesis, is not only legitimate but necessary; it will always remain indispensable in establishing the data of revelation defined and promulgated by the Church, which must be known exactly under pain of compromising faith itself. But it is necessary also to state categorically that this methodical teaching alone does not suffice to form true Christians who live and practice their faith. In the words of Dom Beauduin: "Religious instruction distilled in the soul drop by drop by the collective prayer of the Mystical Body of Christ is the indispensable complement of the catechetical method."[1]

Let us now see in more detail how, in the Church, life of worship and life of faith, liturgy and religious instruction, sustain and complete each other. It is clear that the interdependence of liturgy and catechetics can be considered from one side or the other. Let us first treat of the kerygmatic value of the liturgy, that is to say of its influence on the life of faith. Then we shall deal with the necessity of religious teaching for liturgical life, that is to say what may be called the liturgical value of catechetics. We should avoid thinking of liturgy and catechetics as though they were parallel ways of Christian living: they should be united in a Christian community which daily lives the mystery of Christ in truth and love. It is interesting to note in this context that, already in the Acts of the Apostles, the infant Church is portrayed as a community living by the religious teaching given by the apostles and by the life of worship over which they presided. The first Christians "were occupying themselves continually with the apostles' teaching, their fellowship in the breaking of bread, and the fixed times of prayer" (Acts. 2:42).

Pius XI, in his Encyclical *Quas primas* gave admirable definition to the kerygmatic role of the Church's liturgy, when

[1] *Irenikon,* 1930, p. 655.

he wrote: "For people are instructed in the truths of faith, and brought to appreciate the inner joys of religion far more effectually by the annual celebration of our sacred mysteries than by any pronouncement, however weighty, of the teaching of the Church. Such pronouncements usually reach only a few and the more learned among the faithful; feasts reach them all. The former are spoken but once, the latter speak every year – in fact, for ever. The Church's teaching affects the mind primarily; her feasts affect both mind and hearts, and have a salutary effect upon the whole of man's nature. Man is composed of body and soul, and he needs these external festivities so that the sacred rites, in all their beauty and variety, may stimulate him to drink more deeply of the fountain of God's teaching, that he may make it a part of himself, and use it with profit for his spiritual life."

This amounts to saying that the liturgy has an essential teaching function in the Church, not only by reason of the doctrine contained in liturgical texts, but first and foremost by its very nature. From the very beginning the Church has wished to express through its liturgy and in conjunction with its rites her awareness of the faith given by Christ, and so to lead her faithful, by means of the liturgy, to a conscious Christianity. In the liturgy the Christian revelation shows itself to us in action, precisely because the central teaching of the liturgy in all its rites and in the unfolding of the liturgical year, is to make us better understand, in its historic reality and actuality, the mystery of Christ's redemptive work. Hence the liturgy, by its very nature, is a source of living faith – it is indeed faith expressing itself in concrete fashion.

The liturgy moreover, constitutes a natural and very human method of religious instruction, enabling the Christian to relive the great mysteries of his religion. Thus the liturgy excels as an active method of religious instruction. Also, using as it does very freely the evocative power of symbols, the liturgy is simultaneously a very efficacious method of pictorial teaching.

In fact, if it is true that all prayer is a form of divine education, that it strengthens us in the faith and makes us better understand and live the mysteries of faith, then it is all the more true of the highest form of prayer, prayer in union with Christ and the Church, prayer of the Christian community, liturgical prayer. For prayer and the liturgical cult not only vivify our faith by promoting the continual exercise of the virtue of faith; the liturgy also enables us to participate actively each day of our lives in the various aspects of the mystery of our redemption, and carries within itself special graces for augmenting and vivifying our faith.

In this short discourse there is no time to expatiate on the fundamental role of liturgical symbols. We know that those symbols used by the liturgy and drawn for the most part from scripture are the materials from which dogmas are built up. We know that by means of them we grasp the truth of supernatural realities in which we believe. Divine revelation has chosen the way of images, actions, and events with symbolic value to teach us the truth, precisely because the religious symbol, appealing not only to the speculative intellect but to all our human faculties, is the most efficacious means to bring us daily nearer to religious truth.

The liturgy then has always been one of the authentic forms of the Church's teaching power. It is one of the forms of expression adopted by tradition and by which the scriptural word of God is proclaimed, explained, and expounded. It is therefore a true theological source by means of which appears the content of revelation, a means of knowing revealed truth. For this reason Pope Celestine writing to the bishops of Gaul says this: *Obsecrationum sacerdotalium sacramenta respiciamus, quae ab apostolis tradita in toto mundo atque ad omni ecclesia catholica uniformata celebrantur, ut legem credendi lex statuat supplicandi.* For this same reason the Church has always exercised control over the liturgy, and has taken care that the liturgy should express truly revealed dogma. In the words of the Council of Milevium: *ne forte aliquid contra fidem vel per ignorantiam vel per studium sit compositum.*

It is true that the liturgy is first of all and principally the official cult of the Church, but no less true that it is also one of the essential forms and one of the most efficacious modes taken by the teaching power confided by Christ to his apostles. It is a true catechesis containing the essentials of doctrine and Christian moral law in their most concrete form. Just like the incarnate Word himself, the Church at prayer gives concrete expression to the most sublime ideas and most hidden mysteries of revelation, and brings them within our reach. In the liturgy she expresses these truths in the simple figurative language of the scriptures; by gesture, rite and symbol which touch souls through the normal human channel of the senses, she gives them an essentially practical teaching. As we shall see later, this practical teaching of the liturgy calls for religious instruction properly so called as a necessary complement, for two reasons: first, so that Christian souls may be capable of understanding and living the Christian mystery proposed in the liturgy, and secondly to elaborate and make more explicit the revealed truths presented by the liturgy in symbols, so that the believer may have a correct idea of them, free from intellectual error. It remains true that what one would call basic religious education is given by the Church to her children in the liturgy. We may rightly conclude then that the liturgy is kerygmatic by its very nature, that it is the normal channel by which our faith finds expression and sustenance in the mystery of Christ, and that it is truly the Church's act of faith, the act of the Christian assembly.

The liturgy has an essential teaching function in the Church, not only by reason of its constitution, but also and even more effectively by reason of its content, that is, the liturgical texts.

It is clear, in fact, that in general the liturgical texts appeal very largely to the intelligence and provide, in many instances, genuine instruction. For example we have only to reflect here on the dogmatic and moral teaching of the collects in the missal. In so many instances, we find with Péguy that the texts of the liturgy are *une théologie détendue*.

It is especially by their biblical content that the texts of the liturgy provide the Christian people with solid teaching, teaching which shares in the supernatural efficacy of God's word in the scriptures. If we examine all the different elements which make up the liturgy, such as it was in the early Church and such as it is now, we find that the biblical element is the most outstanding. God's word, as found in the scriptures, is offered to us by Mother Church in many ways in the liturgy.

First of all there are the readings, properly so-called, taken from the Bible. At the International Congress on Pastoral

Liturgy held at Assisi, Cardinal Augustine Bea said: "The intimate connection between liturgical prayer and the eucharistic sacrifice on the one hand, and liturgical readings and their explanation on the other, is a feature characteristic of Christian worship found neither in pagan worship nor in the sacrificial worship of Israel. It was our Lord himself who established the main outlines of the chief liturgical function of his Church. For at the Last Supper, before instituting the holy Eucharist, he explained the meaning of the washing of the feet; and after the offering of the first eucharistic sacrifice he addressed to his apostles his sublime farewell discourse. Throughout the centuries holy Mother Church has followed this plan of our Lord and put together the prayer of the liturgical sacrifice and the reading of holy scripture."

Secondly we have the explanation of these readings from the Bible in the sermon. Later we shall come back to the liturgical role of the sermon.

Thirdly we find the word of God from the scriptures in those psalms and canticles of which the liturgy makes frequent use.

Alongside the biblical extracts in the liturgy we should equally bear in mind the many biblical references to be found in the liturgical texts. Finally (and this is perhaps the most important pedagogical element in the liturgy) there is that primordial fact that the whole liturgy brings before us each day the bible story of the redemption. For this very reason, the great period in the formation of our liturgy (the fourth and fifth centuries) is also the period during which the history of our redemption as told in the Bible was alive in Christian consciousness with a vigour unparalleled at any other time in history. Since liturgy constantly uses texts and events from the Bible in their real context, that is, in the story of the redemption and in the unity of the Christian mystery, liturgy actually gives us the true sense of scripture. As the liturgical year goes by, holy scripture is unfolded before us, showing the divine plan of the redemption. Liturgy not only puts our Blessed Lord in the centre of the Bible, but gives with it the thought of Jesus Christ and the Church on the scriptures, in fact a very clear and sound introduction to the truths of scripture; it teaches us that vital understanding of God and the world without which the Bible will always remain a closed book.

To conclude, with Canon Martimort we say that the whole liturgy is in truth *le lieu de la Bible,* wherein the Christian is given the word of God from the scriptures and from the mouth of the Church.

We must now come back to the place of the sermon in the liturgy. We readily see that the sermon is part of the teaching office, but it is not so evident that it forms part of the liturgy; many a Christian these days would be astonished if he were told that the Sunday sermon is part of the liturgy! Nevertheless, not only is it a fact that the sermon has always been placed within the liturgical celebration, but also it had an intrinsic relation with this celebration, being the explanation of the texts, the symbols and the ceremonies of the liturgical function. Just as the proclaiming of the word of God in the scriptures constitutes an essential part of the liturgy, so does the explanation of this same word of God and the work of preparing the heart to receive the word in sermon and catechesis have an essential connection with this liturgy.

St. Paul, speaking of his evangelical work uses words which are most liturgical; for example, in Rom. 4:15–16 he says, "and yet I have written to you . . . by way of refreshing your memories. So much I owe to the grace which God has given me, in making me a priest *(leitourgos)* of Jesus Christ for the Gentiles, to make the Gentiles an offering worthy of acceptance, consecrated by the Holy Spirit."

This liturgical aspect of religious teaching applies as much to catechesis as it does to the sermon or the homily. The true purpose of catechetics is the initiation into the Christian life, into the Church, into the full incorporation with Christ. This initiation has two forms: a pre-baptismal catechumenate for adults who are converted to the true religion and a post-baptismal catechumenate for baptized children who have still to be taught the truths of Christian life. This teaching of the catechism has its own intrinsic link with the liturgy; because it is intimately joined to the sacraments of Christian initiation, baptism and confirmation, and because it is a preparation for the whole Christian cultual life.

The connection of the sermon with the liturgy is still more intrinsic. The purpose of the homily is not to convert non-Christians, nor to teach the truths of religion for the first time to Christians, but to instruct them in the faith which they already possess and to stimulate them in the morality which they practise already. Its purpose is then to make more explicit faith taught by the liturgy, and to exhort to the practice of Christian life for which the liturgy is a preparation and of which it is the most perfect expression. For this reason, the sermon is normally given during one or other of the sacred offices, and its subject is (or ought to be) the Christian mystery in which Christians participate through the liturgy. The audience is the Christian assembly at worship, the one who preaches is the *leitourgos,* bishop, priest or deacon.

What we have said on the role of the sermon in the liturgy has in fact now brought us to the second point which connects the liturgy and catechetics; namely the liturgical value of catechetics. We would now like to point out briefly what catechetics in its broad sense, the teaching of the faith, contributes to liturgical life.

If we really understand that liturgy is the cult which the Christian assembly offers to God in Christ and with Christ our leader, then we see that the participation of the faithful in the cult is an indispensable element. It is also quite evident that unless the faithful have sufficient Christian instruction they cannot understand and live the liturgy; the *conditio sine qua non* for *participatio actuosa* is religious teaching. Without faith, and moreover living faith, no liturgical life is possible. The liturgical assembly is, to quote Dom Jean Hild, an "Epiphany of the Church"; it is the Church *in actu,* in her most normal activity, in her most intimate and sublime way of acting. But, this assembly is first and foremost made up by its unity in the faith, and the faith is only made possible by evangelization, preaching, and making known of the word of God; *fides ex auditu!* Besides, we have already seen the most important part played in the liturgy by the preaching of the word of God as found in the Bible; and were we to attempt to explain the liturgy without explaining the Bible, it would be a mere contradiction in terms.

In conclusion we shall say, that on the one hand catechetics introduces to cult, and is the one necessary condition for active participation in cult; and on the other hand, liturgy is one of the principal sources of faith, for it gives not only a speculative knowledge of revelation, but especially it forms the faithful for Christian life.

But first and foremost, we must insist that this cannot be true in practice unless liturgy and catechesis are joined in the living unity of the mystery of Christ and his Church. This means:

1. Our religious instruction must once again find the unity of the Christian mystery in the person of Christ.
2. Religious instruction must be a Christian education and not merely a speculative instruction in the truths of faith.
3. Religious instruction must be closely connected with the liturgical year and must make use of texts and symbols from the liturgy.
4. The liturgy has to be made intelligible to the faithful so that they can take an active part in it.
5. Those in charge of souls have to prepare their faithful to understand and live the liturgy.
6. The faithful must be taught to listen to, to understand, and to love the word of God in scripture, which is the essence of liturgical texts.

This integral method of educating the Christian in the union of cult and catechesis will make him understand more and more the mystery of Christ; by it, the Christian educated in the *familia Dei,* in the Christian assembly, will understand and live the mystery of the Church. Then the parish will be what it ought to be, "a community of cult" and "a community of catechesis".

Our contention that, in the intimate union of liturgy and catechesis, pastoral zeal will find the true way of Christian education both for children and for adults, is confirmed by the Church's history. It was certainly during the early Christian centuries, up till about the sixth century, that this mutual penetration of liturgy and catechesis was most complete – and that to an extent such that catechesis was, in practice, almost entirely absorbed into the liturgy. And it was just at this time that the Church had unparalleled success in her task of evangelization; this is shown not merely by the numbers converted, but still more because the primitive Church succeeded in training her catechumens to become convinced and well instructed Christians in a relatively short time and in circumstances that were by no means favourable. Could we not conclude that in large measure this success was due to the method of evangelization? Obviously I do not want to state that during these early centuries the situation with regard to religious knowledge was perfect; there were certainly some who missed Mass on Sundays. And especially I do not propose that we return to the system of those early years when liturgy alone constituted the only means of instruction. We are no longer in the sixth century, and even in our days we must make full use of the work of the scholastics and those great teachers of catechism after the Reformation. What we have to do is to employ the methods used during those two periods and harmonize them.

By way of conclusion, may I, a missionary bishop, point out to you how this question of joining the liturgy and catechetics, preoccupies us in our missionary work. At this crucial moment in the history of world evangelization there are two problems for which we seek a practical solution.

One is the problem of creating real Christian communities without which there can be no genuine implantation of the Church. The other problem is that the new Christian communities in non-western countries are faced with both the theoretical and practical materialism of the communist block and also by the practical materialism and secularism of the western countries. We believe that a liturgical life fully enlightened by solid knowledge of the faith is one of the fundamental solutions to these problems.

In the parish which is at once, "community of the cult" and "community of catechesis", the new Christians will find the answer to that agonizing problem: how to live in a world of new human relations. When they understand the liturgy, the praise of God by men and by creation, they will find the answer to the second problem which also is most troubling: how to live in this new world of material things, the world of modern technique.

If in this they enter into the spirit of the Church, they will understand that it is not only the Church of men but also the Church of material things. Christian life will then become no longer a life of some individuals who are busy trying to save their souls by means of Christianity and by endeavouring to follow a certain moral code, but the life of a Christian community joined in the same faith, the same hope, and the same love, the family of God, whose purpose is to accomplish the essential work of a Christian here on earth; to offer to God the praise due to him in the liturgy of all men and all creation.

# Making the Mass Catechetically more Effective

KARL WEBER, S.V.D.
Bishop of Ichowfu, China

A MISSIONARY must have close ties with his people; so also must the worship by which he is to lead them to God. Hence throughout the course of a long missionary life it was my constant endeavour to integrate into our community worship the traditional customs and usages of the people, so that our neophytes could easily feel at home in God's house.

As an example, let me tell you how we used to celebrate Christmas. The people should be helped to realize that Christ came into this world as its almighty Lord and God. They had already learned how to receive an important personage from the traditional ceremonial used for the reception of a new Mandarin, so why not connect up our Christmas celebrations with this familiar ceremonial?

We devised, therefore, a ceremonial reception for the Christ-Child after the pattern already well known to the people. On his way from heaven to earth, Christ comes to rest in a tent outside the confines of the village. A solemn procession goes out to meet him; fireworks are let off, the smoke of incense rises, music is played, and the little Saviour of the World is placed in a litter and carried ceremonially into the church. Then a child comes forward to greet him, saying: "We have carried your image into our church, to receive it with honour; we ask, now, that you will come into our souls and reign over our hearts as king."

On the same principle we make use of traditional customs on other occasions, such as at funerals and harvest festivals. Thus we are able to bring home to our people the meaning and spirit of quite a number of the Church's celebrations. But

all of these something was done or witnessed by everyone in common, and the singing, which included antiphons repeated by the people again and again, brought home to them the meaning of what was going on, and impressed it vividly on the minds and hearts of all.

Another constituent of the service was the proclamation of God's Word. The readings from holy scripture (which were, of course, in the vernacular), together with the ensuing homily, constantly nourished the people's faith, leading them to the riches of God's revelation and to the depths of the sacred mysteries.

A third constituent was the offertory procession. The material gifts for consecration – bread and wine – were at the same time gifts for those of their brethren who were in need. The offering was thus a regularly recurring communal action by means of which both love of God and love of one's neighbour were expressed and practised. Next came the sacred mystery of the Eucharist itself, in which the faithful were brought into personal contact with the sacrificed and risen Saviour, gave themselves in him and with him to the Father, ate together the Meal of Love, and became united with Christ and with each other. All this was catechesis of a singularly perfect kind; indeed it was better than any catechesis, for it was not mere teaching but also doing and praying and sacrificing. It went even further; for here they met Christ himself and became ever more deeply incorporated into him.

In contrast with this early worship, we have to recognize that in recent times public worship as carried out in the missions has had far too little significance. Its catechetical and missionary power is pitifully limited – especially at Low Mass when the people remain wholly passive. Nothing remains except the sacramental efficacy; but the fruit even of this depends on the receptivity or disposition of the faithful who are present.

That is why it is an imperative necessity that in our own times we must do everything possible to restore full missionary force to the public worship of our people. Newly converted Christians must experience in their worship the solicitude and the understanding love of holy Mother Church, ready to do anything to impart to her children her word of truth, the prayers of her heart and the meaning of her sacred actions, in order to lead them to God.

We cannot evade the serious charge of negligence if we fail, now, to attach much more importance than we have done in the past to the intelligibility of divine worship, which could be such a wonderful means for training and sanctifying our Christian people. Especially by the careful planning and staging of the Sunday Mass we can achieve, more than by any other means, the most extensive effect; for all the faithful come to Mass on Sunday, not merely those of one age group. Here also we can produce the most intensive effect, because in the Mass there is not only teaching, but also prayer, offering, and union with Christ. Finally it is here that we can produce the most lasting effect; for training given at school or by courses of instructions eventually comes to an end, whereas Sunday Mass remains a factor in a Christian's life for the rest of his days.

The problem has become especially topical and urgent because many of our mission schools have been taken away from us, and others are likely to be taken away in the future. Then we shall be left with nothing except the main thing – divine service, public worship. And we know that tremendous strength can be drawn from public worship if it is celebrated communally, carefully prepared, and staged in a meaningful way. The proof of that is the experience gained in the east German diaspora now under the oppression of atheistic communism, where the Catholics derive almost exclusively from this one source the strength which they need to preserve their faith, to suffer, and to witness to Christ.

## The Present

### *Possibilities within the Limits of the Present Rubrics*

Someone might object to the ideas expressed so far by saying that the forms for divine worship are already fixed by rubrics and ecclesiastical laws, and thus that we do not enjoy the freedom in this sphere which existed during the early centuries. The objection is not without substance; but that must not blind us to the considerable possibilities which we still do have, even within the framework of existing legislation, to conduct our services in ways which would increase their missionary efficacy. To achieve this purpose, bishops in many dioceses and countries have already issued directives regulating in detail the forms of public worship. The value of such directives is that, on the one hand, they eliminate all irresponsible tinkerings with the liturgy while, on the other, they promote forms liturgically more worthy and pastorally more efficacious. Some of these forms have already been employed for decades in German dioceses, and have clearly demonstrated their usefulness and formative power, especially during the years of Nazi persecution. Examples are those which the Germans call *Gemeinschaftsmesse* (Community Mass) and *Betsingmesse* (Prayer-hymn-Mass). Pastoral work in Germany would now be unthinkable without them.

What exactly can now be done in practice? That we may form a concrete picture, let us consider briefly some of the main forms of active participation in the Mass.

## LOW MASS

The simplest form of people's participation in Low Mass is attained if the priest addresses his greetings, not merely to the server, but to the entire congregation, so that the people themselves make the appropriate replies. Even this by itself transforms the whole character of the celebration. It is no longer a private action of the priest, but a communal action of priest and people together. In addition a lector, or one of the senior Mass servers, reads out the scripture pericopes in the mother tongue, and the people say, in their own language, the *Sanctus* and *Agnus Dei.*[1] This form should be the very minimum for every Mass at which there is a congregation.

In a more developed form the people say together the entire Ordinary of the Mass, together with the *Gloria* and *Credo* and

[1] This is lawful in Germany and in some mission countries having special privileges; but elsewhere, since the Instruction of the S.C.R. of Sept. 3rd, 1958, the people may not recite literal translations. They are limited to the Latin or to paraphrases.

*Pater noster,* all in the vernacular. A schola or lector reads aloud parts of the Proper,[2] and a lector reads out translations of the Collect, Preface and Postcommunion.[3]

The *Betsingmesse* (Prayer-hymn-Mass) is a form particularly well suited for use on Sundays. The people sing appropriate hymns at the beginning and end of the Mass, during the preparation of the gifts, and during the Communion, in addition to the responses and prayers listed above. This affords a lively variety of activities, and yet makes provision, during the Canon, for the silence needed for personal prayer.

## HIGH MASS

In Germany there is a centuries-old usage which has now become a special privilege for all German dioceses. Even during a High Mass the people are allowed to sing in their own language specially composed hymns corresponding with certain parts of the Ordinary and the Proper. This form is of importance historically, for by its aid whole dioceses were preserved from falling into heresy at the time of the Reformation.

## OTHER DETAILS

In every form of Mass, whether said or sung, the pastoral effect can be intensified by other expedients. The most important of all is careful preparation. This involves the choice of hymns, and consultation to ensure agreement between the celebrant, organist, servers, prayer-leader, lector and schola. It involves also a thorough rehearsal of all those who have any function in the service, as well as attention to such details as the beauty of vestments and sacred vessels – even to the very building of the church. For the church should be so built that the altar is not too far away from the people or obscured from their view. Ideally the altar should be fairly close to them, in a

[2] Note 1. applies here also.

[3] In countries without special privileges the lector may not use translations, but only summaries; and even these may not be read simultaneously with the priest's Latin.

position such that they can really be the *circumstantes* mentioned in the Canon of the Mass.

A further point concerns the offertory procession. The easiest way is to place, near the entrance to the church, a dish for the hosts, or a ciborium, into which each intending communicant puts a host – using a spoon if this be considered desirable. At the proper time, the servers carry up to the altar these offerings from the faithful, together with the wine and water, and the priest receives them. This meaningful action expresses clearly and vividly both the self-surrender of the faithful, and also their union with Christ as victim of the sacrifice, and it helps them greatly to take their part in a prayerful and conscious way at this point of the Mass. They receive at the communion their own offerings now transformed into heavenly food.

The *Oratio fidelium* or "Bidding Prayers", are of special importance. While the liturgy as such transcends time, these prayers invest the worship with a direct relationship to the "here and now". Some form of them is found in most of our diocesan hymnals *(Diözesangesangbücher)* with variations according to the seasons of the liturgical year, and for different intentions, such as "for youth", "for the missions", "for the faithul departed", and so on. The priest, or a lector, leads the prayers before the offertory, and the people answer by saying "We beseech thee to hear us".

For the distribution of communion the use of a communion dish (instead of a ciborium) is becoming more and more widespread. After all, a chalice is really a drinking cup, and a ciborium looks very like a chalice. A dish corresponds far better with what it is to contain, namely, food. Also it avoids all danger of confusion between the chalice and the vessel containing the sacred hosts – a confusion which is not unknown when a ciborium is used.

### SUMMARY

From all this we can see that, when seeking for a more catechetically effective form of Mass, we have no need to look only to the future. In celebrating Mass with our people we have, even now, a considerable margin of freedom. Any bishop can improve the way Mass is celebrated in his diocese by means of directives to his clergy, and specially by making provision for such improvements in his diocesan hymnal. We are no longer groping after ways in which to begin; we have long passed the merely experimental stage. We possess Mass forms already worked out, the fruits of decades of reflection, devised by specialists, critically assessed by liturgists, and widely tested in practice by zealous pastors. They are forms which have stood the test of time, and have already brought forth abundant fruit in pastoral work.

## The Future

### *Privileges to be Sought, for the Future Shaping of the Liturgy*

In spite of all the possibilities we have examined, we constantly come into head-on collision with restrictive and frustrating prohibitions inherent in some of the rubrics and existing laws. And so we ought to have the courage, in a spirit of sincerity and of realism, humbly to question whether these restrictions do in fact serve any useful purpose. No one would deny that a set of rubrics is necessary in order to ensure the dignity and orderliness of divine worship. But is this end truly served by the rubrics as they stand now? Does each of them really achieve its purpose in every single case? To assess this, we have to judge by the right norms.

One such norm is, beyond question, the great commandment given us by Christ that we must love God and love our fellow man. We ought, therefore, to examine the extent to which any given rubric does help people to love God; whether it does in fact draw the faithful closer to God and to the sacred mysteries. We must see, also, whether it measures up to that standard of love for men which takes seriously the needs of the simple man-in-the-street, the humble woman-of-the-people. Does this rubric help them to see and to feel, in their worship, the "goodness and loving kindness of God our Saviour" (Tit. 3:4)?

Another sure norm is the example of Christ our Lord, whose heart so yearned over the simple and humble, and who gave us the Eucharist in the simple and humble form of the sacred meal.

We should also take as a norm the statement of the encyclical *Mediator Dei,* that "the principal aim of ritual laws is to nourish and foster the piety of Christians, and their inner union with Christ and his visible representative; also to engender in us those dispositions of mind and soul whereby we may conform ourselves to the High Priest of the New Covenant". Beyond doubt there are some rubrics which, in the circumstances obtaining today, will not satisfy these criteria.

A further norm is given us by pastoral knowledge and experience that the Church's basic principle is *salus animarum suprema lex*. This pastoral concern recognizes the sensibilities and susceptibilities of our own generation, of the people of our own countries and dioceses; for it is *these* people whom we have to lead to God. Hence their idiosyncracies, the ways in which they react, will not allow us to do anything that would hinder or obstruct their access to the founts of holiness; rather must we open these, and render access to them easy. (An example: in China, white is the colour of mourning, not of joy.)

Finally we have a norm in the love of our holy Mother the Church, who cannot possibly oppose her own will or the will of God who "desires that all men should be saved and should come to the knowledge of the truth" (1 Tim. 2:4).

If now we reflect upon the task which our public worship imposes on us – if we think about it in the spirit of God, of Christ and of the Church – we find ourselves driven forcefully to a number of conclusions. We cannot do other than conceive a whole series of heartfelt desires which, in all sincerity, we should state clearly, and examine dispassionately. And then we should trustfully and insistently petition the Holy See to grant, for the good of souls and for our own good, those which we hold with conviction to be truly necessary.

In doing so we should make it clear that what we ask for would be permissions; that is, we seek approval for forms which would take their place beside the form of the official Roman liturgy of cathedrals and monasteries. We seek them only for the worship of ordinary people in parish churches, and chapels.

The first petition is one which has been voiced many times. It is, that every celebrant should be allowed to read the Epistle and Gospel of the Mass to the people directly, in their own tongue, without having to duplicate them in Latin. Duplicate readings in the vernacular by a lector are only distracting and unsatisfactory substitute forms, which ill befit the dignity of, and reverence due to, the Word of God.

The second petition: that the privilege of singing in the mother tongue during High Masses, already granted to the dioceses of Germany and to certain missions, should be extended to all dioceses.

The third petition concerns the Liturgy of the Word, sometimes called the Mass of the Catechumens, that is, that part of the Mass which extends from the beginning till the Creed. All this should be reformed in ways which would restore its original function, and enable it truly to fulfil the purpose for which it came into being. Such reforms imply a number of sub-petitions. These are as follows.

We ask that, in Masses celebrated for the people, especially in Sunday parochial Masses, the Liturgy of the Word should be in the vernacular throughout.

So that the people may have access to the riches contained in God's Word, and so that in practice no really important item of divine revelation be withheld from them, we ask for an increased selection of pericopes from the Epistles and Gospels which, in the course of a four-year cycle, would familiarize the people with all the principle treasures of revelation contained in Holy Writ. This petition has already received unanimous approval at the Nijmegen Congress, and a draft of the proposed new order of scripture readings has been sent to Rome.

That all duplications should be eliminated from the Liturgy of the Word; that is, that when the people pray, or when the choir sings, the priest should not have to pray anything different, nor should he have to read these parts in Latin parallel with the people or choir.

Wherever it may seem necessary in missionary countries, may the bishops be authorized to work out modifications and adaptations in the Liturgy of the Word, so as to make it better suited to the needs of their people; let them lay before the Holy See the modifications they propose and then, if these be approved, prescribe them for their own dioceses.

So that the importance of the Liturgy of the Word may be recognized, and its pastoral purpose be more surely achieved, may the celebrating priest, during the songs and prayers, be at the *sedile* instead of at the altar which is the place of sacrifice; but for the readings may he go to the *ambo* and face the people. This would be according to the intrinsic nature of the Liturgy of the Word, as is shown by the rubrics governing Vespers. Such a clear distinction between the Liturgy of the Word and the eucharistic Liturgy of Sacrifice would teach an important catechetical lesson to the people, and the manner and the place of each part of the service would better correspond with its nature. The priest would go to the altar itself for the first time only at the offertory.

The fourth petition. It should be recognized that our present form of the Mass has been derived from the highly developed liturgy of the Papal Mass. But in the country places around Rome the Mass used to be celebrated in a much simpler form, suited to their modest circumstances and lack of resources. For this reason it would be desirable that for less developed communities a simpler form of the Mass should be allowed – something which would resemble more closely the Last Supper of our Lord, or the Mass of ancient times described by Justin.[4]

In such a form the three principal parts of the eucharistic sacrifice would be easily and distinctly recognizable. Firstly, the preparation of the gifts, including some form of offertory procession. Secondly, the Eucharistic Prayer, from the beginning of the Preface dialogue to the Great Doxology with its Amen. Thirdly, the Communion, comprising the Our Father, the breaking of Bread, the *Agnus Dei,* the Kiss of Peace and the distribution of the heavenly Food.

In this simple form, all audible parts would be in the vernacular, while the Canon and other silent parts would be recited by the priest in Latin. This permission has already been granted in substance to China, though not yet promulgated.

[4] "When we have finished the prayers, bread, wine and water are brought. The President says prayers and thanksgiving, and the people join in by saying *Amen*. Thereupon the distribution begins; everyone receives his portion of the consecrated gifts, and deacons take a share to those who are absent" (Apol. c. 53).

These heartfelt desires, which imply a number of small details not mentioned here, are by no means revolutionary, for they correspond to the ancient traditions of the Church. Also they are in full consonance with the aim expressed by the Council of Trent, as that of reforming the celebration of the Mass *ad pristinam formam Patrum*. They are, furthermore, in accordance with the spirit of the classical missionary documents issued by Propaganda in 1659 to the Vicars Apostolic on their way to the East: "In no way and under no pretext should you attempt to urge those people to change their customs and habits, so long as they are not in flagrant contradiction with good morals. What would be more absurd than to transplant France, Spain, Italy or any other part of Europe into China? It is not Europe that you are to take with you, but the Christian faith which in no way rejects or condemns any usages or customs so long as they are not immoral, but rather preserves them whole and intact." Finally these proposals fulfil the purpose of the ritual prescriptions already cited from the encyclical *Mediator Dei*.

Hence they are not inspired by any mere archaeological considerations, but solely by the acute pastoral needs of our times, and by a recognition of the duty which we cannot evade even if we will – the duty, namely, of opening the way for the peoples of other cultures to the very heart of our worship. The importance of the proposals, therefore, does not derive from the fact that these forms once did exist in the golden ages of liturgy; it is based squarely on the fact that they are so absolutely necessary for our missionary task.

If anyone raises objections on the grounds that the Latin language is still the symbol and bond of unity of the Church and should therefore continue to be the liturgical language, we have to make a clear distinction. For the clarity of the Church's teaching as proclaimed at her Councils, or for the mutual comprehension of theologians in their scientific studies, or for the univocal terminology of Canon Law, Latin renders an indispensable service. The admirable solemn forms of the Latin liturgy also should never be given up. In all these domains Latin does indeed foster and subserve the unity of the Church.

But when it comes to community worship, including the Mass, the situation is quite different, especially in the mission countries. Here an inflexible conservatism insisting on the exclusive retention of Latin has led to an immense loss of souls, and has done more to divide Christians than to unite them.

Is it not true that one of the chief obstacles to the return of the Oriental churches to the One Fold has been the fear of being latinized? One of the main factors which drove the Evangelical Christians to break away from the Mother Church was their desire to worship in their own tongue. A leading theologian of our days has said that one of the main reasons why millions of the working class have fallen away from the Church during the past century has been a surfeit of Latin in worship.

Even today millions stand just outside the gates of the Church but do not feel drawn to enter because in the Church's worship they do not find the loving embrace of a mother longing to adapt herself to them, to understand them and to be understood by them. They do not come in because they do not perceive the redeeming love of Christ who so mercifully sought out the common people; they see instead a foreign product – a museum piece belonging to the bygone days of European culture and art. Besides the strange language, many ceremonies in the Mass are unintelligible apart from their historical background, and have hardly any contact with the life of today. If we are genuinely concerned with the salvation of souls, we must do all that we possibly can to adapt the forms of divine worship to the pastoral needs of our own times and our own people.

The Church, which progressed from the Aramaic, through the Greek, to the Latin language in her liturgy did not lay the foundations of her unity upon the use of Latin in public worship. External unity has become easier to maintain today by reason of technical advances in communication and administration. The interior unity, however, is the work of the Holy Spirit and of a common faith nourished and expressed in an inspired, meaningful liturgy that speaks to the heart.

Must we not also realize that today we live in a democratic world in which, far more than formerly, everyone feels that he has a right to understand what is going on? Can we sing a Passion lasting half an hour, or an *Exsultet* for twenty minutes in an unintelligible language to layfolk who are supposed to be adult members of the Church? And when the Church lays it down as a natural right of her children that they should receive their religious instruction in their own language, even if they are a linguistic minority, should not the same principle be applied to divine worship, particularly as regards its catechetical parts? Ninety per cent of Catholics throughout the world will never feel themselves called to raise up their hearts when they hear the words *Sursum corda;* nor will they truly wish for the priest that the Lord may be with his spirit when they say *Et cum spiritu tuo*. No amount of explanation and translation will ever alter the fact that the meaning is not really grasped even of the simplest and commonest Latin formulae, and that thereby the whole divine service loses much of its effect.

We are living at a decisive moment in the history of the Church, at a time when the world is threatened with terrifying dangers. But it is also a time of tremendous missionary possibilities, when the Church must show herself to the peoples as the stronghold of love and of truth. This congress itself is a historic occcasion, for never before have so many missionary bishops and specialists in catechetics met together in the spirit of the Good Shepherd, a spirit of consuming anxiety to win mankind for Christ. May the Holy Spirit enlighten us and enable us to recognize what should be done. May our deliberations lead to the ever more complete fulfilment of what the encyclical *Mediator Dei* teaches: that the holy sacrifice should be the summit and centre of all Christian piety; that the faithful should be moved by the beauty of the liturgy, and raise their voices in alternation with those of the priest and choir; that the faithful should pray in the closest union with the priest, in the very same words, according to the mind of the Church. May we then recognize and achieve everything that will render accessible to the peoples of the world the way to the Church, to Christ, to God – everything that will enable them to find their salvation in him.

(Tr. C. H., S.J.)

# Sunday Services without the Priest

WILLIAM JOSEPH DUSCHAK, S.V.D.
Vicar Apostolic of Calapan, Mindoro, Philippines

THE Sunday service without the priest, which forms the topic of the present paper, is discussed here from the standpoint of the mission territories, also of those regions where Catholics are few and far between. We are not concerned with private family devotions but with Sunday community services in out-of-the way places. These are miniature parishes, which cannot regularly be reached by a priest, and which are consequently deprived of the sacrifice of the Mass, for which these services have become substitutes, though naturally, not perfect ones. As to the liturgical character of these services and the obligation to attend them, nothing definite has as yet been laid down.

It is remarkable that both patristic and mission literature, apart from St. Augustine and St. Francis Xavier, have little to say about this service; indeed, only recently has it come to be regarded as a real problem. Nevertheless, this kind of Sunday service has always been of great importance and may well be of immense consequence for our present missionary era. We merely have to focus our attention on China, on other Communist-dominated territories, on the vast mission territories suffering from scarcity of personnel, or on possible developments in the near future, and we shall feel the need of giving the problem our serious consideration. Our task is to conduct this Sunday service in such a manner that it will guarantee the preservation and growth of the faith over large territories both now and in times of persecution. We must also take into consideration the propaganda activity of many religious sects. These sects are extremely active and aggressive and have made much progress in those out-of-the-way places both at home and in the missions where the Sunday service should be established. There is, therefore, on the one hand, an urgent call for a permanent systematic defensive, more or less negative in character, while on the other hand a liturgical, biblio-catechetical, pastoral offensive of a positive kind is necessary. These two tendencies could be effected through this Sunday service. Superficially the services of the sects consist of the same elements which should inform our service. They provide a Bible reading service, sermons, prayers, hymns, and other liturgical ceremonies. Clearly the re-organization of the Sunday service without a priest as the Christian life's means of defence and preservation and its source of strength, is most imperative.

If our concern up to now has been for the catechetical character of the service, this does not mean that we favour the idea of allowing it to degenerate into a mere catechism class, enlivened perhaps by hymns and prayers. The "priestless service" is, like the Mass, first and foremost divine service consisting of petitions, praises, thanksgiving, and acts of surrender. Its catechetical aspect is important but it is not the main aspect, the role it plays being merely contributary to the ultimate purpose, as in the Mass. Quite apart from the catechetical instruction or reading, a well arranged divine service will be catechetically instructive in its entirety. The liturgical, catechetical and pastoral aspects present in the service will complement one another, thus forming a living whole as is to be found in the Mass.

### *Missionary Situations for the Priestless Service*

Ideal solutions of little practical use are not hard to come by. For this very reason it is necessary to bear in mind right from the beginning the prevailing conditions in the missionary countries in which our service is to be introduced. It is true that one mission district differs from another, but everywhere the growth and formation of the Kingdom of God has common distinctive features. We find enormous parishes, both territorially and numerically, which frequently lack adequate transport facilities; quite apart from that, climatic conditions often aggravate already existing problems. The lack of personnel, both priests and catechists, is a perpetual worry. Then there is the constant struggle in the field of education: some governments maintain schools in the curricula of which religious instruction does not feature at all. This is so, more often than not, in mission territories. There are great numbers of people without any serious religious convictions, with whom external compliance to religious obligation goes hand in hand with superstitious piety. There are the communities consisting principally of women and children, subjected to sectarian influences. The sectarian ministers are usually offering precisely what our service is supposed to supply. Then there is the proverbial poverty which seems to be indigenous to the missions; no Church tax, poor collections, income depending on meagre stole fees and the trickle resulting from an occasional begging campaign; to this can be added the lack of a uniform and well-developed language, of a good Bible translation, and the complete absence of good religious literature in general; no diocesan prayer or hymn books, no suitable books for sound and solid catechetical readings.

In the light of these and other conditions it is clear that a twofold obligation arises. First to discover solutions to all tangible problems and secondly to apply the remedies and to do so with regard to the catechetical aims of the Sunday service we want.

In the conditions just outlined it is quite understandable that this service still does not exist in many places where it should exist and also that we have often to content ourselves with the minimum requirements. It would no doubt be instructive to present its growth by statistics and maps. The usual minimum ritual in many places is the Rosary with the Litany of the Blessed Virgin Mary, augmented perhaps by morning or other suitable prayers or hymns and opened or concluded with instruction for the children. In the Vicariate of Mindoro we have a case where one man held such a service on an island for forty years. Later, when the Bible was published in Tagalog, he also read the Gospel and explained it after a fashion, thus preserving the faith, and staving off sectarian influences.

The Belgian missionaries from Scheut in their Manual of Catechetics[1] have offered a solution deserving of our careful attention. The very first chapter concerns itself with the prayer meeting, and in the preface we read; "The prayer meeting takes the place of the holy Mass on Sundays and Holidays of Obligation, when the priest is absent. The catechist leads his prayer meeting in the way suggested by the priest. The catechist should always include the following in every prayer meeting: 1. A lesson on Christian doctrine. 2. Ordinary prayers. 3. The Rosary. 4. Special prayers. 5. Announcements and recommendations." The main part of the Manual consists of fifty-one lessons for prayer meetings on Sundays. They are compiled according to the so-called psychological method and arranged after the manner of the pre-kerygmatic catechism. Two important principles are stressed and adhered to, one requiring catechetical units, the other stressing the personality of the catechist. If he follows the advice of the Manual he will not just read the lessons; he will endeavour to assimilate the subject so as to be able to teach it without the book. However, the structure of the "priestless service" after the manner of the Mass of the Catechumens has not yet been accomplished by the Manual, most probably because at that time the necessary aids were still lacking. Also the catechetical function of the service, called a prayer meeting, seems to be somewhat overstressed and unconnected with the prayer aspect. It must be noted in this connection that the kind of catechist we have in mind must be specially trained. Catechetical courses differ with the different missions. In all cases, however, they ought to concern themselves with the Sunday service and with the double task of providing for it an individual, not only endowed with a thorough knowledge of the truths of our faith, but also qualified for leadership.

In what follows I am referring to my own experiences and endeavours in the Vicariate of Calapan, and anticipating certain points of an ideal Sunday service.

We have at our disposal a Sunday Missal written in the national language of the Philippines, which is generally spoken in Mindoro. This is the *Misal na Panlinggo*. Thus the reading of

[1] Catholic School Press, Bagŭio, Philippines, 1937.

the Epistle and Gospel of each Sunday and feastday is made possible. Then, too, we are provided with a handy and cheap translation of the psalms for the prayer part. "Our little hymnal" contains hymns in Tagalog, English, and Spanish. The catechetical function of our service is taken care of by a booklet edited by Father Henry Demond, entitled *Siya ang inyong Pakinggan* – "Him you shall hear".[2] It provides readings of a catechetical nature and contains a great many scripture quotations. Readings may also be taken from *Pananampalataya at Katuwiran.*[3] They are of a more apologetical nature, although the term "apologetical" may be somewhat resented. It must, however, be emphasized that, due to the massive offensive of the various sects in many parts of the mission-world, our kerygmatical reading and sermon or catechetical instruction has to be largely apologetic. The faithful, even those not particularly zealous, are quite anxious to be able to answer objections and produce scriptural arguments when dealing with non-Catholics.

Since 1956 the Philippines have had their own official catechism. It is kerygmatic in principle, as the president of the episcopal committee for catechetical instruction writes: "It puts Christ, the Son of God, at the very centre of its teaching, and weaves around the living and winning personality of Jesus the obligations and privileges of his followers – the members of his mystical body." A young missionary whose island home is Mindoro and whose mother tongue is Tagalog, has been commissioned to write short and suitable sermons based on this catechism. The sermons should not only be substantial, but also draw largely from scripture.

These sermons which are at present being written and mimeographed provide the young missionary who has not yet acquired a solid command of the language with suitable texts. For our Sunday service they do the same. However, an important factor has been left unconsidered. Reading and scripture texts are not co-ordinated. We can now consider the

[2] Catholic Trade School, Manila, 1935.

[3] "Faith and Justification", Society of St. Paul, Pasay City, Philippines, 1957.

ideal solution, the theory of which presents few difficulties, but the realization of which, in the typical background of mission life requires a great deal of study, energy and sacrifice. The Sunday Mass as it is celebrated by many priests frequently leaves much to be desired, and that not only in missionary districts. Let us not be too demanding or over-expectant when it comes to the carrying out of a plan based largely on ideas.

### *Two Apparently Ideal Proposals*

Attempts have been made to incorporate in the "priestless Sunday" the whole structure of the Mass.[4] It seems preferable to model it only on the Mass of the Catechumens; this might, however, include elements of the actual Mass, but any pedantic or perfunctory imitation of the Mass should be avoided. The faithful must understand that these services are in no way equivalent to a real Mass. Structurally, quite apart from parts taken from the New Testament, the Mass of the Catechumens is modelled on the ancient synagogue services.

A satisfactory structure is found in the so-called *Stationsgottesdienst,* as published in loose leaf form by the *Seelsorgeamt,* Magdeburg, in East Germany. It is designed more for festal seasons than for individual Sundays. It presents a simple but impressive combination of prayers, hymns, readings, and liturgical actions such as collections and requests for blessing. These services fall into three distinct parts: scripture reading, community prayer, union in the Holy Ghost. It is encouraging for us missionaries to see how dexterously the *Seelsorgeamt* in Magdeburg gave the Rosary a central position, for in the beginning the missionary has almost always recourse to the Rosary for his service and might have to retain it for some time to come or for ever, especially if or because the Rosary is such a popular devotion. Scripture reading is introduced by prayer and followed by an appropriate decade of the Rosary which forms a transition to a short meditation. Finally attention is given to

[4] See Father van Helvert's lecture "Sunday service without a priest". Jabalpure.

the task of applying to the Christian life what has been learned.

The combination of prayer, hymns, scripture readings and, finally, meditation on how it can all be applied to the daily life of the Christian, emphasizes the spiritual aspect of this kind of service and leaves the idea of catechetical instruction somewhat in the background. At the same time the catechetical content is as that of a normal catechism class, or even higher. Prayers are said in the responsorial manner. This way of praying is very commendable, since with a little practice it is possible to dispense with the prayer book. In like manner, prayers composed in the form of litanies are very suitable. Finally the third part, genuinely Catholic, makes the small priestless community aware that they are a part of the great family of God and the Church; even the announcements bear this out. The catechetical value of this kind of *Stationsfeier* lies in the fact that the truths of our faith are incorporated in kerygmatic form in the great message of joy, along with prayers, hymns, and ceremonies, into a devotional unit as into a living organism. It is essentially a divine service, which contains also pastoral values not to be under-estimated, which upon this background or in this connection exert a more tangible and lasting influence. Finally this model of our service is not too difficult to organize even in the mission; it is only necessary that a zealous and capable missionary lends his mimeograph.

Another form of Sunday service, a truly ideal structure, which leaves almost nothing to be desired in the line of thoughtful elaboration, was presented by Father J. Kellner, S.J.[5] In the same book Father Hofinger discusses the importance and structure of divine service without a priest.[6] Father Kellner presents a basic plan in which his and Father Hofinger's theory is fully exploited for practical purposes. He illustrates the working of this basic plan, selecting the Fourteenth Sunday after Pentecost. The following basic plan comprises all essential parts of the Mass of the Catechumens and in the same sequence as found in

[5] Joseph Kellner, S.J., "Worship, the Life of the Missions" in *Liturgical Studies,* University of Notre-Dame Press, 1958.

[6] Johannes Hofinger, "Communal worship in the absence of a priest; its importance and its structure", *op. cit.,* Chapter 11.

the Missal; as such it constituted an independent divine service as far back as the time of St. Augustine of Hippo.

### LITURGY OF THE WORD

Opening prayer or appropriate hymn.
1st reading: Epistle of the day or another reading from scripture suitable to the theme of the day.
1st responsory, varying according to the time and circumstances. Father Hofinger would allow the recitation of a prayer here.
2nd reading: Gospel of the day.
2nd responsory, varying, as first responsory.
3rd reading: Instruction on the Sunday or the feast.
Father Hofinger: Catechesis.
The Apostles' Creed.

### LITURGY OF PRAYER

General Prayer (Prayer of petition, *Oratio fidelium*).
Father Kellner calls for special additional prayers proper to the individual Sunday.
Hymn (of supplication).
Collect of the Day. The leader introduces it by saying:
"Let us pray", and then reads it. It is concluded by the *Amen* of the whole congregation.
Father Hofinger makes no mention of this collect. Thanksgiving prayer with *Sanctus* and *Pater Noster*.
These are parts of the Mass which follow, however, spontaneously and organically upon the ministry of the word.
Commemoration of the Holy Sacrifice (invariable). Only Father Kellner mentions this prayer of remembrance. I would call it a lay-anamnesis and suggest that it must never be missing in any such Sunday service. As it is functionally a substitute for the Mass, the essential part of the Mass must find expression in it in some way or other. Therefore the *Pater Noster,* too, belongs here after the lay-anamnesis. Final exhortation, prayer for blessing (invariable), concluding hymn.

The catechetical function of this Sunday service without a priest, not unlike that of the Magdeburg *Stationsgottesdienst,* is not exhausted by the double scripture reading and the catechetical instruction or reading. The entire service is living catechesis.

Also, this second kind can easily be introduced, if, apart from those contained in the Missal, we do not insist on specific prayers for this or that particular Sunday. Furthermore, suitable hymns could take the place of the responsorial recitation of the psalms as long as the latter are not available in good translation, or have not been adopted.

Father Hofinger places great emphasis on the catechetical reading; this is perhaps too idealistic for the beginning and even for a long time after. "The bishop is speaking to his Christians whom he cannot visit personally each Sunday. He gives them the book that contains the catechetical instructions. Taking the Gospel as its starting point and eventually the Epistle as well, it should give an exposition of some important point of our religion in a popular and vital way, always in relation to the Christian life and to the concrete situation of the Christians in the particular mission." Where are the bishops who could and would write such an ideal book? In general, they will leave this to those who are gifted with a special *charisma*. The third part of this paper will deal with the type of book we want.

## *Shaping the Service*

It may not be out of place to propose at the very outset to drop the term "priestless". *Stationsfeier* certainly sounds more dignified, at least until linguistically inclined liturgists and catechetical experts find some more appropriate name. What we need first of all is a manual or guide book, a *directorium* for the entire Church Year. This book could be quite unassuming, containing the unchangeable parts which are not so voluminous, and merely informing us where Gospel, Epistle and hymns can be found if a hymn-book is available. It may also contain some hymns, even prayers that are intended to be regularly said. Sufficient freedom should be given to the individual missionary and catechist to add other changeable parts. It would be better if several such manuals were undertaken – this would eventually lead to the adoption of the ideal manual.

We must not, however, discard the old form of Sunday service before a new form is made available, or rather, a gradual transition from the old to the new form is preferable. Anyone who knows his parishioners is well aware that they are reluctant to abandon a custom which they have come to like. This holds good also for the Sunday service. Hence the need of first training prayer-leaders, cantors, organizers and of only gradually adopting the ideal Sunday service.

It would be better to have the Rosary, litany and some additional prayers only, rather than an empty chapel.

To use the Mass of Catechumens as a basic plan is nowadays quite generally accepted. But it must also be explained to the congregation attending the "priestless" service. Parts of the Mass proper naturally fit in. The Mass of the Catechumens is already long established; originating in the Old Testament, passing through the apostolic era and the epoch of primitive Christianity it has come down to our times. By it the neophytes were trained; it was a weekly refresher course for all Christians, and that is what it should again become. Not only the scripture and catechetical reading, but the entire atmosphere of communal reading and singing, of prayers and ceremonies aim at the renewal and deepening of the knowledge and life of faith.

This part of the Mass, the Mass of the Catechumens, forms the introduction to the Mass proper, of which it takes the place, and thereby makes the community more keenly aware of what they are lacking. It makes them long and prepare for the real Mass. The Mass may not be possible because of impending hardship or persecution, but the Mass of the Catechumens will one day again serve as an introduction to the Mass itself.

We are free in our Sunday service to return to the original plan of the Mass of the Catechumens; consequently more recent pastoral and liturgical tendencies may be taken into its composition. We might use it as a testing ground, provided we do so cautiously and respectfully. If the Mass of the Catechumens should ever be remodelled, it might greatly profit from the attempts made in our service. Above all we have the tremendous advantage of the vernacular.

Readings arranged according to a three or four year plan could be tried and might prove advantageous; the manual could be composed accordingly. Furthermore the catechetical readings could be tuned to the scripture readings, and such responsories and psalms adopted that the whole structure would form an organic and fruitful unit.

The special needs of the individual communities, however, should not be overlooked. There are the burning questions of the day: sectarian propaganda and the uncertainty created by it in the minds of the uninstructed, themes such as the divinity of Christ, the foundation of the Church, Mass, sacraments, infant baptism, Sabbath or Sunday, veneration of Our Lady and the saints. The "priestless Sunday" must afford ample opportunity for such timely tracts. It is of paramount importance that the missionary has a chance to instil into the minds of his people the imperturbable certainty of having the true faith. The kerygmatic nature of our service is no longer a matter of controversy but is universally accepted. Thus both plans for the "priestless" service referred to, are based upon the kerygma – the heralding of glad tidings. It begins with Christ and he remains its centre. It is as if a current coming from God transmitted by Christ reaches the congregation. This is its predominant feature. The faithful sense that the living word of God speaks to them through the scriptures, not merely the cold and dead catechism-theology of former times with its bone-dry enumerations and subtleties. The whole human personality is made to feel the impact of God's love and grace, rather than chiefly and firstly his commandments and punishments. Emphasis is placed on what is essential rather than on completeness. Contents count more than method, Christian living more than perfect knowledge of the creed. As this entire study week is devoted to the kerygma, we need not cite literature and authors dealing with this subject, but one point needs still further elucidation, namely, the book of Glad Tidings.

The outer form of a catechism is in no way suited for our purposes. In the first place it is not intended to be read aloud but to be explained, and it would surely meet with resentment on the part of the adults. This book must contain catechetical readings in the language of scripture. These must be tied up into natural units and attuned to the cycle of scripture readings or at least must have some sort of affinity with these readings.

Such a book should reflect the spirit and language of *A Catholic Catechism*.[7] This book – especially if it were the outcome of many successful endeavours – could be given some kind of official recognition in a similar way, though clearly on a different footing from the Missal or Breviary. Such a book should go hand in hand with the new arrangement of the lessons contemplated for the Mass. Such a book would fill one of the most essential needs of our service. Let us hope that the coming Ecumenical Council will present us with such a book or at least inspire its composition or appoint a commission to that effect.

### *Conclusions*

Supervision by the pastor is required. Father van Helvert remarks: "There is a danger that such popular services might prove more attractive than the Mass itself and even be taken as substitute for the Mass." The remote danger of schism must not be passed over lightly. In our vicariate of Calapan some groups have thus seceded from the Church. If the priest is absent for long periods at a time, certain elements of the congregation might assume rights to which they are in no way entitled and perhaps separate themselves and their group in small sects, at first perhaps only in opposition to the priest but eventually to the congregation and the faith. The results of such a prolonged "priestless" period in Mindoro are some powerful confraternities, the *Cofradias*. Their members consider divine services, bells, processions, collections, even the holy water font, baptisms and funerals as belonging to their jurisdiction. Even today hundreds, perhaps thousands, are found who have been baptized by the *buhos tubig*, a form of lay-baptism often of doubtful validity. The child is not brought to the priest, and it is only on the occasion of first communion that such cases come to the knowledge of the pastor.

The ordinary daily prayers should be integrated into this service. It is one of its catechetical functions to safeguard this deposit of essential prayers.

[7] London and New York, 1953.

Special prayers for feasts and festival seasons should be included in the relevant manuals. They must be short, composed with great care, diligence and expertness and might at the same time serve as family prayers, This, too, is a catechetical function of this service which will bear fruit throughout the following week.

Ceremonies (cult or ceremonial actions), too, should be mentioned in the manual, or recommendations made for developing them where and as conditions are favourable. Some of them are known and introduced in many places, for example, offertory collections, contributions for the sick, for the poor, for refugees, or for the victims of this or that calamity. In the Philippines we have the so-called *Flores de Mayo,* an offering of flowers during the month of May accompanied by a variety of hymns. It could easily be included in the plan of the Mass of the Catechumens or of our service. Many missionaries collect rice in the villages during harvest time. The rice is sold and the money used for the construction or repair of chapels. This rice, called *palay,* could be offered. The Manual for Catechists which we mentioned, lists three different blessings for rice.

Popular devotions could easily be assimilated. They could enliven the service and also make it popular. On the other hand this service could greatly contribute toward the preservation of these popular devotions. The *Mahal na Pasiyon* is perhaps the most ancient native popular devotion in the Philippines. It is an epic poem of quintameters beginning with the creation of the world but principally relating the details of Christ's Passion. It exists in different Filipino dialects, preserving expressions that otherwise have become obsolete. This epic is for many the principal source of religious knowledge and edification. It is both a family and a community devotion cultivated especially during Lent, when the well-known melodies are chanted often from beginning to end, sung by peacefully competing groups, and can be heard sometimes for hours, even days and nights. Some missionaries have deemed it fit to allow parts to be chanted during Mass; they have organized community singing of the *Pasiyon* or at least encouraged it. During the season of Lent it would be quite in place to chant part of it either before or after or even during the service. Unfortunately, the younger generation seems to be dropping the custom of chanting the *Pasiyon*.

We conclude with a mission axiom: "To every village a chapel." People are not anxious to visit private homes. We must also always consider human nature. A chapel is a community affair, it is the house of God and of his little flock. Here the true atmosphere for divine services prevails. Here, too, on rare occasions the priest can say Mass for which the service without a priest is no substitute. For it must not lead away from the Mass; its most noble catechetical function consists precisely in educating the little "priestless" community towards it.

# THE ROLE OF THE CATECHUMENATE IN CHRISTIAN TRAINING

# Reaching the Unbelievers in the Missions

JOSEPH SPAE, C.I.C.M.
Editor of the *Missionary Bulletin,* Tokyo

I TAKE it that the topic which has been assigned to me refers to what is now commonly called "pre-catechesis", or the predisposition of the individual and the masses for the acceptance of the faith. My reflections will concentrate on an approach to the masses rather than to the individual; and my examples will be taken from experience in Japan.

In Japan we are but 264,000 Catholics, or two per thousand of the whole population. We have some ten thousand adult baptisms per year. This little flock is sent to ninety-four million potential pre-catechumens, every one of whom God wills to save. As you know, in the past God has kept faith with our people. We were long without priests, without the Mass, without the Bible. Throughout an unrelenting persecution lasting 250 years thousands gave their lives for Christ. It is among the descendants of these glorious martyrs that we find the highest incidence of vocations to the priesthood and the religious life – higher, indeed, than anywhere else in the world. The conversion of an individual or of a nation is nothing else but the finding of their specific vocation. Missionary activity means helping them to discover vocation. Strictly speaking only God converts. Towards this end God uses the efforts of his apostle, "the one whom he sends", and of the convert, "the one to whom he sends his love". The action of divine grace is not on the same plane as that of human liberty, and we shall not examine here their delicate relationship. We limit ourselves to a consideration of those initial contacts between the apostle and the one to whom he is Christ's ambassador.

### *The Pre-Catechumen*

The pre-catechumen – as an individual or a group – is not an abstraction. The mind and culture of a people is the substratum upon which its supernatural vocation must be built. Hence the importance of a reverent attention to, and respect for, individual and national traits of character.

The spiritual uneasiness of the good pagan betrays his need for God. A certain combative anti-Catholic attitude which looms on the horizon in Japan and other far eastern countries (I do not include China, where it has erupted in all virulence) is often attributed to historical circumstances such as persecution, scientific atheism, resurgent nationalism or the awakening of ancient native creeds. But these causes, either alone or in combination, fail to give a sufficient explanation. More correctly, this sulking antagonism springs from the subconscious, impassioned baulking of pagan mentality at the first effective contact with divine truth. It springs also from an ill-defined resentment against us, as I heard it said, "because you came too late, too slowly, and with too few". It will never quite be cured, no more than the sinful tendency of the individual soul to resist the promptings of divine grace. But it can be overcome by us with God's help – and this, in practice, largely to the extent that we rid ourselves of internal divisions, lack of purpose and of accessories which might becloud the essence of our message.

All nations possess antecedently Catholic religious attitudes. And these we must discover and foster in our first contact with them. These very same attitudes, once ennobled through supernatural life, will blossom into that "native" Christian outlook and, eventually, culture, which are the splendid endowment of a Catholic people. In other words, there is a hierarchy and a method of presentation which we must respect.

Take such a basic attitude as *pantheism* in Oriental religions. We need not run it down as an enemy. We might rather stress, with St. Paul, that "in God we live and breathe" and that he is all in all. And once this general knowledge is established, we might lift it up to its full stature which is that of the incarnation. For Christ, *caro factus,* is the living bridge between the general knowledge of God which is pantheism and the concrete one which is monotheism. In Japan at least, where we find that about one third of the population admits the existence of a personal God, the stage is generally already set where a prudent presentation of our concept of God will meet with little resistance.

Take, further, another basic attitude which holds that action precedes faith. "Action" (literally "to do", "to go", *gyo-hsing*) is that way of the good pagan by which he expresses his *famulatus* to God. We might translate it more correctly by *ascesis* and "penance", rather than by "activity". For it is a spiritual voiding of oneself to make place for God; it is even a passive approach, comparable to the *pati deum* of the mystics; it is a path, *michi-tao-manga* (the classic definition of religion in Japan, China and India) which leads into the realms of the spirit and of contemplation.

Who would doubt but that among those millions who in truth "walk" before God, even though they might but vaguely perceive the first words of the creed, there could be many authentic candidates for conversion? So much the more that many express their *gyo* through acts of charity. To such people, I have often found, the gospel passage of Matt. 25:31–40 on the last judgement, or the enraptured descriptions of St. Paul in 1 Cor. 12:12–13; 13:3 and Ephesians 4:2–6 strike a responsive chord at first reading. They confirm the words of St. Augustine that "through charity we enter into the texture of the body of Christ so that there is but one Christ loving himself in all". *(In 1. Epist. Joan.* 10:3*)*. They also invite us to use a sound catechetical approach: the prospective catechumen will often, at a distance, be invited to imitate our Christian ways of living, as if to give himself a trial run before his real ascent to the Church.

Take, finally, the role of intuition as a preamble to the faith. By intuition I mean that "intellectual and affective sympathy" in the Bergsonian sense; that true knowledge and practical approach to spiritual reality to which St. Thomas would attribute the interior instinct to believe,[1] the *cœur* of Pascal, the

[1] See M. D. Chenu, O.P., "Les catégories affectives dans la langue de l'École: le Cœur" in *Études Carmélitaines* (1950).

*mens* of Augustine and the *cor* of the Bible. Intuition, which pervades human sentimentality, is known by the Oriental philosophers as *jo, ch'ing* (often translated by the word "sentiment"). Without *jo,* intellect *(chi, chih)* and will cannot function. Intuition is at the core of that compassionate knowledge of man which the Japanese express by the word *ningen-mi (sapere hominem)*. It bypasses the usual logical processes and the exigencies of time, and in one fell leap, it reaches that comprehension of its subject, not to change it, but to be changed into it. Intuition accounts, I submit, both for Japan's surprises and summersaults in the ideological field and for her reaching the status of a world power in record time. Through intuition Japan will discover Christ, if only for the reason that the love for a person is more quickly acquired than the knowledge of his teachings and that the way through the heart is shorter than the way through the head. Many, I presume, are those who come to the *baptisma flaminis* without having heard about the *baptisma fluminis*. Many are those who, like one old man I assisted, seeing a priest at their death-bed, exclaim: "I have seen Christ; the God of the Catholics has come!"

But there are also sociological factors to be considered. Whether we like it or not, the western forms of living are conquering the world. The Japanese and other peoples find themselves divided along the course of this mad race for Europeanization into the three strata described by Riesman in his book, *The Lonely Crowd*. Firstly, there are the tradition-directed conservatives who, in ever decreasing numbers, still feed precariously at the well-springs of their old religions; secondly, there are the masses – directed from the outside – that faceless majority, both peasants and city-dwellers, who, through the acceleration of urbanism, fall prey to mass-communications and collective hysteria; and lastly, there is the small band of inner-directed men, driven by their ideals and ideologies, whose enthusiasm foments revolutions, who are willing to lead the shiftless millions – and among whom will be found the great apostles of the age – for good or for evil. These are the men we must befriend with special care.

It is a state of moral indifferentism and relativism which makes our apostolate so difficult. To the extent that ideological currents from the west have abetted this secularization, they have been assimilated. To the extent, in other words, that Christianity contented itself with injecting some moral elements into that syncretism, it has been welcomed. As for Catholicism with its absolutes of truth and love, it has never been seriously tried in modern times, at least not on a scale comparable to that with which other ideologies and especially the techniques of the west have been imported.

How to open a window to their mind, how to offer ourselves as the supreme discovery to their intuition, how to bring them that interior unity which leads to peace and the knowledge of God, remains now to be examined.

### *Our Message: Christ, the Church*

It is imperative that we succeed in bringing knowledge of a love for Christ and his Church to the pagan masses. God has provided us with the spiritual equipment for the task. We – that is, the Universal Church, the priest, the local community, the individual Catholic – we are the *praefigura Christi* and the palpable incarnation of that benignity and humanity through which the Lord reaches out to those who do not know him.

Often one hears it said by workers who have cast out their nets in vain: "No one comes to me!" Perhaps it was forgotten that the pagan ought not first to come, but that the priest ought first to go. He is the one sent, long before they are the ones called. Geographical distances and, even more so, psychological distances must first be bridged. The awareness of this fact, that "we must put ourselves across", is essential for success in precatechetical teaching. Methods are many, and we shall analyse some particular ones in the third part of this paper. Here are some general thoughts on the matter.

We must preach the gospel. The chasm which divides east and west is really of the intellectual order. Fortunately, the communication of supernatural life is not conditioned by one's intellectual habits, or by one's acknowledging the relations between body and soul, or the distinctions between substance and accident. Such notions have their use for a deeper understanding of revealed truth. But they are not to be propounded to all; and as a first contact, at least outside the sphere of western thinking, they should be avoided. It is of the greatest importance to present the whole Christ, but progressively, to the pre-catechumen. While all information should be correct, it cannot be complete all at once. The first impression is of prime importance. It suffers when all that is known about Catholics is that we eat fish on Friday, or are against birth control, or that priests do not marry. Rather, from the very beginning, the pre-catechumen must be, as it were, gently overwhelmed by the basic mark of our religon: that we love God above all else, and that we love one another.

Then there is a negative pre-catechesis: that, which prevents us from giving a false impression. Restraint, silence, common sense are its hallmark. Here I would wish to endorse what Father Schütte said at Nijmegen about the primacy of the spiritual over the material, and I would like to advocate, in the light of what he said, a re-examination in regard to the distribution of our mission funds. The physical growth of our missionary enterprises is at times out of proportion to the local contributions and the training of personnel, both native and foreign. It launches us into a vortex of expansion which keeps us panting and overwhelmed by material cares. This state of affairs is not left unnoticed by the non-Catholic masses. They know us for what they see: a mighty international organization with considerable financial backing. They find us sometimes in competition with their chosen fields, such as charity and hospital works in the welfare state, such as schools in countries with universal education.

A just measure must be observed in all these things, especially if sponsored by foreign men and capital, lest our spiritual message become obscured, personal contacts drowned in institutional machinery, and the human touch be lost. *Cor ad cor non jam loquitur*. We should therefore shun all rivalry in secular matters in order the more to concentrate on the heart of our calling: to be witnesses to the truth, to be channels of grace.

### *We Need a Pre-catechism*

A first introduction to the knowledge and love of Christ and the Church could hardly be gained by reading our traditional catechisms or books of devotion. We all feel that, in Japan at least, the catechism should not be given at first to the prospective catechumen. As for the unwary non-Catholic who might find it accidentally on a seat in the train (and some Japanese writers have gone on record about their experiences here), the traditional catechism might very well be the beginning and also the end of all he wants to know about the Church. The same applies, within limits, to our liturgical ceremonies. On a recent occasion, the priestly jubilee of one of our most respected missionaries, two of the twelve non-Catholic friends whom he had invited to Mass left during the ceremony, protesting they could not stand "the hocus-pocus of the gestures and the strangeness of the words". Such examples are the exception, it is true, but they are instructive. Both the catechism – or shall we say, the pre-catechism – and the liturgy are meant to point to Christ.

Therefore, we need this special book – this pre-catechism – a book that should be cast not in the form of a textbook, but of the Gospel; it should focus on the life and the personality of Christ, not on the organization which he created; it should bring out the light and love of his message, not the objections against it; it should be intuitive, not only notional; it should be personal and yet on a world scale; it should be existential and yet transcending, like Christ, the particularities of any nation; it should be a true image of him who is that unique Chinese, Hindu, Bantu, Japanese, that awe inspiring *homo toto terrarum orbe diffusus*.[2] Such a pre-catechism, I submit, will be as different from the present ones as Deharbe is from the German Catechism and Gibbon's *Faith of Our Fathers* is from the *Autobiography of the Little Flower*.

In Japan, at least, we have nothing of the kind, but modest efforts in that direction (such as a little pamphlet entitled "You and Christ" of which we have distributed half a million copies) have been encouraging.

[2] St. Augustine in Psalms 85 and 122.

### *How to Spread our Message*

We must make contact. To the missionary, nothing in a people, save sin, ought to be alien. The barrier of language and customs ought resolutely to be removed. This starts with the frank acceptance of the other's individuality without trying to reduce him to our own image. To us, brought up in a Catholic atmosphere, such an attitude does not come naturally. After all, we are right, and they must be wrong. And yet, we must not only admit the fact that others are different, but that they ought to be different, so that in them, and in us, the body of Christ may reach its full stature. In other words, our intellectual acceptance of national traits and personal ideosyncracies must have an affective content, in order to become an effective contact. Such a contact, unfortunately, is sometimes absent even between the apostolic workers themselves, and between the missionary and the native clergy. It is sometimes lost by default, victim to the *status quo*. Missioners – those certainly not rebelling against their mission land atmosphere – often complain, in regard to the necessary actual contact: "It's not that we're on bad terms; just on no terms."

Effective contact between us and the masses will largely depend upon the solution of this problem in ourselves. This *mutua subministratio,* to use a word coined by St. Thomas[3], is the key to spiritual perfection, the quintessence of Catholic Action and the sound basis for missionary adaptation and modification. In broad lines, it might be put like this: our faith reaches out for their intellect and intuition, *fides quaerens intellectum*. Thus we shall see to it that a certain strain of political imperialism does not change its hue into ideological imperialism. A new phase will start when Christianity is presented and accepted as part of the national patrimony. In almost every mission country this process is now in laborious gestation. We must deliberately accelerate it through apostolic inventiveness and new formulas of collaboration between all concerned.

Positive pre-catechesis is mainly the work of the laity, both as individuals and as a community. It should be stressed that the

[3] *Summa Theologica,* II II, q. 138, a. 2 ad 1.

essence of Christian life requires that it be propagated spiritually by all. A healthy spirit of conquest is necessary. Where this spirit is inspired by true sympathy as we described above, where it endeavours to meet others on their own ground, to be useful to them, it will bring many to the discovery of Christ. In the mission field, the role of the priest is chiefly in the vertical order of dispensing graces from God to man. The role of the laity, however, is in the horizontal order of human relations. Any contact which they have with their fellowmen should be sanctifying. How much could be achieved through a systematic use of those contacts that Christ be known!

The efficacy of individual testimony, however, is not only increased as the number of witnesses increases, but witness given in community has, by divine will, a peculiar cogency upon the non-believers. It is generally admitted that, if, for example, in France eighty per cent of the 5000 adults who are baptized annually lose the faith, this is chiefly due to the fact that they were not brought to a real meeting with Christ, not incorporated into a real community of Christians.[4] We have come to the same conclusion concerning Japan.[5]

It is almost axiomatic that conversions in a given place are in direct proportion to the number of apostolic contacts and the spiritual fervour of the community which nourishes them. Schematically, this spiritual current of graces, running in both directions, could be presented as follows:

| | | | | |
|---|---|---|---|---|
| The | ↑ | eucharistic community | ↓ | Christ |
| unbeliever | | baptismal community | | approaches |
| approaches | | catechumens' community | | the |
| Christ: | | pre-catechumens' community | | unbeliever: |

The pre-catechumen is a sympathizer who feels subconsciously drawn to an ideal which is held up to him. I know of a Buddhist bonze who became a Catholic after observing a priest for three years. I know of a doctor who did not understand anything of what he read in the catechism, but decided to join the Church upon seeing, every night, a group of nurses at prayer. I know

[4] *Documentation Catéchistique,* Juillet 1957, p. 37

[5] *Lumen Vitae,* viii, 1953, pp. 585–606.

of a famous critic and author who recently told a university audience: "There is but one logical step for all of us to make, and that is to join the Catholic Church. Now, if we do not join it, perhaps, it is because we lack courage. But it is also because it is so hard to find: there is too little Catholicism left in the Catholic Church."

I cannot enter here upon an elaboration of the organization, the spirituality and the methods of small group movements as the most modern and yet very ancient way of influencing non-believers. A renewal of pastoral and catechetical theology is intimately connected with them. In countries where, as in Japan, small group cooperation is, as it were, such a part of the social make-up as to be almost second nature, they can play a providential role. Meanwhile, it is gratifying to see how, in our home countries, they bring new life to old parishes.[6]

In our efforts to contact the millions who are waiting, we have already talked about the role of the individual and the community. We would now like to say a word about the national level, which through modern communications has reached an unprecedented importance.

### *Mass Media*

There are first of all, the different mass media. Press, radio and television need not be in Catholic hands before they can serve our purpose. Catholics can "infiltrate" them, if they will but take advantage of all opportunities and prepare themselves for such an apostolate, both technically and apostolically. This field, indeed, belongs primarily to the Catholic layman. It is unfortunately true that practically no systematic effort is made toward such training, in the form of positive job guidance or financial assistance. It sets one thinking again of a redistribution of funds.

In Japan, we have an incipient radio program which may before long cover the whole nation and which is linked to

[6] Jos. J. Spae, C.I.C.M., *Neighbourhood Association, a Catholic Way for Japan* (Himeji, 1956); Bishop E.-J. de Smedt, *Le Christ dans le quartier* (Bruges, 1960); J. Bulckens, "Adult Catechesis within the context of local meetings" in *Lumen Vitae,* xiv, 1959, pp. 685–694.

correspondence courses. Such correspondence courses can also very profitably be organized on a parish level, as we are doing now. They are then no longer anonymous, but easily find their fulfilment in face to face relationships of the unbeliever with a Catholic, thus becoming his first live contact with the local community.

We also have a nationwide Christmas programme. An average of at least one million pieces of literature are distributed to non-Catholics at the occasion of the Lord's Nativity. And here we have a not-very-respectable ally. A Buddhist paper has commented that, for all their madness, even the pagan Christmas celebrations in Tokyo yet point to the birth of him with whose name they are associated, while no one remembers the birthday of Buddha... .[7]

We have made a start towards presenting Catholic thought and morality to the masses through the use of our youth magazines. It is remarkable how non-Catholic parents appreciate these efforts and attentively read the guide books or special pages which we publish for them. On the occasion of our centenary, Father Roggendorf, S.J., of Sophia University in Tokyo, brought out a symposion on Catholic thought, written for the non-Catholic intelligentsia but specially prepared for Japan by a group of famous foreign Catholic authors. The book received very wide acclaim. In all these efforts, quality counts more than quantity, and any show of strength and financial pressure is carefully avoided.

### *An Institute for the Intellectual Apostolate*

In line with a suggestion of the Holy Father that "the Ordinaries set up a centre of culture, according to the need of the region, where priests, both native and foreign, will be able to put their experience at the service of the nation in which they were born or to which they have given themselves by choice" (John XXIII *Princeps Pastorum*), it is our cherished dream to start in the near future an Institute for the Intellectual Apostolate, built upon a wide co-operation among the mission societies, the native clergy

[7] *Chugainippo,* Dec. 18, 1959.

and an élite of our Catholic laity, and subject to the direct control of the Hierarchy.

We visualize the role of such an institute as follows. Firstly, it would supply information about Japan to the Church in Japan. To this effect, a scientific analysis should be made of public opinion in this country, and of the factors, or rather personalities who influence it.

A second part of the programme would have broad pastoral implications. The findings of this analysis would lead, it is hoped, to the formulation of new methods and catechetical advance. They would show us openings and hitherto unsuspected opportunities. Individual Catholics and communities could be told about the task they might fulfil, encouraged in their contacts with those influential men and invited to participate in a well planned approach over the entire missionary front, towards the public at large.

Such an institute, too, could bring accurate information about the Church to Japan. (The lack of such an organ has, last year, been publicly deplored by the non-Catholic sympathizer.) This could be done not only by its library facilities, conferences and publications, but especially by furnishing appropriate material on current topics to our many Catholic university professors and writers, a methodical pool of whom could easily be set into motion. This information could then be absorbed by them and rewritten for publication in the national or local press.

The institute could powerfully contribute towards the raising of intellectual and apostolic standards among priests, missionaries and laity. Serving, as it would, as clearing house of pastoral, catechetical and religious- sociological information, it would draw an élite of resident students, both Japanese and foreign. These students would then go back to their respective fields with a better grasp of the national situation and with that power of observation which, in turn, could channel local information to the central organ. It is indeed a pity that we have so few specialists in those contact fields among the clergy.

Finally, we believe that such an institute could be of help to other mission countries, and that it is the privilege of Japan to take the lead in carrying out the Holy Father's suggestion. Conceivably, such an institute could be affiliated with *Lumen*

*Vitae* and other similar research centres throughout the world. Japan, being at the crossroads of the missionary world, at the focal point where old and new, east and west, meet, is an ideal testing ground for new experiments, and an outpost whose importance to the development of the Christian ideal throughout the far east and the whole world is becoming increasingly accepted by the Church. The institute we refer to would be our laboratory.

## *Conclusion*

Pre-catechesis is primarily a matter of apostolic contact by the Christian community – including the world Church – and the individual with the nation at large. Lest we lose to Communism, we must organize ourselves and use every means at our disposal. Systematic planning, research and the use of modern group techniques seem particularly indicated. World opinion has a profound impact upon the masses in countries with high literacy. National centres of information, directed both to and from the Church, could immensely improve our effectiveness and show us new methods in the apostolic field. An international centre of apostolic and missionary information seems necessary to coordinate all efforts.

# Instruction and Formation of Adult Catechumens

PAUL BRUGGISSER, S.M.B.
Director of the Mission Seminary, Schöneck, Switzerland

". . . He who believes and is baptized will be saved" (Mark 16:16).

TO believe and then to be reborn in baptism is the original, evangelical gateway to new life in Christ. It is the missionary way, and many a missionary must have found himself secretly envying his adult neophytes their experience of meeting Christ at the prime of life. No wonder that many of them develop the proverbial apostolic zeal of converts!

What I mean to say is that adult catechumens are not so much a problem as a real glory of the missionary Church. But against this positive side, there remains the missionary problem of preparing the way for adult catechumens. The missionary and his helpers must go out and meet the candidates for baptism halfway and even more than halfway. Whereas cradle Catholics grow into their faith, the faith must grow upon our adult catechumens. They bring along with them a definite frame of mind, certain fixed errors and half-truths from their pagan beliefs and surroundings, and half a life's experience not moulded on the pattern of Christian living. Their lot is a con-version, a definite transformation of their mental outlook. Their very age often handicaps them when it comes to learning about the fundamentals of the faith. What missionary has not heard the pathetic complaint from the lips of elderly people: "Yes, Father, I would like to be baptized; but I cannot learn!" By that they mean "learning" after the fashion of school children;

somehow the impression has got abroad that the Catholic faith is only for school children.[1]

In the light of these facts – and with proper consideration of all the preceding talks during this Study Week – this paper intends to set out and present for your deliberation and discussion two particular facets of the problem at hand, namely, the catechetical instruction and the pastoral formation of adult catechumens before and after baptism.

### *Instruction of Adult Catechumens*

In order to determine the nature of catechetical instruction for adults, the aim of the whole course must be borne in mind from the very beginning. The *aim* of the catechumenate is the introduction of unbaptized and newly baptized people into Christian faith and Christian living.[2]

This introduction runs through two phases; firstly, the candidates must be weaned from their deeply rooted pagan beliefs and attitude; secondly, they must be led to discover for themselves the "new life" in Christ. This second phase also is twofold as it calls for an appropriate knowledge of the faith and, secondly, for a corresponding religious and moral training. For the sake of clarity, this latter aspect will be presented in the second part of my paper. Now, the necessary knowledge of the faith is imparted through catechetical instruction properly understood. As the etymology of the Greek word κατηχεῖν (= to sound forth, to provoke an echo) suggests, catechetical instruction must be lively and potent enough to evoke a reasonable echo, an intelligent answer on the part of the candidates.[3]

If we are to achieve that aim, our catechetical approach must possess a positive character. As one missionary from Southern Rhodesia writes: "No builder can construct a solid house without foundation. No farmer will produce a bumper crop

[1] J. Rutishauser, in *Guti,* Periodical for the Missionaries of the Diocese of Gwelo, S.R., 6th Year (1957), p. 140.

[2] Thomas Ohm, *Das Katechumenat in den katholischen Missionen* (Münster, 1959), p. 5.

[3] loc. cit.

without knowing the soil of his fields. Even today, both pagans and Christians are tremendously influenced by their old religion. European missionaries should in the first place acknowledge that there is a section of the African mind which they have not yet been able to enter." It is not right to force the African to erase his own culture and religious background entirely, and to compel him to accept a form of Christianity exactly identical with that of the European missionary. "Can the African be Christian only by giving up his culture, or is there a way by which Christianity can ennoble him?"[4] There can be no doubt in our minds how we would answer this question; let it suffice here to refer to the earlier papers on the character of missionary catechesis and missionary adaptation. At any rate, a flexible attitude is always needed, and if a positive approach must be characteristic of all catechetical instruction, then our adult catechumens are even more entitled to it because pagan beliefs have so far been an essential part of their lives. Moreover, African thought and mentality *(négritude)* is about to re-discover its hastily abandoned sources; and with or without the rising tide of nationalism they would certainly resent it if we were to make light of their national heritage.

Concerning the methods to be adopted for our catechetical presentation of the faith to adult catechumens, much will be remembered again from the previous talks on catechetical methods, the catechetical use of the Bible, and the catechetical value of the liturgy. I shall, therefore, not repeat that, unless it has a special bearing for adult catechumens. To me, the application of the general principles of catechetical methods to adult catechumens reveals these characteristics.

Above all, the instruction of adult catechumens must be as simple as possible. By that I mean a simplicity which gives the unchangeable facts of divine revelation according to the mental capacity of adult people. Father Hofinger who has laboured for decades on this field says[5] that the Bible, the liturgy, some systematic catechesis and the practical orientation towards Christian living, are the main ways by which we introduce our catechu-

[4] J. Braendle in *Guti* (2), p. 36.
[5] In *Heiliger Dienst,* 9th Year (1955), p. 131.

mens into the mystery of Christ. The sequence in which these four ways are listed indicates the essential steps of a progressive initiation. Whoever has acquainted himself with modern catechetical methods will agree that the biblical narration is the cornerstone on which to build up the essentials of Christian doctrine. Care must be taken, however, that the narration is not put in for its own sake but as an illustration of the mystery of Christ. The ferial masses of Lent which were composed especially for the last examination of catechumens before baptism, remain a valid pattern of sound scriptural and liturgical catechesis.

The teaching of adult catechumens must be "alive, *intuitive* and varied". This is saying that the text of the Bible and its subsequent catechetical summary is by itself not sufficient. "The catechist has to endow the skeleton of the catechism with flesh and blood by making use of images, comparisons and new examples borrowed from the people whom he is evangelizing."[6] If we cannot achieve this ourselves we should at least encourage our indigenous co-workers to do it.

Our teaching must be personal in the sense that we build up the personal responsibility of each and every catechumen. With all due respect to the communal, tribal thinking of our African people and because of it, this personal appeal involved in becoming a Christian must reach the mind and will of every catechumen. "The former lives of the Africans in their community were embedded in tradition and communal thinking to such an extent that no personal decisions were ever asked of them".[7] Only now, with the beginning of the catechumenate, personal responsibility awakens and takes on a new meaning towards the new freedom of the children of God. This personal responsibility on which I should like to dwell a little longer matters in two respects. It matters in regard to the idea of God. Many Bantu people have a clear idea of the Supreme Being. Take, for example, the Vashona people of Southern Rhodesia. "They know the Supreme Being as the Creator, supreme above

[6] J. Beckmann, "Missionary Catechesis Yesterday and Today" in *Lumen Vitae,* 12th Year (1957), p. 122.

[7] J. Beckmann, *Die Katholische Kirche im neuen Afrika* (Einsiedeln, 1947), p. 257.

men and the forces of nature. He is the source of all life, the giver of fertility and rain. He does not exist in only one locality. He has existed before creation. He is very powerful, but is far removed from men and concerns himself mainly with the welfare of the tribe. He reveals his presence through awe-inspiring physical phenomena (lightning, thunder) and through fire (like God in the burning bush and in the pillar of fire) and is held in reverence.

They confuse their belief in God with their belief in dynamic forces. Their fear of magic is greater than their pagan belief in God. They should be led to know God as their personal Father through Jesus Christ as their personal saviour. He has to become a personal God. They should be taught that in Christ they possess the spiritual power supreme above all other spiritual forces."[8]

Unless we purify the idea of God in our catechumens, there will forever be a queer coexistence of Christian faith together with pagan beliefs as in the typical example of a missionary from Togo. "A Christian polygamist has just asked for five Masses to be said for a good delivery by one of his wives and for the child to become full of wisdom and grace. At the same time, however, a chicken was given to the witchdoctor".[9] Father Lugira of Uganda, when confronted with such examples of bilateral allegiance to God and to magic forces, said from his own understanding of this mentality: "If the first commandment is not inculcated sufficiently in their minds, they remain with doubts and stick to all the intermediaries of their basic belief in the all-powerful God. Still it is a question of God, not a question of intermediaries." In their approach to God the Bantu people have attached themselves to a great variety of mediators in the world of spirits as well as in the world of men. They have to be taught to approach him through the one Mediator, Jesus Christ.

Individual responsibility must be emphasized also in regard to the moral obligations which Christian living imposes on our adult catechumens. Hitherto, they judged their moral conduct by what they considered to be in the interest of tribal

[8] See (4), p. 37.

[9] F. Delattre, "L'Apostolat en Afrique et ses options" in *Les Missions Catholiques,* No. 69 (1958), p. 33.

life and for the welfare of the world of their ancestral spirits. Morality was something external, and retribution of sin after death was more or less unknown. With their detribalization and with the breakdown of their ancestor worship, the Africans are in dire need of a new set of moral values.

Now "they must see themselves as individually responsible before God and challenged in Christ to a life of loyalty to him, instead of maintaining merely a group-morality. They must come to know that morality is not merely external but has its roots in the inward life. At the same time, the African sense of communal loyalty, if understood in a broader and Christian sense, can bring new warmth in our modern and too individualistic society. We have here an African treasure which has to be purified and preserved."[10]

A final point in catechetical methods must be made concerning the psychology of learning in adult catechumens. Experience shows that it is a matter of discretion how much we can ask of them. If we use some catechetical aids (pictures, suitable textbooks with illustrations, etc.) as they become available, and as long as the doctrinal summary flows from the biblical themes, then we should not have to ask much memory work from our adult catechumens; on the other hand, one might be too lenient and too easily satisfied with a minimum. Especially with illiterates one cannot do entirely without a certain amount of memorization. They need some pegs, as it were, on which to fasten their thoughts and affections; but in hard cases the main Christian prayers and the apostolic creed – if properly brought home to them – will go a long way towards securing the necessary knowledge of the faith before baptism. Group learning and discussion, as in the case of the Inquiry Class designed by the American Paulist Fathers, will also make for readier assimilation.

Whatever methods one may adopt and whatever circumstances may prevail in a given mission, all catechetical instruction has fulfilled its purpose when Cardinal Newman's word is

[10] Rev. W. J. v. d. Merwe, "The Shona Idea of God", N.A.D.A., Vol. 34 (1957), p. 61.
See B. G. M. Sundkler, *Bantu Prophets in South Africa* (London, 1948).

verified: "This is the very definition of a Christian – one who looks for Christ."[11] Once they seriously look for Christ, they can be made to find him by means of our pastoral sollicitude to develop the habits of Christian prayer and of Christian life.

## *Formation of Adult Catechumens*

The separation of these two phases of instruction and formation of adult catechumens seems to be somewhat artificial; it is true that in the practice of the catechumenate they must go together. Nevertheless, a separate treatment is likely to highlight the importance of each aspect in itself. Suitable instruction will give the catechumens the required knowledge of the faith whereas the formation comprises all our efforts to introduce them into Christian living; or again, the instruction is directed to their minds, and the pastoral formation is addressed to their wills so that they may be enabled to love God and their neighbours "with their whole hearts and their whole souls" as well as "with their whole minds" (Matt. 22:37). In this field of formation, some general principles might be briefly stated before two specific applications will be given.

There is, first of all, the time factor. No lasting results could be achieved if one were to shorten the duration of the catechumenate. There is a long way from recognizing and acknowledging the truth of the Christian message to a life which is impregnated by it. A short time of preparation does not allow for the necessary training in Christian living. Although conditions vary from one country to another, the average experience has shown the wisdom of a catechumenate for a period from two to four years.

Closely related to the duration in time is the gradation in intensity of their baptismal preparation. Cardinal Lavigerie's orders on this subject are well known. He prescribed a catechumenate of three grades. "The first grade is those beginners whom he liked to call postulants because they had to give evidence of a serious desire for baptism with all its rights and

[11] Ohm, *op. cit.* (2), p. 110.

duties. In keeping with the old *disciplina arcani,* or rule of secrecy, they were not to be admitted to Mass or any other acts of public worship; instead they would be given restricted general instruction about Christian living. The second group of catechumens properly so called should be introduced into the specifically Christian truths of the Blessed Trinity, the incarnation of Christ, and the sacraments; they were to be admitted to the first part of Mass – the old Mass of the Catechumens, including the homily; only the third group, whom he called *electi* would have access to the whole teaching and cult of the Church into which they were about to enter."[12] Both from the pedagogic and the pastoral point of view, the wisdom of this principle of gradation could not be doubted; it is only in its practical application that the difficulties begin.

A third general principle of this period of formation might be called "learning by doing". Our adult catechumens must notice very soon that becoming a Catholic is not a mere course of learning but a new way of life. Catechetical instruction which does not lead to practical prayer and thanksgiving is academic and vain. All that is meant by "renouncing Satan and all his works and all his pomps" must begin now. The catechumenate is a training ground of Christian living. All relations to spiritual powers other than God and his "household" (Eph. 2:19) must be broken. There is for many catechumens that in-between period of which one student aptly said: "We don't believe in spirits any longer, but we are still afraid of them."[13] Their entire individual and social life, their attitude towards work and leisure must be re-formed in terms of the new faith. "It is", as Father Ohm[14] says, "one of the most important tasks of the missionaries and their helpers . . . to teach the catechumens all that Christ has commanded us", without imposing any unnecessary burdens. It is more important still, as Father Hofinger points out, that the commandments shoud not be treated merely as divine directions but "mainly as our loving response to divine love".[15]

[12] J. Beckmann, *op. cit.* (7), p. 251 et seq.
[13] Ohm, *op. cit.* (2), p. 94².
[14] Ohm, *op. cit.* (2), p. 95.
[15] J. Hofinger, *The Art of Teaching Christian Doctrine* (Univ. of Notre Dame Press, 1957), p. 61.

Against the background of these three principles two specific applications must be made with regard to what I consider to be the two most important fields of formation, namely the initiation into prayer and sacrifice, and the initiation into the new community and the apostolate.

Concerning initiation into prayer and sacrifice, mention was made already of the most common Christian prayers as a means of securing the necessary knowledge of the faith. This is, of course, only a subsidiary function of prayer. We are well advised, anyway, not to rely only on formulated prayers but to encourage our catechumens in their innate forms of prayer. Whoever has seen African women making a day's retreat at a mission and sitting for hours in the deepest of silence cannot doubt that these people are able to find their way to God in prayer.

Care must also be taken to make the catechumens familiar with the great prayers and ceremonies which accompany their baptism, especially where it can be done on the great baptismal days of the Church Year. It is to be hoped that the recommendation of last year's study week at Uden (Holland) may soon be fulfilled: *Ritus Baptismi adultorum de integro restauretur; occasione talis restaurationis ritus baptismi adultorum ad modum antiqui catechumenatus in diversos gradus distribuere liceat, et forma aptior Exorcismorum inveniatur.*

We are equally concerned about the prayers and scripture readings of the Fore-Mass; this prompts us to ask the local Ordinaries to endeavour to have the Mass of the Catechumens restored as a separate unit. It seems desirable to give the catechumens a form of worship which they can really make their own, according to their standing in the Church. In his recent study on the catechumenate, Father Ohm says: If they had appropriate services of their own, the catechumens would not yet come into close contact with the holy rites the meaning of which they cannot possibly grasp. On Sundays special religious services ought to be held for them, after having attended holy Mass up to the Offertory.[16] As the priests are already overburdened with the Sunday services for the faithful, these special services ought to be entrusted to well trained catechists.

[16] Ohm, *op. cit.* (2), p. 92.

In the Christian life of prayer one more thing must be mentioned with regard to our highest act of worship, the Mass. In his study on the Shona (S. Rhodesia) idea of God, a Dutch Reformed minister, W. J. van der Merwe, comes to the conclusion: "From what has been said before, it is clear that Shona worship should be delivered from a superstitious overemphasis on ritual. Nevertheless, any genuine Shona worship will undoubtedly seek appropriate expression in ritual and symbolism. In time to come such worship will call for appropriate African music and appropriate African instruments. There will be the demand for such action in worship as is true to the African. The bringing of gifts as an act of worship, which was such an integral part of the pagan Shona approach to the Supreme Being, should be fitted into Christian worship more appropriately."[17] As a protestant minister he has no Mass.[18] We have it, and surely we must convey to our new Christians the full meaning and beauty of the Christian sacrifice. What an irony and tragedy would it be if "people who have been spiritual as pagans, who have been active in their pagan worship, find themselves lacking as Christians in what they regard as proper means for expressing themselves spiritually!"[19]

The second field in which the formation of our catechumens must not fail is their awareness of the new community into which they enter by baptism, and their obligation to a genuine apostolate of their own. To start with, many of these "underdeveloped" nations have a well-developed sense of community. Once the barriers of tribal and racial egoism are broken down, they are likely to bring their community-mindedness into the one Church from among all nations – a constructive element which ranks among the highest hopes for a Christian solution of the global problems of our time. In connection with the formation of adult catechumens, only a thumb-nail sketch can be given of the structure of their community life. It must begin with the family. In old pagan Africa the families were kept together by their ancestor worship; Christian families receive a

[17] Rev. W. J. v. d. Merwe, *op. cit.* (10), p. 61.

[18] W. van Bekkum, "Sacramental Life in the Missions" in *Christian Living in Mission Lands* (Fordham Univ. Press, 1959), p. 58 et seq.

[19] J. J. Considine, *op. cit.* (19), p. 103.

deeper unity if we give it to them. After the family it is the parish as their *ecclesiola*. It will be as strong as we can make it by impregnating it with the apostolic spirit towards their fellow-men. The various extra-liturgical forms of Catholic action into which the catechumens must be prudently introduced, will give them scope for an apostolate which they can perform. It is up to the older Christians in the community to create an atmosphere in which the adult neophytes will be welcome as an addition to their ranks. The present Pope has made the apostolate of the lay people the main point of his recent encyclical *Princeps Pastorum;* in one place he says almost bluntly: "It will not do to convert people in young Christian communities to the Catholic Faith and to enter them in large numbers in the baptism registers. They must receive a Christian formation which measures up to the circumstances of our times and which enables them to perform responsible tasks for the benefit and growth of the Church today and tomorrow."[20]

## *Conclusion*

In this survey of the instruction and formation of adult catechumens I have tried to point out the actuality of this topic in our present-day Church among the nations. I hope that you will excuse me for having drawn liberally and somewhat onesidedly on my Rhodesian experiences. Even so, the general principles exposed in this paper may be said to sum up the experience of several generations of missionary thought and labour, and of more than one country.

My main finding is that the groundwork is good; there is much to be gained from past and present methods of organizing a catechumenate for adult postulants of our faith. Individuals as well as entire centres of catechetical and religious formation, such as *Lumen Vitae* in Brussels or the *Centre documentaire catéchétique* at Mayidi, Congo, have served our cause well and continue to do so. What is still needed and to my mind quite urgent, is to give each diocese its own centre, especially in the

[20] Pope John XXIII, *Princeps Pastorum,* November 28, 1959.

form of a school for catechists, and one or two specialists who will bring the fruit of the international catechetical and liturgical renewal to our overburdened missionaries labouring in the field.

A second finding from this study points even more to the future. If up to now we could, without arrogance, speak of the missionaries and their indigenous helpers (as I did earlier on), the time is coming fast, also in this field of catechetical instruction, when we shall become the helpers of the indigenous clergy and laity who really hold the keys to the minds and hearts of the people. Nobody could be happier about this change of positions than we foreign missionaries. For all that, we shall not find ourselves out of work; there is still much to be done in passing on the experience and the material from our old Christian countries and in adapting them to new situations. As long as we can do it, we must also school capable laymen in the technique of the apostolate[21], before the schools are taken away from us or perhaps before we are no longer tolerated in certain countries. Even if it were to come to the worst, nothing essential will be lost as long as we shall have deposited our faith in the minds and hearts of our adult catechumens. With them and with their own pastors and catechists, the Christian faith itself will have come 'of age', and we missionaries shall have more reason to say with St. Paul: 'I long to see you, in the hope that I may have some spiritual gift to share with you, so as to strengthen your resolve; or rather, so that the faith we find in each other, you and I, may be an encouragement to you and to me as well." (Rom. 1:11 et seq.)

[21] Ibid.

# Better Training for Parents in the Missions

SISTER PIA, C.P.S.
Mariannhill, South Africa

BETTER religious instruction and training is wanted in both church and school, but while seeking this let us not forget the most important place of Christian formation, namely the home. It is quite evident that God has made the family the basic educational institution. In looking for a better Christian formation, therefore, let us look for improvement to the home: we need better Christian instruction and formation there.

## *How Do Families Fulfil Their Task?*

In our day there has been a serious decline in the holiness of married life. Religious ideals do not influence family affairs sufficiently. As a result Christian family education has been greatly weakened. Evidence for the decline can be seen in lack of preparation for marriage. Emphasis is placed on preparation for a profession or some career in the world. Young people are not being fitted to assume the responsibilities of marriage.

Moreover, after marriage, young couples tend to be too deeply immersed in temporal and materialistic pursuits, they are too caught up in the cares and hurry of everyday life. Parents give too little thought to the spiritual development of their children: in fact, they neither have enough time nor are they inwardly free for the child. Their Christianity too often consists of little more than formal practices; it is much less than daily renewal of life in Christ.

Three hundred questionnaires which we sent to different parishes and schools of the Union of South Africa and Basutoland, brought us enlightening information and at the same time confirmed our own experience. Perhaps our findings apply also to other countries and continents. From an analysis of replies to the questionnaires we drew the following conclusions.

Lack of religious instruction and formation by parents is indicated only too clearly from the fact that half the Catholic children entering school do not even know how to make the Sign of the Cross; about one third do not know any prayers at all. Very often African parents say they do not know how to instruct their children.

Family prayer is neglected. Only about one tenth of the children say their prayers with their mothers; half of them are left to say their prayers alone; about thirty to forty per cent do not say any prayers at all. The latter are usually children of parents who do not practise their faith. In general the children are more regular with night than morning prayers. About ten per cent say the family Rosary; some have scriptural reading.

The replies reveal that parents give little help in preparing the children for first confession and holy communion. The general attitude is that the priest, or sister, or the teacher should do it. Parents excuse themselves by saying they do not know how to do it, that they have no time.

Far too little consideration is given to the sacraments in family life. Baptism has some importance as a family celebration, but first confession does not receive anything like the same attention. In some families first communion ranks high, but here, too, parents are more likely to be concerned with outward things than with inner preparation of the child.

The liturgical seasons are not marked in any special, personal way, even the penitential season of Lent passes almost as the rest of the year. However, I know of some African parishes where most members of the parish abstain from drinking beer during Lent and we should not overlook the significance of this. But in general it seems there is an almost total lack of understanding of the liturgical year.

Approximately seventy-five per cent of the parents whose children attend government schools send them to religious instruction, and of these children only about fifty per cent attend regularly. It must be said that very few parents show any direct interest in the religious instruction of their children. Answers to our questionnaires show that many parents forget they have a mission. They do not use the splendid opportunities given them for the Christian formation of their own flesh and blood.

Yet there is a marked difference between children from different homes. As one would expect, children from good Catholic families are the easiest to instruct. And it is easier to instruct children of mixed marriages where the Catholic parent practises the faith, than it is to instruct the children of careless Catholics. The latter group has no foundation on which to build.

*Christian Formation Begun and Fostered in the Home*

Normally, if religious formation is to be effective it cannot be detached from the family. Here it has to start and take its deepest roots. Why is this so?

The early years of the child are passed almost exclusively within the family. We know that during this time attitudes are formed that can hardly be eradicated in later life. The parents are always with the children; and their influence, if properly used, will outweigh undesirable external influences and safeguard the future of the children.

Christian parents should be to their children what we may call a first picture of God, a "kind of transparency of his presence". In the ideal home, their love, generosity, kindness, piety, and humility coupled with a true Christian dignity will leave indelible marks on the developing personalities of their children and will form stepping-stones to God.

Religious education is entrusted to parents not only during the helpless periods of the child's early years, but for as long as the child needs education and assistance. Hence parents' obligations do not end with attendance at Catholic schools. Not even the best Catholic schools can replace the home. No teacher can be a complete substitute for the parents. Priest or brother can take up and complement the work of parents, they cannot do it themselves. A sister can be the mother's auxiliary, nothing more.

This emphasis on the parents' religious role needs to be stressed particularly now, because already many schools have been nationalized and secularized in missionary countries. Christianity is in danger among the masses. It has to fight for its very existence in the midst of a secular environment in which God no longer has a place, in which science, technology or money are treated as idols. Ranged against it in open combat are the extraordinarily vital and powerful forces of Communism. More than ever our young need religious education in the home: to keep their faith intact, to intensify it, to strengthen their souls against seduction and enslavement.

How are parents to begin? Their first task is to awaken in the child a sense of God. But this will not be done at first in words, nor will there be for a long time any systematic instruction about God. In his own parents the child experiences something of the love and greatness of God. The atmosphere of the home – love, peace, security and respect – should convey the sense of God. But the decisive factor is the living faith of father and mother. Even before the child can understand words, reverent use of tone and signs leave impressions.

As the child grows older, the method used is observation, story-telling and prayer with gestures. I consider the latter as perhaps most effective. When father and mother pray with their child, when they make themselves small before God, praise him and thank him, they convey to the child a sense of the presence of God. At the same time the child prays with them and responds personally to God.

Father and mother need to be on the alert for moments when the child will benefit from a remark, or will be ready to listen to a suitable story. Discretion and tact are indispensible. Frequent repetition is the key to all progress, and so parents have to repeat little lessons continually. Unfolding of the mystery of Christ will take place gradually. Parents will tell the child of the Lord Jesus, who is the Son of God. God our Father sent him to us because he loves us. Jesus is powerful, and he is good. He welcomes everyone, the poor, the sick, the sinners, but especially children.

If the lessons parents teach to children culminate in prayer, their task has been accomplished. They have done what St. Augustine wants teachers and priests to do: "to teach in such a way as to guide the listener from hearing to believing, from believing to hope, and from hope to charity." They have done this because "faith, hope and charity are exercised in prayer, regardless of whether or not these theological virtues are expressly named as such."[1]

In first teaching the child to pray, parents should never begin with the "Our Father", the "Hail Mary", or any other formal prayer. They should help the child to speak to God in his own simple words.

Formation of the moral conscience of the child is also the task of the family. The objective is that the law of God should become the law of his life. The child learns to distinguish between good and bad. He learns by doing. In the natural discipline of daily family life, he develops proper attitudes and virtues.

When the child has come to a positive knowledge of the law of Jesus he should gradually be brought to find out where he has acted wrongly and should ask for forgiveness. This will lead him to trust and humble repentance, which in turn will be a progressive and remote preparation for first confession.

It cannot be overemphasized that the decisive factor in all this is the intangible yet real tone or character of the home. If parents show love and protecting care, humility and piety, a frank and friendly attitude towards others, faith and hope, they help the child to get rid of his own selfishness and to become ready for receiving and giving. The law of God and of Christ which reigns in the home begins to become the law of his young life.

There are other special tasks for parents to various age levels. First confession has already been mentioned. As for first communion, the eucharistic initiation of children must begin when their hearts and minds are completely open to the mysteries, that is, when the children are very young. That means it must be for the most part the work of parents.

Confirmation forms another high point in the child's religious life. Parents should help their children towards a consciousness

[1] Jungmann, *Handing on the Faith* (London and New York, 1959), p. 263.

of their vocation as citizens in the Kingdom of God and as soldiers of God. Educationalists agree that the best sex teaching is a sane, all-round education. In the ideal family we have been picturing, parents have played their part in giving that. Moreover, the products of such a home develop a Christian reverence for their bodies. Having understood the place of sex in God's plan for men and women, and having accepted it, they are already well on the way towards coping with the inevitable problems that arise. If they cannot do so, at least – and this is definitely second best – they must ensure that some other responsible person does. Adolescent boys and girls are often confused by their problems. No one can help them more effectively than an understanding father and a sympathetic mother.

### *How to Help Parents Fulfil Their Tasks Better*

We looked first at the actual state of religious education in Christian families, and we saw there are grave deficiencies. Next we stated by way of contrast what Christian family education ought to be. Now we ask how the family can be helped.

It is obvious from answers to our questionnaires that help is needed. Alone, the family cannot succeed. Parents must be enlightened, supported, helped, encouraged in their task. How ought we to set about this? What is possible and useful to most of our parishes?

Common sense says: "Begin with the beginning" – which means in this case, begin with the training of children in school, begin with the future mothers and fathers. All the same I wish to say: "Begin at the same time with parents, for without their help and example all work done by school and church is little more than patchwork."

Training of future parents begins in fact with their education as children in school. The way they are taught religion there is important for them in the future. Bad teaching methods in primary classes are not likely to help them develop later as adults leading vital Christian lives. The time-worn, dry analysis of lengthy, difficult catechisms certainly does not help.

On the other hand we could hope that parents to whom the truths of religion were heralded as God's good news during their early years at school, would gladly and eagerly convey this treasure to their children in a vital and inspiring way.

This wonderful transition stage is of great importance. It is at once a time of stress, of questioning and of ideal-making. The adolescent should be helped in the "transformation of his faith from the childish forms in which it has been assimilated into adult ideas, and to find the answers to his questions."[2]

It is difficult to reach young people at this age. Yet "to dispense with this third stage of training", says Father Jungmann, "would be tantamount to building a house without a roof."

The topics we should discuss with those we can reach are: the problems that confront them in their work and profession, sex and family difficulties, faith and science. All instructions should converge upon Christ. If we turn aside from this chronological approach, we may consider now the question of direct preparation of future parents for marriage.

Pope Pius XI in his encyclical on Christian Marriage points out the necessity of giving to youth the guidance so much needed to make a wise choice of marriage partner and to achieve lasting happiness in the home. The young people should be helped to understand the supreme importance of choosing the right partner, because it will be decisive for their earthly and even the eternal happiness of themselves and of their children. They must see that the choice should be made with the greatest care, prudence and wisdom. They should be encouraged to have extensive friendship and use the opportunities which Church and society provide. They should know that the purpose of steady company is to learn to know each other, that is, to discover each other's qualities of mind and heart and character, the congeniality of taste, culture and disposition.

Above all the young people should be encouraged to keep courtship on a high plane and to receive the sacraments of penance and the Eucharist frequently.

In the Ranchi mission of India all Catholics have to undergo a "catechumenate" before receiving the sacrament of matri-

[2] Jungmann, *op. cit.*

mony. With us in South Africa not very much has been done in this line. Some years ago a marriage course was conducted in Durban. Since then, with various changes, such courses have been presented in many parts of the Union, being limited, however, in most cases to towns.

What can be done for the indigenous, for the Africans who live in the reserves, in the bush? There are unlimited prospects for a Catholic apostolate. We must save the family. The Africans of to morrow, becoming extreme nationalists, may reject western culture and with it Christianity. We have to convince them that the Christian religion will raise and perfect the natural virtues apparent in the traditions, customs and beliefs of their ancestors. This can only be done by faithful fathers and pious mothers.

Many African families are disrupted by the system of migratory labour, which is frequently the cause of adultery, juvenile delinquency and crime. The African family is in danger. There is great ignorance of the nature, dignity, rights and duties of marriage; many young Africans enter marriage without the adequate mental and moral preparation that are so necessary to fit them for the heavy responsibilities of this sacrament.

A good number of parishes has made the Sodality of Our Lady an apostolic agency for the preparation of young women for adult life, particularly the married state. The methods of the Y.C.W., if given a fuller consideration and application, will prove most helpful, too.

What do we need? A numerous and qualified personnel. The number of the Christian élite of Africans is too small. We do not have enough teachers, nurses, social assistants, nuns, catechists, priests, who, with a knowledge of the sphere of life and native social structure and a thorough grounding in the methods of modern catechesis, can work among their own people, can prepare the parents.

### *Catechetical Training of Married Couples*

Christian marriage preparation courses are most valuable in that they counsel for a happier and more stable Christian marriage and family. But this does not do away with the catechetical training of married couples. Such training is necessary, possible, wanted and appreciated.

Two years ago, after a catechetical weekend refresher course for African teachers at one of the mission stations of the Mariannhill diocese, a Catholic African man approached us with the following request: "Could you not show your method of teaching religion to all our mothers in the country? It would certainly make a difference." We tried to find a solution. As every course was attended by married women teachers, who in most cases were also the office bearers of the Catholic African Women Association, we asked them to carry the new approach into their monthly meetings where most of the Catholic mothers could be reached. We also hope to use the African sisters as agents of the family apostolate in the near future. To them, the African milieu is more fully familiar; they speak the language which the people speak, they are acquainted with their customs, they belong to them. They can more easily make contacts with the people than missionaries who come from foreign countries.

*What Parents Should Know and Do*

Experience shows that the catechetical training of parents should not be considered as complete after attending a marriage preparation course. A follow-up is necessary and should be given soon. It is too late to awaken fathers and mothers to the problems of religious education and formation of their children when these are six or ten years of age. The catechetical training for parents should be offered as soon as the children are born. Parents should be taught how i. to train their children in prayer, ii. to tell a story, iii. to form the conscience, that is, to make God's law the law in the life of their child, iv. to initiate their child into the mystery of the Eucharist, preparing him for first confession and first communion, v. to show him the greatness of being Christ's witness through confirmation, vi. to train him in chastity by giving him an all-round, sane education and by teaching him respect for his own body, vii. to tell him about the facts of life, viii. to guide and help their adolescent sons and daughters, ix. to be the friend of their adult children.

How can this be achieved? At the beginning of this year we started a catechetical course for fathers and mothers whose children we prepared for first confession and communion. The attendance was remarkable, the interest and cooperation was very good. Parents are more willing and eager than we usually think.

It will not always be possible to reach all parents by special courses. The printed word, however, can be brought into every home. Pamphlets, parents' letters, parish letters, suitable books for parents and children will prove most helpful in the family apostolate, in the catechetical training of parents.

However, let us never forget that the parents' most effective teaching will not be in what they say, but in what they do. Their own doing at holy Mass, at family prayer, at dealing with others, will achieve more in the hearts and minds of their children than anything they say.

# TRAINING AND HELPING CATECHISTS

# The Catechetical Training of Missionary Priests

JOHANNES HOFINGER, S.J.
East Asian Pastoral Institute, Manila, Philippines

THE main burden of the catechetical work done in the mission fields lies upon the missionary sisters and the lay catechists. They are far more numerous than the missionary priests; in some missions there are more than twenty sisters and lay catechists for each priest. The programme of the catechetical renewal will remain a dead letter unless this immense army of catechists can be better trained and made familiar with the basic principles and the progress of the modern catechetical renewal.

## *Urgency of the Need*

Undoubtedly catechists must be better trained; but a still more urgent need is that an improved catechetical training be given to future missionary priests. For several reasons their training is more important than that of catechists. Moreover it can be undertaken at once, with less difficulty and greater effect. It will not involve additional and intolerable expenses, or the appointment of new professors so hard to obtain. If those priests who are already out in the missions had been better trained for the catechetical apostolate, strenuous efforts would have been made long ago to procure up-to-date training for the catechists. No one can blame a missionary, whose own catechetical training was inadequate, for not appreciating the necessity for a thorough training of his catechists, for not grasping the deficiencies in their catechetical work, or for being unable to apply remedies.

Here we have the most important of all the reasons why a very thorough catechetical formation should be given to the missionary priest. He has not only to teach catechism himself; nearly always he has to be the responsible director and inspector of the numerous mission schools and catechism classes of his district. It is not enough that he should be constantly behind his catechists to spur them on in their labours by his own fatherly love and determination. He must be able to assess their work, to give them advice and help, to be truly their director. He must be competent himself to give demonstration lessons from which his catechists can learn something to the advantage of their own work. Everyday experience has proved that even competent and zealous catechists sink all too often and easily to a merely mediocre level of work if they find that the missionary cannot offer them the understanding which they need and the help and guidance which they have a right to expect. All this presupposes no mean competence in catechetics on the part of the missionary. And this is not something innate; it has to be acquired during his seminary course. Once he has been sent out to work in the mission he has neither the time nor the energy – and usually lacks the needed books – to undertake the labour of remedying in afterlife those deficiencies caused by the inadequacy of the catechetical training received at the seminary. Usually, in fact, he will not even realize that he stands in need of that further catechetical knowledge which is such an urgent requirement for his apostolate. Probably the seminary course which he did receive was such that it neither awakened nor fostered ideas of this kind.

The education in catechetical science given to missionary priests up till now has left much to be desired. In recent times, and in every missionary region, many instances of inadequate training have come to light. Even highly respected missionary orders have sent out from the home countries young missionary priests who have not been given any suitable catechetical formation, putting them to work at once in the missions. Last autumn, when I was in Africa, the regional superior of a certain renowned order of missionaries made a remark which, at least by implication, expressed a grievance against his higher superiors. "All of us", he said "were sent out to the mission without any kind of special training in catechetics!" That, we may hope, was rather an extreme case. Yet anyone of experience in the missionary world knows full well that such extreme cases are by no means confined to Africa. And it is easy to understand that any deficiencies in the training of present missionaries are wont to exert a deleterious influence on the training of local missionaries. For whatever was made to seem of small importance in the training of the foreign missionaries will be given no stress in that of the local clergy. For it is the same superiors who plan and supervise the syllabus of missionary training for both groups.

As regards our present situation, and the task which we must undertake in the near future, the following experience may perhaps be significant. During the past seven years it has fallen to my lot to give a great many courses on catechetics in a number of different countries. I know from this experience that missionary sisters and lay catechists (I refer mainly to the *élite* among these whom I have been able to address in English) have shown a far greater interest in and understanding of the problems of the catechetical renewal than have the priests. The most frequent objection, brought up again and again in courses and lectures given to sisters and laity, was this: "Yes, Father, that is exactly what we need and what we want. But what will the pastor, the missionary, say about it? How is he going to react? He has never had any opportunity to come to grips with the basic principles of modern catechetics!" This objection came up regularly, not only in mission countries, but elsewhere as well, especially in the United States of America and in Australia. The reason for this is probably that in those countries, just as in the missions, most of the actual work of catechetical teaching is done by sisters and laity; hence it did not seem so necessary to give to the priests any thorough formation in catechetical science.

Fortunately some undeniable progress has been made in the past few years, and hopes for the future are brighter. Seminaries in which students for the priesthood are given no catechetical course whatever are becoming exceptional. The danger is rather one of complacency – that of being content with a course dealing almost exclusively with the pedagogical aspects of catechetics, with mere technique. This would be to stop halfway at a point of unsatisfactory compromise.

### *Catechetical Courses*

A thoroughly sound course in catechetics is an absolute necessity if future missionary priests are to be well prepared for their catechetical work. It will be quite insufficient if they are taught only the technique, or method, of religious instruction. They must have this, of course, but it is only one side of their catechetical education. The other side also is vital; it is that they must acquire a knowledge and understanding of the specific purpose and underlying principles of the catechetical renewal. They must learn to grasp the way in which catechetical methodology has to be completely subservient to the content of that message of Christian salvation which it is our task to impart to Christians and non-Christians alike. The seminarian has to be given a clear view of those basic laws of religious instruction upon which all the tenets and techniques of modern catechetics are ultimately founded.

Later on the missionary, as director of many mission schools and catechism classes, will have to do personally some catechetical work of a high standard. And his education in the science of catechetics must blend harmoniously with his education in general theology. For these reasons the catechetical course given in the seminary needs to be more exhaustive than that required for ordinary catechists. For example, it would not be enough to familiarize a seminarian with the usual structure and technique involved in the giving of a good catechism lesson; we must enlighten him about the fundamental laws of human learning and teaching. From these it will become plain to him why the first step in instruction is to present the matter, the next one is to explain it, and that this should be followed up by its practical application to life. Only if he sees this, and the reasons for it, will he later be able to expound these steps to his catechists and help them to make practical use of them in their teaching. And because of his eventual task as regional inspector of schools, the future missionary must learn in his seminary catechetical course something about the problems involved in drawing up a sound plan of religious instruction.

For the same reasons he has to become absolutely clear about the ultimate purpose of all religious instruction. Missionary sisters and lay catechists are constantly voicing complaints to the effect that missionaries lay far too much stress on the mechanical memorization of the locally used catechism; or that they over-emphasize mere theoretical knowledge, or that they expect the pupils to be able to express themselves in scholastic formulations of the Christian truths. An extreme case – doubtless quite exceptional – came to light in Brisbane not long ago. I had been lecturing about the ultimate purpose and guiding principles of the catechetical movement, and the entire audience seemed enthusiastic about them. But then a missionary sister put a question: "Everything you have said, Father, satisfies me completely. But what am I to do when my parish priest, examining the candidates for first communion, still insists on asking my tiny children about the matter and form of the Eucharist?" And this some fifty years after St. Pius X's Communion Decree!

This example illustrates one particularly important thing which the seminary catechetical course has to do. Precisely because the future missionary, from the days when he began his philosophy, has been taught to think in the manner characteristic of scholasticism, he must now learn in his catechetical course the exact difference between popular and pastoral instruction and scholastic exposition. He must see that the one begins from the concrete and goes thence directly to its application in Christian life, whereas the other begins with the abstract and only reasons its way towards the concrete. It is concerned primarily with analytic penetration of the content of revealed truth, and if it has any bearing at all on Christian living this is implied rather than explicitly mentioned. One of the greatest difficulties besetting the average priest-catechist is that, without doing so consciously or of set purpose, he is far too much involved in categories, syllogisms and concepts pertaining to scholasticism. We can hardly be surprised at this. His position is rather like that of a mathematician who, after years spent industriously studying Integral Calculus, Fourier Analysis and Bessel Functions is now confronted with a class of infants to whom he must teach subtraction. He needs some special coaching so as not to be talking over the heads of his pupils. And this applies even more forcibly to religious teaching. Here it is not enough that the teacher be understood; he is concerned to speak to the heart as well as to the mind, and to form both for Christ.

As regards how much catechetics should be taught in seminaries it is impossible to lay down any hard and fast rule. So much depends on the way in which the main theological subjects are taught. We shall have to return to this important subject later. But if only the teaching of dogmatic and moral theology and of exegesis is properly geared to a balanced grasp of the divine message of salvation and to the communication of this to mankind, then a catechetical course of quite modest proportions can and should suffice. Two or three periods a week during one academic year might well be enough.

Nowadays a man who is appointed professor of any technical subject is expected to have equipped himself with a sufficient technical training. This is true also of the science of catechetics. As a general principle it might be a good thing if the professor of dogmatic theology, especially in a mission seminary, were to be also the professor of catechetics. But this holds good only if he has the right temperament and has undergone sufficient training. Such training is available now; the courses given in Paris and in Brussels can be specially recommended; they are well suited for the training of competent professors of catechetics. The *Lumen Vitae* centre in Brussels offers a "catechetical year", whereas the *Institut Supérieur Catéchétique* in Paris gives a full training spread over two or three years.

## *Practical Experience*

Seminarians need not only instruction in theory, but also some exercise in practice. Without this they may acquire quite useful knowledge of the science of catechetics, and yet never become competent catechists. There are three kinds of practical exercise to be recommended during the years spent at the seminary; they supplement each other, and in planning the catechetical training of the seminarians they should be regarded as an organic unity and related to each other accordingly.

Firstly, there already exists in some seminaries a laudable custom whereby the seminarians give catechism lessons to each other under the guidance of the professor of catechetics. If these practice lessons are to bear due fruit, they have to be guided and planned by someone who is a first class catechetical teacher, well prepared by the students, and then discussed in common. It is important to make a correct choice of subject; for such practice lessons only primary and significant subjects are suitable. With this proviso, and when practice lessons are held through all the years of training for the priesthood, then every seminarist will have plentiful opportunities to become familiar with the various kinds of catechetical teaching and to learn how to use them. There is no reason why the seminarian who is giving one of these practice lessons should not adhere closely to a prepared text provided that it is suited well enough to the fictitious circumstances of the lesson and to his own personality. It will soon appear whether the seminarians have really grasped the basic elements of the psychological method. The main thing is that they have to learn how to appeal, not merely to the minds, but also to the wills of their pupils, winning their entire personalities for God. In such practice lessons, of course, the audience is fictitious in that the seminarians themselves have to "play at" being children as realistically as they can. Hence at times very comic situations can arise. By all means let everyone then have a good laugh; yet the practice lessons should never as a whole descend to the level of comic turns; they demand a certain amount of seriousness and religious earnestness, even in those who play the part of child-audience, if they are to be of real use.

More important than these fictitious catechism lessons are the opportunities for teaching practices with real children which ought to be arranged for seminarians during the course of their training. It is most desirable, especially in the missions, that the seminary should be somewhere within easy reach of one of the larger parish or mission centres. For then the seminarians can be called in to help at the services and catechism classes. Of course this would have to be arranged in some way which would not interfere too much with the lectures and timetable of the seminary, and so that the students should not be distracted from their studies. On the other hand, many would agree that the studies for the priesthood in the seminaries of today have far too little contact with real life. If seminarians are given opportunities to teach catechism to children of the neighbourhood, or to help with youth-work according to a well planned programme and in moderate degree, then the apostolic zeal and catechetical skill of the future missionaries will benefit. Obviously these early experiments in the apostolate will achieve their purpose only if the seminarians have the benefit of sound guidance and fatherly supervision in their work for the children.

The practice lessons in the seminary and the genuine lessons for children of the neighbourhood should be supplemented by demonstration lessons given from time to time by the professor of catechetics himself or by some other experienced catechist. And it might be a good thing to invite occasionally some missionary sister or good lay catechist of known competence. Would it not be a pity if the young seminarians never came to realize that they have a lot to learn from well-trained and experienced sisters or lay catechists?

### *Kerygmatic Orientation of the Main Theological Subjects*

Even the best of courses in catechetics, and the fullest opportunities for practice, will not of themselves suffice to transform the future missionary into the ideal catechist and herald of Christ. It is essential that he be well grounded in the chief theological disciplines – dogma, moral and exegesis. These are the subjects immediately concerned with the study of divine revelation, – that is, with the message of salvation which the seminarist must later on proclaim as Christ's herald. During the years of his training he must absorb them, let his mind become steeped in them and his character formed by them. Then he will find it not so difficult to impart them in an attractive way to others, and by means of this heavenly message to transform others into true Christians.

And now we come to a point which, up till now, has hardly been perceived in the seminaries. And it applies not only to seminaries in mission countries. It is that not even first class lectures in catechetics can fully make up for a lack of explicit kerygmatic orientation in the main theological subjects. Only through the correct presentation of these main subjects can the seminarian obtain an insight, at once clear and joyful, into the organic unity of the Christian message of salvation. He must penetrate into the religious content of each truth of the Christian faith, grasp its connection with the very core of the Good Tidings, and see its bearing upon Christian living. All this he should derive from the way in which dogma, moral and exegesis are presented to him. A one-sided scholastic exposition which neglects religious values and loses itself in minutiac and dessicated theses without imparting an enlightened overall view of God's single and overwhelming plan of salvation is a totally inadequate preparation for the future apostolate. The rector of an excellent mission seminary in Africa expressed the matter thus: "That would not be a *formatio,* but rather a *deformatio;* not education for the priesthood, but perversion." Many priests in mission countries and elsewhere display a woeful lack of interest and understanding for the highest ideals of the catechetical renewal; it is hardly possible to doubt that this is chiefly due to a too exclusively intellectual formation in their seminary days, a training which never opened to these future messengers of the faith the religious depths and beauties of the Christian Good Tidings.

A more kerygmatic treatment of the main theological disciplines in no way implies a watering down of theological science; on the contrary, it demands a deepening and enrichment of theology. If anyone thinks that the kerygmatic orientation of seminary theological courses would be incompatible with a solid scholastic approach, he is entertaining a lamentable misunderstanding. We have shown at length in another place[1] how scholastic teaching and kerygmatic orientation can be

[1] J. Hofinger, *The Art of Teaching Christian Doctrine* (Notre Dame Press, Indiana, U.S.A.), pp. 234–49; J. Hofinger, "Das Problem des Textbuches in Seminarien der Missionsländer" in *Neue Zeitschrift für Missionswissenschaft* (1956), pp. 46–63.

harmoniously combined. We pointed out there the recent efforts made at the Gregorian University in Rome to meet this justifiable demand on scholastic theology.[2]

We cannot enter now into more detail about the way in which the kerygmatic attitude should be taken into account in the various disciplines. At most we can call attention to a few of the chief desiderata. The main task in dogmatic theology will be to enable the seminarian who is studying particular theses to retain his view of the whole. Individual theses must be so handled that they will really contribute to a more complete and deep understanding of the economy of salvation. In this way the seminarians will be in a much better position to grasp the religious content of each truth of our faith and to make it their own.

For an effective catechetical training it would seem absolutely indispensable to make the seminarian see clearly, by means of examples, just why and how a scientific theological exposition and a good catechetical presentation differ from one another. There can, for example, be no objection if the dogma course in the seminary begins with an extensive treatise *De Deo Uno et Trino*; but there is everything to be said against starting the catechism lessons for children in their first year at school with an abstract treatment of the divine attributes or – worse still – with a lesson about the Blessed Trinity! A catechetical presentation must always begin from the concrete, and go only gradually towards abstract truth – and then only so far as abstract formulation is really necessary. One has to start from what is perceived by the senses and thence lead on to imperceptible causes. In speculative analysis it is perfectly in order to go in the opposite direction, from the abstract to the concrete, or to argue from the ultimate cause to its specific effects that these may be ever more deeply and fully understood.

Up till now the seminary course in moral theology was usually centred on things needed for the administration of the sacrament of penance. No one would deny that the future pastor

[2] The organizers of the Eichstätt Congress purposely entrusted the main paper of the first day to a professor from the Gregorian University, asking Fr. Domenico Grasso, S.J., to discuss the decisive question as to what constitutes the essential core of missionary preaching. See page 39.

of souls should have a solid training in moral theology to fit him for his work in the confessional. But he needs much more than that. A missionary must be enabled to expound Christ's law in a persuasive and winning manner, to show "God's way" and to lead his flock along that way. The textbooks of moral theology in current use seem to have overlooked this point altogether. To train effective missionary catechists the moral course must lay far more emphasis on its own connections with Christian dogma and must make the seminarian see this connection. And the positive aspect of Christian morality must be brought out more strongly. For Christ's herald has to proclaim the right way in which we should respond to God's loving invitation. He must explain the meaning of the commandments, and be able to show that a life lived in accordance with the commandments and Christian ideals is a life truly worth living, a life which calls for the fullest personal effort.

Each commandment must, of course, be thoroughly studied at the seminary, and later explained in religious instruction. But such study should never cause the seminarian to be utterly absorbed in minutiae; he must be shown how to see all the commandments, great and small, against the background of that holy vocation which we all share as God's children. The innermost core of missionary preaching is the proclamation of God's plan for salvation (Eph. 3:8); hence the future missionary must be shown, in his course of moral theology, how each and every commandment contributes in some way to the fulfilment of this divine plan by conforming us to the image of God's only-begotten Son so that Christ may be the first-born among many brethren (Rom. 8:29).

The main purpose of the study of holy scripture should be to impart to the seminarian, for his whole future life, a deep and effective love for the Word of God. In the scripture course he should not become bogged down in the solution of innumerable small exegetical problems, but should rather attain some familiarity with the sacred text and an understanding of the religious import of the Bible as a whole. Of course all this must be done on the level of modern Catholic biblical scholarship. Nowadays the priest catechist needs everywhere (including the missions) a clear understanding of the different literary *genres* of the Bible. He must know which books or passages are historical, which are illustrative parables, and so on. His devoted and prayerful study of the Bible must familiarize him with the main themes and fundamental concepts of the revelation given in the holy book. In the mission catechesis given today the Bible certainly does not fulfil the role which it used to play in early Christian missionary preaching and which it can claim, according to the Catholic doctrine that it is the written Word of God. Does not the explanation of this fact lie in the defective biblical training given to the missionaries during their years of study?

Together with the kerygmatic orientation of the courses given in theology there must go a similar kerygmatic attitude in all other spheres which contribute to the education of a priest in the seminary. This is of decisive importance in the formation of the future apostle. In essence the attitude consists in a joyous and wholehearted dedication to Christ, in order to become fitted to be used as his instrument in the life-giving spread of the gospel message. Its characteristics are a sense of mission – of "being sent" – an apostolic zeal and a selfless readiness on the part of the young seminarian to accommodate himself to all circumstances and peoples involved in his vocation as Christ's herald. Its main sources are the Bible and the liturgy. This explicitly missionary spirit that must pervade the whole of seminary life is all the more important because, even with the best will in the world, it is impossible to revolutionize the formal teaching of theology overnight and to bring it into line with the requirements discussed above. To effect this will usually entail finding new men to become professors, and giving them suitable training. It is much easier and quicker to make changes in those spheres of seminary life which lie outside the classroom, and to adapt these to the needs of future missionary life. Nevertheless we cannot expect complete success with the catechetical renewal in the missions and in other countries until the entire system of education in seminaries – both inside and outside the classroom – has been purposively and consistently adapted to form true priests and heralds of Christ.

(Tr. C.H., S.J.)

# The Training of Missionary Sisters and Lay Catechists

P. JACQUEMART, M.E.P.
Regional Superior, Bangalore, India

A SIMPLE occurrence. I walk through a group of huts and see among them a little mud-brick chapel. Its door is open, and nobody is inside. On a low mound nearby, a man is sitting. There are a lot of people round him. He is, it seems, an atheist, a peripatetic propagandist! And obviously he knows his job – the crowd hangs onto his every word.

– Don't we need at least as many catechists as the atheists do for their propaganda? And shouldn't they also win the ears of the people?

This introduces us to the subject of my paper, wherein I propose to speak first of the recruiting of catechists, and then of several aspects of their training. I shall say something, also, about their *missio canonica* and their perseverance.

## *Recruitment*

We need many catechists, and they must be such as to win a hearing from their audiences. This cannot be done unless our propagandists (catechists) come from the same world as their hearers, know their people well and all the problems that beset them. I would not go so far as to recommend that the people should choose their own catechists – that would entail a number of risks. But I do maintain that the prospective catechist should be a man whom others like and approve; one who, from the day he goes to the catechetical training school, is considered by his own people as a desirable candidate.

It is even more important that he be the type of man who will put his heart into his work. If he is going to look on it merely as a way to earn his living, then he lacks a fundamentally necessary quality – zeal for souls. Of what use would be a veritable army of catechists if they are going to be nothing more than honest employees, carrying out peacefully their routine duties, but not otherwise interested?

When he comes to the training school he must already have attained a certain maturity of judgement. But it is also extremely desirable that he possess a lively grasp of Christian doctrine far beyond a mere ability to recite catechism answers by heart.

He will need, too, a certain minimum of mental and moral qualities; among these common sense, trustworthiness and unselfishness are the most obvious. And these must have a solid basis of the virtues of faith, humility and obedience, coupled with genuine piety. It is for competent priests to pick out men of the right type who might become candidates for catechetical training, to set them on the right path, and retain contact with them afterwards.

It should be obvious that any candidates who desire to join religious orders must also have the qualities needed to fulfil the obligations of community life and those entailed by their vows.

### *The Ideal to Be Aimed at: Spiritual Formation*

In his recent encyclical, *Princeps pastorum,* the Holy Father said catechists must be "true Christians". We should think for a moment what this implies. A true Christian is one who has heard God's call and is answering it; one who dedicates himself to Christ in faith and love.

In the training school, therefore, everything – classes, lectures, exhortations, instructions, sermons, meditations, even games, and above all the life to be lived – must be impregnated with this outlook; it is a view with inexhaustible facets. Those in training must be told again and again that the true Christian is aware that he is a son of God, and lives from this conviction by uniting his life with Christ under the influence of the Holy Spirit and the maternal protection of the blessed Virgin Mary; he lives in an atmosphere of prayer, doing always what he ought to be doing at any given time, no matter what it may be.

And if the true Christian is also a catechist, this means something more. It means that God has chosen him to fulfil a particular and well defined task – that of taking an active part in the conversion of the world, which is always a wonderful thing, even if his own part in it may be quite a humble one.

St. Paul said something of deep significance about those engaged in spreading the gospel: "This is how we ought to be regarded – as Christ's servants, and stewards of his mysteries. And this is what we look for in choosing a steward: we must find one who is trustworthy" (1 Cor. 4:1–2). This word "trustworthiness" covers all the duties of our catechists, duties which nowadays are our own as well.

Trustworthiness – fidelity – to the Word of God first of all. This means a determination to know it well ourselves, to absorb it, to use it as a guide for our lives. Fidelity also in transmitting the message in its integrity; it must be adapted, of course, to those who hear it, but it must not be toned down, and nothing of our own is to be added to it.

Fidelity to the Church: to priests, bishops, and to the Holy See. We must accept unconditionally any post which the Church entrusts to us, and carry out loyally and generously whatever tasks are involved in it. Fidelity, also, to souls. Within the limits of our mandate we belong to them, we must give ourselves to them – but in the capacity of guides, of good shepherds. After the example of our Master we must know each and every one, adapt our pace to theirs, encouraging them if they lag behind, gently restraining them if they go too fast, but always serving them. One of our chief responsibilities is to lead them to the Church's own spirit of piety and teach them to savour it; it is a piety simple yet very deep, enshrined chiefly in the liturgy.

Fidelity to the Holy Spirit. It is the Holy Spirit who guides the Church. It is from him that we – like the Church herself – derive light and strength, that light and strength of which we have such a constant and absolute need. So we must have devotion to the Holy Spirit, always careful never to hinder his action, whether this be in our own souls or those of our pupils – as we would be doing if we sought our own satisfaction or glory.

Fidelity to Christ who is the light, the way, the truth and the life. We, above all others, should be living cells in his mystical body and, according to our degree, be also light, way, truth and life, one amongst ourselves, one with those we teach, all one in Christ. All those who approach us should find in us true Christian charity; we must make them feel this by the way we act, by letting them see that every newcomer is welcome. Each of us must do this on his own account; but all of us must do it in common also – in union with the whole Church, with her saints, with their Queen, Mary the Mother of God. Fidelity, therefore, to Mary. But most of all, fidelity to God.

All this shows us in a brilliant light, what great things God asks of us. And these same things he asks – according to their station – of our catechists too. Without these things, nothing worth while can be done. With them, everything . . . even in abundance.

*The Catechist and the Bible*

The Church possesses three different editions, if I may so term them, of God's revelation to man. The first, the original edition, is in the form of scripture; the second – meditated and lived – is the liturgy; the third – studied, analysed, formulated synthesized – is in the form of theology. We shall treat of all three; but first of all, the Bible.

If we look at centuries gone by, we find that all Christian instruction was based on the Bible, God's word. But the use of the Bible in instruction gradually grew less until we have reached the present state of affairs in which it is hardly used at all. It is for us to recover this great loss. We are too apt to be content with mere precision, with accuracy, in our teaching; as a result, it is cold. We have lost the sense – the feeling for – the message, which is Good News. We shall recover it only if we have recourse to the Bible. Having found it again, we shall be equipped once more to pass it on to others.

Our future catechists have to be initiated into the Bible. In my opinion this can be done only by a course which is consecutive, unhurried, and well-balanced so that it may be assimilated. Above all, in its essentials. It must strike a mean between our classical "Bible History" books overloaded with anecdotes, and our modern "Introductions" overloaded with *minutiae*.

The course would follow a chronological order – which is the order of real life; it would divide up the centuries into appropriate eras, indicate the books which belong to each of these, and then impart their contents in the form of general summaries, but with careful reading and commentary on the passages of basic importance. Obviously the lecturer, in doing all this, would lay emphasis on the unfolding of God's message. This will endow his course with unity and power, will reduce complications and will forestall the premature shock of tripping over stumbling blocks. At the beginning and again at the end one lecture, thus given twice, would treat inspiration and inerrancy in a succinct, accurate but attractive explanation appealing to faith. A programme like this could hardly be done in less than a year, with one class on each working day.

But something else remains to be done – something which also takes a long time – to impart a deeper knowledge of the Bible's most important books. Of these, the Gospels and the Acts hold the first place; then – with some freedom of choice – the other books of the New Testament. Finally, any specially useful passages from the Old Testament. In this second-year course the lecturer will dwell with pleasure on this or that longer passage of scripture, showing the richness of its doctrine and its usefulness in catechesis. Under his guidance each pupil will become accustomed to leafing through the Bible in search of particular references, being happy in the thought of the help these will be in future work. He will do it first of all to meet the immediate needs of his studies; but later, and under the influence of grace, he will do it more and more according to his personal taste and the interior needs of his soul. Launched into his career in life he is likely to keep up this practice, loving to have the Bible (or at least the New Testament) as his bedside book, seeking guidance and advice from the priest whenever desirable.

## *The Catechist and the Liturgy*

"Well ordered ceremonies!" we used to think a few years ago, if the word "liturgy" ever occurred to us. We have to thank the late Pope Pius XII for giving us a more enlightened view by defining liturgy as the "entire worship of the Mystical Body of Christ, head and members".

In our present context this "entire worship" has a triple role to play: instruction, personal practice, communal practice.

In olden days, during the Mass of the Catechumens, passages from the Bible were read and commented on by the bishop; in between these readings came songs, also of biblical provenance. The official prayer of the bishop, succinct and sober, embraced the intentions of all and commended them to God through Christ. Then came the Mass of the Faithful in which all the baptized, united around their bishop, celebrated together with him the "sacred mysteries". From reading to commentary, from commentary to personal prayer, from personal prayer to community prayer, from community prayer to sacrifice.

If we look through our missal we shall find that the same structure is still there, even though in shortened form. It is for us to make the best of it. We are not totally without means for doing this, especially in a school or college: a few words in the evening about next day's Mass, meditation in the morning about the Mass which is to follow, a two-minute sermon within the Mass itself, thanksgiving in common under leadership. *Gutta cavat lapidem* – repeated drops of water can wear holes in a stone. How much good can come from these simple practices if they are faithfully kept up throughout the whole year!

And how much more simple and more enriching if we do all this within the framework of the liturgical year. The whole Christmas cycle contemplates the mystery of the incarnation, the whole Easter cycle that of the redemption. We have in mind especially an attentive preparation of each Sunday Mass and, at the appropriate times, of each liturgical season and each major feast.

Even that is not all. Our men have got to be made familiar with the whole course of the liturgical action. Occasionally – perhaps once a month – a more formal instruction could deal with one or other of the main aspects of the Mass: sacrifice, self-dedication, union in charity, sacred banquet. This is best done with the aid of some guide (Parsch?), and about twenty such instructions throughout the period of training would cover the whole matter thoroughly. There is no place more suitable or more worth while for such a course than a catechists' training college.

In addition to all this theory we have to look after the practice too, first on the personal level and then on that of the community. At the school at Tindivanam in India, the form of active participation in the Mass differs each morning of the week. Solemn Mass, Sung Mass, dialogue Mass, commentary, hymns in Tamil, and so on. The men are encouraged also to take part in the baptisms at the neighbouring parish church. These are simple means for helping them to understand and live the liturgy, yet very effective.

One point should be mentioned which is by no means an unimportant detail: the men must be given a vivid consciousness of their baptismal character. It is this, and this alone, which accustoms them to unite themselves closely with the priest and with Christ. It is essential that they have a clear grasp of it if they are to make the most of their dignity as Christians.

## *The Catechist and Theology*

Holy scripture, in handing on to us God's message, strongly accents the Person of Christ our Lord, mediator between God and man. The liturgy takes up the same theme with marked insistence on the practical consequences flowing from it. Now comes theology which examines the whole truth in detail, point by point, intent on the utmost precision. It patiently analyses every advance of God towards man and every duty which follows from it, to bring them all together finally in a synthesis.

This meticulous precision of theology is beyond doubt of great value; it enables us to see things clearly and wards off both error and ignorance. But if we limit it all solely to analysis, we come into danger: each point may now appear to us as something on its own, and its connection with other truths hardly appears while the harmony of the whole cannot be seen at all. Nobody becomes filled with admiration and awe for a cathedral just by studying each of its stones. He has to stand back to get a view of the whole, to see its proportions and the beauty of its lines. So with theology: there has to be a synthesis.

Till recently our catechisms were woefully deficient in this respect, as everyone realizes now. Following the example of Germany, where the new catechism was the fruit of such prolonged and thorough study, all the other Catholic countries are scrapping their old catechisms and writing new ones. We cannot doubt but that practical results will appear soon. Permit me, *à propos* of this matter, to draw your attention to Father Hofinger's book *The Art of Teaching Christian Doctrine*. Under the title of "Our Message" an important chapter of this book develops in a detailed way how we should teach doctrine so that it is seen to be what it really is – the Good Tidings.

This being understood, we must now say a few words about the different levels of doctrinal preparation which our catechists should have according to the type of work to which each one is destined. There are many possibilities: our men may have to work in a *milieu* which is Christian, or else pagan; for children or for adults; in a village or in a town; at an elementary level, or in a university. The diocese of Pondichéry makes provision for four levels of attainment; those needed respectively to prepare candidates for first communion, to teach in elementary or village schools, to teach in secondary schools, to give even more advanced instruction. The preparation given for this highest level is worthy of comment: some thirty episodes from the history of salvation have been chosen; for these the candidate has got to assemble the material to be used for one or more lessons. Each candidate is provided with a note book bearing the title of the subject on its cover. Its pages are mainly empty, but give, in small print, references to the most useful passages of the Bible, to the liturgy, to Church history, to profane history, to science, to Hinduism, etc., and also suggestions for hymns, chants, illustrations. The candidate attends a real class, taught by somebody else; he observes everything carefully and asks how he himself would prefer to treat the subject. He then writes out his own notes at leisure. When he is satisfied with what he has done, he submits his results to the Director for suggestions, criticisms, and so on, and then works over his matter again. When the Director is satisfied with the notes thus compiled on any particular subject, he initials the book. And when at last the candidate possesses thirty such books all bearing the desired signature he is given his diploma without having to take any examination. This method of training is of immense value and marvellously supple. It is a pity that it has not been adopted very widely. But it does demand a great deal of initiative and patience from the candidate.

In recent times all the different Catholic countries have worked out systems for training catechists; the centre *Lumen Vitae* can supply details of them to anyone who asks.

### *The Catechist and Education*

All sorts of methods have been discovered and proved by experience to be useful in catechesis; the beginning of this century saw such a profusion of them as to be, at first sight, bewildering. Very many of them are akin to, and have been allied to, the psychological approach known as the "Munich Method". This, because it is based on human psychology, is in its essence as old as mankind and has won its way everywhere. It proceeds from the senses to the mind, from the mind to the will. At each stage it encourages personal activity of the pupil based on what he already knows, for the purpose of leading him on to further knowledge both known and lived.

As regards the pedagogical formation of catechists, we have to make a difference between those who are already teachers and those who are not. The former have already had training in pedagogy, while the latter have not. In the case of the teachers we have to be careful to see that their former training, which was concerned with secular subjects, does not make them lose sight of the ulterior aim of religious teaching (which is more than mere instruction) and of the religious needs of their pupils. In the case of the others, we have to start more or less from scratch, and so we must take our time. They will need a general description of the method as a whole, and then a patient explanation of each of its elements, with demonstration classes conducted by an experienced catechist. Then they must have the opportunity themselves to give practice lessons, each one observed, criticized and corrected. There is no purpose whatever in taking short cuts in this training; any pupil who has failed to grasp any one of its stages will only relapse into dry and futile routine methods. Some other, who thinks he has got the ideas, will try to work out some "simplified" method of his own which ends by being rigid and inadequate. In both cases they need more time – at least thirty hours of careful work and supervision seems to be the minimum capable of achieving good results. Even after all this, it is very desirable that any catechist who is just beginning his work should, for a while, be under the supervision of some other more experienced catechist.

Besides this training in pedagogy there should also be training in what I shall call practical skills. Many are worth cultivating, for they help to foster a sense of the sacred or a feeling for the community, but there is no time to discuss them now. I will mention just some connected with liturgy. Our catechists should be prepared to fulfil a number of roles in this, and ought to know how to do them well and should appreciate their true value, which is spiritual. In the past we have trained catechists, according to their talents, to be sacristans, organists or cantors. The recent Instruction on Sacred Music and Liturgy by the S.C.R. (1958) widens the field considerably. A catechist may now be called upon to prepare the people for the various degrees of active participation in the Mass, to be a lector or a commentator at Mass. If he is gifted in that direction he may render great service to the Church by introducing native hymns and music. In places which the priest can visit but rarely, the catechist will have to lead the daily prayers, conduct the Sunday service and perform baptisms; he will prepare those intending to marry, give spiritual help to the sick and dying, conduct funerals and lead prayers for the dead. He must be well trained for all these functions – in fact, so well trained that he will be able to get others to do them unter his direction. If he has the right ideals and is also competent in these practical skills, he will be able to do an enormous amount of good to the faithful; hence we should nowadays train him for this, just as in the past we trained him to do good to the catechumens. But above all we must lay stress on his interior formation to the fundamental dispositions of willingness and obedience.

### *The Catechist's Canonical Mission and his Perseverance*

"How shall they preach unless they are sent?" asks St. Paul concerning messengers of the gospel. Unless I am mistaken it is customary to authorize a catechist to teach – that is, to give him a *missio canonica* – on two occasions: when he receives his diploma, and when he is appointed to a post. The question has often been raised as to whether it would not be a good thing to do this in a more formal and solemn manner than hitherto, so as more certainly to confer external authority. I presume we are all in favour of this, as also of securing for the catechist a clearly defined official status.

But is it enough to be concerned only about "exterior" authority? The whole world rightly admires the development of the Confraternity of Christian Doctrine in the United States of America. We might do more than admire . . . we might even imitate! But not a few missionaries wish that we could go beyond this first stage. How about ordaining catechists to one of the minor orders – or even to the major order of the diaconate – and that even for married men? Obviously it is quite beyond the competence of missionaries to put any of these ideas into action. We can but put our desires on record, and exchange views about them; we have to leave anything further to the only authority which is competent to do anything, that is, to Rome.

Now we must glance at a final problem, that of the perseverance of our catechists. We must not delude ourselves about the fact that many catechists now at work did not receive an adequate training, and that some of them are failures. We have to take them in hand again – and the first step is to make them desire it. Days for catechists, exhibitions which include lectures, demonstration classes or other such things might succeed in giving them the shock needed to make them realize their shortcomings and form higher ideals. On another plane, and perhaps with better chances of success, we might get them to days of recollection or retreats. When they have got that far they would be in the right dispositions to undertake some intensive revision course in catechetics. Yet we must not forget that at times their keenness could be an obstacle to their success – they want to do too much and do it too quickly! Hence short courses, but several of these, might be preferable to one longer course. And if they come back again after a year, the results previously obtained would be confirmed.

With catechists who did have an adequate training and are successful, ordinary contacts can be made through periodical visits to the place where they work, through reunions, and through publication of a bulletin. Every year they should have a series of professional conferences well worked out, and also – unless this is quite impossible – a closed retreat. At Tindavanam all the catechists, together with those who taught them at the training school, make a retreat together; afterwards the catechists are treated as guests of honour, and judge an exhibition prepared throughout the course of the year by the present pupils who are destined to join them in the field later. This kills two birds with one stone. After the distribution of the prizes each catechist returns to his own post strengthened and comforted.

And the work of spreading the gospel continues . . . *fideliter*.

(Tr. C.H., S.J.)

# Centres of the Catechetical Apostolate

MARK GOPU
Archbishop of Hyderabad, India

WE have, in most mission countries – if I may give my own analysis of the catechetical situation – some experts who are in remarkable agreement regarding the essentials of catechetics and their adaptation to our missionary problems. But their ideas are far from being accepted by all, not to speak of their realization in practice. On the other hand, some very good attempts are made here and there, exhibitions are held, books are published; but all this remains too often unknown in the same region, even in the same diocese. Thus, efforts are wasted, because dispersed; and the progress made runs the risk of remaining superficial because centred on some secondary aspect of the problem, or copied from a foreign project without due attention to the real local conditions. Where can the pooling of all those individual efforts be done, where can the required work of documentation and research be done, if not in efficient centres of the catechetical apostolate?

Indeed, the International Catechetical Congress of Rome, 1950, uses a striking formula when presenting its conclusion on this very point; *Congressus peculiarissimo modo insistit* – words not found in any of the nine other series of conclusions – *in creatione, recta ordinatione et efficaci actione Officii Catechistici Dioecesani.*[1] This was but an echo, more strongly worded perhaps, of the Decree *Provido sane Consilio,* promulgated in 1935 by the Sacred Congregation of the Council.

[1] *Acta Congressus,* p. 171.

## *The Scope of Catechetical Centres*

Concerning the phrase "Catechetical Apostolate" misunderstanding may have to be avoided. The word "catechism" brings into the minds of many the picture of classes held for children, if not that of a small handbook on religion. A catechetical centre would not, however, be concerned only with this important, but quite partial aspect of the missionary problem. In our missions especially, the task of the "catechesis", of spreading the knowledge of Christ's message, includes much more, such as the continued formation of the faithful, and the extension of the Kingdom. Besides, we cannot have, as in other countries, one centre for the liturgical apostolate, another for pastoral approach, and so on. All these problems, however, must be tackled on a methodical basis, as Monsignor Cordeiro demonstrated last year at Nijmegen concerning liturgy. My own plea now is that all this could, and should, be done in the centres of catechetical apostolate as I see them.

Why, then, not choose another and more general name? First, because the "catechesis", that is, the formation of the Christian adult by means of solid teaching, is at the very centre of our pastoral action, nay is the first mission entrusted by Christ to his Church: *Euntes, docete.* Moreover, Rome, as far as I know, never urged upon us the foundation of any such centre as clearly as it did for the Catechetical Office, by the decree of 1935.

## *Different Kinds of Centres and their Work*

### THE DIOCESAN CENTRE

The bishop is, by divine institution, pastor and teacher. Quite naturally, therefore, Canon Law[2] invests him with the responsibility of religious instruction in his diocese. Hence, in the two texts already referred to, first attention is paid to catechetical work on a diocesan scale. "The local Ordinaries", says the 1935 decree, "will start if possible an office which, under

[2] C.I.C., 1336.

parish. This has been going on for little over one year, but already results are felt, and the priest is only anxious to ensure better and better co-operation. Thus, he has started a cyclostyled "circular letter" for his teacher-catechists, in which they can find some dogmatic or liturgical explanations, the announcements of various competitions, model-lessons prepared by other teachers or trainees, and even models for drawing or cut-outs. This example, in my opinion, shows there is a great advantage in starting our diocesan centre at some training school, if we have any – provided, of course, the director of the centre is not burdened with administrative work in the training school. For there will be mutual profit: the director will come to know, and help to form, those who will later on teach religion to most children in the villages; and he will get their help for making posters, or commentaries of films. Some kind of "permanent catechetical exhibition" can thus be set up, for the profit of every one in the diocese. In dioceses without a training school of their own, at least part of the same results may be achieved if the religious instruction director normally resides in a high school or middle school. Whatever be the government regulations, this director could, without taking regular classes, help the school authorities in religious matters, after an agreement has been drawn up with the Ordinary.

The diocesan centre is not concerned exclusively with lay teachers, far from it. The whole diocese must enter fully into the catechetical movement, so that the knowledge of Christ may permeate the hearts and lives of all. All the trends of modern catechetics must be brought to the notice of priests and religious, in a manner showing that the efforts demanded are worthwhile. Hence, according to the Roman directives, there will be not only some "refresher courses" for lay teachers, but also more advanced "study sessions" for priests and for religious. Indeed, the number of such study-weeks or summer courses nowadays being held in mission countries, is one of the most encouraging features of the present situation.

In brief, the director of religious instruction must be at the centre of a real team-work. He is not, however, a dictator, imposing his ideas on all; his role in the diocesan commission is important, but the other members are no mere silent partners.

They bring into the discussions their viewpoint as the workers in the field, confronting the principles and suggestions exposed by the director, with their own practical knowledge. In this way, the directives of the Ordinary can combine depth with realism; add to this the services rendered by the diocesan office, and those catechetical regulations will then run much less risk of being looked upon as some hasty unwarranted changes and thus quietly left aside.

### NATIONAL CENTRES

Even in the best conditions, the diocesan centres cannot cater for the whole task of information, study, and publication which is essential for catechetical renewal. The need for centres of catechetical apostolate on an interdiocesan basis was expressed in the International Congress of 1950. "Besides the diocesan catechetical offices, it is convenient that, under the authority of the bishops, some regional and national centres exist for catechetical questions, on a national or regional level, so that, by pooling all efforts, a more efficient organization of the religious instruction may be achieved."[4]

In our mission countries, on what must we insist? On national centres, on regional centres, or on both? On the occasion of the International Congress, "some catechetical centres in India", in their answers to a questionnaire, asserted that "the existence (in India) of a national catechetical centre is practically impossible, due to the variety of languages and of culture in a region as vast as Europe."[5]

But, when a few years later, the Indian Bishops' Conference sent round a questionnaire to all Ordinaries, at least a dozen replied that such a national centre should be started. Nowadays, practically all mission countries have a Bishop's Conference, with its Standing Committee. The national centre of catechetical apostolate, in my opinion, will work in constant co-operation with the member of that Standing Committee which is in charge of catechetics. No question, this time, of any "administrative power"

[4] *Acta Congressus,* p. 172.
[5] *Acta Congressus,* p. 409.

invested in such centres. Like the Bishops' Conference itself, the national centre, and the national commission, can at best give suggestions for action, which the Ordinary is free to chose or leave – though the good of the Church often asks for agreement on the practical forms of our work!

The most important task of the national centre will be to help the diocesan centres, to be a link among them and a link with the catechetical movement abroad. The diocesan directors have neither the time nor the money necessary to get all catechetical publications, study them, and make the necessary selection and adaptation to their own needs. They will expect therefore, from the national centre, a service of documentation: general trends of catechetical progress the whole world over; summaries of most important articles or books published in various languages; annotated lists of catechetical material. This documentation could be made available in the shape of circular letters, or even of a regular catechetical magazine published in the language common to the priests of a nation.

In the line of researches, inquiries will show the practical needs on a national basis, while more theoretical studies of theological and psychological principles are continued. The centre is also to train the personnel necessary in the dioceses, by means of summer schools and even, once the work is developed, by means of a real training course meant for directors of religious instructions or for full-time workers in the diocesan centres. Is this a mere day-dream, a utopia? Let us look at some realizations, though no one will deny that these are only the very first steps. The Mayidi Centre, in the Congo, organized several very successful study-weeks, which were attended by delegates from many parts of Africa. And, to speak of what I personally know, the Catechetical Centre of Poona (India) has prepared, besides several liturgical leaflets, a small guide for the participation of the faithful in the Mass, at the demand of the Bishops' Conference. This centre also sent a thorough inquiry on the teaching of moral science in our high schools and colleges; as a result, a series of text books is already in the press.

Rights were secured for printing or adapting some very important books. Father Hofinger's work on "The Art of

Teaching Christian Doctrine", the English edition[6] of the *Katholischer Katechismus der Bistümer Deutschlands,* and Pichler's book for younger children which, though well-known for many years, had not been as yet translated into English. Another text-book, *The Way and the Life,* a catechism for middle school children, aged from 10–13 years, with a liturgical orientation, which serves at the same time as a preliminary step to *A Catholic Catechism* used in the upper forms, was written in Poona itself. With these publications as a basis, a totally new syllabus was introduced in the English language schools of the archdiocese of Bombay; both syllabus and text-books have been highly praised by authorities like Canon Drinkwater, and Father Jungmann and Father Delcuve. Several editions of these books in the vernacular are in preparation; and an inquiry has been held on the results of that first attempt in Bombay, with a view to bring in the necessary adaptation.

Yet, in Poona very much remains to be done before this centre of catechetical apostolate will be able to serve its purpose efficaciously.

## REGIONAL CENTRES

In big countries, a single national centre cannot cater for all the needs, in all the languages spoken by the people. Hence, between the diocesan and the national centres, we often need regional centres founded on a linguistic basis – as were asked for by more than twenty Indian bishops in their answer to the questionnaire already referred to.

The regional centres should, first of all, make available, in the various vernaculars, the gist of what the national centre puts out in the language most common to the clergy of the nation. Both the spread of documentation and the work of further research will be thus rendered easier. Moreover, the "common pool of practical experiences" could be gathered on an interdiocesan basis and be made available immediately to religious or lay teachers themselves.

The establishment of regional centres would also solve a difficult problem for us in the missions: the publication of

[6] *A Catholic Catechism* (London and New York, 1957).

text-books and other catechetical works. I repeat on the regional scale what I said when speaking of the national centre: there is no question of interfering with the rights of each bishop. Yet, given the smallness of the market for books in most dioceses, we all realize that agreement among the Ordinaries of the same linguistic region could lessen the cost of production . . . without the various diocesan presses suffering. For, if there is real co-operation, the high school text, for example, could be printed in one diocese, the text for middle schools in another, and so on for teachers' helps, periodicals in the vernacular, etc. The Regional Director could be the editor of this magazine, and each Diocesan Director could insert some supplement giving the diocesan news and directives.

For practical reasons, I suggest that both national and regional centres be started preferably in some seminary. In most missions, students from several dioceses join the same institution, and there is often a papal seminary where some of the best priests are trained. If catechetical centres were set up in these places, both students and the centre itself would profit: on the one hand, a better theoretical (and even practical) formation, under the guidance of some expert; on the other, essays prepared in study-circles, as well as posters or film commentaries designed with artistic skill by the students, would be a welcome addition to the documentary service of the centre. Through the seminarians, the catechetical problems in the different dioceses can be more easily studied, and a better view of the whole situation reached. Finally, the very presence of the regional or national centre in the seminary can foster the spirit of enthusiasm and co-operation which the seminarians need to acquire to become real apostles in their future catechetical work.

### *Summary*

Allow me to sum up the catechetical organization in mission countries, as I envisage it. The task of the diocesan centre is not only one of inspection, but also of the organization of all the catechetical efforts in the diocese. Its director visits the villages, keeps contact with all the teachers of religion, and encourages and advises them. In the national centre, the ideas of the world-wide catechetical movement are studied, selected and adapted to the general needs of the country. There also the diocesan directors find help for their own work in preparing catechetical magazines and more important publications, organizing courses and study-weeks – all this in the language common to the priests of the whole country. The national centre, though approved by the Bishops' Conference and working for it, has no "administrative power" binding on individual dioceses. The same work is done by regional centres, where they are needed, on a linguistic basis: they help the religious and lay helpers, who often know only their own vernacular, and, still more, they prepare vernacular literature on the subject of catechetics. At every level, a catechetical commission facilitates the work of practical information, and of real adaptation to concrete needs and possibilities. This commission is made up, on the diocesan level, of actual teachers of religion, and on the regional or national level, of some diocesan directors and specialists in one branch or other of the catechetical question. I wish now to insist again on what I think is an essential condition, if this programme is to bear real fruit. At each level, diocesan, regional or national, we must have at least one man set apart entirely for the work. This was the opinion of the experts gathered at Rome in 1950: *Officio Catechistico praesit . . . sacerdos . . . qui, liber ab aliis negotiis, huic gravissimo officio totus incumbat.*[7] I have already explained that some teaching of pedagogy in training school or seminary may not go against this wish.

But a mere appointment is not enough, we must have a well-prepared specialist. *Sacerdos psychologiae, pedagogiae, methodologiae catechisticae vere peritus prudentia et zelo probatus.* It all comes down to this. Catechetics is not some hobby for a busy man; it is a science, and on this science depends much of the future of our faith. Only men scientifically trained will do full justice to the task. I hasten to add, we have means to train specialists. Several countries have a course in catechetics corresponding to a Licentiate or even Doctorate in Theology. In Rome, the

[7] *Acta Congressus,* p. 171.

institute *Pastor Angelicus* trains priests in all branches of pastoral theology. Of particular interest for catechetics in the missions is the formation given in two institutions. The two-year course of the *Institut Supérieur Catéchétique* in Paris provides a highly specialized formation both on the theoretical and the practical planes. Many students from mission countries have already attended it with much fruit. The annual catechetical course organized at the *Lumen Vitae* Centre in Brussels concentrates more on a systematic view of the catechetical problem as a whole and, thanks to the international staff of professors and lecturers, tries to emphasize the universal application of the matters under discussion. Besides, the several study-tours organized in connection with the course greatly enhance its practical value for the future directors of the catechetical apostolate in the missions.

The existence of this Catechetical Year shows the importance, and advantage, of co-operation on higher level still, between the various national centres. This is achieved to a high degree by the Centre *Lumen Vitae,* which is one of the officially mandated Catholic international organizations. We can all profit greatly from the work of Father Delcuve. However, we have some catechetical problems peculiar to us with which *Lumen Vitae* is not necessarily concerned. Why not have our own "International Missionary Centre of the Catechetical Apostolate"? In fact, we have one, namely the East Asian Pastoral Institute in Manila, run by Father Hofinger. This, among other things, is in charge of the catechetical and liturgical section of the *Mission Bulletin* (now *Asia*) published in Hongkong. I am sure that, if all mission territories come to co-operate with the Manila Centre, this will mark a further step in the progress of the catechetical movement in the missions.

### *Conclusion*

I have made many suggestions, expressed many wishes. My last wish is that no one should be discouraged by the efforts required. No quick results will be achieved, but the work must be solid, beginning with the preparation of the personnel necessary for those centres. Meanwhile a start may be made on a small scale: enthusiasm and *practical* desire for co-operation will grow, at the sight of the first results. Thus, I am confident, the seeds planted during this Eichstätt Congress will grow into a mighty tree, "that they may know thee, Father, and the one thou hast sent", Jesus Christ, and thus, that the Kingdom of God may spread and become ever more mighty from end to end of the world.

# The Bishop's Role in the Catechetical Renewal

DENIS E. HURLEY, O.M.I.,
Archbishop of Durban, South Africa

THE role of the bishop in the catechetical renewal is a particular and direct expression of the general role of the bishop in the Church. The bishop forms part of the governing body of the Church under the authority of the Pope. He shares in the power to rule, to teach and to administer the sacraments. It may be argued whether or not the teaching power is an expression of jurisdiction. What is important about this teaching power, this *magisterium,* is the extraordinary emphasis laid on it in the New Testament and the tradition of the Church.

## *Magisterium*

One cannot fail to notice this emphasis in Christ's references to the truth he had come to reveal. The Synoptic Gospels generally convey this in a concrete way by presenting his message in minute detail and with all the moving and appealing imagery with which he clothed it. St. Matthew, however, goes beyond this in one brief passage as he communicates a deep reflection of Jesus on his truthgiving mission: "Father, who art the Lord of heaven and earth, I give thee praise that thou hast hidden all this from the wise and prudent, and revealed it to little children. Be it so, Father, since this finds favour in thy sight. My Father has entrusted everything into my hands; none knows the Son truly except the Father, and none knows the Father truly except the Son, and those to whom it is the Son's good pleasure to reveal him" (Matt. 11:25–27).

But it is St. John who rises to the heights in reporting Christ's self-revelation as infinite and eternal truth. "I am the light of the world. He who follows me can never walk in darkness; he will possess the light which is life" (John 8:12). "If you continue faithful to my word, you are my disciples in earnest; so you will come to know the truth, and the truth will set you free" (John 8:31–32). "Believe me when I tell you this: if a man is true to my word, to all eternity he will never see death" (John 8:51). "What I was born for, what I came into the world for, is to bear witness of the truth. Whoever belongs to the truth listens to my voice" (John 18:37). "I am the way; I am the truth and the life" (John 14:6). Life and light, light and life – interchangeable words under the pen of St. John. They pour themselves out in a torrent when St. John sits down to write, as for instance in the opening passage of his first epistle: "Our message concerns that Word, who is life; what he was from the first, what we have heard about him, what our own eyes have seen of him; what it was that met our gaze, and the touch of our hands. Yes, life dawned; and it is as eye-witnesses that we give you news of that life, that eternal life, which ever abode with the Father and has dawned, now, on us" (1 John 1:1–2). No wonder the meditations of a life-time burst forth into that tremendous prologue: "In the beginning was the Word, and the Word was with God: and the Word was God. The same was in the beginning with God. All things were made by him; and without him was made nothing that was made. In him was life; and the life was the light of men. And the light shineth in the darkness and the darkness did not comprehend it" (John 1:1–5).

Word without beginning or end, Word divine, Word creating, illuminating and vivifying. Such was St. John's vision of the Saviour whom he also heard saying: "If a man believes in me, it is in him who sent me, not in me that he believes; to see me is to see him who sent me (that "true likeness of the God we cannot see" of St. Paul). I have come into the world as a light so that all who believe in me may continue no longer in darkness . . . it was my Father, who sent me, that commanded me what words I was to say, what message I was to utter. And I know well that what he commands is eternal life; everything then, which I utter, I utter as my Father has bidden me" (John 12:44–50). Everything is referred to the Father.

What his Father had bidden him, he in turn will bid his apostles. But first they will receive the truth-giving Spirit who proceeds from the Father, and when he has befriended them, "he whom I will send to you from the Father's side, he will bear witness of what I was; and you, too, are to be my witnesses, you who from the first have been in my company" (John 15:26–7). Jesus prays for them: "Thou hast sent me into the world on thy errand, and I have sent them into the world on my errand; and I dedicate myself for their sakes, that they too may be dedicated through the truth" (John 17:18–19). All these promises and prayers are leading up to the great moment when the most sublime mission of all time is conferred on men: "All authority in heaven and on earth has been given to me; you, therefore, must go out, making disciples of all nations, and baptizing them in the Name of the Father and of the Son and of the Holy Ghost, teaching them to observe all the commandments which I have given you. And behold I am with you all through the days that are coming, until the consummation of the world" (John 28:18–20). "The Holy Spirit will come upon you, and you will receive strength from him; you are to be my witnesses in Jerusalem and throughout Judea, in Samaria, yes, and to the ends of the earth" (Acts 1:8).

How seriously this mandate was taken, the Acts of the Apostles recount. The first apostolic duty after the ascension of Jesus was to elect a man to fill the post vacated by Judas; and what was uppermost in their minds, as Peter put it, was to complete the number of those who would be witnesses of the resurrection of Jesus and all that the resurrection implied. Witnessing, testifying, teaching – that was the important task. After the coming of the Spirit "great was the power", writes St. Luke, "with which the apostles testified to the resurrection of our Lord Jesus Christ, and great was the grace that rested on them all" (Acts 4:33). It was not long before the growth of the infant Church created problems through the practice of that very charity which was its distinguishing mark. The social and benevolent mission of the Church was not long in coming into being and the apostles perceived that preoccupation with it was seriously interfering with their teaching duties. "It is too much that we should have to forego preaching God's word, and bestow our care upon tables" (Acts 4:2). They solved the problem by the appointment of deacons.

They never forgot the importance of the word. "We, his companions on the holy mountain", wrote St. Peter years later, "heard that voice coming from heaven, and now the word of the prophets gives us more confidence than ever. It is with good reason that you are paying so much attention to that word; it will go on shining, like a lamp in some darkened room, until the dawn breaks and the day-star rises in your hearts" (2 Peter 1:18–19).

St. Paul enters fully and enthusiastically into the ministry of the word confided to him. He is "set apart to preach the gospel of God", he tells the Romans. Christ did not send him to baptize, he tells the Corinthians, but to preach the gospel, not with persuasive language, devised by human wisdom, but by the proof he gave of spiritual power; God's power, not man's power was to be the foundation of their faith (1 Cor. 2:4–5). To the Galatians he writes: "And then, he who had set me apart from the day of my birth, and called me by his grace, saw fit to make his Son known to me so that I could preach his gospel among the Gentiles" (Gal. 1:15–16). And to the Ephesians: "With what grace God gives me (and he gives it in all the effectiveness of his power) I am a minister of that gospel; on me, least as I am of all the saints, he has bestowed this privilege of making known to the Gentiles the unfathomable riches of Christ, of publishing to the world the plan of this mystery kept hidden from the beginning of time in the all-creating mind of God" (Eph. 3:7–9).

If the preaching of the gospel was not the only task of the apostles, it was at least of such importance that it could be said to be the characteristic of an apostle. He was a messenger, a prophet, a herald. And when he passed on his mandate and power to others, he did so, as Paul did to Timothy, exhorting him "to preach the word continually, welcome or unwelcome" (2 Tim: 4:2), to make himself "a model of speech and behaviour for the faithful, all love, all faith, all purity. Reading, preaching, instructing, let these be thy constant care while I am absent. . . . Two things claim thy attention, thyself and the teaching of the faith; spend thy care on them; so wilt thou and those who listen to thee achieve salvation" (1 Tim. 4:12–16). Though Paul himself is in prison there is no imprisoning the word of God. "For its sake", says St. Paul, "I am ready to undergo anything; for the love of the elect, that they like us, may win salvation in Christ Jesus and eternal glory with it" (2 Tim. 2:9–10).

This supreme dedication to the faith and the teaching of it will remain a characteristic of the Church through the ages. The *Didache* refers to the preaching of the itinerant missionaries of the early Church "the apostles, prophets and doctors" as well as to the teaching of the local hierarchies of bishops and deacons. St. Ignatius describes the bishop's duty to the truth, his obligation to stand fast before the onslaught of heretics "like the anvil under the hammer". We read Ireneus and Origen on the *magisterium,* Augustine and Chrysostom on the necessity and methods of preaching. The publication of the Christian revelation is the mainspring of the Church's being and growth, and the bishop in his church is the man mainly responsible. For this reason the Church prays at the consecration of a bishop that "there may abound in him constancy in the faith, purity of love, sincerity of peace"; that "by thy gift his feet may be beautiful for the preaching of peace, for the telling of thy good news". "Give him, Lord", she prays, "the ministry of reconciliation in word and in deeds, in the power of signs and wonders. May his speaking and his preaching depend not on persuasive language, devised by human wisdom, but rather on the proof of spiritual power." When, through the consecrator, she hands him the Gospel texts, she exhorts him to "go and preach to the people committed to him; for the Lord is strong, to increase his grace in him." And the sacred canons oblige him to ensure "that the food of Christian doctrine is provided for the faithful, particularly the children and the uninstructed" (Can. 336).

How does all this apply to-day? Is it still true as it was in the days of the apostles and of the early Church that the task occupying most of the bishop's time should be the telling of the good news? It seems it should be. There is, however, the problem that with the continually increasing complexity of modern life and the growth of institutions necessary to cope with it, the bishop finds himself more and more an organizer and administrator and less and less a herald of the gospel.[1] There is a temptation to slip into the routine of the bureaucrat and operate from behind a desk, to keep in motion a curial machine which, through specialized channels, brings the bishop's distant authority to bear on the multiple facets of Church life, particularly the provision of buildings in which and from which the Church's influence can be exerted. The missionary bishop is especially one whose whole life revolves around buildings, begging for them, planning them, paying for them, blessing them and mortgaging them.

Thank God, however, that there are still occasions like confirmations, the laying of foundation stones, the blessing of churches and schools, rallies, conferences, study courses, and special celebrations when we get our opportunity of speaking directly to the flock. We should make the most of it, for the bishop has a special gift from the Spirit for teaching, and his words carry weight. But such occasions will never make us the regular, systematic teachers of the flock, particularly of the little ones, for these occasions occur too seldom. Modern conditions impose upon us the necessity of performing most of our ministry of the word through others; through priests, teachers, catechists and Catholic Action leaders. Our interest in and solicitude for the manner in which they deputize for us should be as keen as the zeal of Peter and Paul for their personal preaching of the word. For the fervour of a church will be in direct proportion to its knowledge of the faith. Fervour is life, and the faith is the light that gives life. The greater the light the greater the life. Our supreme aspiration for ourselves and the flocks committed to our care should be the realization of that prayerful wish expressed by St. Paul to the Christians of Ephesus: "So may he who is the God of our Lord Jesus Christ, the Father to whom glory belongs, grant you a spirit of wisdom and insight, to give you fuller knowledge of himself. May your inward eye be enlightened, so that you may understand to

[1] See Cajetan's treatment of this issue in his commentary on the *Summa* II II q. 185 3 n. IV; quoted by Monsignor Elchinger, Auxiliary Bishop of Strasbourg in his brilliant paper "Catéchèse Autour de l'Évêque" in the series *Vérité et Vie,* Strasbourg.

what hopes he has called you, how rich in glory is that inheritance of his found among the saints, what surpassing virtue there is in his dealing with us who believe" (Eph. 1:17 to 18).

If the bishop must do most of his teaching through deputies, his consuming ambition will be to ensure that these deputies do their work well; that priests, teachers and catechists achieve the highest standards in the teaching of the faith. Much has been said at this conference by eminent lecturers concerning the essential content, the objectives, trends and methods of modern catechetics. It should be our earnest resolution to take all this back with us to our respective territories, to do our best to put it into effect and to urge its enthusiastic acceptance on our brother bishops. But there is so much to be accomplished, at least in territories like my own where the catechetical renewal is still only a glimmer on the horizon, that we need more practical ideas on where and how to start.

Our ultimate objective is clear. We want to provide the little ones under our care with inspired teachers who understand the catechetical message and the methods of conveying it, and who have the necessary materials at their disposal: syllabus, teacher manuals, pupils' textbooks and teaching aids. Briefly: skilled workers and efficient tools. Fortunate indeed is the bishop who has well-trained and well-equipped catechists at his disposal. My words are not for him, but for those like myself who feel that their catechetical apostolate is hopelessly out-of-date.

### *Basic Requirements for Catechetical Renewal*

The advice I have to offer is merely a repetition of some of the recommendations made by the Archbishop of Hyderabad in his excellent paper entitled "Centres of Catechetical Apostolate". The three basic essentials would appear to be: a realization by the hierarchy that catechetical reform is an urgent necessity; trained personnel to do the job; a catechetical institute through which to do it. In the case of some territories it may be possible to undertake the catechetical renewal on a diocesan basis because the diocese is large enough to engage the necessary staff, establish the institute and finance the printing or buying of the books and teaching aids that are required. But in the case of most missionary dioceses it will be essential to operate on provincial, regional or national level. On the assumption that this is the only practical way for most of us to go to work, I shall talk in terms of a hierarchy and not of individual bishops.

Our first necessity, then, is to convince the members of our hierarchy that catechetical renewal is one of the vital necessities of our day. Along with the liturgical movement and Catholic Action it forms part of the vigorous reaction of the Church to present-day atheism, whether communistic or merely secularistic. Most hierarchies will not require much convincing. They know the inadequacy of the old methods. They are anxious to be introduced to the new ones.

Our second necessity is trained personnel. The catechetical renewal is not just a matter of revising a few words in a catechism, or changing the order of the questions and answers or re-arranging the syllabus. The catechetical renewal, as has so frequently been emphasized during the course of this Study Week, is concerned with a fundamental reorientation in the very content of the catechetical message and with a vast change in the pedagogical methods of presentation. Such reorientation, such changes will not be easily achieved without the services of competent people trained in the modern catechetical outlook. At least one well-trained priest is essential and around him must be built up a commission of intelligent and experienced people who can learn from him and at the same time provide the advice and practical assistance that he will require for the realization of the project. I speak now as one who has had some experience of a catechetical commission, a willing, eager and enthusiastic commission, but one lacking the services of a full-time trained and experienced director.

No matter how expert the director, no matter how capable and willing the commission, it is vitally necessary for the hierarchy to remain in very close association with the catechetical commission, and the best way of doing this would appear to be by providing an episcopal chairman. For the hierarchy must have a concrete and practical realization of what the catechetical renewal is and what is involved in planning syllabuses, choosing books and training teachers. Commissions are impersonal things and they have no authority in the Church. Unless the hierarchy assumes its just responsibility and maintains the sense of urgency, long and discouraging delays may result, and apathy and open opposition may kill the undertaking before it achieves any significant results. The commission must have a bishop that can be blamed if meetings are not held and money not provided and work not executed. Commissions are essential in modern life but they do not dispense with the need for authority, authority embodied in one man who sees that the job is done and the means provided to get it done.

I need not go into details about the terms of reference of the commission. It must deal with the entire catechetical field; syllabus, teacher manuals, pupils' textbooks, teaching aids, training centres, training courses, refresher courses; the lot. Under the authority of the hierarchy it must aim at producing well-trained and well-equipped catechists in all fields: in the Catholic school and outside the Catholic school. It must aim at producing the workers and the tools. And it must not forget that the trained catechist is not the only worker, he is perhaps only the secondary worker: the principal worker is the Catholic parent, the Catholic father and mother, who must be given every assistance to understand and fulfil his or her function in the religious formation of youth. There is a certain wholeness about the work of catechetical commission. It does only half its job if it points out how parents and teachers must be trained without providing them with the means of fulfilling their task, or if it provides the means and omits to indicate how the means are to be used. The commission's task is two-fold: training and tools.

Without a commission and its expert director little progress will be made in catechetical renewal. But a commission cannot work without headquarters, and so we come to the third necessity: a catechetical institute, a place where books and reviews can be accumulated, where the director, with the assistance of at least one secretary, can carry on the routine work from one meeting of the commission to another, from which courses can be organized and information supplied. An institute at the disposal of the director guarantees the basic facilities necessary for the continuity of the task and the accomplishment of steady results. Expecting a commission and its director to function without an institute is like trying to run a university without lecture rooms and a library. There are many present here more capable than I of emphasizing the importance of a catechetical institute in each country or region. There are some who can speak from the experience of successfully running an institute. I speak only as a member of a hierarchy that feels the need and hopes to satisfy it in the near future.

If, through the help of God, all this is realized: commission, trained personnel, institute, syllabuses, teacher manuals, pupils' textbooks, teaching aids, training courses, refresher courses, courses for parents and all that pertains to a vigorous and efficient catechetical apostolate; one thing may still be wanting for the success of that apostolate, one thing the lack of which could ruin it completely: the whole-hearted and devoted co-operation of the clergy. None of us here needs to be told that no successful apostolic venture is ever launched without the support of the priests. Unless the priests are body and soul in the catechetical movement, it will not succeed. A bishop can reach his flock only through his priests. Whatever he wants to accomplish he will accomplish through his priests. It is, of course, quite possible that a little time may elapse before the clergy of a territory understand and whole-heartedly support a change in catechetical methods. We are all creatures of habit. We follow the established system. And it is not easy for anyone to relinquish a system that has grown into his personality and to take up something new. Custom is initially more powerful than logic. But if the logic has inherent value and is cogently and persistently pursued it will triumph in the end. The clergy must be given a chance to learn about the new methods. Courses for priests are as necessary if not more necessary than those for religious and lay teachers. Success will not be one hundred per cent, for we cannot expect everybody to change to new ideas. After all, most of today's clergy were trained according to a system that needs some adjusting if it is to be perfectly consonant with modern requirements, both in preaching and catechetics.

### *Seminary Studies*

That brings us to another point, and a very important point: seminaries. Those of us at this conference whose ecclesiastical studies are of a generation removed from the present time have probably all undergone quite a substantial mental transformation in our theological outlook. We left our books twenty years ago and more with the firm conviction that the comprehension of essences was the fulfilment of all knowledge. Our ability to grasp essences and our appetite for the task were developed in a course of philosophy. Then we were trained to apply the ability and the appetite to God's revelation. The aim of theology was the dissection of revealed truth into manageable parts and the definition of them by means of the concepts and terminology that philosophy had supplied. We explored the essence of the Trinity, of the Hypostatic Union, the Redemption, the Church, sacramental instrumentality and the sacrifice of the Mass, and, in the process, we lopped off many of the untidy fringes of great mysteries. We sometimes claimed that our theological precision enabled us to rebut the arguments of unbelievers by demonstrating that a mystery was not a contradiction, but this never sounded very convincing; he who demonstrates non-contradiction demonstrates compatibility and dissolves the mystery.

It was an invaluable experience, this pursuit of philosophical and theological essences. It provided an indispensable discipline of the mind, a brilliant sharpening of thought. It helped us to share in an achievement of the Church, an accomplishment of Catholic mental culture. But it had the great drawback of leaving us with the impression that he who defines the essence has reached the end of the pursuit of truth, whereas he is only half-way. The other half of the task consists in fitting the accidents back on the substance, particularly the accidents of "action" and "passion", the movement and dynamism, the transforming and being transformed, the resulting joy and satisfaction, hurt and suffering. In a word – life. For life, though it has an essence, is complete only in action and passion, through which it reaches out to become an integral part of the vast stream of life flowing out from and returning to the inexhaustible Fountain of Everlasting Life. We left our studies with a mental outlook divorced from time and space, static in a world of eternal essences. In the hard school of experience we had to learn how to re-enter the world of movement. Many never succeed. Their philosophy and theology remain like a sediment on the bed of a canal rarely sufficiently disturbed to mix with the flowing waters of mental experience and reaction. It is not their fault. It is the fault of the system.

The discomfort felt in the Church at the contrast between static theology and dynamic reality led to stirrings in many quarters which are now joining forces to flow in a great stream of biblical, theological, liturgical, catechetical and apostolic renewal. It is good to plunge into the stream and feel the excitement of its flow. The renewal is involving the biblical scholar and the theologian, the religious teacher, the lay teacher and the Catholic actionist, the pastoral priest and the parishioners in the liturgical parish. The person it must involve above all is the seminarian. For he is the one who is going to make the renewal a universal reality when he comes out as a priest.

Twenty-five years ago if you had asked the average seminarian in what way he was being trained, he would have given you a reply reflecting his philosophical or theological exertion. His reply would certainly not have reflected the conviction that his studies were aimed at one great objective: announcing the glad tidings of Christ's redemption. I do not know if the position is any different today in a great number of cases. Possibly it is in parts of Europe. So much depends on the seminarian that we should well ask ourselves whether he is receiving the proper training to become a zealous and effective herald of the gospel, a man filled to the brim with a conviction and fairly vibrating with enthusiasm to communicate it. Perhaps our study system is so dry and analytical that it takes all the dynamism out of our faith. Perhaps we neglect so tragically the art of communication that we turn out boring and monotonous theorizers instead of apostles whose conviction and fire and imagery compel attention. At the opening of this Study Week we heard Canon Brien emphasize the importance of making our catechesis personal, complete and relevant to the world in which we live. If we want to achieve that, must we not begin in the seminary and make the education of future priests personal, complete and relevant?

Many of you must have thought a lot about this problem: of how to combine with the essential systematic studies in philosophy and theology, the acquisition of a warm and integral understanding of the mystery of Christ and the desire and the ability to communicate it. I cannot speak with any authority on the subject but a suggestion that has occurred to me is that the first year of ecclesiastical studies should be devoted to giving our students a comprehensive vision of the mystery of Christ and the beginnings of a thorough training in communication by speech and writing. Such an introductory year would fix in their minds, a little vaguely no doubt but convincingly enough, the content of the message they will be dealing with for the rest of their lives and the realization that their great objective is to be communicators and not merely contemplators. Emphasis on the importance of communication would ensure that far greater attention is paid to preaching and catechetics, which are often sadly neglected in some of our seminaries and yet occupy seventy-five per cent of the priestly lives of those who are trained in them. Few men are born to be enthusiastic about theories. Show them how theory takes on the flesh and blood of action and life, and enthusiasm rises. Much boredom in ecclesiastical study would disappear if the students saw more clearly how that study serves the mystery of Christ and the proclamation of it.

Again and again it has been impressed upon us in the course of this week that one of the great necessities of our preaching and catechesis is adaptation; adaptation to what already exists in the mental and moral universe of those to whom we address our message. I ask myself if the traditional course of scholastic philosophy fosters adaptability. Does it not impress upon the youthful mind of the seminarian that here is the way all human intelligence functions and this is the method by which all men are to be won? A detailed consideration of the problems of philosophical studies in seminaries is beyond my scope; so I merely ask a few questions and make a few tentative suggestions in all due submission to what is prescribed in the matter by the Holy See.

Should we not, for example, re-arrange the division of philosophical matter into philosophy of the universe (or physical philosophy), philosophy of man (or human philosophy) and metaphysics? And should we not introduce our philosophy of the universe with a bird's eye view of how the universe appears to modern scientific man? Evolution should receive fair treatment, for it colours all modern thought. After that we may have some difficulty in convincing students of the validity of hylomorphism and the immutability of species, but that would be better than giving them a cosmology that has no point of contact with modern science. Philosophy of man would be a vast subject. It should begin like the philosophy of the universe with a bird's eye view of the picture of man in modern science. Certain characteristic topics from modern psychology and sociology could contribute to this. And from these the students could be taken on to rational psychology and critics, to ethics and political science. Metaphysics would remain the keystone of the arch. History of philosophy would play an essential role in fostering adaptability. It would help students to understand the minds of other men and how error flourishes very often because of the kernel of truth it contains. History classes would also pay a great deal of attention to the particular intellectual atmosphere, whether uncultivated or sophisticated, which the young priests are likely to experience when they leave the seminary. What Doctor Bühlmann has said about Bantu philosophy has its importance here and the same applies to Hindu and other vital and influential systems of thought.

The main objection to this magnificent programme is that it would take six years to complete. Obviously, therefore, the most that could be done would be to give our seminarians a sufficiently enlightening introduction to the problems of the modern world, the principles of Thomistic philosophy and the relation between the two to enable them to do their own personal and realistic thinking. All the while they are coping with philosophy they will be fully aware of the part it is playing in their formation, that is, its subsidiary role as a technique designed to make them better ministers of the word. They will be fully aware of this because of the introductory year dealing with the mystery of Christ. Only too often it is to be feared that under the traditional system, philosophy has no relevance to the life of the seminarian. He suspects it will play a very minor role in his priestly life. He accepts it as a course of mental gymnastics designed to sharpen his wits, but he finds it very hard to be enthusiastic about gymnastics so far removed from the arena of life. Furthermore the cast-iron methods of modern scholastic philosophy colour his whole approach to subsequent ecclesiastical studies. He is inclined to continue the mental gymnastics in theology and thus fails to provide himself with a living doctrine.

You have been detained long enough with these amateur suggestions for seminary improvement. I shall not spend much time on theology but shall limit myself to an expression of the hope that after the year of apprenticeship in the mystery of Christ and the philosophy course closely related to the problems of our time, our seminarians will come to theology eager for a fuller grasp of the mystery of Christ that is to save the world and the humanity they have been studying, and that they will receive a presentation of that mystery characterized by those very elements that have been described as essential for good catechesis: Christ-centredness and concern for the Bible, the Kingdom, history and liturgy. And while they are absorbing all this, time must be found to give them a very good practical course in preaching and catechesis. It seems quite evident that there will be but slow progress in catechetical renewal if the training of our most important catechists remains remote from the spirit of that renewal.

Forgive me if I have presumed too much on your patience or revealed too embarrassingly my ignorance of what may be under discussion or in the process of implementation in the sphere of seminary training. Out in the missions some of us are inclined to be a generation behind the times. Forgive me, too, if I have added to the mountain of proposals emanating from this Study Week without indicating what practical steps can be taken. I know that sometimes local hierarchies in the missions have little say in the conduct of seminaries, particularly regional seminaries, and that direct control over such seminaries is exercised by the Holy See. All I can suggest in the line of practical steps is that we begin discussions with our seminary staffs on the catechetical renewal and its implications for the seminary, and submit our findings to the Holy See if they appear to involve substantial alterations to the present organization.

This treatment of the bishop's role in the catechetical renewal has covered three points: the importance of the episcopal *magisterium,* concern for the catechetical expression of the *magisterium,* particularly in regard to the provision of means for revitalizing the catechetical apostolate and, finally, seminary improvement. In some ways the task of the twelve apostles in the first century looks simple by comparison with ours. Yet, no doubt if we make a start, the Lord himself will provide the increase and the results, and we shall have the satisfaction of knowing that we are giving a new and dynamic dimension to the *magisterium* in which we share.

# Links between the Catechetical Apostolate in the Home and the Mission Countries

GEORGE DELCUVE, S.J.
Director of *Lumen Vitae* Centre, Brussels

IN a paper entitled "Missionary Catechesis yesterday and today", Father Beckmann, Director of the *Nouvelle Revue de Science missionnaire,* expressed the results of his researches: "This historical survey brings to light the incessant efforts, however variable in intensity according to difference in time and place, which have been made by missionaries to improve and adapt their religious instruction; it shows also that the decisive impulses have come from Christian countries."

These conclusions invite us to give credit to the missionaries for the adaptations they have made; but they bring out, too, the preponderant role played by the Christian countries. In view of this, the title of my paper may occasion surprise because it puts forth a different view. Anyone can understand how catechesis in Christian countries can help that of the mission countries. But is there any truth in the converse statement? Can poverty come to the aid of riches?

It may be useful to recall the celebrated sermon preached by Bossuet in 1659 on "the eminent dignity of the poor within the Church". For we can transpose it and apply it to our subject. Bossuet speaks of three contrasts between the relative positions of rich and poor in the world and in the Church. "In the world", he says, "the rich have all the advantages and hold the place of honour; but in the Kingdom of Christ this place of honour belongs to the poor. In the world the poor are subject to the rich, and seem to be born only to serve them; but in the Church the rich are admitted only if they are willing to serve the poor. In the world graces and favours are only for the rich; the poor have a share only by their help. But in the Church of Christ graces and blessings are for the poor; the rich have none except by their aid."

If we take a wide view of the question, we shall be able to see that catechesis in the home countries and in the mission lands can indeed help each other, and that, in a certain sense, catechesis anywhere induces and helps catechesis anywhere else. But we must not yield to the temptation to discuss the question solely in terms of practical aids, even though we will mention these in due course. We must pass over neither of the two levels on which mutual aid is possible – for there are, indeed two. I will call the first type "directive aid", meaning thereby help to discover the ultimate object, the channels and the spirit of catechesis. Aid of this kind should normally precede that of the second type, which I will call "practical aid", directed to the formation of catechists and the facilitation of their work.

I will make no attempt to define the expressions "mission countries" and "Christian countries", for we all know well enough what we mean by them. But I would like to draw your attention to two features which they both have: neither exists in a unadulterated state, and both are always in a state of change. In all Christian countries there are missionary territories, just as in the mind and heart of every Christian there remain secret depths still pagan! Moreover both Christian and missionary countries are continuously developing. When fervour grows cold in a Christian community formalism takes its place, and this paves the way for superstition. And it may be said that, in general, the advance of missionary countries towards Christianity consists in passing through these stages in the opposite sequence.

This is how Father Beckmann describes Christian and missionary countries. "In Christian countries the catechist normally finds a *milieu* favourable to his work; the spirit of the home, the parish and even the atmosphere of public life all help him. But in mission countries he is up against a hostile paganism which still has a tenacious influence even on the children of Christian parents." And he observes that even the dechristianized areas of Europe have retained traditions of Christian origin to an extent far greater than many people would imagine. The French sociologist Wilbois writes that "in many instances an atheistic Frenchman puts more Christianity into his daily life than a baptized negro". Upon which Father Beckmann remarks: "This opinion will be confirmed by all those who know both Christian and mission countries."

Now that we have explained our terms I would like to submit to you some thoughts on "directive aid" and "practical aid". Several of us worked them out together; and I would like publicly to acknowledge how much this paper owes to Father Xavier Seumois, W. F., missionary at Ruanda-Urundi and director of the African discussion group at *Lumen Vitae,* and also to Father Ivan Extross, professor at the Seminary in Allahabad, India, who is a visiting professor at *Lumen Vitae*.

## *Directive Mutual Aid*

Making the faith known, heralding the faith, is in essence transmitting to mankind the message of salvation, *verbum salutis*. It is a form of mediation which, if it is to be really effective, implies three things: firstly, fidelity to God from whom the message comes, secondly, a proper understanding of man to whom the message is addressed, and thirdly, competent mediation – that is the proper exercise of the art of putting man in contact with God by the way in which we proclaim the faith. Under these three headings we will now consider the way in which the Christian and mission countries can give directive aid to each other.

It is against fidelity to God to water down or distort God's word, to neglect the channels through which God continues to speak to man (Bible, liturgy, systematic teaching of the Church, Christian life), or to disregard the Holy Ghost whose work it is to guide souls to a knowledge of the truth.

But the proclamation of the faith can suffer also through lack of fidelity to man, that is, by paying insufficient attention to human psychology. The Christian message must be like a leaven, influencing the whole of men's lives; how can it do that if it is only laid upon the exterior like a veneer, and never penetrates their psychological states which are partly innate and partly formed by their ever changing environment? How can it ever go into them if we do not understand their personal dispositions and the spirit of their *milieu?*

Finally it is not enough to understand what God says and also to understand man to whom he says it. There must also be competent mediation; we have to master the art of communication by learning, from Bible and liturgy, the principles of God's pedagogy – of the ways in which God teaches.

Unless we see clearly all the factors involved in heralding the faith we are not in a position to discuss in detail the directive aids which Christian and mission countries can give to each other in catechesis.

### *What Can Christian Countries Contribute?*

Two things: reflection on the life of the Church and of man, and experience – that is, application of the results of reflection. These two are closely connected, as I shall now attempt to explain.

Proclamation of the faith requires, as I have just said, that we be faithful to God who is speaking to man – speaking through the Church. And that implies many things. The Church is not something static, immobile; she is animated by the Holy Spirit whose creative spontaneity is inexhaustible. He is always at work leading the Church further and further into the mystery of salvation. If she begins to go the wrong way, he draws her back again to the life-giving sources which are the Bible and the liturgy. He helps the Church to discover the particular task she has to perform in any given era of the history of salvation.

But the voice of the Holy Ghost cannot be heard except in peace and quiet. Normally his messages resound through the Church only as uttered by human voices. They push their way through as the fruit of persistent labour of theologians who combine prayer with their thought, who have access to libraries where they can study the thought of the Fathers and consult the major works of the past, who live in the midst of a community filled with faith and thus feel their own faith in the Church ever strengthened, and who – finally – have sufficient peace and quiet to be able to commit to paper the fruits of their studies.

How much prayerful labour must have gone into the writing of the three volumes of *Missarum Solemnia,* into the regular publication of the *Liturgisches Jahrbuch,* into the recent translation of the *Bible de Jérusalem* and that of the late Ronald Knox. The same may be said of all the books and articles which have contributed so much to the vigour of the liturgical and biblical movements. And what a tremendous amount of work lies behind the activities of the *Centre Pastorale Liturgique* of Paris, the *Liturgisches Institut* of Trier, the *Apostolat Liturgique* of St. André and the Liturgical Press of Collegeville!

It is difficult to imagine such books and articles being produced in the mission fields where pastoral work absorbs the missionaries' whole time, where seminary professors – far too few in numbers – find it all they can do to keep up with their personal studies, and where the task of establishing the material conditions (buildings, etc.) needed for the Church's work is not only an urgent necessity but may even be a temptation deflecting energies from the task which is really primary. And who can be surprised if, in such unfavourable circumstances, catechesis in the missions if left to its own devices should fail to return to its sources and be content, in certain areas, to carry on with out-dated methods and ancient catechetical textbooks drawn up or translated half a century ago?

Proclamation of the faith requires, as I have also said, that we be faithful to man, in the sense that it must obtain a hearing from man through an understanding of the psychology of persons and groups, and of what Newman so aptly called "dispositions favourable and unfavourable to the faith". Now all this presupposes much reflective study, analyses, questionnaires, reports. No one can carry out such work properly unless he has been adequately trained for it and has the time for it. Even though Christian countries are not in a position to carry out direct research on the characteristic mentality of this or that mission country, they can nevertheless work out techniques and devise instruments to be used in such research. Moreover they can carefully observe in their own countries contemporary ideological movements which will later spread abroad and affect mission countries. In Africa, for example, the missionaries are now confronted with social problems which cropped up long ago in the home countries; and in Japan they are up against currents of scientific and existentialist thought of which the same may be said. True enough, there is usually a time-lag; but sooner or later ideologies from the west spread to the rest of the world including the mission countries and there have influence in moulding their outlook on nationalism, communism, humanism and all the rest. Evangelization will remain merely superficial if it does nothing more than dab a few Christian notions on top of minds already saturated with these other ideologies, and if it fails to distinguish between the elements in these which are legitimate and those others which are merely poison for the mind. It is clear, then, that advance in psychology and religious sociology and the discussion of streams of contemporary thought at home can be of real service to the proclamation of the faith in the missions. The superior of a mission in Asia said recently: "We have to turn to the western universities if we are to understand the mentality of our own students, because their minds are nourished on the literature of the western world."

Proclamation of the faith requires competent mediation – a mastery of the technique of communication. Without this we would be painfully disillusioned; even if we have already drunk deep from the sources newly opened up by the Holy Spirit and channelled by the theologians, and even if we have attained sympathy and understanding with those who must hear us, we still have to transmit our message. An excellent theologian is not necessarily a good teacher; it is possible to grasp the religious aspirations and limitations of persons or nations, and yet fail to impart the answer which meets their case. No doubt the Bible and liturgy have immense catechetical value, but it takes a great deal of work and also special training before a man can exploit them properly, use them judiciously in catechesis, to supplement them and harmonize them with other branches of learning. In all these things the Christian countries have an important part to play.

*A Catholic Catechism* was not written in a day. Before writing it, its authors, Klemens Tilmann and Franz Schreibmayr, had to acquire, by experience, a thorough mastery of the art of religious teaching; all the time they were writing the book they were helped by a group of teachers and also, in a very real sense, by an immense number of Catholic children. Now what missionaries – no matter how gifted – could have achieved a work of this kind which has already received so much acclaim both in home countries and missions? One could say much the same about other books written in Christian countries such as *Life in Christ,* by the American priests, James Killgallon and Gerard Weber, or the earlier *Religionsbüchlein* by Monsignor Pichler.

The help which Christian countries can give as a result of continuous and unremitting mental toil is in fact very great. But there is something even more vital in view of the present situation in the missions. This situation was very ably discussed by Monsignor Blomjous in the paper he read at Nijmegen. The Good News of salvation, he said, has indeed been announced; yet the Church has not thereby been implanted. It will be implanted and securely rooted only as the result of action in two spheres, the liturgical and the social.

If a man is attracted by the ideal of holiness, he will learn far more from actually meeting a saint than he will from any number of books or lectures. If a nation is approaching the ideal of becoming a Christian community (in the full sense of that word) then nothing can be so helpful as experience of a genuine Christian community – a community united by eucharistic sacrifice, by living and missionary faith, by charity. Such a community is, in any given place, the Church, the sign set up amongst the nations. It is a manifestation of the mystery of the Church; it is the most eloquent and most complete proclamation of the faith, and the one most longed for by the mission countries because, in it, faith is not separated from the liturgy which is its own expression and nourishment, and is not divorced from its social efflorescence. The experience of Christian life lived to the utmost is the second, and perhaps the greatest service which Christian countries can give to catechesis in the missions. Some Christian countries are, I admit, mis-leading in the literal sense of that word; instead of showing the right way they lead people astray. But alongside these instances of inconsequent Christianity there are also magnificent examples of Christian vitality. There are homes which make a deep impression on married couples who have come from mission countries; there are parish communities like that of St. Sévérin in Paris, there are youth movements and adult sodalities living up to their ideals, and there are towns where the whole atmosphere is Christian (I think of Uden where we gathered last year for our Study Week on Liturgy in the Missions). Any priest or layman who has experience of such a Christian community comes face to face with the true Church in her prophetic, sacramental and charitable mission.

To sum up: the proclamation of the faith in Christian countries can help its counterpart in the missions by all the thought and study devoted to God's revelation and the ways in which it is expressed, to man who is to receive this revelation, and to the ways in which it can best be handed on. In practice this means the initiatives, books, biblical and liturgical reviews, works on psychology and religious sociology and, above all, catechetical institutes and the instructional books which they produce. And this proclamation of the faith in Christian countries is particularly effective when exemplified in the entire life of a community. If we seek a single word to express this thought, it would be the word "incarnation".

### *What Can the Mission Countries Contribute?*

As counterpart to the word "incarnation" applied to the ultimate result of catechesis in the home countries, I would suggest "dynamism" to describe that of catechesis in the missions. For this is the way it appears when viewed in the light of the same three headings we used before: God's message and the way he gives it, man who hears it, and the ways used to proclaim it. The great service which the mission countries can offer to catechesis in the home countries is to prevent sclerosis, complacency, degeneration into mere formalism. For on the one hand missionary catechesis, by its effort to cast off inessentials, restores to the Christian message its universal validity; and on the other hand, by its work of integrating the values found in mission countries, it achieves new "incarnations" of Christianity.

In mission countries fidelity to God's message and to the ways in which he makes it known leads to a casting off of superfluous elements and a concentration on the essentials of the faith and its decisive goal, conversion.

In the course of his theological studies the future missionary will have made a synthesis in his mind; it will contain truths derived from tradition, but also a philosophy inherited from Aristotelianism, a western epistemology and cosmology often rendered out of date by later developments, and a style of expression rooted in the past. When he comes into a different cultural *milieu* in the missions he realizes the need to react against taking the easy way by just passing on, even in condensed form, his personal synthesis. He strives to discover the very core of the message in its authentic and original form. And so for him the kerygma regains its impact. One who bears the Good News of salvation is correspondingly careful to develop, with the aid of God's grace not only the mental acceptance of the entire content of revelation but also its volitional acceptance – the involvement of the entire man.

Catechesis in mission countries can also contribute much to the biblical and liturgical renewals, though in ways somewhat different from catechesis in the home countries. Precisely because it should help persons and groups to find their way along the path which leads to Christ and to his Church, missionary catechesis will seek to show clearly the main lines of the history of salvation which culminate in Christ and in the Church. It will stress also the steps taken by "biblical man" – who heard God's call, left his home, and walked in God's presence.

Missionaries will lay before higher authorities urgent petitions that the liturgy may be restored to its clarity of structure, and that certain parts of it may be in the mother tongue of the people. For only by such reforms can the liturgy fulfil its role as the worship, in spirit and in truth, of the Mystical Body of Christ, a conscious exercise of the priesthood of the faithful; only thus can the liturgy regain its full catechetical value. The African, for instance, is much influenced by the ritual side of religion; but this is true only in so far as the rites appeal to his whole nature – his body, his intelligence, his senses and his heart. By reason of the special interest of the Holy See in the missions, such requests coming from missionaries are more likely to be granted than if they come from the home countries.

And liturgical life well developed in the missions will inspire a renewal of liturgical life at home. A number of rites and ceremonies have degenerated in the home countries to become mere formalities; for instance, the catechumenate and the role of godfathers and godmothers at baptism and confirmation, which are in themselves of great value for growth and perseverance in the faith. In the missions these are regaining their former vigour, and are reacting on people at home. There are many who think that the contact which the missions have with the home countries will do much to imbue our own religious instruction with a more devotional spirit by combining prayer with instruction.

Catechesis in the missions casts off many adventitious and superfluous elements in order to bring out the essentials; but it does not stop there. It has a tendency also to seek integration. Attempting to grow as close as possible to the people whom he is evangelizing, the bearer of the Good News learns to share in the religious aspirations of these people, and does his best to teach them Christian practices in forms adapted to their own culture. In this way missionary catechesis renders great service to the Christian countries. For on the one hand it gives a forcible reminder of something incumbent on every teacher of religion – seeking for that *preparatio evangelica* in the hearers on which the Fathers laid such stress. On the other hand, as Monsignor Blomjous pointed out last year, the people whose outlook this effort brings to light are frequently religious-minded, poor in spirit, receptive to symbolism, and particularly gifted for contemplation and mysticism. Their religious ideals, when fulfilled in Christianity, may do much to rescue our own world from excessive desire for mere technical advances carrying with them a danger of materialism. And these people have an admirable sense of community, and many attendant qualities which strongly resemble evangelical virtues far too little practised in the west. They have, for instance, a traditional respect for parents, mutual helpfulness, solicitude for the sick, hospitality, all developed in a marked degree.

Efforts to cast off inessentials, efforts to integrate: these are two manifestations of the dynamism of missionary catechesis. But there is a third, which helps Christian countries to evaluate correctly their own apostolic tasks. I refer to an enthusiasm which inspires even the laity to devote themselves to the spreading of God's word. It is through their generosity that the Church fulfils her true mission and shows forth her true countenance.

Father Pierre Charles once said to us: "We shall understand St. John's Gospel much better when some commentary on it is written by an oriental." Many biblical ideas regain their full force only in a missionary context. Father Xavier Seumois says this applies, for instance, to the idea of the Kingship of Christ over all creatures, material and spiritual. In Africa a fear of evil spirits can almost bring tribal life to a standstill; for such people the triumph of Jesus over Satan and his dignity as the One Mediator bears the same full meaning as it did for St. Paul's disciples. This can help us to put new meaning for ourselves into expressions which no longer make much impact, such as the idea of the covenant. For Africans such things as the shedding of blood in sacrifice, and sharing in a fraternal meal (communion) have the same significance as they did for Abraham and Moses.

At other times light comes not from similarities but from contrasts. But the result is the same – a deepened understanding of biblical customs and ideas.

We see, then, that catechesis in the home countries and catechesis in the missions are able to complement and help each other. Who can say which of the two is poorer and which the richer? One gives a picture of an established church which, however, does not always avoid the danger of complacency; the other shows a church harried by a thousand spiritual and temporal needs, pressing for certain urgent reforms and adaptations. Each needs the other. If missionary catechesis is cut off from catechesis in the home countries, it looses all the results of study and reflection on the Christian message, human psychology, and the arts of communication. But if catechesis at home is cut off from that of the missions, it looses enthusiasm and is in danger of complacency and routine.

A second thought before we go on to the second part of this paper: on a map of the world we can pick out mission countries from Christian countries; though we cannot do that on maps of our home dioceses or parishes we should remember that they also, in most cases, are simultaneously Christian territories and mission territories! And just as home and missions should help each other, so also should the good and bad areas of our dioceses and parishes. A sound eucharistic community in a parish attracts enquirers – whom we may term catechumens. And these, in turn, attract sympathizers. As between each group and the next one, there should be mutual aid.

### *Practical Mutual Aid*

Let us begin with three considerations of some importance. The second part of this paper is closely related to the first, as a conclusion is related to premises. Next, we must not be afraid of the immensity of the task facing us. It is useless merely to tinker with it; for great problems nothing short of radical solutions will suffice. And finally, though we must take a wide view, we must also adopt a flexible approach. There is such a diversity of conditions to be taken into account. With these preliminaries in mind, let us consider the first kind of practical mutual assistance which I suggest.

### *A Campaign to Make Catholics Realize their Responsibility to Work for Spreading the Faith*

The Second World Congress of the Lay Apostolate exhorted all its participants to practise "the charity of the faith" as something vital to the Church. This phrase was coined by Jean Guitton. He points out that at different times in history Christian charity has been exercised in different fields. And he adds, "In our time the misery of ignorance and religious error is far worse than the misery of material poverty. In these circumstances, in this new state of affairs, one cannot deny that the form of charity most needed is charity towards men's minds . . . one might call it a 'charity of the faith'."

Yet many Catholics are not convinced of this. They do not see the scope of action directed at arousing a living faith, or the supreme importance of such educative *milieux* as the family, the parish, the school, the youth organizations. If they are generous souls they may devote themselves to some form of indirect apostolate, but they leave entirely to priests, brothers and nuns all responsibility for direct apostolate by working for conversions or undertaking catechism lessons. This is true above all in Christian countries, where the indirect apostolate is well developed, or where – at least apparently – everyone can find opportunity if he desires it to hear Christ's message. I say "apparently" because many Catholics seem quite blind to the rapid changes which have transformed some parts of such countries into veritable mission areas. These changes were vividly described recently by Father Jean Dimet, director of religious instruction for the *Mission de France*.

Our first task is to make Catholics aware of their duty to spread the faith. When I was invited to some preliminary meetings before the Second World Congress of the Lay Apostolate I was able to see there the good influence which the mission countries could exert in the accomplishment of this task. It became apparent at one of these sessions that general opinion was wholly in favour of the indirect apostolate. One of the speakers was defending with conviction his thesis that, though the laity should endeavour to facilitate the Church's apostolate by means of their influence in temporal affairs, the actual proclamation of the faith did not concern them at all – it was a matter for the clergy only! I shall always remember what an effect was produced when someone else rose and passed the simple comment: "How disappointed they would be in the missions if they could hear what we are saying now. Surely one of the principle forms of the lay apostolate is catechizing – helping with the task of religious instruction!"

For the campaign I have proposed I now suggest three practical points. Firstly, we should do everything possible to make people realize the "prophetic mission" given to them by the sacrament of confirmation, and make known as widely as possible what the Popes have said about the importance of spreading the faith. No doubt Pope John XXIII will find opportunities, as did his predecessors, to make pronouncements on this subject.

Secondly, perhaps this congress might send up a suggestion that the subject for the next International Congress of the Lay Apostolate should be "Bearers of the Good News". The theme has already been listed among the possible subjects, when the matter was raised at a recent preliminary meeting. It would be highly desirable that the matter should be discussed throughout the whole Church, at local congresses on the diocesan, national and regional levels, during the time still remaining before the Third International Congress.

And, lastly, perhaps one of the concrete objects of our present assembly might be the establishment everywhere, in some modernized form, of the Confraternity of Christian Doctrine which does such fine work in the United States of America.

### *A Campaign to See That Catechesis Is Both Adequate and Balanced, and Related to Present Conditions of Life*

Two dangers are threatening catechesis today. One of them is a risk of narrowness through the use of a single approach to the mystery of salvation, to the neglect of the others. For example, attempting to make catechesis exclusively biblical, exclusively liturgical, or exclusively apostolic; any one of these approaches by itself would result in an unbalanced and only partial understanding of the faith. The other danger is that of being divorced from reality; sometimes the faith is taught as if it had little or nothing to do with the life which we must live here below. The result of this is a kind of "departmentalism" putting religion and life into separate mental compartments.

Both dangers could be avoided, I think, if we based the training of lay apostles on two principles, namely, no training for the direct apostolate of teaching the faith without some knowledge also of the main forms of indirect apostolate in economic and civic life, the family, and so on; no training for the indirect apostolate without a solid formation in the main spheres of the direct apostolate – Bible, liturgy, doctrine.

With these two principles there must go also three practical steps. Firstly making known a Catholic view of life (adapted to each country) whereby our religion can be seen as a unity both dynamic and integrated. Secondly, mutual help between institutions (such as the *Mission de France*) concerned with dechristianized parts of the country, and the foreign missions. Thirdly, close collaboration between catechetical institutes *(sensu lato)* and international Catholic organizations.

### *Mutual Aid in the Catechetical and Pastoral Training of Seminarians and Priests*

Catechesis is dependent on the priest because he is bound to it by duty and also has the task of training other messengers of the Good News. The catechetical training of future priests is, therefore, of the greatest importance; it will involve theoretical and practical courses, but needs above all a kerygmatic orientation of the theology courses.

Those who plan studies in the seminaries are apt to view progress solely in terms of knowledge acquired, rather than in the kerygmatic value of this knowledge. To bring about a kerygmatic orientation the professors of the home countries should collaborate with those in mission seminaries. They might do it by arranging for the occasional exchange of professors; this would be of immense benefit to the professors themselves and to their students. Also by encouraging the collaboration of home and mission professors in the production of theological textbooks imbued with the kerygmatic outlook. Some have already appeared and others are even now in preparation. Father Hofinger has brought out the books of Father Maurice Heinrichs, published from Hongkong. In France they are working on a whole series. Such books could be adapted where necessary, or at least will inspire others.

Concerning the training of professors for catechetics and pastoral theology, although we must avoid the pitfall of thinking we have solved the problem by merely adding a course or two, we must also be careful not to underestimate the importance of such courses and practical exercises in catechetics and pastoral theology. The proper training of professors is vital and urgent. Here also home countries and mission countries can help each other greatly. Future professors should be chosen from among those who already have some experience of the pastoral conditions of the country; and this means that those destined for different countries must have courses also differing in certain ways. For the reasons developed in the first part of this paper, it would be of great advantage to them if they did some advanced studies in the home countries, taking part in the Catholic community life there and getting to know key-institutions and people. And it would profit all if those who teach catechetics and pastoral theology at home could go to spend at least some time in the missions.

Another immensely useful piece of work would be the writing, by a team of men drawn from each sphere, of a textbook of missionary catechesis.

In mission countries could not some form of "refresher course" be given after the priests have already been brought together for their annual retreat? The retreat itself could be an occasion for recalling to them "the primacy of the spiritual", a theme so ably handled by Father J. Schütte at Nijmegen. The refresher courses need not be for priests only; nuns and lay catechists could be admitted to them also.

In the home countries suitable courses might be organized for missionaries who are on home leave.

*Servatis servandis* all these ideas could be applied also to the religious orders of brothers and nuns for the training given in their own houses. In Rome there are courses available to nuns at *Regina Mundi* and for brothers at *Jesus Magister*. There are encouraging signs that the kerygmatic orientation will become increasingly perceptible in the courses given in both these institutions.

### *Mutual Help in Understanding the Mentalities of the Peoples of Mission Countries*

For this purpose the home countries have worked out methods of research; also they have already collected and studied many facts such as the difference to be found between rural and urban mentalities. They could help missionaries to a better understanding of their own people by sending out to them sociological and ethnical experts, help them to prepare questionnaires, to found research institutes and to work out a textbook of religious sociology. They could foster contacts with the International Conference of Religious Sociology. In return the knowledge and experience gained by missionaries will help the progress of religious sociology at home.

### *Mutual Aid in Running Catechetical Institutes*

I am thinking here of those institutes which have an international reputation, such as pontifical institute *Pastor Bonus* in Rome, the Pastoral Institute at the Gregorian University, the *Institut Supérieur Catéchétique* in Paris, the Catechetical Year run by *Lumen Vitae* in Brussels, and various Summer Schools held in the United States. Experience shows that such institutes help catechesis in the mission fields by the training of priests, brothers and nuns who later will rejuvenate the schools for catechists run in the missions, organize local courses and found diocesan, national or regional centres. In the main European catechetical institutes a large proportion – perhaps even as many as half – of the audiences consists of people who have come from the missions. It is thus very desirable that among them there should be organized an African *séminaire,* an Asian *séminaire* (and so on) directed by some priest who has experience in the continent concerned. These priests would render a great service to the students from their own countries, but in addition would themselves profit from many contacts with specialists and opportunities for ascertaining facts.

These primary institutes would be twice as useful as they are now if only they would retain contact with their *alumni* afterwards, giving them advice, encouragement and help in all possible ways, including the offer of hospitality if they return for any form of refresher course.

### *Mutual Aid in Founding and Developing New Catechetical Centres*

To awaken a new spirit is more important than to create a new institution. Nevertheless an institution is usually required to keep this spirit alive, to stabilize it and give it the powers needed to make further progress in such matters as the foundation of schools for catechists, the working out of programmes and the publication of reviews. In the beginning, at least, it would seem best that any institute newly founded should concern itself with several spheres such as catechetics, liturgy, sociology, having a section for each. Local conditions often permit of no other way.

Now what can the home countries, and in particular the well-established institutes which they already have, do to help the foundation and running of new centres in the mission lands? Four things occur to me. Firstly, they can help with the training of those destined to run them. Secondly, they can give good advice about equipping them, especially by sending out bibliographies appropriate to their sphere of action. Thirdly they can keep them informed of all new developments whether in the way of new books or new ideas and experiments made elsewhere, and, finally, they can help the new centre in organizing sessions of various kinds, perhaps providing, or at least giving advice about, subjects and speakers.

In return the centres in mission countries can help the home centres; for the interest they arouse by reporting their efforts and what they have been able to achieve will keep alive the kerygmatic ideals of those at home. There will be a similar effect as regards the study of the outlook and culture of mission peoples.

The work done towards adaptation, whether in teaching or in cult, will be both stimulating and suggestive. I am thinking, for example, of the work of Father Tempel and of the three small volumes by Father Seumois on adaptation of the liturgy for Africa.

### *Mutual Help in Bringing out Publications*

This will cover such matters as the adaptation of textbooks, the launching and improvement of periodicals of various kinds, and even printing – which may be done better or more cheaply in one place rather than in another.

## *Conclusions*

Our first concern, as I said at the beginning of the second part of this paper, must be to mobilize all the forces available to the Church, whether at home or in the missions, for this task of proclaiming the faith. And among these forces are two, of extreme importance, which I have not mentioned until now in order that they may be "the last word". I mean prayer and suffering; or, in the concrete, contemplative religious orders, and the sick.

Catechesis in the mission needs the help of the Holy Ghost in a very special way; it is therefore easy to understand that one of the greatest services which the home countries can perform for mission countries is to cause the foundation, out in the missions, of contemplative communities. And we must never forget that Jesus did not enter into his glory, and was not able to send down the Holy Spirit, until after his Passion. The Paschal mystery and the Pentecost mystery are both continued amongst us and are ever active. What Father Perreyve once said remains always true: "Of all the powers which can save the world, the Cross is the most powerful of all."

(Tr. C.H., S.J.)

# Concluding Address

VALERIAN CARDINAL GRACIAS
Archbishop of Bombay

WE have concluded our labours, happily indeed, and I think wisely and profitably, not however without healthy differences of opinion. For me, it has been one of the greatest experiences of my life – especially the close contact with the Church in Africa. The eyes of the world today are set on Africa, with its *uncertain* future, politically; with its *certain* future, religiously – with the certainty born of Christian hope.

As last year at Nijmegen, so on this occasion, our experts, whether it be in the field of catechetics or liturgy, have suffered gladly those of us who are not, so that, in the heartening words of one of the participants, this conference has resulted in being a two-way traffic.

The greatest gain of this Study Week has been the formulation of a very *positive* attitude in catechetics in relation to the missions. This has been possible largely because of the complete *unanimity forged among* the experts – which in itself is one of the eight wonders of the world! It has proved beyond doubt how untrue is the saying *Quot capita, tot sententiae*. So much of our time has been devoted to the formulation of the Basic Principles and the Rules of Guidance. To those who have not been engaged in this Study Week, the Principles and Rules may appear commonplace, but those who will be entrusted with the explanation of the implications, will be in the best position to point out how necessary they were and how significant they are. For our problem in the missions has ever been that, though there has been an abundance of good will, there has been lack of guidance.

## *The Aim of Catechetics*

For obvious reasons, I had to cut short, or rather mutilate, my Inaugural Address. That did not matter, for the full text of the Address (for whatever it is worth) is in the *Dossier* possessed by each participant. But in this concluding speech, I should like to speak out my mind, and also, if I may so express myself, my heart, – the more so as it has been dinned into our ears during these days that the aim of catechetics is not merely intellectual knowledge, but above all, the conquest of the heart, issuing into right conduct – the love of God and the love of our neighbour; life rooted in Jesus Christ and the Church he founded; uniting us not only to God but also among ourselves. We are living in an age when, I am afraid, such importance is given to the mind as to neglect or to prejudice the claims of the heart, and yet the heart has its reasons which the mind cannot perceive.

I accepted Father Hofinger's pressing invitation to preside over this Study Week, even as I had done last year over the Nijmegen Conference in Holland, and – I might add – happening to be a Cardinal, I accepted to do so on both occasions only after the "Line Clear" had been given by the Sacred Congregation of Propaganda through Father Hofinger.

Even though neither in the sphere of liturgy nor of catechetics have I any particular competence or any appreciable degree of practical experience, I accepted the invitation, because I felt that by associating myself with the great work achieved in this sphere, it would serve to offer some encouragement to the organizers, who have worked for so long and so strenuously, and to the participants, drawn from over seventy countries, who have undertaken journeys to give to the cause of catechetics the benefit of their study and experience. Moreover, as last year, I would be in a far better position to give a personal report to the Holy Father, whom I hope to see again on 6th September.

Having disposed of preliminaries at the very outset I should like to place on record our deepest appreciation of the excellent services of the Organizers in the preparation and the conduct of this Week. Obviously the lions's share of our great gratitude goes to Father Hofinger, S.J., who, to fulfil his mission, has been seven times round the world, and is threatening to undertake an eighth world tour! God has blessed him with a slender frame – a sign of health and energy, without any encumbrances, with an infinite capacity for study and work, a consuming zeal, a gift for driving hard his secretaries; and with the inestimable, priceless ability to sleep to order! To them who have fed our minds by their learned Addresses and to the experts, who were like "hawks" during our deliberations, we are greatly indebted.

### *The Procedure Adopted*

In accepting the presidency, I had resolved to deliver myself body and soul in the hands of Father Hofinger, for he is best fitted to direct operations. It was a case of reigning, but not ruling. I perfectly understand his reasons for the procedure he has adopted. Time was short, and much had to be covered if we were to have at the end of the Week some concrete conclusions.

### *The Great Problem Today*

One of the speakers remarked "that between the two – liturgy and catechetics – catechetics was more fundamental. Yet we do wish to emphasize that outward accommodation, whether in Church art and architecture, in liturgical rites and vestments, or in the missionary's way of living, is of secondary importance. The most important thing is the way in which spiritual values are presented". I agree. For our great problem today is to produce enlightened Catholics, such as will be able to give a reason for the faith that is in them. And this can be secured only if the foundations are laid early in life when catechism will be taught to our children in such a way that, growing in age, they do grow in wisdom and grace. The Church today is confronted with a multiple challenge; and among its various manifestations is the intellectual and moral challenge. Men's minds, restless in experimentation, are led to believe that the search in the realm of thought has to be endless, to ensure increasing intellectual growth. The special danger of our age is one that springs more from thought than from passion. It lies in the rivalry of new ideas fighting against the old ones; it lies in the circulation of new ideas claiming to be true and at the same time destructive of the old; it lies in the view that nothing is in possession and that faith itself needs justification and must secure it if faith is to remain. Again, today, unfortunately everywhere there is the same pretence to recast ancient religions, and age-consecrated codes of morality; everywhere there is infatuation for all that is novel; identification of the latest with the truest and the best; a silly fear of being held or being called oldfashioned, orthodox, out-of-date. No one is satisfied with pouring out the bath water. The baby must be thrown out with it.

In the course of my reading, I came across this passage – "Never in the history of Christianity has the Christian religion been under such an individual attack as it is at the present time. We have more fine minds, more learning pitted against us than ever before in history." To meet this intellectual challenge is not easy. It needs time and learning. We are not losing because we lack good will, but because of the indifference of Catholics to the claims of enlightened Catholicism. And again, "Christianity faces today its most serious crisis since the Church came out of the catacombs." Against this, I would like to observe – while the Moslem threat in previous centuries, and certainly also in Africa today, was no less severe than the present danger of Communism, the Moslems were, and perhaps are, by no means without an appreciation of spiritual values. The Communists are the godless ones, and also given to compromising ways. As some one has said, "Communism is like a hat which has lost its shape because everyone wears it". But we have nothing to fear, even when the Church is on her knees. The Church has always to be on her knees, for she knows that her strength is from above. Nor should we be afraid of crises.

Looking through the Christian literature of the past, one gets the impression, rightly or wrongly, that there has always been a crisis, that Christianity has always lived in the world in a state of continual crisis. It would be paradoxical to say that the Church has never known any world except one in a state of crisis. The Church has faced many crises since she first came into existence; she has, on more than one occasion, seemed to be swallowed up by the waves, and each time she has escaped shipwreck and re-embarked on her way to the future, to the surprise of those who judge her by purely human standards, or even of Christians when they have not been enlightened by hope. In the history of the Church there have been falls, rises, lulls. There are catacomb eras, basilica eras, cathedral eras. We must keep to the way of the Cross, but we must go on hoping, and seeking for the Resurrection and the Life of Glory. Human beings today are mad about technical power conferred on them by science – excited, and at the same time appalled by it. At one moment their pride in their achievements makes them quite crazy, and at the next they are nearly as crazy with fear. Bergson in a well-known phrase has said that modern man needs a bit more soul, and this bit more can only be given by the Church, because the Church is the representative upon earth of God, who strengthens by the gift of faith, and frees freedom from its shackles by the action of his grace.

### *The Knowledge that Edifies*

I must confess that never have I learnt so much about catechetics (rather late in the day though!) as during this Study Week. The various addresses were so well prepared and delivered. In the case of some it was heavy artillery, shattering all our preconceived, outmoded ideas. In the case of others, it was learned stuff interspersed with light interludes. In all cases, one could note that the speakers had their heart in those subjects with which they dealt. With one expert continually by my side, and so many of the same category in the assembly, I was breathing continually the air of catechetics, and at times perhaps to suffocation! It has helped me to realize how much we, who were born in a different age, have been the losers, and how much those of today stand to gain. And yet, let me express this fear: I wonder whether with all our modern techniques we shall succeed in producing a generation of Catholics stronger in the faith and more warmhearted in their love of

God and Our Lady than their predecessors. Greater knowledge they will certainly have, but will it be the knowledge that edifieth? That is certainly our aim. Or will they need, as it is happening today in increasing measure, the help of a strong devotional life, to which the rank and file are having recourse today in abundant measure. Obviously I do not speak as an expert, but as a pastor of souls.

This has been an international conference especially in relation to the missions. It has been the third one over which I have presided – Manila, Nijmegen, Eichstätt. The greatest advantage I find of cultural profit in such gatherings is the opportunity to know one another – the universality of the Church *circumdata varietate*. But there will always be this drawback when an international conference concerns the missions – Africa, Asia, Japan, Philippines, Vietnam, Korea, Formosa, etc. We have seen here, as we observed last year in Holland, how different are the cultural, social, religious, political levels in all these countries. Moreover, as time progresses, and the pace of industrialization gains momentum, what we decide on today will in a few years be out-of-date. This observation is being made merely to indicate how the conclusions we arrive at today are not to be considered final.

### *Grace Builds on Nature*

At this stage let me raise a fundamental issue. It is absolutely necessary to lay due emphasis on the natural in modern catechetics. We say, grace does not supplant nature. It is necessary to affirm boldly and clearly that grace builds on nature. Many years ago we had Father Ernest Hull, S.J., who was Editor of the *Bombay Catholic Examiner* for over twenty-five years. In the course of his career he had many publications to his credit, and among them were several essays on the teaching of religion and moral instruction. He maintained that in our programme of instruction not sufficient importance was given to natural virtues. Cardinal Newman said that a perfect Christian must be a perfect gentleman – not one who has just the veneer of certain social accomplishments, but one who applies himself seriously to the cultivation of the virtues of justice, honesty, politeness. The neglect of due emphasis on the natural has led to the practice of raising a supernatural edifice on weak natural foundations, with the result that often there are collapses in adult life. We are often asking ourselves, why is it that so many who have been brought up in our schools make a poor show of their Catholic upbringing – cheating, violation of charity, scandal in conversation, etc.? A young Parsi who had recently made a tour of Europe asked me why it is that in the Catholic countries he visited, he came across so many cases of the violation of the purely natural virtues in spite of the supernatural atmosphere of those places; whereas in the purely Protestant countries – and he mentioned Scandinavia – he was greatly impressed by the sense of decency, honesty, gentleness manifested by the people.

Cardinal Newman has a classic sermon on the 'Religion of the Natural Man' and the 'Religion of the World'. He draws a contrast between the Pharisee and the Publican, not so much to highlight the hypocrisy of the Pharisee as to indicate that he set up for himself the ideal of a narrow range of duties, and thus he was easily satisfied when fulfilled. So it is – he argues – with the Natural Man – that his religion is good, but not good enough; that it goes far, but not far enough. The point is that there was something good, and it is on this something naturally good that the greater had to be built, raised and perfected. Exactly as when we say that *grace must build on nature*.

It may have been noticed that in the course of our discussions in this Study Week, as last year in Nijmegen, speaking generally, it is the European missionaries much more than the non-European, who are eager to advance the cause, for example, of the vernacular in the liturgy. It has been the same experience in the fields of art, architecture, music, where adaptation is concerned. What is the explanation? It is manifold:

Undoubtedly it is a reaction against the past. That in the past in all mission countries, speaking generally, there was a tendency, quite understandable and even natural on the part of the European missionary, to transplant his own culture, is an inescapable fact. Else, there would have been no need for the Instruction of Propaganda Fide as early as 1659; and for what is stated in *Evangelii Praecones*.

Yet, it cannot be denied that European missionaries have shown greater vision, as is evidenced by the studies they have undertaken in the field of missiology, than the indigenous clergy.

On the other hand, the hesitancy on the part of non-European missionaries is understandable, for being of the people, and knowing their own – for better or for worse – quite intimately, they are hesitant to take the plunge, even though their minds may be convinced up to a point of launching out into the deep. They are, therefore, grateful and encouraged when the European missionary, for an experiment, takes the initiative; for this must be acknowledged that when it is a question of battling against complexes, deep-rooted likes and dislikes, the European missionary has a far better chance of "going down" among our own people than we ourselves. In spite of our vaunted progress and new-found freedoms, speaking generally, our people yet put a premium on the way of thinking, judging and acting on the part of a European.

Therefore, I would say to our European pioneers, whether it be in the field of liturgy or catechetics, philosophy or art, architecture or music or dramatics: Go ahead, yet *festina lente;* take sufficient note of the hesitancy of non-European bishops and priests, after all it may be healthy conservation, even if the number be small, and slowly you will find that we shall fall in line. This is what is actually happening in certain spheres. Though I myself have never belonged to the advanced school of thought, I must confess that under the force of circumstances, and encouraged by the lead given by others, I have been drawn, almost in spite of myself, into movements which I believe to be essential to the life of the Church in mission countries. For one thing, I feel that the Indian group of dancers who are going to perform in Munich under the training and direction of Father George Proksch, S.V.D., a European missionary, will be instrumental in making decisively an Indian contribution to the cultural and spiritual value of the Congress – even more than, let us say, what a public address on the position of the Church in the countries delivered by an Asian or African prelate would achieve.

*Catechetical Centres*

We have secured agreement on the principles, which are to form a Code of Guidance. The problem will be in different areas to apply these principles to concrete circumstances. Such situations demand the creation and existence of catechetical centres. As last year for the liturgical movement, so this year for the catechetical movement, it would be helpful if experts from time to time come to the missions, not merely on a whirlwind tour, but tarry for some time, so that they may get – in some degree – at the actual state of affairs.

# APPENDICES

I

# General Conclusions

## *I. Catechetical Revival*

At the present time we are faced in our mission apostolate with an extremely urgent and responsible task. Complete success in this task will never be achieved by any mere increase in catechetical activity. What we need is something more: a reform that takes account of the findings of modern psychology and the conclusions reached by the recent kerygmatic renewal.

The chief aim of this kerygmatic renewal is to present the truth of our faith as an organic whole. Its core is the Good News of our redemption in Christ. Its fruit should be the grateful response of our love.

It is in the light of this central message of Christian catechesis that all other truths of the faith must be viewed, presented, and made fruitful for Christian life.

## *II. Need for a Clearly-outlined Programme*

We need a general but clearly-outlined programme for the catechetical apostolate. Such a programme should meet the special catechetical needs in the mission lands today, but in no way neglect such needs in every country. To draw up this programme, ten specialists in catechetics have been chosen. These men shall work under the guidance of an episcopal commission consisting of Archbishop Hurley, Archbishop Mark Gopu, Archbishop Young, and Bishop Yougberé.

## *III. Liturgy*

There is latent in the liturgy a colossal wealth of meaning and a tremendous instructive power. These lie in its prayers, songs, and readings; in the actions of the priest and people, the frequency of its celebration and the assembly for it of all the faithful. Therefore, the liturgy should be celebrated in a manner which will bring out to the full its catechetical content, and which will enable the people to take an active part in it devoutly and intelligently. Hence, in order that the liturgy may produce its due catechetical effect, it should display its intrinsic excellences by means of its intelligibility, beauty and clarity. Only thus can its full catechetical value be exploited. But this cannot be done unless certain reforms are introduced. Some proposals will be found set forth in a separate document.

## *IV. Bible*

The Bible must be given a very prominent place in catechetical teaching because it is the inspired Word of God, and the most important of all the Church's didactic books. It sets forth the divine actions whereby God has revealed himself; its method of presentation is so vivid and lively that it is suited to man's capacities, and it is explicitly ordered towards man's salvation.

Hence catechetics must be solidly built up on a biblical foundation; every age group should be taught biblical texts and made familiar with events in biblical history.

## *V. Textbooks*

Good textbooks are an absolute necessity for catechetical work. The suggestions which are most important for their compilation have been set forth in a special section.

Those who teach religion in the missions need a teacher's aid book even more than do those similarly engaged in countries where Christianity has already been established. These aid books should not only provide the necessary material, but also give guidance for its use.

The mere revision or modification of former textbooks or catechisms which are not drawn up according to the principles of the catechetical renewal cannot produce a work which fulfils the basic demands of catechetics.

Good new textbooks can be composed only by authors who are thoroughly acquainted with the findings of modern catechetics.

## *VI. Postulata on the Catechetical Centres*

To ensure the practical co-operation of all in the catechetical apostolate, the participants in this Study Week wish 1 to see a catechetical office functioning in each diocese, according to the decree *Provido sane concilio*. Besides the appointment of a diocesan commission, this implies the formation of a catechetical centre, from where teachers of religion can get both advice and catechetical material.

2 The director of this diocesan centre must be prepared for his task by special studies, and be given time and opportunity to promote the catechetical renewal in an efficient manner.

3 In each country, a national centre shall serve as a link between the various diocesan centres and the catechetical movement abroad. Such a centre may organize efforts towards a better adapted catechesis, by means of enquiries, study sessions, publication of books and magazines, and the like.

4 Wherever necessary the national centres should work in close co-operation with regional centres fulfilling the same task on a linguistic basis.

5 The various national centres, especially those in the mission countries, should help one another by pooling their documentation and the fruits of their experiments in the catechetical apostolate.

6 In particular, the help already given by several institutes for the formation of specialists in catechetics, should be still increas-

ed, so that all future directors of religious instruction in the missions would be really able to obtain the special preparation they need.

### *VII. Catechists (Lay-teachers)*

All catechists should have at least one year of solid training. This must impart to them above all a complete grasp of the fundamentals of Christian doctrine concerning man's salvation, together with an adequate competence in catechetical methods.

At the same time great stress must be laid on the spiritual training and character formation given to catechists as well as on their social behaviour, so that they may become not only good teachers, but also "witnesses to Christ".

In their religious training, the Bible and the liturgy must be given the prominent place due to them in the catechetical apostolate later on.

### *VIII. Catechetical Training in Seminaries*

The catechetical renewal has not as yet brought forth its due fruit in the missions. The chief reason for this is the inadequate training in catechetics of the future missionaries. This applies not merely to indigenous priests, but also to those from the home countries.

It is absolutely essential that future missionaries be given a training in catechetics suited to the needs of our own day. This would involve a series of lectures and also sufficient training in practice; the course would have to familiarize the future missionary with the aims, viewpoint and technique of the modern catechetical movement, would be designed expressly in the light of the missionary apostolate, and impart to him a certain degree of competence in teaching catechism.

It is just as important that the major subjects of theology (dogma, moral, exegesis) should be presented to the future missionary from the same angle, so that he may grasp vividly and clearly the organic unity of the Christian message of salvation, the religious content of each doctrine, and its application to Christian life.

## *IX. Co-operation*

Catechetical co-operation of Christian countries with mission countries will assume various forms, notably developing intercommunication between catechetical centres and experts in missionary countries among themselves, and also with centres and experts in Christian countries; helping one another in the catechetical and pastoral training of seminarians and priests, in the study of psychology of the peoples to be evangelized, and in addition to this, in the studies of missiology and ethnology, in the progress of catechetical institutions, in the foundation of catechetical centres, and in the improvement of books and periodicals.

II

## Special Conclusions on Catechesis and Liturgy

I. As is noted in the general conclusions of this Study Week, it seemed necessary to the Congress that some reformation of the liturgy be undertaken to bring its catechetical value to light.

That this reform be prudently elaborated, this Congress first requests that the whole matter be properly examined by the forthcoming Ecumenical Council.

II. Regarding questions of a particular nature, the Study Week proposes the following conclusions of its deliberations.

1. The Study Week adopts as its own the conclusions of the First International Study Week on Mission and Liturgy held in the past year at Nijmegen. The conclusions are:
   a. that it be permissible for all chants belonging to the people and choir to be sung in the vernacular;
   b. that the readings be given directly in the vernacular by the appropriate minister or celebrating priest;
   c. that the pericopes of readings should be enlarged and spread over several years by means of an appropriate cycle;
   d. that the Prayer of the Faithful be restored in a proper form;
   e. that all duplications be avoided so that the celebrating priest need not recite in a low voice those parts which are duly carried out by others.
2. The greater part of the Study Week desires a further reform of the liturgy of the word, or Mass of the Cate-

chumens, which is especially destined for the catechetical instruction of those present. The catechetical efficacy of this part of the Mass might well be augmented if, in every Mass celebrated in the presence of the people, be it a low or a high Mass,

a. the vernacular be employed in the entire Mass of the Catechumens.
b. Since the Mass of the Catechumens is the liturgy of the word, it could be celebrated not at the altar but at a sedile and lectern as is now the case in the restored Easter Vigil.

3. It seemed to not a few of the participants that attention should be given by experts to the question of whether the entire Mass could be reduced to some simpler form in order to bring out its catechetical efficacy and cause its structure to stand out more clearly.
4. Finally, it was generally agreed that permission be sought to adapt certain ceremonies of the Mass originating in western usage to the prevalent and meaningful customs of mission countries.

It was also noted that many things which answer the needs of the missions may even now be introduced by the local Ordinaries themselves, on their own authority, as *Pia Exercitia*.

III. Comments.

1. These proposals do not intend that Latin, which is acknowledged as a symbol of the unity of the Church, should be excluded from the liturgy, but rather that permission would be given to employ the vernacular along with Latin, in those places where, in the judgement of the Ordinary, the mother tongue appears useful or necessary.
2. For places where a variety of tongues or other reasons hinder the use of the vernacular in the liturgy, no change should be imposed.
3. To avoid too much variety in a particular territory, it is likewise agreed that the Ordinaries of the region should proceed according to their common consensus.

III

# Programme of the Catechetical Apostolate

## A. BASIC PRINCIPLES OF MODERN CATECHETICS

*Our Aim*

### I. Catechesis carries out the command of Christ to proclaim God's message of salvation to all men

Christ carried out the will of his Father by giving his Church the commission "to preach the gospel to every creature", "to make disciples" for him and to provide him with "witnesses throughout the world" (Mark 16:15; Matt. 28:19; Acts 1:8). The catechist does what Christ did and commissioned the Church to do: he proclaims the Good News of salvation, he helps men to accept it and to become disciples who will give witness to it. Catechesis then does more than teach the doctrines of the Church; it wins men (children, adolescents, adults) for Christ and after baptism unites them further to him. All principles and methods of catechizing flow from the missionary command of Christ.

*Our Message*

### II. Catechesis proclaims the merciful love of the Father for us and the Good News of God's Kingdom

Carrying out the commission of Christ, the Church brings a message from God which surpasses by far what the heart of men can conceive or hope for (1 Cor. 2:10; Eph. 3:20).

The Church proclaims to all people that the eternal and grace-giving Kingdom of God is at hand, a Kingdom prefigured in the Old Testament, begun by Christ in the New and growing towards the fullness of glory at the end of time. (Mark 1:15; Matt. 24:14; 25:34). All men are invited to the wedding feast prepared by the King of Kings from all eternity. (Matt. 22:2ff.).

This message proclaims that God is not merely an idea or a remote and silent being, but a living personal God, the almighty Creator and the eternal Father. It tells of a world not drifting into chaos but being transformed into "a new heaven and a new earth" (Apoc. 21:1). It speaks not of the dissolution of all things but of a "new creature" and of an eternal and living union with our Father in heaven.

## III. Catechesis is Christ-centred, reflecting the fulfilment in and through Christ of the Father's loving design

God the Father carried out his plan through Christ, his Son, born of the Virgin Mary, our Saviour and Lord. Salvation is found only in him (Acts 4:12). Through Christ we know about the Father and receive the Good News of the Father's Kingdom. By his death, resurrection and ascension, Christ saves us from our sins. He works in us through the Holy Spirit and leads us towards that day when he will judge all men and bring the world to its perfection. He is the Word (John 1:1), the Mediator (1 Tim. 2:5), the Way and the Life (John 14:16).

Catechesis gives due importance to the historical treatment of God's design: how God prepared for Christ's coming in the Old Testament, how his coming brought about our salvation, and how Christ continues to communicate himself through the Holy Spirit till he returns as the Lord of glory.

## IV. Catechesis proclaims that Christ continues to live and work in his Church through the Holy Spirit and the ministry of his shepherds

By the action of the Holy Spirit in the Church and particularly in the hierarchy, Christ gathers men together through his word, sanctifies and gives them life through the mystery of his passion, resurrection and ascension communicated in the sacraments and gives them power to be witnesses before the world.

The Church is truly Christ's Body. He unites the members to himself, the Head, and to one another, and assigns to each member a specific function. The Church is the chosen race, a people God means to have for himself, a holy people called to priestly service in the world (1 Pet. 2:9). The Church is the city built on the mountain top, lightened by Christ's light and shining brightly for all nations to see (Matt. 5:14; Is. 2). It is the family of God on earth, the home which the Father offers to all wanderers, the community of men advancing to its eternal destiny.

### V. Catechesis emphasizes that worship is the heart of Christian community life

Whenever the Church celebrates liturgy, she assembles as a holy people. Christ is in her midst and she is vivified by the Holy Spirit. In the service of the word (Mass of the Catechumens) Christ nourishes his Church by the word of life and carries her prayer up to the Father. In the celebration of the Eucharist (Mass of the Faithful) Christ engulfs her in the sacrifice of the redemption and saturates her anew with his life. By the one eucharistic Bread, the many are made one body (1 Cor. 10:17). By the Good Tidings, the prayer and the sacramental celebration, the people are filled with inner strength, spiritual knowledge and understanding enabling them to proclaim the word of God without fear (Acts 4:31).

Worship is primarily directed to the praise of God. At the same time it is the supreme expression of catechesis. Catechesis leads to worship and draws its life from worship. Worship is the inexhaustible source of faith, grace and the apostolate.

*Our Response*

### VI. Catechesis teaches us to respond to God's call by an inner change of heart manifested in a life of faith and hope and of loving obedience to his commands

Man's first response to the message of salvation is that inner change of heart described in the Gospel as absolutely necessary to enter the Kingdom. Turning to God, man begins to realize all that God has done, is doing, and will do for him. In this acceptance of Christ, which must be made by catechumen and Christian alike, man recognizes the God of Love who will save him from his sins. Repenting of his sins and filled with joy at the recognition of his Saviour, he is moved to obey the commandment of love. "The man who loves God is the man who keeps the commandments he has from me" (John 14:21).

## VII. Catechesis makes the Christian aware of his responsibility for the world and the betterment of its condition

The Christian sees the world as the work and possession of the Father in heaven, and feels responsible for it as "son and heir". What is called the "profane" or "natural" order is no less from the hand of God. The Christian must value it in itself if he is to contribute to its sanctification in Christ. This is particularly true of the social order. If the Christian does not endeavour to restore it to its proper condition in regard to family, professional, economic, civic and cultural life, he is betraying the trust of his heavenly Father.

## VIII. Catechesis leads the Christian to share the faith with others

Catechesis makes the Christian keenly aware that the growth and welfare of God's kingdom depend on him. It stimulates the missionary spirit so that the followers of Christ strive for sanctity, not only for the sake of their own salvation and greater happiness, but also that their fellowmen may see their good example and praise the Father who is in heaven (Matt. 5:16). It is the Holy Spirit who makes them witnesses of his word and life, and enables each one according to the measure of his faith and the gifts he has received from God, to communicate the message of salvation with its spiritual values to all with whom he comes in contact. Sanctity of life, the praise, the joy of Christians, their contentment and assurance, their willingness and ability to share the message and especially their love, which embraces even enemies, are the signs by which others are led to experience the realities and values of God's Kingdom.

*Our Method*

**IX. Catechesis, following God's method, proclaims "the wonderful works of God", which show forth the truth and especially the love contained in them, moving the heart and inspiring the whole of life**

Catechesis follows God's method of proclaiming the Glad Tidings of salvation. The wonderful works of God as narrated in the Old Testament, the miracles, discourses, and events in the New Testament, lead us to an understanding of the divine message and of its impact in our lives (Heb. 1:1). In these events God has come close to us, has revealed and united himself to us and has shown us the way to live through him and in him. Catechesis is at the service of this divine revelation and adapts itself to God's own way of winning men.

**X. Catechesis embraces a four-fold presentation of the faith: through liturgy, Bible, systematic teaching aud the testimony of Christian living**

Each of these forms of presentation has its own specific function in the winning of the non-Christian and the development of the Christian. Catechesis strives to combine liturgy, Bible, doctrine and the testimony of Christian living, so that the organic unity of the Christian message is more clearly presented.

The *liturgy* does more than communicate the Christian mystery to the mind of the participant. It uses sound pedagogical principles, namely the intuitive process, activity, teaching by experience the imparting of values. It appeals to the entire person, the sensibilities, the intellect and the will. It is the means of impregnating the whole life with the Spirit of Christ. For, in the liturgy, the mystery of redemption is not only proclaimed through the words of holy scripture, but is also expressed in prayers and hymns, presented in sacred signs and rendered sacramentally present and efficacious.

Catechesis is as inseparable from the *Bible,* the inspired word of God, as a plant from its roots. The Bible is the basis of the Church's proclamation and thus also of her catechesis. We use the Bible to follow the history of salvation in the way God himself made it known. These sacred books take us from the creation of the world to its end and show us how Christ is the fulfilment of all.

The *systematic presentation* of the faith has its roots in the creeds and preaching of the early Christian proclamation, and has derived its organic development from the authoritative teaching of the Church throughout the ages. The catechism gives the learner spiritual insight into the relationship between the faith and Christian life and enables him to cope with the questions of the day as an articulate Christian, and to express his faith to those who enquire about it.

The Christian message and teaching is borne out through the *witness of a Christian life*. The life of the Church and her saints show us repeatedly that Christ lives and works in the Church. The witness of a Christian life by individuals and by the community of the faithful, not only nourishes the faith of Catholics, but is the way that ordinarily leads the non-Christian to Christ and to the Church.

## XI. Catechesis adapts itself to the life and thought of peoples, shows due appreciation of their laudable views and customs and integrates them harmoniously into a Christian way of life

The message of the living God should contact the living man, move his innermost heart, and convert him from within. Before the catechist begins his task God has already worked in the individuals and nations of his creation through his truth and grace, moving them to seek and attain their salvation in Christ (Acts 17:26–27). In the love of the Good Shepherd, the catechist seeks to recognize the special character, manner of thought, outlook, customs and culture of his catechumens. Beginning at the point where they can follow him, he seeks to instruct them according to the psychology of age-group, sex and special circumstances. Guided by the Holy Spirit he enters into their hidden problems and leads them to adopt Christ's way of thinking as the best solution. He seeks in patience to correct whatever is false and erroneous, but humbly endeavours to mould into the Christian way of life "whatever things are true, whatever honorable, whatever just, whatever holy, whatever lovable, whatever of good repute, if there be any virtue, if anything worthy of praise" (Phil. 4:8).

## XII. Catechesis introduces the catechumen into a living community and helps him to strike root in it

The life of faith is a life in the community of believers. The apostles received their formation in the community which Christ gathered around himself as the family of God (Matt. 12:19). Those who were converted at the sermon of St. Peter were "taken into the community of the faithful which was inspired by the Holy Spirit" (Acts 2:41ff.). They found a home in the communal life of the primitive Church. Likewise, believers today should welcome and embrace the newly baptized. Special groups may be needed, apart from the family and the parish, to sustain and stimulate the new Catholic in his faith. For only in the community can a Christian recognize the full meaning of the Lord's message and experience the bonds of charity which unite all men in Christ.

## B. THE PRACTICE OF CATECHETICS

### *I. The Dispositions of a Catechist*

**The sense of prayer.** The catechist speaks in the name of God, and it is God alone who will give him the words of truth and open the hearts of his hearers.

**Purity of intention.** The actions of the catechist must radiate the love of Christ in his own life, so that his hearers will recognize the message of our Lord in his words.

**Fidelity to the Church.** The catechist has the right to preach or teach only because it has been given to him by the bishop in the name of the Church. He does not preach his own ideas, but the doctrine of the Church.

**The desire to communicate a living faith to others.** The goal of the catechist is to win not only the intelligence, but, even more, the heart of his hearers and to lead them to live by Christ in his Church. A mere acquaintance with the faith which does not show itself in action is not a living faith.

### *II. The Period of Pre-catechesis*

**Pre-catechesis.** For the instruction of those who are not yet believers, it is necessary to have a period of pre-catechesis more or less long, before the complete formulation of the doctrine is given to them. During this period, the catechist should endeavour, with the help of grace, to awaken in the catechumen a desire for God, to stir up his unquenched spiritual longings, and to show how these longings find their fulfilment in the divine truth. He must help them to realize whatever is disorderly in their lives, as well as their attachment to earthly values. He should arouse in them a longing for forgiveness and a desire to give themselves to God. In this way, he will prepare the soil for the sowing of the word of God. Unless these spiritual powers are awakened in them, the catechumens will remain incapable of understanding the meaning of the Christian message.

### *III. The Main Points in a Lesson*

**Awaken interest.** This cannot be done in a superficial manner. In the beginning, the catechist must reach the secret aspirations and problems of the hearers, to awaken in them a spiritual interest. It is important that his opening words be not commonplace or depressing, but the answer to an interior need. This is especially important when the catechumen is still far from the faith.

**Present a living reality.** Take an event, a passage from the Bible, a liturgical action, an incident from Church history, the life of a saint, or daily life. Expose it in a simple, calm manner, direct enough to touch the heart.

When giving a biblical catechesis, the teacher may start by reading the text aloud, slowly and impressively, and then bring out its deep significance.

**Bring out the sense of what has been told,** always in such a manner that it will reach the mind and heart. That is why the catechist must avoid making a purely intellectual exposition. The best effect comes from a simple and lively discussion in which the listeners have full freedom to participate. Such a dialogue enables each one to seek with the catechist and to express in his own words the truth discovered. The catechist directs and develops these findings until the truth is clear and alive. He tries to have all the points understood, and then ends by a clear summary of the different steps.

**Stimulate a personal response to the call of God.** It does not suffice that the catechumens have understood the truth, but they must be led by the catechist to answer it. He must show them how to pray, either spontaneously, or by using a prepared formula, or by a short liturgical ceremony. He must invite them to review their lives, to see more clearly the duties which await them, and to make the resolutions they need.

**Some memorization is demanded** (especially for children) of certain biblical passages and texts essential to the lesson, not only that they be rooted in the memory, but that they may penetrate the thinking and life of the person. The memory must always be at the service of the faith. That is why the catechist should never cause passages to be memorized which have not been explained in the lesson or clearly understood by the hearers. A mechanical memorization of formulas is not sufficient to grasp the vitality of the Christian doctrine.

**Avoid rigidity** in the use of the above steps. The catechist should employ the above method with a certain suppleness and freedom according to the matter to be explained and the age or mentality of the catechumens.

### *IV. Some Concrete Points on Pedagogical Techniques and Method*

**Have recourse to pedagogical techniques** in order to give variety to the lesson and to stimulate the interior awakening and the exterior activity of the hearers. The use of techniques offers the catechist the possibility of winning not only the intellect but the whole being of the person, namely, mind, heart, imagination, creative ability and power of expression.

He must always remember that these diverse means have one goal, to help the catechumen to open wide his heart to the activity of the Holy Spirit.

**Means to awaken interior activity.** Create an atmosphere; present a reality, bring forward its meaning, show its bearing, define it; establish comparisons with other facts or truths, a motivation, proofs; draw conclusions, present a clear summary, a repetition; drive home a point, an application, bring the lesson into contact with daily life, lead to action, arouse consent.

**Means to stimulate exterior activity.** Narrate an event, make observations, ask questions, elucidate, show an object, cause reflection, give an explanation, start a discussion, read aloud, make others read (each one by himself, or one reading aloud, or several in turn), a recitation, learning by heart, interrogate, direct practical exercises, choral recitation, drawing either in the copybook or on the blackboard. Assign tasks and make the pupils look for facts, classify them, reflect on them, formulate them sometimes before and sometimes after the class. Assign home-work, and make them keep a note book.

Also, hold a singing practice, recollect oneself, pray; exhort them to examine their conscience, meditate, hold a liturgical service. Celebrate a feast, stage a playlet with different actors, prepare an exhibition. Finally, use audio-visual aids, wall pictures, flannel-boards, slides, tape-recordings, gramophone records.

### *V. Prayer, Action, Community-consciousness*

**Religious formation is not only instruction but education;** therefore it must be directed towards prayer, action and community consciousness.

The catechist will cultivate a taste for *prayer* in his hearers, if he encourages them to pray in their own words and to use formulas which they understand. To this end, he will offer them a certain number of prayers which they can slowly make their own. Naturally, the common prayers of a Christian, the daily prayers, the psalms, and texts from the Missal, should be the foundation of this collection, which should reflect the faith and prayer of the Church. It should be, at the same time, an expression of personal piety.

There is no genuine religious formation without education to *action*, and above all, formation of conscience. The catechist must continually and persistently inculcate this in his hearers. He must likewise endeavour to lead them to personal maturity, to self-reliance, and to the sense of responsibility.

Moreover, because Christian life unfolds itself day by day in the Church, the catechist must avoid forming in his hearers an individualistic personality. To this end, he must bring them into contact with the parish *community*, and above all with its liturgical life. He must make them realize the duties they will have to perform for the community and he will encourage them to take part in the groups or associations proper to youth or adults. In this way he will introduce them into a concrete and realistic charity, and he will give them a sense of apostolate among Christians and non-Christians.

**Catechesis does not stop** with the reception of the sacraments nor with the end of the years at school. Catechesis must constantly grow and deepen throughout the whole life a person, as a child, an adolescent, and during the years of adulthood. The catechist must lead his catechumens or Christians to a more intimate union with God and to a more personal conviction of the Christian truths. This will bring them gradually to become adults in the faith, in order that through their lives and actions they may share in the fulness of Christ (Eph. 4:13).

**It is by study, reflection, written notes and prayer** that the catechist should prepare his lessons. He must be constantly thinking in terms of those to whom he will speak. Before addressing his hearers, the catechist should recall three questions. What am I going to teach (content)? Where should I be leading my hearers (pedagogy of the living faith)? How shall I arrange my lesson?

A lesson of catechesis is a work of art which is acceptable only if it is well prepared. Without constant effort it is impossible to be a good catechist.

## C. SOME SUGGESTIONS FOR THOSE COMPILING TEXTBOOKS OF RELIGIOUS INSTRUCTION

### *Basic Considerations*

Those who write religion textbooks must have a clear idea for whom they are writing, and know what they want their books to accomplish. The purpose of religious instruction books is to facilitate catechesis. Hence, before drawing up a catechetical textbook, two questions must be answered.

**For whom is this book intended** (for the catechist, for the pupils, or for both and, for what age-group)?

What part should it play in the religious instruction?

The lessons in the book should **not be based on mere abstract notions and definitions.** Rather, they should correspond with the way in which God has given us his revelation. He revealed himself above all through his living word and his great deeds, and aimed always at the salvation and life of mankind.

The lessons in the books should have an **organic unity.** Catechetical books should not present the content of faith as a series of disconnected units, but as an organic whole, as an unfolding of God's great plan of salvation with Jesus Christ as its heart and centre.

The content of the lessons should **stress the message of salvation, not mere moral obligations.** The books should show how God revealed himself to us personally, how he saved us through the death and resurrection of Jesus Christ, how he gathers us in the Church and operates in us through the Holy Spirit. The life of Christians should appear as a glad and grateful answer to God, by following Christ our Saviour and Lord and by participating in the community life of the Church.

Religion textbooks should be **adapted** like catechesis in general, to the age, psychology, and mentality of the catechumens. It is, therefore, contradictory to the basic principles of catechetics to use the same book for every age-group. Nor is it sufficient just to add new matter to what has already been learned, while keeping the same structure of the book. On the contrary, one must exert a serious effort to present the content of Christian belief in its wholeness, but in adapted forms varying with the age-group.

Textbooks must proclaim in a clear manner the message of salvation and be based on sound psychological principles. A **mere modification** of those textbooks which no longer fulfil the basic principles of the proclamation of faith and the demands of modern pedagogy, **will not serve the purpose.**

### *Different Types of Catechetical Textbooks*

A first type of religion textbook can **follow the liturgical year** in its main lines. In that way, it can treat the chief events of the history of salvation, as well as the fundamental truths of Christian belief and life, in the order in which they are celebrated. This form is particularly well suited to that age when the children begin to receive their elementary education and are being initiated into religious services and the reception of sacraments.

Another type may consist of lessons **based on the Bible.** Such a textbook can present in historical sequence a choice of abridged and simplified texts from the Old and New Testaments. It is not advisable to recount the Bible story in one's own words. To each passage should be appended appropriate explanatory lessons, texts for memory work, prayers and other aids. The practical initiation into an active and conscious participation at holy Mass and into the reception of sacraments, may be treated in a separated section.

**The lesson form,** in a systematic catechism, should consist of certain integral parts, structured so as to be more effective, and not exclusively of questions and answers. In particular, a textbook which exposes the content of faith in a systematic elaboration is suited for older children, adolescents and adults. Such a type of catechism in lesson form is in accordance with the way in which God has given us his revelation, and with the laws of psychology. For this reason, it is desirable that each lesson contain a section presenting the matter, an explanatory section, texts to be memorized, and a section for practical applications of the content taught. To present all truths exclusively in a question-and-answer form would hardly do justice to the rich treasure of our faith.

**The actual text of the Bible** should be used especially by older pupils. Older children and adolescents (as well as adults) should make use of a book of biblical passages. This book should, as far as possible, contain unaltered passages from the Bible, the authentic Word of God. But some abbreviations or condensations of less important parts, especially of the Old Testament, may well be inevitable. Explanatory paragraphs, inserted between the biblical extracts, should clarify the connection of one with another, and, wherever necessary, should point out what bearing a given passage has on the economy of salvation, as also its literary genre. The book of biblical passages should be representative of the Bible as a whole. It should contain not only historical extracts, but also doctrinal discourses, passages from the psalms, the prophetical writings, the epistles and the Apocalypse. As early as is deemed profitable, everyone should have a personal copy of the complete New Testament. This should serve not only as a source and reference book during religious instruction periods, but also for personal reading.

**Adult catechumens need a special textbook,** which answers their particular problems. For adult catechumens, neither a children's book nor an adult catechism for Catholics is sufficient. Rather, the book they use must serve to lead them to the faith and take into account the problems of adults which arise out of their religious and cultural environment.

Catechetical books should, as far as possible, contain **pictures** which have a formative religious value. These pictures should aim not only at visualizing the lesson but at conveying a message of their own. They should not stop at depicting merely external events, but should communicate the sacred inner meaning of the lesson. Finally, they should respect the sensibility proper to each nation and be artistically genuine, because they deeply affect the world of religious imagination. Pictures are of invaluable help especially for the little children.

As far as possible each country or diocese should follow a **uniform and graded course of studies.** This syllabus should determine and allot the subject matter for catechism classes in schools or outside it, as well as for the adult catechumenate. For instructing baptized children and adolescents in school, the syllabus should contain plans that correspond to each year of religious instruction. It should also indicate how the subject matter in the textbooks ought to be divided and co-ordinated, and how the liturgical year, religious homework, and prayers and hymns, can be properly incorporated. Moreover, it should give advice on how to give religion classes under adverse conditions.

Besides graded textbooks for the students, there should be a **teacher's manual** for every grade. This manual must present the methods for developing the content of catechesis in the classroom.

IV

## Catechetical Periodicals

*Boletín Nacional de Información Catequística* – Alfonso XI, 4, Madrid 14, Spain

*Catéchèse* – 19, rue de Varenne, Paris VIIe, France

*Catechesi* – Via Maria Ausiliatrice, 32, Turin, Italy

*Catéchistes* – 78, rue de Sèvres, Paris VIIe, France

*Catequista* – Apartado 170, Morelia, Mich., Mexico

*Catequista* – Córdoba 56, Mexico 7, D.F.

*Catholic Education* – 27 Great James Street, London, W.C.1, England

*Christlich-Pädagogische Blätter* – Vienna I, Stephansplatz 3/IV, Austria

*Didascalia* – Presidente Roca, 150, Rosario, Argentine

*Katecheta* – Ul. Freta 48, Warsaw, Poland

*Katechetische Blätter* – Munich 2, Maxburgstrasse 2/IV, Germany

*Lumen Vitae* – 184, rue Washington, Brussels 5, Belgium (two editions, in English and French)

*Met Brandend Hart* – Malmberg, 's Hertogenbosch, Holland

*The Japan Missionary Bulletin* – Tokyo, Japan

*Notre Catéchèse* – Abbaye de St-André-les-Bruges, Belgium

*Op Wen* – Nieuwe Gracht, 16, Utrecht, Holland

*Orientación Catequística* – Serapio Rendon, 56-B, Mexico D.F., Mexico

*Our Apostolate* – Lasallian Publications, Castle Hill, N.S.W., Australia

*Rasgando as Trevas* – Rua de Oliveira Monteiro, 833, Oporto, Portugal

*Religionsunterricht an höheren Schulen* – Merten bei Bonn, Kreuzstrasse 12 (H), Germany

*Religious Education* – (Interconfessional journal), 545 West 111th Street, New York 25, N.Y., U.S.A.
*Revista Catequística* – rua Silva Gaio, 34 e 39, Viseu, Portugal
*Revue du Clergé Africain* – Mayidi, Congo
*Rivista del Catechismo* – Via Galilei, 65, Brescia, Italy
*School en Godsdienst* – Arksteestraat, 1, Nijmegen, Holland
*Sinite* – Estudios Lasalianos, Tejares, Salamanca, Spain
*The Sower* – 11 Cavendish Square, London, W.1, England
*Sussidi* – via Botticelli, Milan, Italy
*Verbum* – Arksteestraat, 1, Nijmegen, Holland
*Vérité et Vie* – 1, rue de la Comédie, Strasbourg, France

## V

# Catechetical Centres Throughout the World

### *Africa*

| | |
|---|---|
| Congo | – Centre Documentaire Catéchétique, Grand Séminaire, Mayidi, via Inkisi, B.P. 6 |
| | – Centre d'Études Pastorales, B.P. Limite 724, Léopoldville |
| South Africa | – National Catechetical Commission, P.O. Box 941, Pretoria |
| Tanganyika | – Catechist Training Centre, Catechetical Department of Tanganyika, Bukumbe, P.O. Box 139, Mwanza |

### *North America*

| | |
|---|---|
| Canada | – Office Catéchistique Provincial, Saint-Jean, P. Quebec |
| | – Foyer Documentaire Catéchétique, Chemin Sainte-Foy, 2360, Quebec |
| U.S.A. | – Catholic Information Centre, 5 Park Street, Boston 8, Mass. |
| | – Confraternity of Christian Doctrine, 1312 Massachusetts Ave., N.W. Washington 5, D.C. |
| | – Pius XII Religious Education Resource Centre, 610 Elm Street, Monro (Michigan) |

### *Latin America*

| | |
|---|---|
| Brasil | – Centro Nacional Catequético, Rua Farani, 75, Botafogo, Rio de Janeiro |

Columbia – Celam, Primer Subsecretariado, Ap. aéreo 5278, Bogotá

Cuba – Junta Catequística, Ap. 594, Havana

*Asia*

India – Catechetical Centre, De Nobili College, Poona 6
– Catechist Training Centre, Tindivanam, South Arcot
– Catechist Training Centre, Tongo, Dist. Ranchi

Indonesia – Catechetical Centre, Seminari Tinggi, Djalan, Telomojo 2, Jogjakarta

Japan – Committee of the Apostolate, Takanawa, P.O. Box 21, Tokyo
– "Missionary Department" of the National Catholic Committee, Tokyo
Catechist Training Centre, 30 Hayatocho Showa-ku, Nagoya

Philippines – East Asian Pastoral Institute, P.O. Box 1815, Manila

Singapore – Catechetical Centre, II-1, Holland Road, Singapore

*Australia*

Victoria – Catholic Education Office, 18, Brunswick Street, Melbourne, N. 6.

*Europe*

Austria – Katechetisches Institut, Vienna 1, Stephansplatz 3/IV

Belgium – There are no national centres, but various diocesan centres. Brussels: Centre International d'Études de la Formation Religieuse (Lumen Vitae), 184, rue Washington, Brussels 5

France – Centre National Catéchétique, 19, rue de Varenne, Paris VII
– Institut Supérieur Catéchétique de Paris, 61, rue Madame, Paris VI

| | |
|---|---|
| Germany | – Deutscher Katechetenverein, Munich 2, Maxburgstrasse 2/IV |
| | – Christliches Bildungswerk "Die Hegge", Die Hegge bei Warburg, Westphalia |
| | – Katechetisches Institut, Würzburg, Domerschulstrasse 18 |
| Greece | – Centre Documentaire Catéchétique, Michel Voda 28, Athens |
| Great Britain | – Catholic Catechetical Centre, 11 Cavendish Square, London, W.1 |
| Holland | – Katechetisch Centrum Canisianum, Arksteestraat, 1, Nijmegen |
| Italy | – Istituto Superiore di Pedagogia del Pontificio Ateneo Salesiano di Roma, Rome |
| | – Magisterio di Maria Assunta, Rome |
| | – Centro Catechistico Salesiano, Turin |
| | – Katechetisches Amt, Bolzano, Pfarrplatz 27 |
| Norway | – St. Olav, Akersveien 5, Oslo |
| Poland | – See "Katecheta" in the list of periodicals |
| Portugal | – Centro Documentário Catequético, Rua de Oliveira Monteiro, 833, Oporto |
| Spain | – Segretariado Catequístico Nacional, Alfonso XI, 4, Madrid |

Appendices IV and V were compiled by Fr. G. Delcuve, S.J., Director of the International Centre for Religious Instruction *(Lumen Vitae)*, Brussels

# INDEX